JOHN G. PATON

JOHN G. PATON, D.D.

JOHN G. PATON
MISSIONARY TO THE NEW HEBRIDES

An Autobiography edited by his brother
JAMES PATON

THE BANNER OF TRUTH TRUST

THE BANNER OF TRUTH TRUST
3 Murrayfield Road, Edinburgh EH 12 6EL
PO Box 621, Carlisle, Pennsylvania 17013, USA

*

Autobiography first published in two parts
Part First   January 1889
Part Second   October 1889

Popular edition in one volume first published 1891

Seventh Popular edition with Part Third added
first published 1898

First Banner of Truth Trust edition reprinted from
Twelfth Popular edition 1965

Reprinted 1994

ISBN 0 85151 667 X

*

Printed in Great Britain at the University Press, Cambridge

EDITOR'S PREFACE.

THE Autobiography of my brother, Dr. John G. Paton has now, at my urgent entreaty, been continued by him, and carried on to the present year, 1897.

The addition of Part Third (pp. 445–497) constitutes therefore the distinctive feature of this Popular Edition; and tells the Story of the Life during the twelve years that have elapsed since Part First and Part Second were completed by the Author, and separately given to the world.

The following words from the *Preface* to the Single-Volume Edition of the Autobiography, published in 1891, are equally applicable to present circumstances :— " The Public hailed it from the first with a welcome so uncommon, and God has in many ways so signally owned and blessed it, that it would be no modesty, but sheer stupidity, on my part, to fail in recognising that it has been voted a Missionary Classic by the great and free Community of Readers. I have therefore spared no pains in making it as perfect as it is in my power to do, with the help of many minute corrections from friends here and abroad, and also happy suggestions as to matters of detail from the honoured Missionary himself."

In the original *Preface* when the book was first published in 1889, I said : " The Manuscript of this Volume, put together in a rough draft amid ceaseless and exacting toils, was placed in my hands and left absolutely to my disposal by my beloved brother, the Missionary. It has

v

been to me a labour of perfect love to re-write and revise the same, pruning here and expanding there, and, preparing the whole for the press. In the incidents of personal experience, constituting the larger part of the book, the reader peruses in an almost unaltered form the graphic and simple narrative as it came from my brother's pen. But, as many sections have been re-cast and largely modified, especially in those Chapters of whose events I was myself an eye-witness, or regarding which I had information at first hand from the parties concerned therein,—and as circumstances make it impossible to submit these in their present shape to my brother before publication,—I must request the Public to lay upon me, and not on him, all responsibility for the final shape in which the Autobiography appears. I publish it because Something tells me there is a blessing in it."

That wish too was abundantly fulfilled. The book has had a great circulation, not only at Home, but also in America, as well as in all our Colonies, and it has been translated, in whole or in part, into many Modern Languages.

In issuing this Enlarged Popular Edition of the Autobiography, now carefully adjusted and completed, my prayer continues to be in terms of the *Preface* of 1891 : " That the Lord may use it for still further deepening the interest in, and kindling an enthusiasm for, the CONVERSION OF THE HEATHEN WORLD. So shall the supreme aim be realized, which moved my brother in consenting to draw up these biographical notes for me, and which inspired me in preparing them for the public eye."

JAMES PATON.

GLASGOW,
February, 1898.

CONTENTS.

PART FIRST

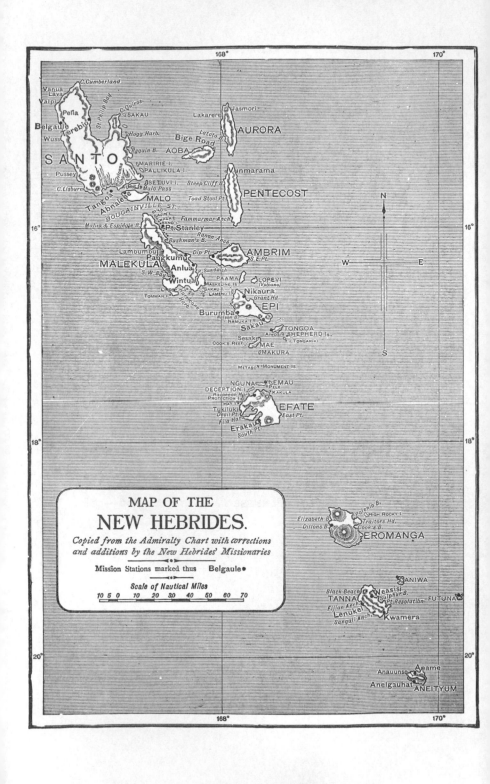

MAP OF THE
NEW HEBRIDES.

*Copied from the Admiralty Chart with corrections
and additions by the New Hebrides' Missionaries*

Mission Stations marked thus   Belgaule●

Scale of Nautical Miles
10 5 0   10   20   30   40   50   60   70

PART FIRST.

CHAPTERS I.—X.

A. D. 1824—1862.

ÆT. I—38

1

INTRODUCTORY NOTE.

WHAT I write here is for the glory of God. For more than twenty years have I been urged to record my story as a Missionary of the Cross; but always till now, in my sixty-fourth year, my heart has shrunk from the task, as savouring too much of self. Latterly the conviction has been borne home to me that if there be much in my experience which the Church of God ought to know, it would be pride on my part, and not humility, to let it die with me. I lift my pen, therefore, with that motive supreme in my heart; and, so far as memory and entries in my note-books and letters of my own and of other friends serve or help my sincere desire to be truthful and fair, the following chapters will present a faithful picture of the life through which the Lord has led me. If it bows any of my readers under as deep and certain a confidence as mine, that in "God's hand our breath is, and His are all our ways," my task will not be fruitless in the Great Day.

CHAPTER I.

THE HOME LIFE.

A.D. 1824—1834. ÆT. I—10.

Kirkmahoe.—Torthorwald Village.—Our Villagers.—Nithsdale Scenes
—Our Cottage Home.—Our Forebears.—An Idyll of the Heart.—
A Consecrated Father.—Accepted Vows.—Happy Sabbath Days.—
Golden Autumn of Life.

I WAS born in a cottage on the farm of Braehead, in the
parish of Kirkmahoe, near Dumfries, in the south of Scotland, on the 24th May, 1824.   My father, James Paton, was
a stocking manufacturer in a small way ; and he and his young
wife, Janet Jardine Rogerson, lived on terms of warm personal
friendship with the " gentleman farmer," so they gave me his
son's name, John *Gibson ;* and the curly-haired child of the
cottage was soon able to toddle across to the mansion, and
became a great pet of the lady there.   More than once, in my
many journeyings, have I met with one or another, in some
way connected with that family, and heard little incidents not
needing to be repeated here, showing how beautiful and tender
and altogether human was the relationship in those days
betwixt the landlord and the cottars on his estate.   On my
last visit to Scotland, sixty years after, I drove to Braehead
in company with my youngest brother James and my cousin
David,—the latter born the same week as I, and the former
nearly twenty years my junior ; and we found no cottage, nor
trace of a cottage, but amused ourselves by supposing that we
could discover, by the rising of the grassy mound, the outline
where the foundations once had been !   Of ten thousand
homes in Scotland, once sweet and beautiful, each a little
possible Paradise in its own well-cultivated plot, this is true

3

to-day; and where are the healthy, happy peasant boys and girls that such homes bred and reared? They are sweltering and struggling for existence in our towns and cities. I am told that this must be—that it is all the result of economic laws; but I confess to a deepening conviction that it need not be, and that the loss to the nation as a whole is vital, if not irreparable.

While yet a mere child, five years or so of age, my parents took me to a new home in the ancient village of Torthorwald, about four and a quarter miles north from Dumfries on the road to Lockerbie. At that time, about 1830, Torthorwald was a busy and thriving village, and comparatively populous, with its cottars and crofters, large farmers and small farmers, weavers and shoemakers, cloggers and coopers, blacksmiths and tailors. Fifty-five years later, when I last visited the scenes of my youth, the village proper was literally extinct, except for five thatched cottages where the lingering patriarchs were permitted to die slowly away,—when they too would be swept into the large farms, and their garden plots ploughed over, like sixty or seventy others that had been obliterated! Of course the Village Smithy still survives, but its sparks are few and fading,—the great cultivators patronizing rather the towns. The Meal Mill still grinds away,—but nothing like what it did when every villager bought or cultivated his few acres of corn, and every crofter and farmer in the parish sent all his grist to the mill. The Grocer's Shop still recalls the well-known name of Robert Henderson; but so few are the mouths now to be fed, that his warm-hearted wife and universal favourite, the very heroine of our village life, " Jean Grier," declared to me in her graphic Doric tongue: " Thae Tory lairds and their big farms hae driven our folks a' awa'! They hae spoiled the Schule and the Shop and the Smiddy; they hae spoiled the Kirk and the Mill." And verily the School is robbed of its children, and the Parish Church of its worshippers, when five families are only reared where twenty once flourished! Political economy may curse me, if it will; but I heard with grim satisfaction that this system of large farming, which extinguishes our village homes, and sends our peasantry to rear their children in lanes and alleys, in attics and cellars of populous towns, was proving ruinous at length to the landlords and factors, who had in many cases cruelly forced it on an unwilling people for mere selfish gain.

The Villagers of my early days—the agricultural servants, or occasional labourers, the tradesmen, the small farmers—were, generally speaking, a very industrious and thoroughly independent race of people. Hard workers they had to be, else they would starve ; yet they were keen debaters on all affairs both in Church and State, and sometimes in the "smiddy" or the "kiln," sometimes in a happy knot on the "village green" or on the road to the "kirk" or the "market," the questions that were tearing the mighty world beyond were fought over again by secluded peasants with amazing passion and bright intelligence.

From the Bank Hill, close above our village, and accessible in a walk of fifteen minutes, a view opens to the eye which, despite several easily understood prejudices of mine that may discount any opinion that I offer, still appears to me well worth seeing amongst all the beauties of Scotland. At your feet lay a thriving village, every cottage sitting in its own plot of garden, and sending up its blue cloud of "peat reek," which never somehow seemed to pollute the blessed air ; and after all has been said or sung, a beautifully situated village of healthy and happy homes for God's children is surely the finest feature in every landscape ! There nestled the Manse amongst its ancient trees, sometimes wisely, sometimes foolishly tenanted, but still the "man's-house," the man of God's house, when such can be found for it. There, close by, the Parish School, where rich and poor met together on equal terms, as God's children ; and we learned that brains and character make the only aristocracy worth mentioning. Yonder, amid its graves that date back on crumbling stone five hundred years, stands the Village Church ; and there, on its little natural hill, at the end of the village, rises the old tower of Torthorwald, frowning over all the far-sweeping valley of the Nith, and telling of days of blood and Border foray. It was one of the many castles of the Kirkpatricks, and its enormous and imperishable walls seem worthy of him who wrote the legend of his family in the blood of the Red

Comyn, stabbed in the Greyfriars Church of Dumfries, when he smote an extra blow to that of Bruce, and cried, " I mak' siccar " (=sure). Beyond, betwixt you and the Nith, crawls the slow-creeping Lochar towards the Solway, through miles and miles of moss and heather,—the nearest realization that I ever beheld of a " stagnant stream." Looking from the Bank Hill on a summer day, Dumfries with its spires shone so conspicuous that you could have believed it not more than two miles away ; the splendid sweeping vale through which Nith rolls to Solway, lay all before the naked eye beautiful with village spires, mansion houses, and white shining farms ; the Galloway hills, gloomy and far-tumbling, bounded the forward view, while to the left rose Criffel, cloud-capped and majestic ; then the white sands of Solway, with tides swifter than horsemen ; and finally the eye rested joyfully upon the hills of Cumberland, and noticed with glee the blue curling smoke from its villages on the southern Solway shores. Four miles behind you lie the ruins of the Castle of the Bruce, within the domains of his own Royal Burgh of Lochmaben ; a few miles in front, the still beautiful and amazing remains of Caerlaverock Castle, famous in many a Border story ; all around you, scattered throughout the dale of Nith, memories or ruins of other baronial " keeps," rich in suggestion to the peasant fancy ! Traditions lost nothing in bulk, or in graphic force, as they were retold for the thousandth time by village patriarchs around the kindly peat fire, with the younger rustics gaping round. A high spirit of patriotism, and a certain glorious delight in daring enterprises, was part of our common heritage.

There, amid this wholesome and breezy village life, our dear parents found their home for the long period of forty years. There too were born to them eight additional children, making in all a family of five sons and six daughters. Theirs was the first of the thatched cottages on the left, past the " miller's house," going up the " village gate," with a small garden in front of it, and a large garden across the road ; and it is one of the few still lingering to show to a new generation what the homes of their fathers were. The architect who planned that cottage had no ideas of art, but a fine eye for durability ! It consists at present of three, but originally of four, pairs of "oak couples" (Scotticé *kipples*), planted like solid trees in the ground at equal intervals, and gently sloped inwards till they meet or are "coupled" at the ridge, this coupling being managed not by rusty iron, but by great solid pins of oak. A roof of oaken wattles was laid across these, till within eleven or twelve feet of the ground, and from the ground upwards a stone wall was raised, as perpendicular as was found practicable, towards these overhanging wattles, this wall being roughly "pointed" with sand and clay and lime. Now into and upon the roof was woven and intertwisted a covering of thatch, that defied all winds and weathers, and that made the cottage marvellously cosy,—being renewed year by year, and never allowed to remain in disrepair at any season. But the beauty of the construction was and is its durability, or rather the permanence of its oaken ribs! There they stand, after probably not less than four centuries, japanned with "peat reek" till they are literally shining, so hard that no ordinary nail can be driven into them, and perfectly capable of service for four centuries more on the same conditions. The walls are quite modern, having all been rebuilt in my father's time, except only the few great foundation boulders, piled around the oaken couples ; and part of the roofing also may plead guilty to having found its way thither only in recent days ; but the architect's one idea survives, baffling time and change—the ribs and rafters of oak.

Our home consisted of a "but" and a "ben" and a "mid room," or chamber, called the "closet." The one end was my mother's domain, and served all the purposes of dining-room and kitchen and parlour, besides containing two large wooden erections, called by our Scotch peasantry "box-beds"; not holes in the wall, as in cities, but grand, big, airy beds, adorned with many-coloured counterpanes, and hung with natty curtains, showing the skill of the mistress of the house. The other end was my father's workshop, filled with five or six "stocking frames," whirring with the constant action of five or six pairs of busy hands and feet, and producing right genuine hosiery for the merchants at Hawick and Dumfries. The "closet" was a very small apartment betwixt the other two, having room only for a bed, a little table, and a chair, with a diminutive window shedding diminutive light on the scene. This was the Sanctuary of that cottage home. Thither daily, and oftentimes a day, generally after each meal, we saw our father retire, and "shut to the door"; and we children got to understand by a sort of spiritual instinct (for the thing was too sacred to be talked about) that prayers were being poured out there for us, as of old by the High Priest within the veil in the Most Holy Place. We occasionally heard the pathetic echoes of a trembling voice pleading as if for life, and we learned to slip out and in past that door on tiptoe, not to disturb the holy colloquy. The outside world might not know, but we knew, whence came that happy light as of a new-born smile that always was dawning on my father's face : it was a reflection from the Divine Presence, in the consciousness of which he lived. Never, in temple or cathedral, on mountain or in glen, can I hope to feel that the Lord God is more near, more visibly walking and talking with men, than under that humble cottage roof of thatch and oaken wattles. Though everything else in religion were by some unthinkable catastrophe to be swept out of memory, or blotted from my understanding, my soul would wander back to those early scenes, and shut itself up once again in that Sanctuary Closet, and, hearing still the echoes of those cries to God, would hurl back all doubt with the victorious appeal, "He walked with God, why may not I?"

A few notes had better here be given as to our "Forebears," the kind of stock from which my father and mother sprang. My father's mother, Janet Murray, claimed to be descended from a Galloway family that fought and suffered for Christ's Crown and Covenant in Scotland's "killing time," and was herself a woman of a pronouncedly religious development. Her husband, our grandfather, William Paton, had passed through a roving and romantic career, before he settled down to be a douce deacon of the weavers of Dumfries, like his father before him.

Forced by a press-gang to serve on board a British man-of-war, he was taken prisoner by the French, and thereafter placed under Paul Jones, the pirate of the seas, and bore to his dying day the mark of a slash from the captain's sword across his shoulder for some slight disrespect or offence. Determining with two others to escape, the three were hotly pursued by Paul Jones's men. One, who could swim but little, was shot, and had to be cut adrift by the other two, who in the darkness swam into a cave and managed to evade for two nights and a day the rage of their pursuers. My grandfather, being young and gentle and yellow-haired, persuaded some kind heart to rig him out in female attire, and in this costume escaped the attentions of the press-gang more than once; till, after many hardships, he bargained with the captain of a coal sloop to stow him away amongst his black diamonds; and thus, in due time, he found his way home to Dumfries, where he tackled bravely and wisely the duties of husband, father, and citizen for the remainder of his days. The smack of the sea about the stories of his youth gave zest to the talks round their quiet fireside, and that, again, was seasoned by the warm Evangelical spirit of his Covenanting wife, her lips "dropping grace."

Of their children, two reproduced the disposition of their father, and three that of their mother. William took to the soldier's career, and died in Spain; May, the only daughter, gave her heart and hand to John Wood, a jolly and gallant Englishman, who fought at Waterloo, and lived to see his hundredth birthday. John, James, and Spiers learned the stocking manufacturing business of their fathers, and also followed their mother's piety—becoming from early teens at once pronounced and consistent disciples of the Lord.

On the other side, my mother, Janet Rogerson, had for parents a father and mother of the Annandale stock. William Rogerson, her father, was one of many brothers, all men of uncommon strength and great force of character, quite worthy of the Border Rievers of an earlier day. Indeed, it was in some such way that he secured his wife, though the dear old lady in after-days was chary about telling the story. She was a girl of good position, the ward of two unscrupulous uncles who had charge of her small estate, near Langholm; and while attending some boarding school she fell devotedly in love with the tall, fair-

haired, gallant young blacksmith, William Rogerson. Her
guardians, doubtless very properly, objected to the "connection"; but our young Lochinvar, with his six or seven stalwart
brothers and other trusty "lads," all mounted, and with some
ready tool in case of need, went boldly and claimed his bride,
and she, willingly mounting at his side, was borne off in the
light of open day, joyously married, and took possession of her
" but and ben," as the mistress of the blacksmith's castle.

The uncles had it out with him, however, in another way.
While he was enjoying his honeymoon, and careless of mere
mundane affairs, they managed to dispose of all the property
of their ward, and make good their escape with the proceeds
to the New World. Having heard a rumour of some such sale,
our young blacksmith on horseback just reached the scene
in time to see the last article—a Family Bible—put up for
auction. This he claimed, or purchased, or seized, in name
of the heiress—but that was all that she ever inherited! It
was used devoutly by her till her dying day, and was adorned
with the record of her own marriage and of the birth of a large
and happy family, whom by-and-bye God gave to her.

Janet Jardine bowed her neck to the self-chosen yoke, with
the light of a supreme affection in her heart, and showed in
her gentler ways, her love of books, her fine accomplishments
with the needle, and her general air of ladyhood, that her lot
had once been cast in easier, but not necessarily happier, ways.
Her blacksmith lover proved not unworthy of his lady bride,
and in old age found for her a quiet and modest home, the
fruit of years of toil and hopeful thrift, their own little property,
in which they rested and waited a happy end. Amongst those
who at last wept by her grave stood, amidst many sons and
daughters, her son the Rev. James J. Rogerson, clergyman of
the Church of England, who, for many years thereafter, and till
quite recently, was spared to occupy a distinguished position
at ancient Shrewsbury, and has left behind him there an
honoured and beloved name.

One thing else, beautiful in its pathos, I must record of that
dear old lady. Her son, Walter, had gone forth from her, in
prosecution of his calling, had corresponded with her from
various counties in England, and then had suddenly disap-

peared ; and no sign came to her, whether he was dead or
alive. The mother-heart in her clung to the hope of his
return; every night she prayed for that happy event, and before
closing the door, threw it wide open, and peered into the darkness with a cry, "Come hame, my boy Walter, your mither
wearies sair ; " and every morning, at early break of day, for
a period of more than twenty years, she toddled up from her
cottage door, at Johnsfield, Lockerbie, to a little round hill,
called the "Corbie Dykes," and, gazing with tear-filled eyes
towards the south for the form of her returning boy, prayed
the Lord God to keep him safe and restore him to her yet
again. Always, as I think upon that scene, my heart finds
consolation in reflecting that if not here, then for certain *there*,
such deathless longing love will be rewarded, and, rushing into
long-delayed embrace, will exclaim—"Was lost and is found."

From such a home came our mother, Janet Jardine Rogerson,
a bright-hearted, high-spirited, patient-toiling, and altogether
heroic little woman ; who, for about forty-three years, made
and kept such a wholesome, independent, God-fearing, and
self-reliant life for her family of five sons and six daughters,
as constrains me, when I look back on it now, in the light of all
I have since seen and known of others far differently situated,
almost to worship her memory. She had gone with her
high spirits and breezy disposition to gladden, as their companion, the quiet abode of some grand- or great-grand-uncle
and aunt, familiarly named in all that Dalswinton neighbourhood " Old Adam and Eve." Their house was on the outskirts
of the moor, and life for the young girl there had not probably
too much excitement. But one thing had arrested her attention. She had noticed that a young stocking maker from the
" Brig End," James Paton, the son of William and Janet there,
was in the habit of stealing alone into the quiet wood, book
in hand, day after day, at certain hours, as if for private study
and meditation. It was a very excusable curiosity that led the
young bright heart of the girl to watch him devoutly reading
and hear him reverently reciting (though she knew not then,
it was Ralph Erskine's " Gospel Sonnets," which he could say
by heart sixty years afterwards, as he lay on his bed of death) ;
and finally that curiosity awed itself into a holy respect, when

she saw him lay aside his broad Scotch bonnet, kneel down under the sheltering wings of some tree, and pour out all his soul in daily prayers to God.   As yet they had never spoken. What spirit moved her, let lovers tell—was it all devotion, or was it a touch of unconscious love kindling in her towards the yellow-haired and thoughtful youth?   Or was there a stroke of mischief, of that teasing, which so oftens opens up the door to the most serious step in all our lives?   Anyhow, one day she slipped in quietly, stole away his bonnet, and hung it on a branch near by, while his trance of devotion made him oblivious of all around ; then, from a safe retreat, she watched and enjoyed his perplexity in seeking for and finding it !   A second day this was repeated ; but his manifest disturbance of mind, and his long pondering with the bonnet in hand, as if almost alarmed, seemed to touch another chord in her heart—that chord of pity which is so often the prelude of love, that finer pity that grieves to wound anything nobler or tenderer than ourselves.   Next day, when he came to his accustomed place of prayer, a little card was pinned against the tree just where he knelt, and on it these words :—

"She who stole away your bonnet is ashamed of what she did ; she has a great respect for you, and asks you to pray for her, that she may become as good a Christian as you."

Staring long at that writing, he forgot Ralph Erskine for one day !   Taking down the card, and wondering who the writer could be, he was abusing himself for his stupidity in not sus-pecting that some one had discovered his retreat and removed his bonnet, instead of wondering whether angels had been there during his prayer,—when, suddenly raising his eyes, he saw in front of old Adam's cottage, through a lane amongst the trees, the passing of another kind of angel, swinging a milk-pail in her hand and merrily singing some snatch of old Scottish song. He knew, in that moment, by a Divine instinct, as infallible as any voice that ever came to seer of old, that she was the angel visitor that had stolen in upon his retreat—that bright-faced, clever-witted niece of old Adam and Eve, to whom he had never yet spoken, but whose praises he had often heard said and sung—"Wee Jen."   I am afraid he did pray "for her," in more senses than one, that afternoon ; at any rate, more than a

Scotch bonnet was very effectually stolen; a good heart and true was there virtually bestowed, and the trust was never regretted on either side, and never betrayed.

Often and often, in the genial and beautiful hours of the autumntide of their long life, have I heard my dear father tease " Jen " about her maidenly intentions in the stealing of that bonnet; and often have heard her quick mother-wit in the happy retort, that had his motives for coming to that retreat been altogether and exclusively pious, he would probably have found his way to the other side of the wood, but that men who prowled about the Garden of Eden ran the risk of meeting some day with a daughter of Eve!

Somewhere in or about his seventeenth year, my father passed through a crisis of religious experience; and from that day he openly and very decidedly followed the Lord Jesus. His parents had belonged to one of the older branches of what is now called the United Presbyterian Church; but my father, having made an independent study of the Scotch Worthies, the Cloud of Witnesses, the Testimonies, and the Confession of Faith, resolved to cast in his lot with the oldest of all the Scotch Churches, the Reformed Presbyterian, as most nearly representing the Covenanters and the attainments of both the first and second Reformations in Scotland. This choice he deliberately made, and sincerely and intelligently adhered to; and was able at all times to give strong and clear reasons from Bible and from history for the principles he upheld. Still his sympathies and votes always went with the more progressive party in that ancient Church. He held it to be right that Cameronians, like other citizens, should exercise the municipal and political franchise, and he adhered to the " Majority Synod," which has since been incorporated with the Free Church of Scotland. While glorying in the Psalms, he rejoiced to sing other hymns and spiritual songs (thanks to Ralph Erskine's " Sonnets," perhaps, for that !) from his earliest days, at least everywhere except in the ordinary Public Worship ; and long before he died, though he still held the Psalms to be supreme, he had learned to hear with glowing delight vast congregations singing the hymns of modern days, had learned joyfully to join in these songs of Zion, and was heard often to confess his belief that God had greatly owned and blessed the ministry of song in the service of the Gospel.

Besides his independent choice of a Church for himself there was one other mark and fruit of his early religious decision, which looks even fairer through all these years. Family Worship had heretofore been held only on Sabbath Day in his father's house ; but the young Christian, entering into conference with his sympathising mother, managed to get the household persuaded that there ought to be daily morning and evening prayer and reading of the Bible and holy singing. This the more readily, as he himself agreed to·take part regularly in the same, and so relieve the old warrior of what might have proved for him too arduous spiritual toils ! And so began in his seventeenth year that blessed custom of Family Prayer, morning and evening, which my father practised probably without one single avoidable omission till he lay on his deathbed, seventy-seven years of age ; when, even to the last day of his life, a portion of Scripture was read, and his voice was heard softly joining in the Psalm, and his lips breathed the morning and evening Prayer,—falling in sweet benediction on the heads of all his children, far away many of them over all the earth, but all meeting him there at the Throne of Grace. None of us can remember that any day ever passed unhallowed thus ; no hurry for market, no rush to business, no arrival of friends or guests, no trouble or sorrow, no joy or excitement, ever prevented at least our kneeling around the family altar, while the High Priest led our prayers to God, and offered himself and his children there. And blessed to others, as well as to ourselves, was the light of such example ! I have heard that, in long after-years, the worst woman in the village of Torthorwald, then leading an immoral life, but since changed by the grace of God, was known to declare, that the only thing that kept her from despair and from the Hell of the suicide, was when in the dark winter nights she crept close up underneath my father's window, and heard him pleading in Family Worship that God would convert "the sinner from the error of wicked ways, and polish him as a jewel for the Redeemer's crown." " I felt," said she, " that I was a burden on that good man's heart, and I knew that God would not disappoint *him*. That thought kept me out of Hell, and at last led me to the only Saviour."

My father had a strong desire to be a Minister of the Gospel ; but when he finally saw that God's will had marked out for him another lot, he reconciled himself by entering with his own soul into this solemn vow,—that if God gave him sons, he would consecrate them unreservedly to the Ministry of Christ, if the Lord saw fit to accept the offering, and open up their way. It may be enough here to say that he lived to see three of us entering upon and not unblessed in the Holy Office ;—myself, the eldest born ; my brother Walter, several years my junior ; and my brother James, the youngest of eleven, the Benjamin of the flock.

Our place of worship was the Reformed Presbyterian Church at Dumfries, under the ministry, during most of these days, of Rev. John McDermid—a genuine, solemn, lovable Covenanter, who cherished towards my father a warm respect, that deepened into apostolic affection when the yellow hair turned snow-white and both of them grew patriarchal in their years. The Minister, indeed, was translated to a Glasgow charge ; but that rather exalted than suspended their mutual love. Dumfries was four miles fully from our Torthorwald home ; but the tradition is that during all these forty years my father was only thrice prevented from attending the worship of God—once by snow, so deep that he was baffled and had to return ; once by ice on the road, so dangerous that he was forced to crawl back up the Roucan Brae on his hands and knees, after having descended it so far with many falls ; and once by the terrible outbreak of cholera at Dumfries. All intercourse betwixt the town and the surrounding villages, during that awful visitation, was publicly prohibited ; and the farmers and villagers, suspecting that no cholera would make my father stay at home on Sabbath, sent a deputation to my mother on the Saturday evening, and urged her to restrain his devotions for once ! That, however, was needless ; as, where the life of others was at stake, his very devotion came to their aid.

Each of us, from very early days, considered it no penalty, but a great joy, to go with our father to the church ; the four miles were a treat to our young spirits, the company by the

way was a fresh incitement, and occasionally some of the
wonders of city-life rewarded our eager eyes. A few other pious
men and women, of the best Evangelical type, went from the
same parish to one or other favourite Minister at Dumfries,—
the Parish Church during all those years being rather miserably
served ; and when these God-fearing peasants "foregathered"
in the way to or from the House of God, we youngsters had
sometimes rare glimpses of what Christian talk may be and
ought to be. They went to the church, full of beautiful
expectancy of spirit—their souls were on the outlook for God ;
they returned from the church, ready and even anxious to
exchange ideas as to what they had heard and received of the
things of life. I have to bear my testimony that religion was
presented to us with a great deal of intellectual freshness, and
that it did not repel us, but kindled our spiritual interest.
The talks which we heard were, however, genuine ; not the
make-believe of religious conversation, but the sincere outcome of their own personalities. That, perhaps, makes all the
difference betwixt talk that attracts and talk that drives away.

We had, too, special Bible Readings on the Lord's Day
evening,—mother and children and visitors reading in turns,
with fresh and interesting question, answer, and exposition, all
tending to impress us with the infinite grace of a God of love
and mercy in the great gift of His dear Son Jesus, our Saviour.
The Shorter Catechism was gone through regularly, each
answering the question asked, till the whole had been explained,
and its foundation in Scripture shown by the proof-texts
adduced. It has been an amazing thing to me, occasionally
to meet with men who blamed this "catechizing" for giving
them a distaste to religion ; every one in all our circle thinks
and feels exactly the opposite. It laid the solid rock-foundations
of our religious life. After-years have given to these questions
and their answers a deeper or a modified meaning, but none
of us have ever once even dreamed of wishing that we had
been otherwise trained. Of course, if the parents are not
devout, sincere, and affectionate,—if the whole affair on both
sides is taskwork, or worse, hypocritical and false,—results
must be very different indeed !

Oh, I can remember those happy Sabbath evenings ; no

blinds down, and shutters up, to keep out the sun from us, as some scandalously affirm; but a holy, happy, entirely human day, for a Christian father, mother, and children to spend. How my father would parade across and across our flag-floor, telling over the substance of the day's sermons to our dear mother, who, because of the great distance and because of her many living "encumbrances," got very seldom indeed to the church, but gladly embraced every chance, when there was prospect or promise of a "lift" either way from some friendly gig! How he would entice us to help him to recall some idea or other, praising us when we got the length of "taking notes" and reading them over on our return; how he would turn the talk ever so naturally to some Bible story or some Martyr reminiscence, or some happy allusion to the "Pilgrim's Progress"! And then it was quite a contest, which of us would get reading aloud, while all the rest listened, and father added here and there a happy thought, or illustration, or anecdote. Others must write and say what they will, and as they feel; but so must I. There were eleven of us brought up in a home like that; and never one of the eleven, boy or girl, man or woman, has been heard, or ever will be heard, saying that Sabbath was dull or wearisome for us, or suggesting that we have heard of or seen any way more likely than that for making the Day of the Lord bright and blessed alike for parents and for children. But God help the homes where these things are done by force and not by love!

The very discipline through which our father passed us was a kind of religion in itself. If anything really serious required to be punished, he retired first to his "closet" for prayer, and we boys got to understand that he was laying the whole matter before God; and that was the severest part of the punishment for me to bear! I could have defied any amount of mere penalty, but this spoke to my conscience as a message from God. We loved him all the more, when we saw how much it cost him to punish us; and, in truth, he had never very much of that kind of work to do upon any one of all the eleven—we were ruled by love far more than by fear.

As I must, however, leave the story of my father's life— much more worthy, in many ways, of being written than my own—I may here mention that his long and upright life made him a great favourite in all religious circles far and near within the neighbourhood, that at sick-beds and at funerals he was constantly sent for and much appreciated, and that this appreciation greatly increased, instead of diminishing, when years whitened his long, flowing locks and gave him an apostolic beauty ; till finally, for the last twelve years or so of his life, he became by appointment a sort of Rural Missionary for the four contiguous parishes, and spent his autumn in literally sowing the good seed of the Kingdom as a Colporteur of the Tract and Book Society of Scotland. His success in this work, for a rural locality, was beyond all belief. Within a radius of five miles, he was known in every home, welcomed by the children, respected by the servants, longed for eagerly by the sick and aged. He gloried in showing off the beautiful Bibles and other precious books, which he sold in amazing numbers. He sang sweet Psalms beside the sick, and prayed like the voice of God at their dying beds. He went cheerily from farm to farm, from cot to cot ; and when he wearied on the moorland roads, he refreshed his soul by reciting aloud one of Ralph Erskine's "Sonnets," or crooning to the birds one of David's Psalms. His happy partner, "Wee Jen," died in 1865, and he himself in 1868, having reached his seventy-seventh year,*—an altogether beautiful and noble episode of human existence having been enacted, amid the humblest surroundings of a Scottish peasant's home, through the influence of their united love by the grace of God; and in this world, or in any world, all their children will rise up at mention of their names and call them blessed !

---

* See Appendix A, "The White-Souled Peasant."

CHAPTER II.

SCHOOL AND EARLY COLLEGE DAYS.

A.D. 1834—1847. ÆT. 10—23.

A Typical Scottish School.—A School Prize.—A Wayward Master.—
Learning a Trade.—My Father's Prayers.—Jehovah Jireh.—With
Sappers and Miners.—Harvest Field.—On the Road to Glasgow.—
A Memorable Parting.—Before the Examiners.—Killing Work.—
Deep Waters.—Maryhill School.—Rough School Scenes.—Aut Cæsar,
Aut Nullus.—My Wages.

IN my boyhood Torthorwald had one of the grand old
typical Parish Schools of Scotland; where the rich and
the poor met together in perfect equality; where Bible and
Catechism were taught as zealously as grammar and geography;
and where capable lads from the humblest of cottages were
prepared in Latin and Mathematics and Greek to go straight
from their Village class to the University bench.   Besides, at
that time, an accomplished pedagogue of the name of Smith,
a learned man of more than local fame, had added a Boarding
House to the ordinary School, and had attracted some of the
better class gentlemen and farmers' sons from the surrounding
country ; so that Torthorwald, under his *régime*, reached the
zenith of its educational fame.   In this School I was initiated
into the mystery of letters, and all my brothers and sisters after
me, though some of them under other masters than mine ;—
my youngest brother James, trained there under a master
named William Lithgow, going direct from the Village School
to the University of Glasgow in his fourteenth year !
My teacher punished severely—rather, I should say, savagely
—especially for lessons badly prepared.   Yet, that he was in
some respects kindly and tender-hearted, I had the best of
reasons to know.   Seeing me not so " braw " as the well-to-do

19

fellows of my year, and taking a warm interest in me as a pupil, he, concluding probably that new suits were not so easily got in my home as in some of the rest, planned a happy and kind-hearted surprise—a sort of unacknowledged school prize.   One evening, when my father was "taking the books," and pouring out his heart in Family Worship, the door of our house gently opened on the latch, and gently closed again.   After prayer, on rushing to the door, I found a parcel containing a new suit of warm and excellent clothes,—seeing which my mother said that "God had sent them to me, and I should thankfully receive them as from His hand, whoever might have brought them."   Appearing in them at school next morning, the teacher cheerily saluted and complimented me on my "braws." I innocently told him how they came and what my mother said; and he laughingly replied:

"John, whenever you need anything after this just tell your father to 'tak' the Book,' and God will send it in answer to prayer!"

Years passed by before I came to know, what the reader has already guessed, that the good-hearted schoolmaster's hand lifted the latch that evening during my father's prayer.

All his influence, however, was marred by occasional bursts of fierce and ungovernable temper, amounting to savagery. His favouritism, too, was sometimes disheartening,—as when I won a Latin prize for an exercise by the verdict of the second master, yet it was withheld from me, and prizes were bestowed without merit on other and especially wealthier boys; so at least I imagined, and it cooled my ambition to excel.   Favouritism might be borne, but not mere brutality when passion mastered him.   Once, after having flogged me unjustly, on my return only at my mother's entreaty, he ran at me again, kicked me, and I fled in pain and terror from his presence, rushing home.   When his passion subsided, he came to my parents, apologized, and pled with me to return; but all in vain,— nothing would induce me to resume my studies there.   Undoubtedly at that time I had a great thirst for education, and a retentive memory, which made all lessons comparatively easy; and, as no other school was within my reach, it was a great loss that my heart shrank from this teacher.

Though still under twelve years of age, I started to learn my father's trade, in which I made surprising progress. We wrought from six in the morning till ten at night, with an hour at dinner-time and half an hour at breakfast and again at supper. These spare moments every day I devoutly spent on my books, chiefly in the rudiments of Latin and Greek; for I had given my soul to God, and was resolved to aim at being a Missionary of the Cross, or a Minister of the Gospel. Yet I gladly testify that what I learned of the stocking frame was not thrown away; the facility of using tools, and of watching and keeping the machinery in order, came to be of great value to me in the Foreign Mission field.

How much my father's prayers at this time impressed me I can never explain, nor could any stranger understand. When, on his knees and all of us kneeling around him in Family Worship, he poured out his whole soul with tears for the conversion of the Heathen World to the service of Jesus, and for every personal and domestic need, we all felt as if in the presence of the living Saviour, and learned to know and love Him as our Divine Friend. As we rose from our knees, I used to look at the light on my father's face, and wish I were like him in spirit,—hoping that, in answer to his prayers, I might be privileged and prepared to carry the blessed Gospel to some portion of the Heathen World.

One incident of this time I must record here, because of the lasting impression made upon my religious life. Our family, like all others of peasant rank in the land, were plunged into deep distress, and felt the pinch severely, through the failure of the potato, the badness of other crops, and the ransom-price of food. Our father had gone off with work to Hawick, and would return next evening with money and supplies; but meantime the meal barrel ran low, and our dear mother, too proud and too sensitive to let any one know, or to ask aid from any quarter, coaxed us all to rest, assuring us that she had told God everything, and that He would send us plenty in the morning. Next day, with the carrier from Lockerbie came a present from her father, who, knowing nothing of her circumstances or of this special trial, had been moved of God to send at that particular nick of time a love-offering to his daughter, such as they still send to each other in those kindly Scottish shires—a bag of new potatoes, a stone of the first ground meal or flour, or the earliest home-made cheese of the season—which largely supplied all our need. My mother, seeing our surprise at such an answer to her prayers, took us around her knees, thanked God for His goodness, and said to us :

"O my children, love your Heavenly Father, tell Him in faith and prayer all your needs, and He will supply your wants so far as it shall be for your good and His glory."

Perhaps, amidst all their struggles in rearing a family of eleven, this was the hardest time they ever had, and the only time they ever felt the actual pinch of hunger; for the little that they had was marvellously blessed of God, and was not less marvellously utilized by that noble mother of ours, whose high spirit, side by side with her humble and gracious piety, made us, under God, what we are to-day.

I saved as much at my trade as enabled me to go for six weeks to Dumfries Academy; this awoke in me again the hunger for learning, and I resolved to give up that trade and turn to something that might be made helpful to the prosecution of my education. An engagement was secured with the Sappers and Miners, who were mapping and measuring the county of Dumfries in connection with the Ordnance Survey of Scotland. The office hours were from 9 a.m. till 4 p.m. ; and though my walk from home was above four miles every morning, and the same by return in the evening, I found much spare time for private study, both on the way to and from my work and also after hours. Instead of spending the mid-day hour with the rest, at football and other games, I stole away to a quiet spot on the banks of the Nith, and there pored over my book, all alone. Our lieutenant, unknown to me, had observed this from his house on the other side of the stream, and after a time called me into his office and inquired what I was studying. I told him the whole truth as to my position and my desires. After conferring with some of the other officials there, he summoned me again, and in their presence promised me promotion in the service, and special training in Woolwich at the Government's expense, on condition that I would sign an engagement for seven years. Thanking him most gratefully for his kind offer, I agreed to bind myself for three years or four, but not for seven.

Excitedly he said, "Why? Will you refuse an offer that many gentlemen's sons would be proud of?"

I said, "My life is given to another Master, so I cannot engage for seven years."

He asked sharply, "To whom?"

I replied, "To the Lord Jesus; and I want to prepare as soon as possible for His service in the proclaiming of the Gospel."

In great anger he sprang across the room, called the paymaster, and exclaimed, "Accept my offer, or you are dismissed on the spot!"

I answered, "I am extremely sorry if you do so, but to bind myself for seven years would probably frustrate the purpose of my life; and though I am greatly obliged to you, I cannot make such an engagement."

His anger made him unwilling or unable to comprehend my difficulty; the drawing instruments were delivered up, I received my pay, and departed without further parley. The men, both over me and beside me, were mostly Roman Catholics, and their talk was the most profane I had ever heard. Few of them spoke at any time without larding their language with oaths, and I was thankful to get away from hearing their shocking speech. But to me personally both officers and men had been extremely kind, for which, on leaving, I thanked them all very cordially, and they looked not a little surprised,—as if unused to such recognitions!

Hearing how I had been treated, and why, Mr. Maxwell, the Rector of Dumfries Academy, offered to let me attend all classes there, free of charge, so long as I cared to remain; but that, in lack of means of support, was for the time impossible, as I would not and could not be a burden on my dear father, but was determined rather to help him in educating the rest. I went therefore to what was known as the Lamb Fair at Lockerbie, and for the first time in my life took a "fee" for the harvest. On arriving at the field when shearing and mowing began, the farmer asked me to bind a sheaf; when I had done so, he seized it by the band, and it fell to pieces! Instead of disheartening me, however, he gave me a careful lesson how to bind; the second that I bound did not collapse when shaken, and the third he pitched across the field, and on finding that it still remained firm, he cried to me cheerily :

" Right now, my lad ; go ahead ! "

It was hard work for me at first, and my hands got very sore ; but, being willing and determined, I soon got into the way of it, and kept up with the best of them. The harvesters, seeing I was not one of their own workers, had an eager dispute as to what I was, some holding that I was a painter, and some a tailor; but the more 'cute observers denied me the rank of tailor from the lack of " jaggings " on my thumb and finger ; so I suppose they credited me with the brush. The male harvesters were told off to sleep in a large hay-loft, the beds being arranged all along the side, like barracks. Many of the fellows were rough and boisterous; and I suppose my look showed that I hesitated in mingling with them, for the quick eye and kind heart of the farmer's wife prompted her to suggest that I, being so much younger than the rest, might sleep with her son George in the house—an offer, oh, how gratefully accepted ! A beautiful new steading had recently been built for them ; and during certain days, or portions of days, while waiting for the grain to ripen or to dry, I planned and laid out an ornamental garden in front of it, which gave great satisfaction—a taste inherited from my mother, with her joy in flowers and garden plots. They gave me, on leaving, a handsome present, as well as my fee, for I had got on very pleasantly with them all. This experience, too, came to be valuable to me, when, in long-after days, and far other lands, Mission buildings had to be erected, and garden and field cropped and cultivated without the aid of a single European hand.

Before going to my first harvesting, I had applied for a situation in Glasgow, apparently exactly suited for my case; but I had little or no hope of ever hearing of it further. An offer of £50 per annum was made by the West Campbell Street Reformed Presbyterian Congregation, then under the good and noble Dr. Bates, for a young man to act as district visitor and tract distributor, especially amongst the absentees from the Sabbath School ; with the privilege of receiving one year's training at the Free Church Normal Seminary, that he might qualify himself for teaching, and thereby push forward to the Holy Ministry. The candidates, along with their application and certificates, were to send an essay on some subject, of their own composition, and in their own hand-writing. I sent in two long poems on the Covenanters, which must have exceedingly amused them, as I had not learned to write even decent prose ! But, much to my surprise, imme-diately on the close of the harvesting experience, a letter arrived, intimating that I, along with another young man, had been put upon the short leet, and that both were requested to appear in Glasgow on a given day and compete for the appointment.

Two days thereafter I started out from my quiet country home on the road to Glasgow. Literally " on the road," for from Torthorwald to Kilmarnock—about forty miles—had to be done on foot, and thence to Glasgow by rail. Railways in those days were as yet few, and coach travelling was far beyond my purse. A small bundle, tied up in my pocket-handkerchief, contained my Bible and all my personal belongings. Thus was I launched upon the ocean of life. I thought on One who says, " I know thy poverty, but thou art rich."

My dear father walked with me the first six miles of the way. His counsels and tears and heavenly conversation on that parting journey are fresh in my heart as if it had been but yesterday ; and tears are on my cheeks as freely now as then, whenever memory steals me away to the scene. For the last half-mile or so we walked on together in almost unbroken silence,—my father, as was often his custom, carrying hat in hand, while his long, flowing yellow hair (then yellow, but in later years white as snow) streamed like a girl's down his shoulders. His lips kept moving in silent prayers for me ; and his tears fell fast when our eyes met each other in looks for which all speech was vain ! We halted on reaching the appointed parting place ; he grasped my hand firmly for a minute in silence, and then solemnly and affectionately said :

" God bless you, my son ! Your father's God prosper you, and keep you from all evil ! "

Unable to say more, his lips kept moving in silent prayer ;

in tears we embraced, and parted. I ran off as fast as I could; and, when about to turn a corner in the road where he would lose sight of me, I looked back and saw him still standing with head uncovered where I had left him—gazing after me. Waving my hat in adieu, I was round the corner and out of sight in an instant. But my heart was too full and sore to carry me further, so I darted into the side of the road and wept for a time. Then, rising up cautiously, I climbed the dyke to see if he yet stood where I had left him ; and just at that moment I caught a glimpse of him climbing the dyke and looking out for me! He did not see me, and after he had gazed eagerly in my direction for a while he got down, set his face towards home, and began to return—his head still uncovered, and his heart, I felt sure, still rising in prayers for me. I watched through blinding tears, till his form faded from my gaze ; and then, hastening on my way, vowed deeply and oft, by the help of God, to live and act so as never to grieve or dishonour such a father and mother as He had given me. The appearance of my father, when we parted—his advice, prayers, and tears—the road, the dyke, the climbing up on it and then walking away, head uncovered—have often, often, all through life, risen vividly before my mind, and do so now while I am writing, as if it had been but an hour ago. In my earlier years particularly, when exposed to many temptations, his parting form rose before me as that of a guardian Angel. It is no Pharisaism, but deep gratitude, which makes me here testify that the memory of that scene not only helped, by God's grace, to keep me pure from the prevailing sins, but also stimulated me in all my studies, that I might not fall short of his hopes, and in all my Christian duties, that I might faithfully follow his shining example.

I reached Glasgow on the third day, having slept one night at Thornhill, and another at New Cumnock ; and having needed, owing to the kindness of acquaintances upon whom I called by the way, to spend only three-halfpence of my modest funds. Safely arrived, but weary, I secured a humble room for my lodging, for which I had to pay one shilling and six-pence per week. Buoyant and full of hope and looking up to God for guidance, I appeared at the appointed hour before the examiners, as did also the other candidate; and they having carefully gone through their work, asked us to retire. When recalled, they informed us that they had great difficulty in choosing, and suggested that the one of us might withdraw in favour of the other, or that both might submit to a more testing examination. Neither seemed inclined to give it up, both were willing for a second examination; but the patrons made another suggestion. They had only £50 per annum to give; but if we would agree to divide it betwixt us, and go into one lodging, we might both be able to struggle through; they would pay our entrance fees at the Free Normal Seminary, and provide us with the books required; and perhaps they might be able to add a little to the sum promised to each of us. By dividing the mission work appointed, and each taking only the half, more time also might be secured for our studies. Though the two candidates had never seen each other before, we at once accepted this proposal, and got on famously together, never having had a dispute on anything of common interest throughout our whole career.

As our fellow-students at the Normal were all far advanced beyond us in their education, we found it killing work, and had to grind away incessantly, late and early. Both of us, before the year closed, broke down in health; partly by hard study, but principally, perhaps, for lack of nourishing diet. A severe cough seized upon me; I began spitting blood, and a doctor ordered me at once home to the country and forbade all attempts at study. My heart sank; it was a dreadful disappointment, and to me a bitter trial. Soon after, my companion, though apparently much stronger than I, was similarly seized. He, however, never entirely recovered, though for some years he taught in a humble School; and long ago he fell asleep in Jesus, a devoted and honoured Christian man.

I, on the other hand, after a short rest, nourished by the hill air of Torthorwald and by the new milk of our family cow, was ere long at work again. I rented a house, and began to teach a small School at Girvan. There I received the greatest kindness from Rev. Matthew G. Easton of the Reformed Presbyterian Church, now Dr. Easton of the Free Church, Darvel, and gradually but completely recovered my health.

Having saved £10 by my teaching, I returned to Glasgow, and was enrolled as a student at the College; but before the session was finished my money was exhausted—I had lent some to a poor student, who failed to repay me—and only nine shillings remained in my purse. There was no one from whom to borrow, had I been willing; I had been disappointed in attempting to secure private tuition; and no course seemed open for me, except to pay what little I owed, give up my College career, and seek for teaching or other work in the country. I wrote a letter to my father and mother, informing them of my circumstances; that I was leaving Glasgow in quest of work, and that they would not hear from me again till I had found a suitable situation. I told them that if otherwise unsuccessful, I should fall back on my own trade, though I shrank from that as not tending to advance my education; but that they might rest assured I would do nothing to dishonour them or my own Christian profession. Having read that letter over again through many tears, I said,—I cannot send that, for it will grieve my darling parents; and therefore, leaving it on the table, I locked my room door and ran out to find a place where I might sell my few precious books, and hold on a few weeks longer. But, as I stood on the opposite side and wondered whether these folks in a shop with the three golden balls would care to have a poor student's books, and as I hesitated, knowing how much I needed them for my studies, conscience smote me as if for doing a guilty thing; I imagined that the people were watching me like one about to commit a theft; and I made off from the scene at full speed, with a feeling of intense shame at having dreamed of such a thing! Passing through one short street into another, I marched on mechanically; but the Lord God of my father was guiding my steps, all unknown to me.

A certain notice in a window, into which I had probably never in my life looked before, here caught my eye, to this effect—"Teacher wanted, Maryhill Free Church School; apply at the Manse." A coach or 'bus was just passing, when I turned round; I leapt into it, saw the Minister, arranged to undertake the School, returned to Glasgow, paid my landlady's lodging score, tore up that letter to my parents, and wrote another full of cheer and hope; and early next morning entered the School and began a tough and trying job. The Minister warned me that the School was a wreck, and had been broken up chiefly by coarse and bad characters from mills and coal-pits, who attended the evening classes. They had abused several masters in succession; and, laying a thick and heavy cane on the desk, he said:

" Use that freely, or you will never keep order here ! "

I put it aside into the drawer of my desk, saying, " That will be my last resource."

There were very few scholars for the first week—about eighteen in the Day School and twenty in the Night School. The clerk of the mill, a good young fellow, came to the evening classes, avowedly to learn book-keeping, but privately he said he had come to save me from personal injury.

The following week, a young man and a young woman began to attend the Night School, who showed from the first moment that they were bent on mischief. By talking aloud, joking, telling stories, and laughing, they stopped the work of the School. On my repeated appeals for quiet and order, they became the more boisterous, and gave great merriment to a few of the scholars present. I finally urged the young man, a tall, powerful fellow, to be quiet or at once to leave, declaring that at all hazards I must and would have perfect order; but he only mocked at me, and assumed a fighting attitude. Quietly locking the door and putting the key in my pocket, I turned to my desk, armed myself with the cane, and dared any one at his peril to interfere betwixt us. It was a rough struggle—he smashing at me clumsily with his fists, I with quick movements evading and dealing him blow after blow with the heavy cane for several rounds—till at length he crouched down at his desk, exhausted and beaten, and I ordered him to turn to his book, which he did in sulky silence. Going to my desk, I addressed them, and asked them to inform all who wished to come to the School, That if they came for education, everything would be heartily done that it was in my power to do ; but that any who wished for mischief had better stay away, as I was determined to conquer, not to be conquered, and to secure order and silence, whatever it might cost.

Further, I assured them that that cane would not again be lifted by me, if kindness and forbearance on my part could possibly gain the day, as I wished to rule by love and not by terror. But this young man knew he was in the wrong, and it was that which had made him weak against me, though every way stronger far than I. Yet I would be his friend and helper, if he was willing to be friendly with me, the same as if this night had never been. At these words a dead silence fell on the School ; every one buried face diligently in book ; and the evening closed in uncommon quiet and order.

Next morning, two of the bigger boys at the Day School, instead of taking their seats like the rest, got in under the gallery where coals and lumber were kept, and made a great noise as if dog and cat were worrying each other. Pleading with them only increased the uproar ; so I locked the doors, laid past the keys, and proceeded with the morning's work. Half an hour before the mid-day rest, I began singing a hymn, and marched the children round as if to leave ; then the two young rascals came out, and, walking in front, sang boisterously. Seizing the first by the collar, I made him stagger into the middle of the floor, and, dragging the other beside him, I raised my heavy cane and dared them to move. Ordering the children to resume their seats, I appointed them a jury to hear the case and to pass sentence. The two were found guilty, and awarded a severe lashing. I proposed, as this was their first offence, and as I only used the cane for a last resource, to forego all punishment, if they apologized and promised to be attentive and obedient in the future. They both heartily did so, and became my favourite scholars. Next evening I had little difficulty, as the worst characters did not at once return, guessing that they had got a bit of lion in the new " dominie," that was more likely to subdue than to be subdued.

On the following day, the parents of some children, getting alarmed by the rumours of these exploits, waited on me accompanied by the Minister, and said their children were terrified to come. I said that no *child* had been beaten by me, but that I insisted upon order and obedience ; I reminded the Minister that of my immediate predecessors three had suffered from these rowdies in the evening class—one actually going wrong in the mind over the worry, another losing his health and dying, and the third leaving in disgust; and finally I declared that I must either be master, at whatever cost, or leave the School. From that time perfect order was established, and the School flourished apace. During next week, many of the worst characters returned to their class work in the evening; but thenceforward the behaviour of all towards me was admirable. The attendance grew, till the School became crowded, both during the day and at night. During the mid-day hour even, I had a large class of young women who came to improve themselves in writing and arithmetic. By-and-bye the cane became a forgotten implement; the sorrow and pain which I showed as to badly done lessons, or anything blameworthy, proved the far more effectual penalty.

The School Committee had promised me at least ten shillings per week, and guaranteed to make up any deficit if the fees fell short of that sum; but if the income from fees exceeded that sum, all was to be mine. Affairs went on prosperously for a season; indeed, too much so for my selfish interest. The Committee, regarding the arrangement with me as only temporary, took advantage of the large attendance and better repute of the School, to secure the services of a master of the highest grade. The parents of many of the children, resenting this, offered to take and seat a hall, if I would remain and carry on an opposition School; but, besides regarding this as scarcely fair to the Committee, however unhandsomely they had treated me, I knew too well that I had neither education nor experience to compete with an accomplished teacher, and so declined the proposal, though grateful for their kind appreciation. Their children, however, got up a testimonial and subscription, in token of their gratitude and esteem, which was presented to me on the day before I left; and this I valued chiefly because the presentation was made by the young fellows who at first behaved so badly, but were now my devoted friends.

Once more I committed my future to the Lord God of my father, assured that in my very heart I was willing and anxious to serve Him and to follow the blessed Saviour, yet feeling keenly that intense darkness had again enclosed my path.

CHAPTER III.

IN GLASGOW CITY MISSION.

A.D. 1847—1856. ÆT. 23—32.

He leadeth me."—A Degraded District.—The Gospel in a Hay-Loft. — New Mission Premises.—At Work for Jesus.—At War with Hell.— Sowing Gospel Seeds.—Publicans on the War Path.—Marched to the Police Office.—Papists and Infidels.—An Infidel Saved.—An Infidel in Despair.—A Brand from the Burning.—A Saintly Child.— Papists in Arms.—Elder and Student.

BEFORE undertaking the Maryhill School, I had applied to be taken on as an agent in the Glasgow City Mission ; and the night before I had to leave Maryhill, I received a letter from Rev. Thomas Caic, the superintendent of the said Mission, saying that the directors had kept their eyes on me ever since my application, and requesting, as they understood I was leaving the School, that I would appear before them the next morning, and have my qualifications for becoming a Missionary examined into. Praising God, I went off at once, passed the examination successfully, and was appointed to spend two hours that afternoon and the following Monday in visitation with two of the directors, calling at every house in a low district of the town, and conversing with all the characters encountered there as to their eternal welfare. I had also to preach a " trial " discourse in a Mission meeting, where a deputation of directors would be present, the following evening being Sunday ; and on Wednesday evening they met again to hear their report and to accept or reject me.

All this had come upon me so unexpectedly, that I almost anticipated failure ; but looking up for help I went through with it, and on the fifth day after leaving the School they called me before a meeting of directors, and informed me that

I had passed my trials most successfully, and that the reports were so favourable that they had unanimously resolved to receive me at once as one of their City Missionaries. It was further explained that one of their number, Matthew Fairley, Esq., an elder in Dr. Symington's congregation, had guaranteed the half of my salary for two years, the other half to be met by the resources of the Mission voluntarily contributed,—the whole salary at that time amounting to £40 per annum. The district allocated to me was one especially needful and trying, that had never been thus heretofore occupied, in and around the Green Street of Calton, and I was enjoined to enter upon my duties at once. After receiving many good and kind counsels from these good and kind men, one of them in prayer very solemnly dedicated me and my work to the Lord ; and several of them were appointed to introduce me to my district, taking a day each by turns, and to assist me in making arrangements for the on-carrying of the work. Deeply solemnized with the responsibilities of my new office, I left that meeting praising God for all His undeserved mercies, and seeing most clearly His gracious hand in all the way by which He had led me, and the trials by which He had prepared me for this sphere of service. Man proposes—God disposes.

Most of these directors were men of God, adapted and qualified for this special work, and very helpful in counsel as they went with me from day to day, introducing me to my district, and seeing the character and surroundings of the people dwelling there. Looking back upon these Mission experiences, I have ever felt that they were, to me and many others, a good and profitable training of students for the office of the Ministry, preparing us to deal with men of every shade of thought and of character, and to lead them to the knowledge and service of the Lord Jesus.

I found the district a very degraded one. Many families said they had never been visited by any Minister ; and many were lapsed professors of religion who had attended no church for ten, sixteen, or twenty years, and said they had never been called upon by any Minister, nor by any Christian visitor. In it were congregated many avowed infidels, Romanists, and drunkards,—living together, and associated for evil, but apparently

3

without any effective counteracting influence. In many of its closes and courts sin and vice walked about openly—naked and *not* ashamed. We were expected to spend four hours daily in visiting from house to house, holding kitchen prayer-meetings amongst those visited, calling them together also in the evenings for worship or instruction, and trying by all means to do whatever good was possible amongst them. And the only place in the whole district available for a Sabbath evening Evangelistic Service was a hay-loft, under which a cow-feeder kept a large number of cows, and which was reached by an outside rickety wooden stair.

After nearly a year's hard work, I had only six or seven non-church-goers, who had been led to attend regularly there, besides about the same number who met on a week evening in the ground-floor of a house kindly granted for the purpose by a poor and industrious but ill-used Irishwoman. She supported her family by keeping a little shop, and selling coals. Her husband was a powerful man—a good worker, but a hard drinker ; and, like too many others addicted to intemperance, he abused and beat her, and pawned and drank everything he could get hold of. She, amid many prayers and tears, bore everything patiently, and strove to bring up her only daughter in the fear of God. We exerted, by God's blessing, a good influence upon him through our meetings. He became a Total Abstainer, gave up his evil ways, and attended Church regularly with his wife. As his interest increased, he tried to bring others also to the meeting, and urged them to become Abstainers. His wife became a centre of help and of good influence in all the district, as she kindly invited all and welcomed them to the meeting in her house, and my work grew every day more hopeful.

Seeing, however, that one year's hard work showed such small results, the directors proposed to remove me to another district, as in their estimation the non-church-goers in Green Street were unassailable by ordinary means. I pleaded for six months' longer trial, as I had gained the confidence of many of the poor people there, and had an invincible faith that the good seed sown would soon bear blessed fruit. To this the directors kindly agreed. At our next meeting I

informed those present that, if we could not draw out more
of the non-church-goers to attend the services, I should be
removed to another part of the city. Each one there and
then agreed to bring another to our next meeting. Both our
meetings at once doubled their attendance. My interest in
them and their interest in me now grew apace ; and, for fear
I might be taken away from them, they made another effort,
and again doubled our attendance. Henceforth Meeting and
Class were both too large for any house that was available for
us in the whole of our district. We instituted a Bible Class,
a Singing Class, a Communicants' Class, and a Total Abstinence
Society ; and, in addition to the usual meetings, we opened
two prayer-meetings specially for the Calton division of the
Glasgow Police—one at a suitable hour for the men on day
duty, and another for those on night duty. The men got up
a Mutual Improvement Society and Singing Class also amongst
themselves, weekly, on another evening My work now
occupied every evening in the week ; and I had two meetings
every Sabbath. By God's blessing they all prospered, and
gave evidence of such fruits as showed that the Lord was
working there for good by our humble instrumentality.

The kind cow-feeder had to inform us—and he did it with
much genuine sorrow—that at a given date he would require
the hay-loft, which was our place of meeting; and as no other
suitable house or hall could be got, the poor people and I
feared the extinction of our work. On hearing this the ostlers
and other servants of Menzies, the coach-hirer, who had
extensive premises near our place of meeting, of their own
accord asked and obtained liberty to clear out a hay-loft of
theirs that was seldom in use, and resolved, at their own
expense, to erect an outside wooden stair for the convenience
of the people. This becoming known, and being much talked
of, caused great joy in the district, arrested general attention,
and increased the interest of our work. But I saw that,
however generous, it could be at the best only another
temporary arrangement, and that the premises might again at
any moment be required. After prayer I therefore laid the
whole case before my good and great-hearted friend, Thomas
Binnie, Sen., Monteith Row, and he, after inquiring into all

the circumstances, secured a good site for a Mission Hall in
a piece of unoccupied ground near our old hay-loft, on which
he proposed to build suitable premises at his own expense.

At that very time, however, a commodious block of buildings,
that had been Church, Schools, Manse, etc., came into the
market. Mr. Binnie persuaded Dr. Symington's congregation,
Great Hamilton Street, in connection with which my Mission
was carried on, to purchase the whole property for Mission
purposes. Its situation at the foot of Green Street gave it a
control of the whole district where my work lay; and so the
Church was given to me in which to conduct all my meetings,
while the other Halls were adapted as Schools for poor girls
and boys, where they were educated by a proper master, and
were largely supplied with books, clothing, and sometimes
even food, by the ladies of the congregation. The purchasing
and using of these buildings for an Evangelistic and Educational
Mission became a blessing—a very conspicuous blessing—to
that district in the Calton of Glasgow ; and the blessing still
perpetuates itself, not only in the old premises, now used
for an Industrial School, but still more in the beautiful and
spacious Mission Halls, erected immediately in front of the
old, and consecrated to the work of the Lord in that poor and
crowded and clamant portion of the city.

Availing myself of the increased facilities, my work was all
re-organized. On Sabbath morning, at seven o'clock, I had
one of the most deeply interesting and fruitful of all my Classes
for the study of the Bible. It was attended by from seventy
to a hundred of the very poorest young women and grown-up
lads of the whole district. They had nothing to put on except
their ordinary work-day clothes,—all without bonnets, some
without shoes. Beautiful was it to mark how the poorest
began to improve in personal appearance immediately after
they came to our Class ; how they gradually got shoes and one
bit of clothing after another, to enable them to attend our
other Meetings, and then to go to Church; and, above all,
how eagerly they sought to bring others with them, taking a
deep personal interest in all the work of the Mission. Long
after they themselves could appear in excellent dress, many of
them still continued to attend in their working clothes, and to

bring other and poorer girls with them to that Morning Class, and thereby helped to improve and elevate their companions.

My delight in that Bible Class was among the purest joys in all my life, and the results were amongst the most certain and precious of all my Ministry. Yet it was not made successful without unceasing pains and prayers. What would my younger brethren in the Ministry, or in the Mission, think of starting out at six o'clock every Sunday morning, running from street to street for an hour, knocking at the doors and rousing the careless, and thus getting together, and keeping together, their Bible Class? This was what I did at first; but, in course of time, a band of voluntary visitors belonging to the Class took charge of all the irregulars, the indifferents, and the new-comers, and thereby not only relieved and assisted me, but vastly increased their own personal interest in the work, and became warmly attached to each other.

I had also a very large Bible Class—a sort of Bible-Reading —on Monday night, attended by all, of both sexes and of any age, who cared to come or had any interest in the Mission. Wednesday evening, again, was devoted to a Prayer-Meeting for all; and the attendance often more than half-filled the Church. There I usually took up some book of Holy Scripture and read and lectured right through, practically expounding and applying it. On Thursday I held a Communicants' Class, intended for the more careful instruction of all who wished to become full members of the Church. Our constant text-book was " Paterson on the Shorter Catechism " (Nelson & Sons), than which I have never seen a better compendium of the doctrines of Holy Scripture. Each being thus trained for a season, received from me, if found worthy, a letter to the Minister of any Protestant Church which he or she felt inclined to join. In this way great numbers became active and useful communicants in the surrounding congregations; and eight young lads of humble circumstances educated themselves for the Ministry of the Church—most of them getting their first lessons in Latin and Greek from my very poor stock of the same! Friday evening was occupied with a Singing Class, teaching Church music, and practising for our Sabbath meetings.

On Saturday evening we held our Total Abstinence meeting, at which the members themselves took a principal part, in readings, addresses, recitations, singing hymns, etc. Great good resulted from this Total Abstinence work. Many adults took and kept the pledge, thereby greatly increasing the comfort and happiness of their homes. Many were .led to attend the Church on the Lord's Day, who had formerly spent it in rioting and drinking. But, above all, it trained the young to fear the very name of Intoxicating Drink, and to hate and keep far away from everything that led to intemperance. From observation, at an early age I became convinced that mere Temperance Societies were a failure, and that Total Abstinence, by the grace of God, was the only sure preventive as well as remedy. What was temperance in one man was drunkenness in another; and all the drunkards came, not from those who practised total abstinence, but from those who practised or tried to practise temperance. I had seen *temperance* men drinking wihe in the presence of others who drank to excess, and never could see how they felt themselves clear of blame; and I had known Ministers and others, once strong temperance advocates, fall through this so-called "moderation," and become drunkards. Therefore it has all my life appeared to me beyond dispute, in reference to intoxicants of every kind, that the only rational temperance is Total Abstinence from them as beverages, and the use of them exclusively as drugs, and then only with extreme caution, as they are deceptive and deleterious poisons of the most debasing and demoralising kind. I found also, that when I tried to reclaim a drunkard, or caution any one as to intemperate habits, one of the first questions was:

" Are you a pledged Abstainer yourself?"

By being enabled to reply decidedly, "Yes, I am," the mouth of the objector was closed; and that gave me a hundred-fold more influence with him than if I had had to confess that I was only "temperate." For the good of others, and for the increase of their personal influence as the servants of Christ, I would plead with every Minister and Missionary, every Office-bearer and Sabbath-school Teacher, every one who wishes to work for the Lord Jesus in the Family, the

Church, and the World, to be a Total Abstainer from all intoxicating drinks as common beverages.

I would add my testimony also against the use of tobacco, which injures and leads many astray, especially lads and young men, and which never can be required by any person in ordinary health. But I would not be understood to regard the evils that flow from it as deserving to be mentioned in comparison with the unutterable woes and miseries of intemperance. To be protected, however, from suspicion and from evil, all the followers of our Lord Jesus should, in self-denial (how small!) and in consecration to His service, be pledged Abstainers from both of these selfish indulgences— which are certainly injurious to many, which are no ornament to any character, and which can be no help in well-doing. Praise God for the many who are now so pledged! Happy day for poor Humanity, when all the Lord's people adopt this self-denying ordinance for the good of the race!

Not boastfully, but gratefully, let me record that my Classes and Meetings were now attended by such numbers that they were amongst the largest and most successful that the City Mission had ever known; and by God's blessing I was enabled to develop them into a regular, warmly-attached, and intelligent Congregation. My work, however exacting, was full of joy to me. From five to six hundred people were in usual weekly attendance; consisting exclusively of poor working persons, and largely of the humbler class of mill-workers. So soon as their circumstances improved, they were constantly removing to more respectable and healthy localities, and got to be scattered over all the city. But wherever they went, I visited them regularly to prevent their falling away, and held by them till I got them interested in some Church near where they had gone to live. On my return, many years after, from the Foreign Mission field, there was scarcely a congregation in any part of the city where some one did not warmly salute me with the cry, "Don't you remember me?" And then, after greetings, came the well-remembered name of one or other member of my old Bible Class.

Such toils left me but small time for private studies. The

City Missionary was required to spend four hours daily in visitation-work; but often had I to spend double that time, day after day, in order to overtake what was laid upon me. About eight or ten of my most devoted young men, and double that number of young women, whom I had trained to become Visitors and Tract Distributors, greatly strengthened my hands. Each of the young men by himself, and the young women two by two, had charge of a portion of a street, which was visited by them regularly twice every month. At a monthly meeting of all our Workers, reports were given in, changes were noted, and all matters brought under review were attended to. Besides, if any note or message were left at my lodging, or any case of sickness or want reported, it was looked after by me without delay. Several Christian gentlemen, mill-owners and other employers in the Calton, Mile-end, and Bridgeton of Glasgow, were so interested in my work that they kindly offered to give employment to every deserving person recommended by me, and that relieved much distress and greatly increased my influence for good.

Almost the only enemies I had were the keepers of Public-Houses, whose trade had been injured by my Total Abstinence Society. Besides the Saturday night meetings all the year round, we held, in summer evenings and on Saturday afternoons, Evangelistic and Total Abstinence services in the open air. We met in Thomson's Lane, a short and broad street, not open for the traffic of conveyances, and admirably situated for our purposes. Our pulpit was formed by the top of an outside stair, leading to the second flat of a house in the middle of the lane. Prominent Christian workers took part with us in delivering addresses; an intimation through my Classes usually secured good audiences; and the hearty singing of hymns by my Mission Choir gave zest and joy to the whole proceedings. Of other so-called "attractions" we had none, and needed none, save the sincere proclamation of the Good Tidings from God to men!

On one occasion, it becoming known that we had arranged for a special Saturday afternoon demonstration, a deputation of Publicans complained beforehand to the Captain of the Police—that our meetings were interfering with their legitimate trade. He heard their complaints and promised to send officers to watch the meeting, prevent any disturbance, and take in charge all offenders, but declined to prohibit the meetings till he received their reports. The Captain, a pious Wesleyan, who was in full sympathy with us and our work, informed me of the complaints made and intimated that his men would be present; but I was just to conduct the meeting as usual, and he would guarantee that strict justice would be done. The Publicans having announced amongst their sympathizers that the Police were to break up and prevent our meeting and take the conductors in charge, a very large crowd assembled, both friendly and unfriendly, for the Publicans and their hangers-on were there "to see the fun," and to help in " baiting " the Missionary. Punctually, I ascended the stone stair, accompanied by another Missionary who was also to deliver an address, and announced our opening hymn. As we sang, a company of Police appeared, and were quietly located here and there among the crowd, the serjeant himself taking his post close by the platform, whence the whole assembly could be scanned. Our enemies were jubilant, and signals were passed betwixt them and their friends, as if the time had come to provoke a row. Before the hymn was finished, Captain Baker himself, to the infinite surprise of friend and foe alike, joined us on the platform, devoutly listened to all that was said, and waited till the close. The Publicans could not for very shame leave, while he was there at their suggestion and request, though they had wit enough to perceive that his presence had frustrated all their sinister plans. They had to hear our addresses and prayers and hymns; they had to listen to the intimation of our future meetings. When all had quietly dispersed, the Captain warmly congratulated us on our large and well-conducted Congregation, and hoped that great good would result from our efforts. This opposition, also, the Lord overruled to increase our influence, and to give point and publicity to our assaults upon the kingdom of Satan.

Though disappointed thus, some of the Publicans resolved to have revenge. On the following Saturday evening, when a large meeting was being addressed in our Green Street

Church, which had to be entered by a great iron gateway, a spirit merchant ran his van in front of the gate, so that the people could not leave the Church without its removal. Hearing this, I sent two of my young men to draw it aside and clear the way. The Publican, watching near by in league with two policemen, pounced upon the young men whenever they seized the shafts, and gave them in charge for removing his property. On hearing that the young men were being marched to the Police Office, I ran after them and asked what was their offence? They replied that they were in charge for injuring the spirit merchant's property; and the officers tartly informed me that if I further interfered I should be taken too. I replied, that as the young men only did what was necessary, and at my request, I would go with them to prison.

The cry now went through the street, that the Publicans were sending the Missionary and his young men to the Police Office, and a huge mob rushed together to rescue us; but I earnestly entreated them not to raise disturbance, but allow us quietly to pass on. At the Office, it appeared as if the lieutenant on duty and the men under him were all in sympathy with the Publicans. He took down in writing all their allegations, but would not listen to us. At this stage a handsomely dressed and dignified gentleman came forward and said, "What bail is required?"

A few sharp words passed; another and apparently higher officer entered, and took part in the colloquy. I could only hear the gentleman protest, in authoritative tones, the policemen having been quietly asked some questions, "I know this whole case, I will expose it to the bottom; expect me here to stand by the Missionary and these young men on Monday morning."

Before I could collect my wits to thank him, and before I quite understood what was going on, he had disappeared; and the superior officer turned to us and intimated in a very respectful manner that the charge had been withdrawn, and that I and my friends were at liberty. I never found out exactly who the gentleman was that befriended us; but from the manner in which he asserted himself and was listened to,

I saw that he was a Citizen well known in official quarters. From that day our work progressed without further open opposition; and many, who had been slaves of intemperance, were not only reformed but became fervent workers in the Total Abstinence cause.

Though Intemperance was the main cause of poverty, suffering, misery, and vice in that district of Glasgow, I had also considerable opposition from Romanists and Infidels, many of whom met in clubs, where they drank together, and gloried in their wickedness and in leading other young men astray. Against these I prepared and delivered lectures, at the close of which "discussion" was invited and allowed; but I fear they did little good. These men embraced the opportunity of airing their absurdities, or sowing the seeds of corruption in those whom otherwise they could never have reached, while their own hearts and minds were fast shut against all conviction or light.

One infidel Lecturer in the district became very ill. His wife called me in to visit him. I found him possessed of a Circulating Library of infidel books, by which he sought to pervert unwary minds. Though he had talked and lectured much against the Gospel, he did not at all really understand its message. He had read the Bible, but only to find food there for ridicule. Now supposed to be dying, he confessed that his mind was full of terror as to the Future. After several visits and frequent conversations and prayers, he became genuinely and deeply interested, drank in God's message of salvation, and cried aloud with many tears for pardon and peace. He bitterly lamented the evil he had done, and called in all the infidel literature that he had in circulation, with the purpose of destroying it. He began to speak solemnly to any of his old companions that came to see him, telling them what he had found in the Lord Jesus. At his request I bought and brought to him a Bible, which he received with great joy, saying, "This is the book for me now;" and adding, "Since you were here last, I gathered together all my infidel books; my wife locked the door, till she and my daughter tore them to pieces, and I struck the light that reduced the pile to ashes.

As long as he lived, this man was unwearied and unflinching in testifying, to all that crossed his path, how much Jesus Christ had been to his heart and soul; and he died in the possession of a full and blessed hope.

Another Infidel, whose wife was a Roman Catholic, also became unwell, and gradually sank under great suffering and agony. His blasphemies against God were known and shuddered at by all the neighbours. His wife pled with me to visit him. She refused, at my suggestion, to call her own priest, so I accompanied her at last. The man refused to hear one word about spiritual things, and foamed with rage. He even spat at me, when I mentioned the name of Jesus. "The natural man receiveth not the things of the Spirit of God; for they are foolishness unto him!" There is a "wisdom" which is at best earthly, and *at worst* "sensual and devilish." His wife asked me to take care of the little money they had, as she would not entrust it to her own priest. I visited the poor man daily, but his enmity to God and his sufferings together seemed to drive him mad. His yells gathered crowds on the streets. He tore to pieces his very bed-clothes, till they had to bind him on the iron bed where he lay, foaming and blaspheming. Towards the end I pled with him even then to look to the Lord Jesus, and asked if I might pray with him? With all his remaining strength, he shouted at me, "Pray for me to the devil!"

Reminding him how he had always denied that there was any devil, I suggested that he must surely believe in one now, else he would scarcely make such a request, even in mockery. In great rage, he cried, "Yes, I believe there is a devil, and a God, and a just God, too; but I have hated Him in life, and I hate Him in death!"

With these awful words, he wriggled into Eternity; but his shocking death produced a very serious impression for good, especially amongst young men, in the district where his character was known.

How different was the case of that Doctor who also had been an unbeliever as well as a drunkard! Highly educated, skilful, and gifted above most in his profession, he was taken into consultation for specially dangerous cases, whenever they could find him tolerably sober. After one of his excessive "bouts," he had a dreadful attack of *delirium tremens*. At one time, wife and watchers had a fierce struggle to dash from his lips a draught of prussic acid; at another, they detected the silver-hafted lancet concealed in the band of his shirt, as he lay down, to bleed himself to death. His aunt came and pled with me to visit him. My heart bled for his poor young wife and two beautiful little children. Visiting him twice daily, and sometimes even more frequently, I found the way somehow into his heart, and he would do almost anything for me, and longed for my visits. When again the fit of self-destruction seized him, they sent for me; he held out his hand eagerly, and grasping mine said, "Put all these people out of the room, remain you with me; I will be quiet, I will do everything you ask!"

I got them all to leave, but whispered to one in passing to "keep near the door."

Alone I sat beside him, my hand in his, and kept up a quiet conversation for several hours. After we had talked of everything that I could think of, and it was now far into the morning, I said, "If you had a Bible here, we might read a chapter, verse about."

He said dreamily, "There was once a Bible above yon press; if you can get up to it, you might find it there yet."

Getting it, dusting it, and laying it on a small table which I drew near to the sofa on which we sat, we read there and then a chapter together. After this, I said, "Now, shall we pray?"

He replied heartily, "Yes."

I having removed the little table, we kneeled down together at the sofa; and after a solemn pause, I whispered, "You pray first."

He replied, "I curse, I cannot pray; would you have me curse God to His face?"

I answered, "You promised to do all that I asked; you must pray, or try to pray, and let me hear that you cannot."

He said, "I cannot curse God on my knees; let me stand and I will curse Him; I cannot pray."

I gently held him on his knees, saying, "Just try to pray, and let me hear you cannot.'

Instantly he cried out, "O Lord, Thou knowest I cannot pray," and was going to say something dreadful as he strove to rise up. But I took up gently the words he had uttered as if they had been my own, and continued the prayer, pleading for him and his dear ones as we knelt there together, till he showed that he was completely subdued and lying low at the feet of God. On rising from our knees he was manifestly greatly impressed, and I said, "Now, as I must be at College by daybreak and must return to my lodging for my books and an hour's rest, will you do one thing more for me before I go?"

"Yes," was his reply.

"Then," said I, "it is long since you had a refreshing sleep; now, will you lie down, and I will sit by you till you fall asleep?"

He lay down, and was soon fast asleep. After commending him to the care and blessing of the Lord, I quietly slipped out, and his wife returned to watch by his side. When I came back later in the day, after my Classes were over, he, on hearing my foot and voice, came running to meet me, and clasping me in his arms, cried, "Thank God, I can pray now! I rose this morning refreshed from sleep, and prayed with my wife and children for the first time in my life; and now I shall do so every day, and serve God while I live, who hath dealt in so great mercy with me!"

After delightful conversation, he promised to go with me to Dr. Symington's church on Sabbath Day; there he took sittings beside me; at next half-yearly Communion he and his wife were received into membership, and their children were baptized; and from that day till his death he led a devoted and most useful Christian life. Henceforth, as a medical man, he delighted to attend all poor and destitute cases which we brought under his care; he administered to them for Jesus' sake, and spoke to them of their blessed Saviour. When he came across cases that were hopeless, he sent for me to visit them too, being as anxious for their souls as for their bodies. He died, years after this, of consumption, partly at least the fruit of early excesses; but he was serenely prepared for death, and happy in the assured hope of eternal blessedness with

Christ. He sleeps in Jesus ; and I do believe that I shall meet him in Glory as a trophy of redeeming grace and love !

In my Mission district, I was the witness of many joyful departures to be with Jesus,—I do not like to name them " deaths " at all. Even now, at the distance of nearly forty years, many instances, especially amongst the young men and women who attended my Classes, rise up before my mind. They left us rejoicing in the bright assurance that nothing present or to come " could ever separate them or us from the love of God which is in Christ Jesus our Lord." Several of them, by their conversation even on their death-bed, were known to have done much good. Many examples might be given ; but I can find room for only one. John Sim, a dear little boy, was carried away by consumption. His child-heart seemed to be filled with joy about seeing Jesus. His simple prattle, mingled with deep questionings, arrested not only his young companions, but pierced the hearts of some careless sinners who heard him, and greatly refreshed the faith of God's dear people. It was the very pathos of song incarnated to hear the weak quaver of his dying voice sing out,—

> " I lay my sins on Jesus,
> The spotless Lamb of God."

Shortly before his decease he said to his parents, " I am going soon to be with Jesus ; but I sometimes fear that I may not see you there."

" Why so, my child ? " said his weeping mother.

" Because," he answered, " if you were set upon going to Heaven and seeing Jesus there, you would pray about it, and sing about it ; you would talk about Jesus to others, and tell them of that happy meeting with Him in Glory. All this my dear Sabbath School teacher taught me, and she will meet me there. Now why did not you, my father and mother, tell me all these things about Jesus, if you are going to meet Him too ? " Their tears fell fast over their dying child ; and he little knew, in his unthinking eighth year, what a message from God had pierced their souls through his innocent words.

One day an aunt from the country visited his mother, and their talk had run in channels for which the child no longer felt any interest. On my sitting down beside him, he said, "Sit you down and talk with me about Jesus; I am tired hearing so much talk about everything else but Jesus; I am going soon to be with Him. Oh, do tell me everything you know or have ever heard about Jesus, the spotless Lamb of God!"

At last the child literally longed to be away, not for rest, or freedom from pain—for of that he had very little—but, as he himself always put it, "to see Jesus." And, after all, that was the wisdom of the heart, however he learned it. Eternal life, here or hereafter, is just the vision of Jesus.

Amongst many of the Roman Catholics in my Mission district, also, I was very kindly received, and allowed even to read the Scriptures and to pray. At length, however, a young woman who professed to be converted by my Classes and Meetings brought things to a crisis betwixt them and me. She had renounced her former faith, was living in a Protestant family, and looked to me as her pastor and teacher. One night, a closed carriage, with two men and women, was sent from a Nunnery in Clyde Street, to take her and her little sister with them. She refused, and declined all authority on their part, declaring that she was now a Protestant by her own free choice. During this altercation, a message had been sent for me. On arriving, I found the house filled with a noisy crowd. Before them all, she appealed to me for protection from these her enemies. The Romanists, becoming enraged, jostled me into a corner of the room, and there enclosed me. The two women pulled her out of bed by force, for the girl had been sick, and began to dress her, but she fainted among their hands.

I called out, "Do not murder the poor girl! Get her water, quick, quick!" and leaving my hat on the table, I rushed through amongst them, as if in search of water, and they let me pass. Knowing that the house had only one door, I quickly slipped the key from within, shut and locked the door outside, and with the key in my hand ran to the Police Office.

Having secured two constables to protect the girl and take the would-be captors into custody, I returned, opened the door, and found, alas! that these constables were themselves Roman

Catholics, and at once set about frustrating me and assisting their own friends. The poor sick girl was supported by the arms into the carriage; the policemen cleared the way through the crowd; and before I could force my way through the obstructives in the house, the conveyance was already starting. I appealed and shouted to the crowds to protect the girl, and seize and take the whole party to the Police Office. A gentleman in the crowd took my part, and said to a big Highland policeman in the street, " Mac, I commit that conveyance and party to you on a criminal charge, before witnesses; you will suffer, if they escape."

The driver lashing at his horse to get away, Mac drew his baton and struck, when the driver leapt down to the street on the opposite side, and threw the reins in the policeman's face. Thereupon our stalwart friend at once mounted the box, and drove straight for the Police Office. On arriving there, we discovered that only the women were inside with the sick girl —the men having escaped in the scuffle and the crush. What proved more disappointing was that the lieutenant on duty happened to be a Papist, who, after hearing our statement and conferring with the parties in the conveyance, returned, and said,—

" Her friends are taking her to a comfortable home; you have no right to interfere, and I have let them go." He further refused to hear the grounds of our complaint, and ordered the police to clear the Office.

Next morning, a false and foolish account of the whole affair appeared in the Newspapers, condemnatory of the Mission and of myself; a meeting of the directors was summoned, and the Superintendent came to my lodging to take me before them. Having heard all, and questioned and cross-questioned me, they resolved to prosecute the abductors of the girl. The Nunnery authorities confessed that the little sister was with them, but denied that the other had been taken in there, or that they knew anything of her case. Though the girl was sought for carefully by the Police, and by all the members of my Class, for nearly a fortnight, no trace of her or of the coachman or of any of the parties could be discovered; till one day from a cellar, through a grated

4

window, she called to one of my Class girls passing by, and
begged her to run and let me know that she was confined
there. At once, the directors of the City Mission were informed by me, and Police were sent to rescue her; but on
examining that house they found that she had been again
removed. The occupiers denied all knowledge of where she
had gone, or who had taken her away from their lodging. All
other efforts failed to find her, till she was left at the Poor
House door, far gone in dropsy, and soon after died in that
last refuge of the destitute and forsaken.

Anonymous letters were now sent, threatening my life ; and
I was publicly cursed from the altar by the priests in Aber-
cromby Street Chapel. The directors of the Mission, fearing
violence, advised me to leave Glasgow for a short holiday,
and even offered to arrange for my being taken for work in
Edinburgh for a year, that the fanatical passions of the Irish
Papists might have time to subside. But I refused to leave
my work. I went on conducting it all as in the past. The
worst thing that happened was, that on rushing one day past a
row of houses occupied exclusively by Papists, a stone thrown
from one of them cut me severely above the eye, and I fell
stunned and bleeding. When I recovered and scrambled to
my feet, no person of course that could be suspected was to be
seen ! The doctor having dressed the wound, it rapidly healed,
and after a short confinement I resumed my work and my
studies without any further serious annoyance. Attempts were
made more than once, in these Papist closes, and I believe by
the Papists themselves, to pour pails of boiling water on my
head, over windows and down dark stairs, but in every case I
marvellously escaped ; and as I would not turn coward, their
malice tired itself out, and they ultimately left me entirely at
peace. Is not this a feature of the lower Irish, and especially
Popish population ? Let them see that bullying makes you
afraid, and they will brutally and cruelly misuse you; but defy
them fearlessly, or take them by the nose, and they will crouch
like whelps beneath your feet. Is there anything in their
religion that accounts for this ? Is it not a system of alter-
nating tyranny on the one part, and terror, abject terror, on
the other ?

About this same time there was an election of Elders for Dr. Symington's congregation, and I was by an almost unanimous vote chosen for that office. For years now I had been attached to them as City Missionary for their district, and many friends urged me to accept the eldership, as likely to increase my usefulness, and give me varied experience for my future work. My dear father, also, himself an Elder in the congregation at Dumfries, advised me similarly; and though very young, comparatively, for such a post, I did accept the office, and continued to act as an Elder and member of Dr. Symington's Kirk Session, till by-and-bye I was ordained as a Missionary to the New Hebrides—where the great lot of my life had been cast by the Lord, as yet unknown to me.

All through my City Mission period, I was painfully carrying on my studies, first at the University of Glasgow, and thereafter at the Reformed Presbyterian Divinity Hall; and also medical classes at the Andersonian College. With the exception of one session, when failure of health broke me down, I struggled patiently on through ten years. The work was hard and most exacting; and if I never attained the scholarship for which I thirsted—being but poorly grounded in my younger days—I yet had much of the blessed Master's presence in all my efforts, which many better scholars sorely lacked; and I was sustained by the lofty aim which burned all these years bright within my soul, namely,—to be qualified as a preacher of the Gospel of Christ, to be owned and used by Him for the salvation of perishing men.

CHAPTER IV.

FOREIGN MISSION CLAIMS.

A.D. 1856—1857. ÆT. 32—33.

The Wail of the Heathen.—A Missionary Wanted.—Two Souls on the
Altar.—Lions in the Path.—The Old Folks at Home.—Successors in
Green Street Mission.—Old Green Street Hands.—A Father in God.

HAPPY in my work as I felt, and successful by the blessing
of God, yet I continually heard, and chiefly during my
last years in the Divinity Hall, the wail of the perishing Heathen
in the South Seas ; and I saw that few were caring for them,
while I well knew that many would be ready to take up my
work in Calton, and carry it forward perhaps with more
efficiency than myself. Without revealing the state of my
mind to any person, this was the supreme subject of my daily
meditation and prayer ; and this also led me to enter upon
those medical studies, in which I purposed taking the full
course ; but at the close of my third year, an incident occurred,
which led me at once to offer myself for the Foreign Mission
field.

The Reformed Presbyterian Church of Scotland, in which
I had been brought up, had been advertising for another Missionary to join the Rev. John Inglis in his grand work in the
New Hebrides. Dr. Bates, the excellent convener of the
Heathen Missions Committee, was deeply grieved, because for
two years their appeal had failed. At length, the Synod, after
much prayer and consultation, felt the claims of the Heathen
so urgently pressed upon them by the Lord's repeated calls,
that they resolved to cast lots, to discover whether God would
thus select any Minister to be relieved from his home·charge,

and designated as a Missionary to the South Seas. Each member of Synod, as I was informed, agreed to hand in, after solemn appeal to God, the names of the three best qualified in his esteem for such a work, and he who had the clear majority was to be loosed from his Congregation, and to proceed to the Mission field—or the first and second highest, if two could be secured. Hearing this debate, and feeling an intense interest in these most unusual proceedings, I remember yet the hushed solemnity of the prayer before the names were handed in. I remember the strained silence that held the Assembly while the scrutinizers retired to examine the papers; and I remember how tears blinded my eyes when they returned to announce that the result was so indecisive, that it was clear that the Lord had not in that way provided a Missionary. The cause was once again solemnly laid before God in prayer, and a cloud of sadness appeared to fall over all the Synod.

The Lord kept saying within me, " Since none better qualified can be got, rise and offer yourself ! " Almost overpowering was the impulse to answer aloud, " Here am I, send me." But I was dreadfully afraid of mistaking my mere human emotions for the will of God. So I resolved to make it a subject of close deliberation and prayer for a few days longer, and to look at the proposal from every possible aspect. Besides, I was keenly solicitous about the effect upon the hundreds of young people and others, now attached to all my Classes and Meetings ; and yet I felt a growing assurance that this was the call of God to His servant, and that He who was willing to employ me in the work abroad, was both able and willing to provide for the on-carrying of my work at home. The wail and the claims of the Heathen were constantly sounding in my ears. I saw them perishing for lack of the knowledge of the true God and His Son Jesus, while my Green Street people had the open Bible and all the means of grace within easy reach, which, if they rejected, they did so wilfully, and at their own peril. None seemed prepared for the Heathen field; many were capable and ready for the Calton service. My medical studies, as well as my literary and divinity training, had specially qualified me in some ways for the Foreign field, and from every aspect at which I could look the whole facts in the face, the voice within me sounded like a voice from God.

It was under good Dr. Bates of West Campbell Street that I had begun my career in Glasgow—receiving £25 per annum for district visitation in connection with his Congregation, along with instruction under Mr. Hislop and his staff in the Free Church Normal Seminary—and oh, how Dr. Bates did rejoice, and even weep for joy, when I called on him, and offered myself for the New Hebrides Mission! I returned to my lodging with a lighter heart than I had for some time enjoyed feeling that nothing so clears the vision, and lifts up the life, as a decision to move forward in what you know to be entirely the will of the Lord. I said to my fellow-student, who had chummed with me all through our course at college, "I have been away signing my banishment" (a rather trifling way of talk for such an occasion). "I have offered myself as a Missionary for the New Hebrides."

After a long and silent meditation, in which he seemed lost in far-wandering thoughts, his answer was, "If they will accept of me, I am also resolved to go!"

I said, "Will you write the Convener to that effect, or let me do so?"

He replied, "You may."

A few minutes later his letter of offer was in the post office. Next morning, Dr. Bates called upon us early, and after a long conversation, commended us and our future work to the Lord God in fervent prayer.

This fellow-student, Mr. Joseph Copeland, had also for some time been a very successful City Missionary in the Camlachie district, while attending along with me at the Divinity Hall. The leading of God, whereby we both resolved at the same time to give ourselves to the Foreign Mission field, was wholly unexpected by us, as we had never once spoken to each other about going abroad. At a meeting of the Foreign Missions Committee, held immediately thereafter, both were, after due deliberation, formally accepted, on condition that we passed successfully the usual examinations required of candidates for the Ministry. And for the next twelve months we were placed under a special committee for advice as to medical experience, acquaintance with the rudiments of trades, and anything else which might be thought useful to us in the Foreign field.

When it became known that I was preparing to go abroad as Missionary, nearly all were dead against the proposal, except Dr. Bates and my fellow-student. My dear father and mother, however, when I consulted them, characteristically replied, that " they had long since given me away to the Lord, and in this matter also would leave me to God's disposal." From other quarters we were besieged with the strongest opposition on all sides. Even Dr. Symington, one of my professors in divinity, and the beloved Minister in connection with whose congregation I had wrought so long as a City Missionary, and in whose Kirk Session I had for years sat as an Elder, repeatedly urged me to remain at home. He argued, that " Green Street Church was doubtless the sphere for which God had given me peculiar qualifications, and in which He had so largely blessed my labours ; that if I left those now attending my Classes and Meetings, they might be scattered, and many of them would probably fall away ; that I was leaving certainty for uncertainty—work in which God had made me greatly useful, for work in which I might fail to be useful, and only throw away my life amongst Cannibals."

I replied, that " my mind was finally resolved ; that, though *i* loved my work and my people, yet I felt that I could leave them to the care of Jesus, who would soon provide them a better pastor than I ; and that, with regard to my life amongst the Cannibals, as I had only once to die, I was content to leave the time and place and means in the hand of God, who had already marvellously preserved me when visiting cholera patients and the fever-stricken poor ; on that score I had positively no further concern, having left it all absolutely to the Lord, whom I sought to serve and honour, whether in life or by death."

The house connected with my Green Street Church was now offered to me for a Manse, and any reasonable salary that I cared to ask (as against the promised £120 per annum for the far-off and dangerous New Hebrides), on condition that I would remain at home. I cannot honestly say that such offers or opposing influences proved a heavy trial to me ; they rather tended to confirm my determination that the path of duty was to go abroad.   Amongst many who sought to deter me, was one dear old Christian gentleman, whose crowning argument always was, "The Cannibals ! you will be eaten by Cannibals ! "

At last I replied, " Mr. Dickson, you are advanced in years now, and your own prospect is soon to be laid in the grave, there to be eaten by worms ; I confess to you, that if I can but live and die serving and honouring the Lord Jesus, it will make no difference to me whether I am eaten by Cannibals or by worms ; and in the Great Day my resurrection body will arise as fair as yours in the likeness of our risen Redeemer."

The old gentleman, raising his hands in a deprecating attitude, left the room exclaiming, " After that I have nothing more to say ! "

My dear Green Street people grieved excessively at the thought of my leaving them, and daily pled with me to remain. Indeed, the opposition was so strong from nearly all, and many of them warm Christian friends, that I was sorely tempted to question whether I was carrying out the Divine will, or only some headstrong wish of my own.   This also caused me much anxiety, and drove me close to God in prayer. But again every doubt would vanish, when I clearly saw that all at home had free access to the Bible and the means of grace, with Gospel light shining all around them, while the poor Heathen were perishing, without even the chance of knowing all God's love and mercy to men.   Conscience said louder and clearer every day, " Leave all these results with Jesus your Lord, who said, ' Go ye into all the world, preach the Gospel to every creature, and lo ! I am with you alway.' " These words kept ringing in my ears ; these were our *marching orders.*

Some retorted upon me, " There are Heathen at home ; let us seek and save, first of all, the lost ones perishing at our doors."   This I felt to be most true, and an appalling fact ; but I unfailingly observed that those who made this retort neglected these Home Heathen themselves ; and so the objection, as from them, lost all its power.   They would ungrudgingly spend more on a fashionable party at dinner or tea, on concert or ball or theatre, or on some ostentatious display, or worldly and selfish indulgence, ten times more, perhaps in a single day, than they would give in a year, or in half a lifetime, for the conversion of the whole Heathen World, either at home or abroad. Objections from all such people must, of course, always count for nothing among men to whom spiritual things are realities. For these people themselves—I do, and always did, only pity them, as God's stewards, making such a miserable use of time and money entrusted to their care.

On meeting with so many obstructing influences, I again laid the whole matter before my dear parents, and their reply was to this effect:—" Heretofore we feared to bias you, but now we must tell you why we praise God for the decision to which you have been led. Your father's heart was set upon being a Minister, but other claims forced him to give it up. When you were given to them, your father and mother laid you upon the altar, their first-born, to be consecrated, if God saw fit, as a Missionary of the Cross ; and it has been their constant prayer that you might be prepared, qualified, and led to this very decision ; and we pray with all our heart that the Lord may accept your offering, long spare you, and give you many souls from the Heathen World for your hire." From that moment, every doubt as to my path of duty for ever vanished. I saw the hand of God very visibly, not only preparing me for, but now leading me to, the Foreign Mission field.

Well did I know that the sympathy and prayers of my dear parents were warmly with me in all my studies and in all my Mission work ; but for my education they could, of course, give me no money help. All through, on the contrary, it was my pride and joy to help them, being the eldest in a family of eleven ; though I here most gladly and gratefully record that all my brothers and sisters, as they grew up and began to earn a living, took their full share in this same biessed privilege. First, I assisted them to purchase the family cow, without whose invaluable aid my ever-memorable mother never could have reared and fed her numerous flock ; then, I paid for them the house-rent and the cow's grass on the Bank Hill, till some of the others were more able, and relieved me by paying these in my stead; and finally, I helped to pay the school-fees and to provide clothing for the younger ones—in short, I gave, and gladly, what could possibly be saved out of my City Mission salary of £40, ultimately advanced to £45 per annum. Self-educated thus, and without the help of one shilling from any other source, readers will easily imagine that I had many a staggering difficulty to overcome in my long curriculum in Arts, Divinity, and Medicine; but God so guided me, and blessed all my little arrangements, that I never incurred one farthing of personal debt.

There was, however, a heavy burden always pressing upon me, and crushing my spirit from the day I left my home, which had been thus incurred. The late owner of the Dalswinton estate allowed, as a prize, the cottager who had the tidiest house and most beautiful flower-garden to sit rent-free. For several years in succession, my old seafaring grand-father won this prize, partly by his own handy skill, partly by his wife's joy in flowers. Unfortunately no clearance-receipt had been asked or given for these rents—the proprietor and his cottars treating each other as friends, rather than as men of business. The new heir, unexpectedly succeeding, found himself in need of money, and threatened prosecution for such rents as arrears. The money had to be borrowed. A money-lending lawyer gave it at usurious interest, on condition of my father also becoming responsible for interest and principal. This burden hung like a millstone around my grandfather's neck till the day of his death; and it then became suspended round my father's neck alone. The lawyer, on hearing of my giving up trade and entering upon study, threatened to prosecute my father for the capital, unless my name were given along with his for security. Every shilling that I or any of our family could save, all through these ten years, went to pay off that interest and gradually to reduce the capital; and this burden we managed, amongst us, to extinguish just on the eve of my departure for the South Seas. Indeed, one of the purest joys connected with that time was that I received my first Foreign Mission salary and outfit money in advance, and could send home a sum sufficient to wipe out the last penny of a claim by that money-lender or by any one else against my beloved parents, in connection with the noble struggle they had made in rearing so large a family in sternly-noble Scottish independence. And that joy was hallowed by the knowledge that my other brothers and sisters were now both willing and able to do more than all that would in future be required—for we stuck to each other and to the old folks like burs, and had all things "in common," as a family in Christ—and I knew that never again, howsoever long they might be spared through the peaceful autumn of life, would the dear old father and mother lack any joy or comfort that the willing hands and loving hearts of all their children could singly or unitedly provide. For all this I did praise the Lord ! It consoled me, beyond description, in parting from them, probably for ever, in this world at least.

The Directors of Glasgow City Mission, along with the Great Hamilton Street congregation, had made every effort to find a suitable successor to me in my Green Street work, but in vain. Despairing of success, as no inexperienced worker could with any hope undertake it, Rev. Mr. Caie, the super-intendent, felt moved to appeal to my brother Walter,—then in a good business situation in the city, who had been of late closely associated with me in all my undertakings,—if he would not come to the rescue, devote himself to the Mission, and prepare for the Holy Ministry. My brother resigned a good position and excellent prospects in the business world, set himself to carry forward the Green Street Mission, and did so with abundant energy and manifest blessing, persevered in his studies despite a long-continued illness, and became an honoured Minister of the Gospel, in the Reformed Presbyterian Church first of all, and thereafter in the Free Church of Scotland.

On my brother withdrawing from Green Street, God provided for the district a devoted young Minister, admirably adapted for the work, Rev. John Edgar, M.A., who succeeded in drawing together such a body of people that they hived off and built a new church in Landressy Street, which is now, by amalgamation, known as the Barrowfield Free Church of Glasgow. For that fruit too, while giving all praise to other devoted workers, we bless God as we trace the history of the

Green Street Mission. Let him that soweth and him that reapeth rejoice unfeignedly together! The spirit of the old Green Street workers lives on too, as I have already said, in the new Halls erected close thereby; and in none more conspicuously than in the son of my staunch patron and friend, another Thomas Binnie, who in Foundry Boy meetings and otherwise devotes the consecrated leisure of a busy and prosperous life to the direct personal service of his Lord and Master. The blessing of Jehovah God be ever upon that place, and upon all who there seek to win their fellows to the love and service of Jesus Christ!

When I left Glasgow, many of the young men and women of my Classes would, if it had been possible, have gone with me, to live and die among the Heathen. Though chiefly working girls and lads in trades and mills, their deep interest led them to unite their pennies and sixpences, and to buy web after web of calico, print, and woollen stuffs, which they themselves shaped and sewed into dresses for the women, and kilts and pants for men, on the New Hebrides. This continued to be repeated year by year, long after I had left them; and to this day no box from Glasgow goes to the New Hebrides Mission which does not contain article after article from one or other of the old Green Street hands. I do certainly anticipate that, when they and I meet in Glory, those days in which we learned the joy of Christian service in the Green Street Mission Halls will form no unwelcome theme of holy and happy converse!

That able and devoted Minister of the Gospel, Dr. Bates, the Convener of the Heathen Missions, had taken the deepest and most fatherly interest in all our preparations. On the morning of our final examinations he was confined to bed with sickness, yet could not be content without sending his daughter to wait in an adjoining room near the Presbytery House, to learn the result, and instantly to carry him word. When she, hurrying home, informed him that we both had passed successfully, and that the day of our ordination as Missionaries to the New Hebrides had been appointed, the apostolic old man praised God for the glad tidings, and said his work was now done, and that he could depart in peace—

having seen two devoted men set apart to preach the Gospel to these dark and bloody Islands, in answer to his prayers and tears for many a day. Thereafter he rapidly sank, and soon fell asleep in Jesus. He was from the first a very precious friend to me, one of the ablest Ministers our Church ever had, by far the warmest advocate of her Foreign Missions, and altogether a most attractive, white-souled, and noble specimen of an ambassador for Christ, beseeching men to be reconciled to God.

CHAPTER V.

THE NEW HEBRIDES.

A.D. 1857—1858.   ÆT. 33—34.

License and Ordination.—At Sea.—From Melbourne to Aneityum.—
Settlement on Tanna.—Our Mission Stations.—Diplomatic Chiefs.—
Painful First Impressions.—Bloody Scenes.—The Widow's Doom.

ON the first of December, 1857, the other Missionary-designate and I were "licensed" as preachers of the Gospel. Thereafter we spent four months in visiting and addressing nearly every Congregation and Sabbath School in the Reformed Presbyterian Church of Scotland, that the people might see us and know us, and thereby take a personal interest in our work. That idea was certainly excellent, and might well be adapted to the larger Churches, by allocating one Missionary to each Province or to so many Presbyteries, sending him to address these, and training them to regard him as their Missionary and his work as theirs. On the 23rd March, 1858, in Dr. Symington's church, Glasgow, in presence of a mighty crowd, and after a magnificent sermon on "Come over and help us," we were solemnly ordained as Ministers of the Gospel, and set apart as Missionaries to the New Hebrides. On the 16th April, 1858, we left the Tail of the Bank at Greenock, and set sail in the *Clutha* for the Foreign Mission field.

Our voyage to Melbourne was rather tedious, but ended prosperously, under Captain Broadfoot, a kindly, brave-hearted Scot, who did everything that was possible for our comfort. He himself led the singing on board at Worship, which was always charming to me, and was always regularly conducted—on deck when the weather was fair, below when it was rough.

I was also permitted to conduct Bible Classes amongst both the crew and the passengers, at times and places approved of by the Captain—in which there was great joy. Nearly thirty years after, when I returned the second time to Scotland, a gentleman of good position, and the father of a large family in the West, saluted me warmly at the close of one of my meetings, and reminded me that he was my precentor in the Bible Class on board the *Clutha !* It was gratifying to hear him say that he had never forgotten the scene and the lessons there.

Arriving at Melbourne, we were welcomed by Rev. Mr. Moor, Mr. and Mrs. Samuel Wilson, and Mr. Wright, all Reformed Presbyterians from Geelong. Mr. Wilson's two children, Jessie and Donald, had been under our care during the voyage; and my young wife and I went with them for a few days on a visit to Geelong, while Mr. Copeland remained on board the *Clutha* to look after our boxes and to watch for any opportunity of reaching our destination on the Islands. He heard that an American ship, the *Francis P. Sage*, was sailing from Melbourne to Penang; and the Captain agreed to land us on Aneityum, New Hebrides, with our two boats and fifty boxes, for £100. We got on board on the 12th August, but such a gale blew that we did not sail till the 17th. On the *Clutha* all was quiet, and good order prevailed; in the *F. P. Sage* all was noise and profanity. The Captain said he kept his second mate for the purpose of swearing at the men and knocking them about. The voyage was most disagreeable to all of us, but fortunately it lasted only twelve days. On the 29th we were close up to Aneityum; but the Captain refused to land us, even in his boats; some of us suspecting that his men were so badly used, that had they got on shore they would never have returned to him! In any case he had beforehand secured his £100.

He lay off the island till a trader's boat pulled across to see what we wanted, and by it we sent a note to Dr. Geddie, one of the Missionaries there. Early next morning, Monday, he arrived in his boat, accompanied by Mr. Mathieson, a newly-arrived Missionary from Nova Scotia; bringing also Captain Anderson in the small Mission schooner, the *John Knox*, and

a large Mission boat called the *Columbia*, well manned with
crews of able and willing Natives.　Our fifty boxes were soon
on board the *John Knox*, the *Columbia*, and our own boats—
all being heavily loaded and built up, except those that had
to be used in pulling the others ashore.　Dr. Geddie, Mr.
Mathieson, Mrs. Paton, and I were perched among the boxes
on the *John Knox*, and had to hold on as best we could.　On
sheering off from the *F. P. Sage*, one of her davits caught and
broke the mainmast of the little *John Knox* by the deck; and
I saved my wife from being crushed to death by its fall, through
managing to swing her instantaneously aside in an apparently
impossible manner.　It did graze Mr. Mathieson, but he was
not hurt.　The *John Knox*, already overloaded, was thus quite
disabled; we were about ten miles at sea, and in imminent
danger; but the Captain of the *F. P. Sage* heartlessly sailed
away, and left us to struggle with our fate.

We drifted steadily in the direction of Tanna, an island of
Cannibals, where our goods would have been plundered and
all of us cooked and eaten.　Dr. Geddie's boat and mine
had the *John Knox* in tow; and Mr. Copeland, with a crew of
Natives, was struggling hard with his boat to pull the *Columbia*
and her load towards Aneityum.　As God mercifully ordered
it, though we had a stiff trade wind to pull against, we had a
comparatively calm sea; yet we drifted still to leeward, till Dr.
Inglis going round to the harbour in his boat, as he had heard
of our arrival, saw us far at sea, and hastened to our rescue.
All the boats now, with their willing Native crews, got fastened
to our schooner, and to our great joy she began to move ahead.
After pulling for hours and hours, under the scorching rays of
a tropical sun, we were all safely landed on shore at Aneityum,
about six o'clock in the evening of August 30th, just four
months and fourteen days since we sailed from Greenock.　We
got a hearty welcome from the Missionaries' wives, Mrs.
Geddie, Mrs. Inglis, and Mrs. Mathieson, and from all our
new friends, the Christian Natives of Aneityum; and the great
danger in which both life and property had been placed at the
close of our voyage, made us praise God all the more that He
had brought us to this quiet resting-place, around which lay
the Islands of the New Hebrides, to which our eager hearts

had looked forward, and into which we entered now in the name of the Lord.

Mr. Copeland, Mrs. Paton, and I went round the island to Dr. Inglis's Station, where we were most cordially received and entertained by his dear lady, and by the Christian Natives there. As he was making several additions to his house at that time, we received for the next few weeks our first practical and valuable training in Mission house-building, as well as in higher matters. Soon after, a meeting was called to consult about our settlement, and, by the advice and with the concurrence of all, Mr. and Mrs. Mathieson from Nova Scotia were located on the south side of Tanna, at Umairarekar, now Kwamera, and Mrs. Paton and I at Port Resolution, on the same island. At first it was agreed that Mr. Copeland should be placed along with us; but owing to the weakly state of Mrs. Mathieson's health, it was afterwards resolved that, for a time at least, Mr. Copeland should live at either Station, as might seem most suitable or most requisite. Till the close of the sailing season, his time was spent chiefly in the *John Knox*, helping Captain Anderson in loading and disloading the wood and house-building materials betwixt Aneityum and Tanna; while I was occupied chiefly with the house-building and preparatory arrangements.

Dr. Inglis and a number of his most energetic Natives accompanied us to Kwamera, Tanna. There we purchased a site for Mission House and Church, and laid a stone foundation, and advanced as far as practicable the erection of a dwelling for Mr. and Mrs. Mathieson. Thence we proceeded to Port Resolution, Tanna, and similarly purchased a site, and advanced, to a forward stage, the house which Mrs. Paton and I were to occupy on our settlement there. Lime for plastering had to be burned in kilns from the coral rocks; and thatch, for roofing with sugar-cane leaf, had to be prepared by the Natives at both Stations before our return; for which, as for all else, a price was duly agreed upon, and was scrupulously paid. Unfortunately we learned, when too late, that both houses were too near the shore, exposed to unwholesome miasma, and productive of the dreaded fever and ague,—the most virulent and insidious enemy to all Europeans in those Southern Seas.

5

At both Stations, but especially at Port Resolution, we found the Natives in a very excited and unsettled state. Threatened wars kept them in constant terror—war betwixt distant tribes, or adjoining villages, or nearest neighbours. The Chiefs, at both Stations, willingly sold sites for houses, and appeared to desire Missionaries to live amongst them; but perhaps it was with an eye to the axes, knives, fishhooks, blankets, and clothing, which they got in payment, or hoped for in plunder, rather than from any thirst for the Gospel, as they were all Savages and Cannibals. They warily declined to promise protection to the Mission families and the Teachers; but they said they would not themselves do them any harm, though they could not say what the Inland people might do;—not a bad specimen of diplomacy, leaving an open door for any future emergency, and neither better nor worse than the methods by which the civilized European nations make and break their treaties in peace and in war! Such promises meant, and were intended to mean, nothing. The Natives, both on Tanna, and on my second home at Aniwa, believed that they had kept their promise, if they inflicted no injury with their own hands, even though they had hired others to do so. No Heathen there could be trusted one step beyond what appeared to be his own self-interest for the nonce; and nothing conceivable was too base or cruel to be done, if only it served his turn. The "depths of Satan," outlined in the first chapter of the *Romans*, were uncovered there before our eyes in the daily life of the people, without veil and without excuse.

My first impressions drove me, I must confess, to the verge of utter dismay. On beholding these Natives in their paint and nakedness and misery, my heart was as full of horror as of pity. Had I given up my much-beloved work and my dear people in Glasgow, with so many delightful associations, to consecrate my life to these degraded creatures? Was it possible to teach them right and wrong, to Christianize, or even to civilize them? But that was only a passing feeling! I soon got as deeply interested in them, and in all that tended to advance them, and to lead them to the knowledge and love of Jesus, as ever I had been in my work at Glasgow. We were surprised and delighted at the remarkable change produced on the Natives of Aneityum through the instrumentality of Drs. Geddie and Inglis in so short a time; and we hoped, by prayerful perseverance in the use of similar means, to see the same work of God repeated on Tanna. Besides, the wonderful and blessed work done by Mrs. Inglis and Mrs. Geddie, at their Stations, filled our wives with the buoyant hope of being instruments in the hand of God to produce an equally beneficent change amongst the savage women of Tanna. Mrs. Paton had been left with Mrs. Inglis to learn all she could from her of Mission work on the Islands, till I returned with Dr. Inglis from the house-building operations on Tanna; during which period Mr. and Mrs. Mathieson were also being instructed by Dr. and Mrs. Geddie.

To the Tannese, Dr. Inglis and I were objects of curiosity and fear; they came crowding to gaze on our wooden and lime-plastered house; they chattered incessantly with each other, and left the scene day after day with undisguised and increasing wonderment. Possibly they thought us rather mad than wise!

Party after party of armed men going and coming in a state of great excitement, we were informed that war was on foot; but our Aneityumese Teachers were told to assure us that the Harbour people would only act on the defensive, and that no one would molest us at our work. One day two hostile tribes met near our Station; high words arose, and old feuds were revived. The Inland people withdrew; but the Harbour people, false to their promises, flew to arms and rushed past us in pursuit of their enemies. The discharge of muskets in the adjoining bush, and the horrid yells of the Savages, soon informed us that they were engaged in deadly fights. Excitement and terror were on every countenance; armed men rushed about in every direction, with feathers in their twisted hair,—with faces painted red, black, and white, and some, one cheek black, the other red; others, the brow white, the chin blue—in fact, any colour and on any part,—the more grotesque and savage-looking, the higher the art! Some of the women ran with their children to places of safety; but even then we saw other girls and women, on the shore close by, chewing sugar-cane and chaffering and laughing, as if their fathers and brothers had been engaged in a country dance, instead of a bloody conflict.

In the afternoon, as the sounds of the muskets and the yelling of the warriors came unpleasantly near to us, Dr. Inglis, leaning against a post for a little while in silent prayer, looked on us and said, "The walls of Jerusalem were built in troublous times, and why not the Mission House on Tanna? But let us rest for this day, and pray for these poor Heathen."

We retired to a Native house, that had been temporarily granted to us for rest, and there pled before God for them all. The noise and the discharge of muskets gradually receded, as if the Inland people were retiring; and towards evening the people around us returned to their villages. We were afterwards informed that five or six men had been shot dead; that their bodies had been carried by the conquerors from the field of battle, and cooked and eaten that very night at a boiling spring near the head of the bay, less than a mile from the spot where my house was being built. We had also a more graphic illustration of the surroundings into which we had come, through Dr. Inglis's Aneityum boy, who accompanied us as cook. When our tea was wanted next morning, the boy could not be found. After a while of great anxiety on our part, he returned, saying, "Missi, this is a dark land. The people of this land do dark works. At the boiling spring they have cooked and feasted upon the slain. They have washed the blood into the water; they have bathed there, polluting everything. I cannot get pure water to make your tea. What shall I do?"

Dr. Inglis told him that he must try for water elsewhere, till the rains came and cleansed away the pollution; and that, meanwhile, instead of tea, we would drink from the cocoa-nut, as they had often done before. The lad was quite relieved. It not a little astonished us, however, to see that his mind regarded their killing and eating each other as a thing scarcely to be noticed, but that it was horrible that they should spoil the water! How much are even our deepest instincts the creatures of mere circumstances! I, if trained like him, would probably have felt like him.

Next evening, as we sat talking about the people and the dark scenes around us, the quiet of the night was broken by a wild wailing cry from the villages around, long-continued and unearthly. We were informed that one of the wounded men, carried home from the battle, had just died; and that they had strangled his widow to death, that her spirit might accompany him to the other world, and be his servant there, as she had been here. Now their dead bodies were laid side by side, ready to be buried in the sea. Our hearts sank to think of all this happening within earshot, and that we knew it not! Every new scene, every fresh incident, set more clearly before us the benighted condition and shocking cruelties of these Heathen people, and we longed to be able to speak to them of Jesus and the love of God. We eagerly tried to pick up every word of their language, that we might, in their own tongue, unfold to them the knowledge of the true God and of salvation from all these sins through Jesus Christ.

Dr. Inglis and I, with the help of the Natives from Aneityum, having accomplished all that could be done for lack of lime and sawn wood to finish the new Mission House on Tanna, made an agreement with the Natives for knives, calico, and axes, to burn lime and prepare other things for our return. We then hastened back to Aneityum, that we might, if possible, get ready for settling on Tanna before the Rainy Season set in. That was rapidly approaching, and it brings with it discomfort and unhealth to Europeans throughout all these Pacific Isles.*

---

* See Appendix B, "Notes on the New Hebrides."

CHAPTER VI.

LIFE AND DEATH ON TANNA.

A.D. 1858—1859. ÆT. 34—35.

Our Island Home.—Learning the Language.—A Religion of Fear.—With or Without a God.—Ideas of the Invisible.—Gods and Demons.—My Companion Missionary.—Pioneers in the New Hebrides.—Missionaries of Aneityum.—The Lord's Arrowroot.—Unhealthy Sites.—The Great Bereavement.—Memorial Tributes.—Selwyn and Patteson at a Tannese Grave.—Her Last Letter.—Last Words.—Presentiment and Mystery.

OUR small Missionary schooner, the *John Knox*, having no accommodation for lady passengers, and little for anybody else except the discomfort of lying on deck, we took advantage of a trader to convey us from Aneityum to Tanna. The Captain kindly offered to take us and about thirty casks and boxes to Port Resolution for £5, which we gladly accepted. After a few hours' sailing, we were all safely landed on Tanna on the 5th November, 1858.   Dr. Geddie went for a fortnight to Umairarekar, now known as Kwamera, on the south side of Tanna, to assist in the settlement of Mr. and Mrs. Mathieson, and to help in making their house habitable and comfortable. Mr. Copeland, Mrs. Paton, and I were left at Port Resolution to finish the building of our house there, and work our way into the goodwill of the Natives as best we could.   On landing, we found the people to be literally naked and painted Savages; they were at least as destitute of clothing as Adam and Eve after the fall, when they sewed fig-leaves for a girdle ; and even more so, for the women wore only a tiny apron of grass, in some cases shaped like a skirt or girdle, the men an indescribable affair like a pouch or bag, and the children absolutely nothing whatever !

At first they came in crowds to look at us, and at everything we did or had. We knew nothing of their language; we could not speak a single word to them, nor they to us. We looked at them, they at us; we smiled, and nodded, and made signs to each other; this was our first meeting and parting. One day I observed two men, the one lifting up one of our articles to the other, and saying, " Nungsi nari enu ? "

I concluded that he was asking, "What is this?" Instantly, lifting a piece of wood, I said, " Nungsi nari enu ? "

They smiled and spoke to each other. I understood them to be saying, " He has got hold of our language now." Thei they told me their name for the thing which I had pointed to I found that they understood my question, What is this ? or, What is that ? and that I could now get from them the name of every visible or tangible thing around us ! We carefully noted down every name they gave us, spelling all phonetically, and also every strange sound we heard from them; thereafter, by painstaking comparison of different circumstances, we tried to ascertain their meanings, testing our own guess by again cross-questioning the Natives. One day I saw two males approaching, when one, who was a stranger, pointed to me with his finger, and said, " Se nangin ? "

Concluding that he was asking my name, I pointed to one of them with my finger, and looking at the other, inquired, " Se nangin ? "

They smiled, and gave me their names. We were now able to get the names of persons and things, and so our ears got familiarized with the distinctive sounds of their language; and being always keenly on the alert, we made extraordinary progress in attempting bits of conversation and in reducing their speech for the first time to a written form—for the New Hebrideans had no literature, and not even the rudiments of an alphabet. I used to hire some of the more intelligent lads and men to sit and talk with us, and answer our questions about names and sounds; but they so often deceived us, and we, doubtless, misunderstood them so often, that this course was not satisfactory, till after we had gained some knowledge of their language and its construction, and they themselves had become interested in helping us. Amongst our most interested helpers, and most trustworthy, were two aged chiefs—Nowar and Nouka—in many respects two of Nature's noblest gentlemen, kind at heart to all, and distinguished by a certain native dignity of bearing. But they were both under the leadership of the war-chief Miaki, a kind of devil-king over many villages and tribes. He and his brother were the recognised leaders in all deeds of darkness : they gloried in bloodshedding, and in war, and in cannibalism; and they could always command a following of desperate men, who lived in or about their own village, and who were prepared to go anywhere and do anything at Miaki's will.

The Tannese had hosts of stone idols, charms, and sacred objects, which they abjectly feared, and in which they devoutly believed. They were given up to countless superstitions, and firmly glued to their dark heathen practices. Their worship was entirely a service of fear, its aim being to propitiate this or that Evil Spirit, to prevent calamity or to secure revenge. They deified their chiefs, like the Romans of old, so that almost every village or tribe had its own Sacred Man, and some of them had many. They exercised an extraordinary influence for evil, these village or tribal priests, and were believed to have the disposal of life and death through their sacred ceremonies, not only in their own tribe, but over all the Islands. Sacred men and women, wizards and witches, received presents regularly to influence the gods, and to remove sickness, or to cause it by the *Nahak, i.e.*, incantation over remains of food, or the skin of fruit, such as banana, which the person has eaten on whom they wish to operate. They also worshipped the spirits of departed ancestors and heroes, through their material idols of wood and stone, but chiefly of stone. They feared these spirits and sought their aid; especially seeking to propitiate those who presided over war and peace, famine and plenty, health and sickness, destruction and prosperity, life and death. Their whole worship was one of slavish fear ; and, so far as ever I could learn, they had no idea of a God of mercy or grace.

Let me here give my testimony on a matter of some importance—that among these Islands, if anywhere, men might be found destitute of the faculty of worship, men absolutely without idols, if such men exist under the face of the sky. Everything seemed to favour such a discovery; but the New Hebrides, on the contrary, are full of gods. The Natives, destitute of the knowledge of the true God, are ceaselessly groping after Him, if perchance they may find Him. Not finding Him, and not being able to live without some sort of God, they have made idols of almost everything: trees and groves, rocks and stones, springs and streams, insects and beasts, men and departed spirits, relics such as hair and finger nails, the heavenly bodies and the volcanoes; in fact, every being and every thing within the range of vision or of knowledge has been appealed to by them as God,—clearly proving that the instincts of Humanity, however degraded, prompt man to worship and lean upon some Being or Power outside himself, and greater than himself, in whom he lives and moves and has his being, and without the knowledge of whom his soul cannot find its true rest or its eternal life. Imperfect acquaintance with the language and customs of certain tribes may easily have led early discoverers to proclaim that they have no sense of worship and no idols, because nothing of the kind is visible on the surface. But there is a sort of freemasonry in Heathen Religions; they have mysterious customs and symbols, which none even amongst themselves understand, except the priests and Sacred Men. It pays these men to keep their devotees in the dark—and how much more to deceive a passing inquirer! Nor need we hold up our hands in surprise at this; it pays also nearer home to pretend and to perpetuate a mystery about beads and crucifixes, holy water and relics—a state of mind not so very far removed from that of the South Sea islander, not disproving but rather strongly proving that, whether savage or civilized, man must either know the true God, or must find an idol to put in His place.

Further, these very facts—that they did worship, that they believed in spirits of ancestors and heroes, and that they cherished many legends regarding those whom they had never seen, and handed these down to their children—and the fact that they had ideas about the invisible world and its inhabitants, made it not so hard as some might suppose to convey to their

minds, once their language and modes of thought were understood, some clear idea of Jehovah God as the great uncreated
Spirit Father, who Himself created and sustains all that is.
But it could not be done off-hand, or by a few airy lessons.
The whole heart and soul and life had to be put into the enterprise. The idea that man disobeyed God, and was a fallen
and sinful creature,—the idea that God, as a Father, so loved
man that He sent His only Son Jesus to this earth to seek and
to save him,—the idea that this Jesus so lived and died and
rose from the dead as to take away man's sin, and make it
possible for men to return to God, and to be made into the
very likeness of His Son Jesus,—and the idea that this Jesus
will at death receive to the mansions of Glory every creature
under heaven that loves and tries to follow Him,—these ideas
had to be woven into their spiritual consciousness, had to
become the very warp and woof of their religion. But it could
be done—that we believed because they were men, not beasts ;
it had been done—that we saw in the converts on Aneityum ;
and our hearts rose to the task with a quenchless hope !

The Tannese called Heaven by the name Aneai; and we
afterwards discovered that this was the name of the highest
and most beautifully situated village on the island. Their best
bit of Earth was to them the symbol and type of Heaven ;
their Canaan, too, was a kind of prophecy of another country,
even a heavenly Canaan. The fact that they had an Aneai,
a promised land, opened their minds naturally to our idea of
the promised land of the future, the Aneai of the Gospel hope
and faith. The universal craving to know the greater and
more powerful gods, and to have them on their side, led them,
whenever we could speak their language, to listen eagerly to
all our stories about the Jehovah God and His Son Jesus, and
all the mighty works recorded in the Bible. But when we
began to teach them that, in order to serve this Almighty and
living Jehovah God, they must cast aside all their idols and
leave off every heathen custom and vice, they rose in anger
and cruelty against us, they persecuted every one that was
friendly to the Mission, and passed us through the dreadful
experiences to be hereafter recorded. It was the old battle of
History ; light had attacked darkness in its very stronghold, and

it almost seemed for a season that the light would be finally eclipsed, and that God's day would never dawn on Tanna!

My companion Missionary, Mr. Copeland, had to go to Aneityum and take charge of Dr. Inglis's Station, during the absence of that distinguished Missionary and his devoted wife, while carrying through the press at home the first complete Aneityumese New Testament. He succeeded admirably in taking up and carrying forward all their work, and gave vital assistance in translating the Old Testament into the language of Aneityum, for his was an exact and scholarly mind. After their return, he similarly occupied the station of Dr. Geddie on another part of the same island, while he sought re-invigoration in Nova Scotia on a well-merited furlough. Thereafter, he was placed on the island of Fotuna; and there, with Mrs. Copeland, he laboured devotedly and zealously, till at last she died and his own health gave way to such an extent as compelled him to retire from the Mission field. He found congenial employment in editing, with great acceptance, the Sydney *Presbyterian Witness*, and thereby still furthering the cause of the Gospel and of Missions.

A glance backwards over the story of the Gospel in the New Hebrides may help to bring my readers into touch with the events that are to follow. The ever-famous names of Williams and Harris are associated with the earliest efforts to introduce Christianity amongst this group of islands in the South Pacific Seas. John Williams and his young Missionary companion Harris, under the auspices of the London Missionary Society, landed on Erromanga on the 30th of November, 1839. Alas! within a few minutes of their touching land, both were clubbed to death; and the savages proceeded to cook and feast upon their bodies. Thus were the New Hebrides baptized with the blood of Martyrs; and Christ thereby told the whole Christian world that He claimed these Islands as His own. His cross must yet be lifted up, where the blood of His saints has been poured forth in His name! The poor Heathen knew not that they had slain their best friends; but tears and prayers ascended for them from all Christian souls, wherever the story of the martyrdom on Erromanga was read or heard.

Again, therefore, in 1842, the London Missionary Society sent out Messrs. Turner and Nisbet to pierce this kingdom of Satan. They placed their standard on our chosen island of Tanna, the nearest to Erromanga. In less than seven months, however, their persecution by the Savages became so dreadful, that we see them in a boat trying to escape by night with bare life. Out on that dangerous sea they would certainly have been lost, but the Ever-Merciful drove them back to land, and sent next morning a whaling vessel, which, contrary to custom, called there, and just in the nick of time. They, with all goods that could be rescued, were got safely on board, and sailed for Samoa. Say not their plans and prayers were baffled ; for God heard and abundantly blessed them there, beyond all their dreams. Dr. Turner has been specially used of God for educating many Native Teachers and Missionaries, and in translating and publishing edition after edition of the Bible, besides giving them many other educational and religious books in their own language ;—blessed work, in which, while I am writing these words, he and his gifted wife are still honourably and fruitfully engaged in the holy autumn of their days.*

After these things, the London Missionary Society again and again placed Samoan Native Teachers on one or other island of the New Hebrides; but their unhealthiness, compared with the more wholesome Samoa or Rarotonga, so afflicted them with the dreaded ague and fever, besides what they endured from the inhospitable Savages themselves, that no effective Mission work had been accomplished there till at last the Presbyterian Missionaries were led to enter upon the scene. Christianity had no foothold anywhere on the New Hebrides, unless it were in the memory and the blood of the Martyrs of Erromanga.

The Rev. John Geddie and his wife, from Nova Scotia, were landed on Aneityum, the most southerly island of the New Hebrides, in 1848 ; and the Rev. John Inglis and his wife, from Scotland, were landed on the other side of the same island, in 1852. An agent for the London Missionary

---

* Alas, he has just fallen asleep ! And yet not Alas, for his work was nobly done, and his rest is sweet.—*Editor, May* 1891.

Society, the Rev. T. Powell, accompanied Dr. Geddie for about a year, to advise as to his settlement and to assist in opening up the work. Marvellous as it may seem, the Natives on Aneityum showed interest in the Missionaries from the very first, and listened to their teachings ; so that in a few years Dr. Inglis and Dr. Geddie saw about 3,500 Savages throwing away their idols, renouncing their Heathen customs, and avowing themselves to be worshippers of the true Jehovah God. Slowly, yet progressively, they unlearned their Heathenism ; surely and hopefully they learned Christianity and civilization. In course of time a simple form of Family Worship was introduced into and observed by every household on the island ; God's blessing was asked on every meal ; peace and public order were secured ; and property was perfectly safe under the sanctifying and civilizing Gospel of Christ. And by-and-bye these Missionaries lived to see the whole Bible, which they and Mr. Copeland had so painfully translated, placed in the hands of the Aneityumese by the aid of the British and Foreign Bible Society—that noblest handmaid of every Missionary enterprise. But how was this accomplished ? As a boon of charity ? Listen !

These poor Aneityumese, having glimpses of this Word of God, determined to have a Holy Bible in their own mother tongue, wherein before no book or page ever had been written in the history of their race. The consecrated brain and hand of their Missionaries kept toiling day and night in translating the book of God ; and the willing hands and feet of the Natives kept toiling through fifteen long but unwearying years, planting and preparing arrowroot to pay the £1,200 required to be laid out in the printing and publishing of the book. Year after year the arrowroot, too sacred to be used for their daily food, was set apart as the Lord's portion ; the Missionaries sent it to Australia and Scotland, where it was sold by private friends, and the whole proceeds consecrated to this purpose. On the completion of the great undertaking by the Bible Society, it was found that the Natives had earned so much as to pay every penny of the outlay ; and their first Bibles went out to them, purchased with the consecrated toils of fifteen years ! Some of our friends may think that the sum was large ; but I know, from experience, that if such a difficult job had been carried through the press and so bound by any other printing establishment, the expense would have been greater far. One book of Scripture, printed by me in Melbourne for the Aniwans at a later day, under the auspices of the Bible Society too, cost eight shillings per leaf, and that was the cheapest style ; and this the Aniwans also paid for by dedicating their arrowroot to God.

Let those who lightly esteem their Bibles think on those things. Eight shillings for every leaf, or the labour and proceeds of fifteen years for the Bible entire, did not appear to these poor converted Savages too much to pay for that Word of God, which had sent to them the Missionaries, which had revealed to them the grace of God in Christ, and which had opened their eyes to the wonders and glories of redeeming love ! They had felt, and we had observed, that in all lands and amongst all branches of the human family, the Holy Bible is, wheresoever received and obeyed, the power of God unto salvation ; it had lifted them out of savagery, and set them at the feet of the Lord Jesus. Oh that the pleasure-seeking men and women of the world could only taste and feel the real joy of those who know and love the true God— a heritage which the world and all that pertains thereto cannot give to them, but which the poorest and humblest followers of Jesus inherit and enjoy !

My first house on Tanna was on the old site occupied by Turner and Nisbet, near the shore for obvious reasons, and only a few feet above tide-mark. So was that of Mr. Mathieson, handy for materials and goods being landed, and, as we imagined, close to the healthy breezes of the sea. Alas ! we had to learn by sad experience, like our brethren in all untried Mission fields. The sites proved to be hot-beds for Fever and Ague, mine especially ; and much of this might have been escaped by building on the higher ground, and in the sweep of the refreshing trade-winds. ,For all this, however, no one was to blame ; everything was done for the best, according to the knowledge then possessed. Our house was sheltered behind by an abrupt hill about two hundred feet high, which gave the site a feeling of cosiness. It was surrounded, and much shaded, by beautiful bread-fruit trees, and very large cocoa-nut trees; too largely beautiful, indeed, for they shut out many a healthy breeze that we sorely needed! There was a long swamp at the head of the bay, and, the ground at the other end on which our house stood being scarcely raised perceptibly higher, the malaria almost constantly enveloped us. Once, after a smart attack of the fever, an intelligent Chief said to me, " Missi, if you stay here, you will soon die! No Tanna-man sleeps so low down as you do, in this damp weather, or he too would die. We sleep on the high ground, and the trade-wind keeps us well. You must go and sleep on the hill, and then you will have better health."

I at once resolved to remove my house to higher ground, at the earliest practicable moment; heavy though the undertaking would necessarily be, it seemed my only hope of being able to live on the island.

My dear young wife, Mary Ann Robson,—daughter of Peter Robson, Esquire, a well-known and highly-esteemed gentleman, at Coldstream on the Borders,—and I were landed on Tanna on the 5th November, 1858, in excellent health and full of all tender and holy hopes. On the 12th February, 1859, she was confined of a son; for two days or so both mother and child seemed to prosper, and our island-exile thrilled with joy! But the greatest of sorrows was treading hard upon the heels of that joy! My darling's strength showed no signs of rallying. She had an attack of ague and fever, a few days before her confinement; on the third day or so thereafter it returned, and attacked her every second day with increasing severity for a fortnight. Diarrhœa ensued, and symptoms of pneumonia, with slight delirium at intervals; and then in a moment, altogether unexpectedly, she died on the 3rd March. To crown my sorrows, and complete my loneliness, the dear baby-boy, whom we had named after her father, Peter Robert Robson, was taken from me after one week's sickness, on the 20th March. Let those who have ever passed through any similar darkness as of midnight feel for me; as for all others, it would be more than vain to try to paint my sorrows!

I knew then, when too late, that our work had been entered

on too near the beginning of the Rainy Season. We were both, however, healthy and hearty ; and I daily pushed on with the house, making things hourly more comfortable, in the hope that long lives were before us both, to be spent for Jesus in seeking the salvation of the perishing Heathen. Oh, the vain yet bitter regrets, that my dear wife had not been left on Aneityum till after the unhealthy Rainy Season ! But no one advised this course ; and she, high-spirited, full of buoyant hope, and afraid of being left behind me, or of me being left without her on Tanna, refused to allow the thing to be suggested. In our mutual inexperience, and with our hearts aglow for the work of our lives, we incurred this risk which should never have been incurred ; and I only refer to the matter thus, in the hope that others may take warning.

Stunned by that dreadful loss, in entering upon this field of labour to which the Lord had Himself so evidently led me, my reason seemed for a time almost to give way. Ague and fever, too, laid a depressing and weakening hand upon me, continuously recurring, and reaching oftentimes the very height of its worst burning stages. But I was never altogether forsaken. The ever-merciful Lord sustained me, to lay the precious dust of my beloved Ones in the same quiet grave, dug for them close by at the end of the house ; in all of which last offices my own hands, despite breaking heart, had to take the principal share ! I built the grave round and round with coral blocks, and covered the top with beautiful white coral, broken small as gravel ; and that spot became my sacred and much-frequented shrine, during all the following months and years when I laboured on for the salvation of these savage Islanders amidst difficulties, dangers, and deaths. Whensoever Tanna turns to the Lord, and is won for Christ, men in after-days will find the memory of that spot still green,—where with ceaseless prayers and tears I claimed that land for God in which I had " buried my dead " with faith and hope. But for Jesus, and the fellowship He vouchsafed me there, I must have gone mad and died beside that lonely grave !

The organ of the Church to which we belonged, *The Reformed Presbyterian Magazine*, published the following words of condolence :—" In regard to the death of Mrs. Paton, one feeling of grief and regret will fill the hearts of all who knew her. To add a sentence to the singularly just and graceful tribute Mr. Inglis pays to the memory of the deceased, would only mar its pathos and effect. Such language, from one accustomed to weigh carefully every word he pens, bespeaks at once the rare excellences of her that is gone, as well as the heavy loss our Mission and our Church have sustained in her death. Her parents, who gave her by a double baptism to the Lord, have this consolation, that her death may exert a more elevating and sanctifying influence for good, than the longest life of many ordinary Christians. Deep sympathy with Mr. Paton will pervade the Church, in the sore trial with which he has been visited."

Dr. Inglis, my brother Missionary on Aneityum, wrote to the same Magazine:—" I trust all those who shed tears of sorrow on account of her early death will be enabled in the exercise of faith and resignation to say, ' The Will of the Lord be done ; the Lord gave and the Lord hath taken away : blessed be the Name of the Lord ! ' I need not say how deeply we sympathize with her bereaved parents, as well as with her sorrowing husband. By her death the Mission has sustained a heavy loss. We were greatly pleased with Mrs. Paton, during the period of our short intercourse with her. Her mind, naturally vigorous, had been cultivated by a superior education. She was full of Missionary spirit, and took a deep interest in the Native women. This was seen further when she went to Tanna, where, in less than three months, she had collected a class of eight females, who came regularly to her to receive instruction. There was about her a maturity of thought, a solidity of character, a loftiness of aim and purpose, rarely found in one so young. Trained up in the fear of the Lord from childhood, like another Mary she had evidently chosen that good part, which is never taken away from those possessed of it. When she left this island, she had to all human appearance a long career of usefulness and happiness on Earth before her, but the Lord has appointed otherwise. She has gone, as we trust, to her rest and her reward. The Lord has said to her, as He said to David, ' Thou didst well in that it was in thine heart to build a House

6

for My Name.' Let us watch and pray, for our Lord cometh as a thief in the night."

The Missionaries assembled at Tanna, on April 27th, 1859, passed the following resolution :—"That this meeting deeply and sincerely sympathizes with Mr. Paton in the heavy and trying bereavement with which the Lord has seen meet to visit him in the death of his beloved wife and child ; and the Missionaries record their sense of the loss this Mission has sustained, in the early, sudden, and unexpected death of Mrs. Paton. Her earnest Christian character, her devoted Mission-ary spirit, her excellent education, her kind and obliging disposition, and the influence she was fast acquiring over the Natives, excited expectations of great future usefulness. That they express their heartfelt sympathy with the parents and other relatives of the deceased ; that they recommend Mr. Paton to pay a visit to Aneityum for the benefit of his health ; that they commend him to the tender mercies of Him who was sent to comfort all who mourn ; and that they regard this striking dispensation of God's providence as a loud call to themselves, to be more in earnest in attending to the state of their own souls, and more diligent in pressing the concerns of eternity on the minds of others."

Soon after her death, the good Bishop Selwyn called at Port Resolution, Tanna, in his Mission Ship. He came on shore to visit me, accompanied by the Rev. J. C. Patteson. They had met Mrs. Paton on Aneityum in the previous year soon after our arrival, and, as she was then the picture of perfect health, they also felt her loss very keenly. Standing with me beside the grave of mother and child, I weeping aloud on his one hand, and Patteson—afterwards the Martyr Bishop of Nakupu—sobbing silently on the other, the godly Bishop Selwyn poured out his heart to God amidst sobs and tears, during which he laid his hands on my head, and invoked Heaven's richest consolations and blessings on me and my trying labours. The virtue of that kind of Episcopal consecra-tion I did and do most warmly appreciate ! They urged me by many appeals to take a trip with them round the Islands, as my life was daily in great danger from the Savages ; they generously offered to convey me direct to Aneityum, or wherever I wished to go, I greatly needed rest and change. But, with a heart full of gratitude to them, I yet resolved to remain, feeling that I was at the post of duty where God had placed me ; and besides, fearing that if I left once the Natives would not let me land again on returning to their island, I determined to hold on as long as possible, though feeling very weak and suffering badly from ague.

Sorrow and love make me linger a little to quote these extracts, printed in the *Reformed Presbyterian Magazine* for January 1860, from Mrs. Paton's last letter to her friends at home. It is dated from Port Resolution, Tanna, 28th December, 1858.

"MY DEAR FATHER, MOTHER, AND SISTERS,—

"When I wrote last, we were just about to leave Aneityum for Tanna, the sphere of our future labours. One can have no idea of the dark and degraded state of these poor Heathen, unless really living amongst them. Still we trust that the cloud which has so long enveloped Tanna will soon be rolled away, and the light of the Sun of Righteousness irradiate this dark land. We have been here about two months, and so far the people among whom we live appear to be friendly. A numerous priesthood reside in the neighbourhood of the Volcano, from whom we anticipate much opposition, as they know that wherever the Missionary gains a footing among the people, their influence is lost. The Tannese are very avaricious. If one renders the least assistance, he demands a most exorbitant pay ; indeed, we can hardly satisfy them. We have a number of male, but very few female visitors, the latter being just slaves to do all the work. The men disfigure their faces with red and black paint, and always carry spears and clubs. At first I was quite shocked with their appearance, but one soon becomes accustomed to such sights. They likewise possess powder and muskets,—guns and tobacco being the chief objects of their ambition. Indeed, such is their degraded condition that, were not the power and grace of God all-sufficient, one might almost despair of ever making any impression on them. All the Natives are in a state of entire nudity, with this exception, that females wear short petticoats made of grass. Young girls are very fond of beads, and sometimes have their necks quite covered with them. They likewise bore holes in the ear, from which they suspend large rolls (circles) of tortoise-shell. Two or three little girls come about me, whom I am teaching to sew and sing ; but no great good can be accomplished till we master their language. We have picked up a good many words, and I trust, with the blessing of God, will soon be able to speak to them of things pertaining to their everlasting peace.

"Port Resolution is a most beautiful Bay. I have never seen such a lovely spot. Indeed, everything around delights the eye, and 'only man is vile.' Our house is at the head of the Bay, on the foundation of Dr. Turner's, from which he had to fly fifteen years ago. The sea, at full tide, comes within a few yards of the door. Mr. Copeland is staying with us now. During the Rainy Season, he is to be sometimes with us, and at other times with Mr. Mathieson, who is in delicate health. The thermometer averages from 80° to 85°. The Rainy Season having now set in, it is not likely we will have any opportunity of sending or receiving letters for three or four months. I am wearying very much to hear from you. I can hardly realize that nine months have rolled away since I left bonnie Scotia! How many changes will take place before I again revisit it! Both my husband and I are in excellent health, and, though the heat feels oppressive, we like the climate very well. A Happy New Year to you all, and many happy returns! I am writing hurriedly, as a vessel has called, and leaves to-morrow morning. I expect to get all the news when you write, for my interest in and affection for home and home-folks have not in the least abated.

"Now I must conclude ; with love to you all, and to all my old companions, believe me ever your loving daughter and sister,

"MARY ANN PATON."

Her last words were, "Oh that my dear mother were here ! She is a good woman, my mother, a jewel of a woman."

Then, observing Mr. Copeland near by, she said, "Oh, Mr. Copeland, I did not know you were there ! You must not think that I regret coming here, and leaving my mother. If I had the same thing to do over again, I would do it with far more pleasure, yes, with all my heart. Oh, no! I do not regret leaving home and friends, though at the time I felt it keenly."

Soon after this, looking up and putting her hand in mine, she said,—

"J. C. wrote to our Janet saying, that young Christians under their first impressions thought they could do anything or make any sacrifice for Jesus, and he asked if she believed it, for he did not think they could, when tested; but Janet wrote back that she believed they could, and " (added she with great emphasis) " *I believe it is true !* "

In a moment, altogether unexpectedly, she fell asleep in Jesus, with these words on her lips. "Not lost, only gone before to be for ever with the Lord "—my heart keeps saying or singing to itself from that hour till now.

Ever since the day of our happy marriage, a strange presentiment possessed my heart that I should lose her soon and suddenly. Perhaps I am not the first who has wrestled through such unworthy forebodings—that that which was so precious and blessed was about to be withdrawn! Our short united life had been cloudless and happy; I felt her loss beyond all conception or description, in that dark land. It was very difficult to be resigned, left alone, and in sorrowful circumstances; but feeling immovably assured that my God and Father was too wise and loving to err in anything that He does or permits, I looked up to the Lord for help, and struggled on in His work. I do not pretend to see through the mystery of such visitations,—wherein God calls away the young, the promising, and those sorely needed for His service here; but this I do know and feel, that, in the light of such dispensations, it becomes us all to love and serve our blessed Lord Jesus so that we may be ready at His call for death and Eternity.

CHAPTER VII.

MISSION LEAVES FROM TANNA.

A.D. 1859—1860.   ÆT. 35—36.

IN the first letter, sent jointly by Mr. Copeland and myself
from Tanna to the Church at home, the following statements occur :—

"We found the Tannese to be painted Savages, enveloped
in all the superstition and wickedness of Heathenism. All the
men and children go in a state of nudity. The older women
wear grass skirts, and the young women and girls, grass or leaf
aprons like Eve in Eden. They are exceedingly ignorant,
vicious, and bigoted, and almost void of natural affection.
Instead of the inhabitants of Port Resolution being improved
by coming in contact with white men, they are rendered much
worse ; for they have learned all their vices, but none of their
virtues,—if such are possessed by the pioneer traders among
such races ! The Sandalwood Traders are as a class the most
godless of men, whose cruelty and wickedness make us
ashamed to own them as our countrymen. By them the poor,
defenceless Natives are oppressed and robbed on every hand ;
and if they offer the slightest resistance, they are ruthlessly
silenced by the musket or revolver. Few months here pass

without some of them being so shot, and, instead of their murderers feeling ashamed, they boast of how they despatch them. Such treatment keeps the Natives always burning under a desire for revenge, so that it is a wonder any white man is allowed to come among them. Indeed, all Traders here are able to maintain their position only by revolvers and rifles; but we hope a better state of affairs is at hand for Tanna."

The novelty of our being among them soon passed away, and they began to show their avarice and deceitfulness in every possible way. The Chiefs united and refused to give us the half of the small piece of land which had been purchased, on which to build our Mission House, and when we attempted to fence in the part they had left to us, they "tabooed" it, *i.e.*, threatened our Teachers and us with death if we proceeded further with the work. This they did by placing certain reeds stuck into the ground here and there around our house, which our Aneityumese servants at once knew the meaning of, and warned us of our danger; so we left off making the fence, that we might if possible evade all offence. They then divided the few bread-fruit and cocoa-nut trees on the ground amongst themselves, or demanded such payment for these trees as we did not possess, and threatened revenge on us if the trees were injured by any person. They now became so unreasonable and offensive, and our dangers so increased, as to make our residence amongst them extremely trying. At this time a vessel called; I bought from the Captain the things for payment which they demanded; on receiving it, they lifted the Taboo, and for a little season appeared to be friendly again. This was the third payment they had got for that site, and to yield was teaching them a cruel lesson; all this we felt and clearly saw, but they had by some means to be conciliated, if possible, and our lives had to be saved, if that could be done without dishonour to the Christian name.

After these events, a few weeks of dry weather began to tell against the growth of their yams and bananas. The drought was instantly ascribed to us and our God. The Natives far and near were summoned to consider the matter in public assembly. Next day, Nouka, the high chief, and Miaki, the war-chief, his nephew, came to inform us, that two powerful Chiefs had openly declared in that assembly that if the Harbour people did not at once kill us or compel us to leave the island, they would, unless the rain came plentifully in the meantime, summon all the Inland people and murder both our Chiefs and us. The friendly Chiefs said, " Pray to your Jehovah God for rain, and do not go far beyond your door for a time; we are all in greatest danger, and if war breaks out, we fear we cannot protect you."

But this friendliness was all pretence; they themselves, being Sacred Men, professed to have the power of sending or withholding rain, and tried to fix the blame of their discomfiture on us. The rage of the poor ignorant Heathen was thereby fed against us. The Ever-Merciful, however, again interposed on our behalf. On the following Sabbath, just when we were assembling for worship, rain began to fall, and in great abundance. The whole inhabitants believed, apparently, that it was sent to save us in answer to our prayers; so they met again, and resolved to allow us to remain on Tanna. Alas! on the other hand, the continuous and heavy rains brought much sickness and fever in their train, and again their Sacred Men pointed to us as the cause. Hurricane winds also blew and injured their fruits and fruit-trees,—another opportunity for our enemies to lay the blame of everything upon the Missionaries and their Jehovah God! The trial and the danger daily grew of living among a people so dreadfully benighted by superstition, and so easily swayed by prejudice and passion.

On Sabbath afternoon, the 6th of January, 1860, in a severe gale, we were surprised to see a large Sydney vessel come to anchor in the Harbour at Port Resolution, right opposite our house. Though wind and sea were both dangerously high, the Captain and all hands, as we were afterwards informed, coolly went to sleep. Gradually, but quite perceptibly, the vessel was allowed to drift as if by deliberate intention, till she struck on the beach at the head of the Bay, and there was soon broken up and became a total wreck. For this also the ignorant Natives gave us credit, as for everything uncommon or disagreeable on Tanna; but we were ever conscious that our Lord Jesus was near us, and all trials that lead us to cling closer in fellowship with our Saviour are really blessings in disguise. The Captain of that vessel, known to us as " Big Hays," and his wife, said to be the wife of a man in Sydney who had run away with him, and his like-minded crew became by their shocking conduct a horrible curse to our poor Islanders, and greatly embittered the feeling against us. They were armed with deadly weapons, and did their wicked will amongst our Natives, who durst not attack so large a party of desperate and well-armed men. But they were white people, and so were the Missionaries; to the savage mind that was enough, and revenge would be taken upon the first white faces, however innocent, who came within their power.

The Natives of Tanna were well-nigh constantly at war amongst themselves, every man doing that which was right in his own eyes, and almost every quarrel ending in an appeal to arms. Besides many battles far inland, one was fought beside our house, and several around the Harbour. In these conflicts, many men were bruised with clubs and wounded with arrows, but few lives were lost, considering the savage uproar and frenzy of the scene. In one case, of which we obtained certain information, seven men were killed in an engagement; and according to Tannese custom, the warriors and their friends feasted on them at the close of the fray, the widows of the slain being also strangled to death, and similarly disposed of. Besides those who fell in war, the Natives living in our quarter had killed and feasted on eight persons, usually in sacrificial rites.

It is said, that the habitual Cannibal's desire for human flesh becomes so horrible that he has been known to disinter and feast upon those recently buried. Two cases of this revolting barbarism were reported as having occurred amongst the villagers living near us. On another occasion the great chief Nouka took seriously unwell, and his people sacrificed three women for his recovery! All such cruel and horrifying practices, however, they tried to conceal from us; and many must have perished in this way of whom we, though living at their doors, were never permitted to hear.

Amongst the Heathen, in the New Hebrides, and especially on Tanna, *woman* is the down-trodden slave of man. She is kept working hard, and bears all the heavier burdens, while he walks by her side with musket, club, or spear. If she offends him, he beats or abuses her at pleasure. A Savage gave his poor wife a severe beating in front of our house and just before our eyes, while in vain we strove to prevent it. Such scenes were so common that no one thought of interfering. Even if the woman died in his hands, or immediately thereafter, neighbours took little notice, if any at all. And their children were so little cared for, that my constant wonder was how any of them survived at all ! As soon as they are able to knock about, they are left practically to care for themselves ; hence the very small affection they show towards their parents, which results in the aged who are unable to work being neglected, starved to death, and sometimes even more directly and violently destroyed.

A Heathen boy's education consists in being taught to aim skilfully with the bow, to throw the spear faultlessly at a mark, to wield powerfully the club and tomahawk, and to shoot well with musket and revolver when these can be obtained. He accompanies his father and brothers in all the wars and preparations for war, and is diligently initiated into all their cruelties and lusts, as the very prerequisite of his being regarded and acknowledged to be a *man* and a warrior. The girls have, with their mother and sisters, to toil and slave in the village plantations, to prepare all the materials for fencing these around, to bear every burden, and to be knocked about at will by the men and boys.

Oh, how sad and degraded is the position of Woman, where the teaching of Christ is unknown, or disregarded though known ! It is the Christ of the Bible, it is His Spirit entering into Humanity, that has lifted Woman, and made her the helpmate and the friend of Man, not his toy or his slave.

To the best of our observation, the Heathen, though vaguely following some division of the week into seven days, spent the Sabbath on Tanna much the same as their other days were spent. Even when some were led to give up manual labours on that day, they spent it, like too many Christians elsewhere, in visiting friends and in selfish pleasures, on feasting and drinking. After we had been about one year on the island, we had a morning Church Service, attended by about ten Chiefs and as many women and children belonging to them; though, once the Service was over, they paid no more attention to the Lord's Day. On some of the more Northern Islands of the group, the Heathen had a sacred day. Twice, sailing with the *Dayspring*, we cast anchor at an Island, but could not see a single Native till next day, when one who could speak broken English informed us that none of the people had been seen moving about because they were "keeping their Sunday." A number of the Tannese spoke a little English, but they were the worst and most treacherous characters of all. They had imbibed the profane Trader's language and his hatred of Missionaries and their work; and these, added to their own Heathen prejudices, made them the most troublesome and dangerous of men.

After the Sabbath Morning Service we used to walk many miles, visiting all the villages within reach, even before we had got so much of their language as to be able to speak freely to the people. Sometimes we made a circuit amongst them, ten or twelve miles away and as many back again. We tried to talk a little to all who were willing to listen; and we conducted the Worship of Jehovah, wherever we could find two or three disposed to gather together and to sit or kneel beside us. It was to flesh and blood weary work, and in many ways disheartening—no responsive faces and hearts there to cheer us on and lift us up into fellowship with the Lord! But it helped us to see the people, and to get acquainted with the districts around; it also secured for us very considerable audiences, except when they were engaged in war.

No real progress could be made in imparting to them spiritual knowledge, till we had attained some familiarity with their language. By finding out, as before recorded, the Tannese for "What is this?" and "What is his or her name?" we got the names of things and people, and made amazing progress towards mutual intelligence. We soon found out that there were two distinct languages spoken in and around Port Resolution; but we confined ourselves to that which was understood as far as the other Mission Station; and, by God's help and great diligence we were able ere long to speak to them of sin and of salvation through Jesus Christ.

Twelve Aneityumese Teachers were at this time living on Tanna, but they had no Schools, and no Books in Tannese, for that language had never yet been reduced to forms that could be printed. The work of the Teachers, besides telling to the people around all that they could regarding Christ and the Christian religion, found its highest value in presenting through their own spirit and character a nobler type of life than any that Heathenism could show.

When a Missionary arrives, the Teacher's first duty is to help him in house-building, fencing, and the many manual and other toils required in organizing the new Station, besides accompanying him on the inland journeys, assisting him in regard to the language as far as possible, and in general furthering the cause. But in altogether virgin soil like that of Tanna, the Aneityumese Teacher, or one from any other island, had the language to acquire first of all, not less than the European Missionary, and was therefore of little use except for manual labour, and that too had to be carried on by signs much more than by words. Not only has every island its own tongue, differing widely from and unintelligible to all the others, but even the people on one side of an island could not sometimes understand or converse with the people on the opposite side of the same. This rendered our work in the New Hebrides not only exceptionally difficult, but its progressive movement distressingly slow.

Word had reached Tanna, that, in a quarrel with Sandal-wooders, the Erromangans had murdered three white men and a number of Natives in their employment, in revenge for the white men's shamefully entreating and murdering the Erromangans. On Tanna all such news were reported and talked over, when the Chiefs and their men of war met for their evening repast—an event accompanied by the excessive drinking of *Kava*, which first produced intoxication, like whisky, and then stupefaction like a dose of laudanum. Excited by the rumours from Erromanga, they had drunk more than usual, and lay about their Village Drinking-Hall—a helpless host. Enemies from an inland tribe stealthily drew near, and discharged their muskets amongst them in the dark, killing one man ; and so, according to their custom, war was known to be declared.

Early next morning, Miaki, the war-chief, despatched his herald to sound the Conch and summon the people to battle. He made the Harbour and all the country resound with it for six miles around, and the savage hordes gathered to the call. Putting our trust in God, we quietly resolved to attend as usual to our work and await the result. Excitement and terror drove the Natives hither and thither. One man close to us being nearly killed, his friends assembled in great force, and with clubs and spears, tomahawks and muskets, drove the offending tribe more than a mile into the bush. They, in turn, being reinforced, drove their enemies back again to the beach. There, seated within hearing distance, they carried on a grand sort of barbarous-Homeric scolding match, and exhausted their rage in javelins of reproach. A great relief seemed thereby to ensue, for the rival Chiefs thereon approached our house and entreated me to dress their wounds ! I did so, and appealed to them for peace, and got their promise to let that conflict come to an end. Alas for the passing influence of such appeals,—for I learned shortly after this, on my return from Aneityum, where I had gone for a fortnight to recruit from the effects of an almost three months' continuance of recurring ague and fever, that eight of the Harbour people had been murdered near our house at Port Resolution. The Natives got into a dreadfully unsettled state, each one wondering in terror who would be the next to fall.

About the time of my dear wife's death, our brother Missionary, Mr. Mathieson, also became exceedingly unwell. His delicate frame fast gave way, and brought with it weakness of the mind as well ; and he was removed to Aneityum apparently in a dying condition. These sad visitations had a bad effect on the Natives, owing to their wild superstitions about the cause of death and sickness. We had reason to fear that they would even interfere with the precious grave, over which we kept careful watch for a season ; but God mercifully restrained them. Unfortunately, however, one of my Aneityumese Teachers who had gone round to Mr.

Mathieson's Station took ill and died there, and this rekindled all their prejudices. He, poor fellow, before death said, " I shall not again return to Port Resolution, or see my dear Missi ; but tell him that I die happy, for I love Jesus much, and am going to Jesus ! "

Hearing these things, the Natives insolently demanded me to tell them the cause of this death, and of Mr. Mathieson's trouble, and of the other deaths. Other reasoning or explanation being to them useless, I turned the tables, and demanded them to tell me why all this trouble and death had overtaken us in their land, and whether they themselves were not the cause of it all ? Strange to say, this simple question turned the whole current of their speculations. They held meeting after meeting to discuss it for several days, and returned the message, " We do not blame. you, and you must not blame us, for causing these troubles and deaths ; but we believe that a Bushman must have got hold of a portion of something we had eaten, and must have thrown it to the great Evil Spirit in the volcano, thereby bringing all these troubles and curses."

Another Chief vindicated himself and others thus :—" Karapanamun, the Aurumanu or great Evil Spirit of Tanna, whom we all fear and worship, is causing these troubles ; for he knows that if we become worshippers of your Jehovah God, we cannot continue to fear him, or present him with the best of everything, as our forefathers have always done ; he is angry at you and at us all."

The fear of the deaths and troubles being ascribed to them silenced their talk against us for a season ; but very little made them either friends or foes, as the next event will too painfully show.

Nowhat, an old Chief of the highest rank from Aneityum, who spoke Tannese and was much respected by the Natives all round the south side of Tanna, came on a visit to our island. After returning home, he became very ill and died in a few days. The deluded Tannese, hearing of his death, ascribed it to me and the Worship, and resolved to burn our house and property, and either murder the whole Mission party, or compel us to leave the island. Nowhat's brother was sent from Aneityum to talk to the Tannese and conciliate them, but unfortunately he could not speak the language well; and the Aneityumese Teachers felt their lives to be at this time in such danger, that they durst not accompany him as interpreters, while I, on the other hand, did not understand his language, nor he mine. Within two days after landing, he had a severe attack of ague and fever; and, though the vessel he came in remained eight days, he was prostrated all the time, so that his well-intentioned visit did us much harm. The Tannese became furious. This was proof positive, that we were the cause of all their sickness and death! Inland and all along the weather side of the island, when far enough away from us, they said that the Natives were enjoying excellent health. Meeting after meeting was held; exciting speeches were delivered; and feasts were given, for which it was said that several women were sacrificed, cooked, and eaten,—such being the bonds by which they entered into covenant with each other for life or death.

On the morning of the following Sabbath, we heard what were said to be the dying shrieks of two woman-sacrifices; but we went not near,—we had no power to save them, and the Savages only waited such a chance of sacrificing us too. Soon after, three women came running to the Mission House, and in tears implored us to try and protect them from being killed by their husbands. Alas, we could only plead for them, the Tannese and Aneityumese Teachers warning us that if we even pled we would be instantly murdered, as the men were raging mad with the thirst of blood. At another time, eight inland girls came running to us and sat in front of our house all day, saying they were afraid to go home, as the men were fighting with their women and killing them. At night-fall, however, the poor creatures withdrew, we knew not to what fate.

The inhabitants for miles around united in seeking our destruction, but God put it into even savage hearts to save us. Old Nowar, the Chief under whom we lived, and the Chief next under him, Arkurat, set themselves to rescue us. Along with Manuman and Sirawia they opposed every plan in the public assembly for taking our lives. Some of their people also remained friendly to us, and by the help of our Aneityumese

Teachers, warned us of danger and protected our lives. Determined not to be baffled, a meeting of all our enemies on the island was summoned, and it was publicly resolved that a band of men be selected and enjoined to kill the whole of those friendly to the Mission, old Nowar among the rest, and not only to murder the Mission party, but also a Trader who had lately landed to live there, that no one might be left to give information to the white men or bring punishment on the Islanders. Frenzy of excitement prevailed, and the blood-fiend seemed to over-ride the whole assembly ; when, under an impulse that surely came from the Lord of Pity, one great warrior Chief who had hitherto kept silent, rose, swung aloft a mighty club, and smashing it earthwards, cried aloud, " The man that kills Missi must first kill me,—the men that kill the Mission Teachers must first kill me and my people,—for we shall stand by them and defend them till death."

Instantaneously, another Chief thundered in with the same declaration ; and the great assembly broke up in dismay. All the more remarkable was this deliverance, as these two Chiefs lived nearly four miles inland, and, as reputed disease makers and Sacred Men, were regarded as amongst our bitterest enemies. It had happened that, a brother of the former Chief having been wounded in battle, I had dressed his wounds and he recovered, for which perhaps he now favoured us. But I do not put very much value on that consideration ; for too clearly did our dear Lord Jesus inter-pose directly on our behalf that day. I and my defenceless company had spent it in anxious prayers and tears ; and our hearts overflowed with gratitude to the Saviour who rescued us from the lions' jaws.

The excitement did not at once subside, men continuing to club and beat the women for the smallest offence. At every opportunity I denounced their conduct and rebuked them severely,—especially one wretch, who beat his wife just in front of our house, as well as one of the women who tried to protect her. On the following day, he returned with an armed band, and threatened our lives ; but I stood up in fron of their weapons, and firmly condemned their conduct, telling that man particularly that his conduct was bad and cowardly.

At length his wrath gave way; he grounded his club in a penitent mood, and promised to refrain from such evil ways.

Leaving all consequences to the disposal of my Lord, I determined to make an unflinching stand against wife-beating and widow-strangling, feeling confident that even their natural conscience would be on my side. I accordingly pled with all who were in power to unite and put down these shocking and disgraceful customs. At length, ten Chiefs entered into an agreement not to allow any more beating of wives or strangling of widows, and to forbid all common labour on the Lord's Day; but alas, except for purposes of war or other wickedness, the influence of the Chiefs on Tanna was comparatively small. One Chief boldly declared, "If we did not beat our women, they would never work; they would not fear and obey us; but when we have beaten, and killed, and feasted on two or three, the rest are all very quiet and good for a long time to come!"

I tried to show him how cruel it was, besides that it made them unable for work, and that kindness would have a much better effect; but he promptly assured me that Tannese women "could not understand kindness." For the sake of teaching by example, my Aneityumese Teachers and I used to go a mile or two inland on the principal pathway, along with the Teachers' wives, and there cutting and carrying home a heavy load of firewood for myself and each of the men, while we gave only a small burden to each of the women. Meeting many Tanna-men by the way, I used to explain to them that this was how Christians helped and treated their wives and sisters, and then they loved their husbands and were strong to work at home; and that as men were made stronger, they were intended to bear the heavier burdens, and especially in all labours out of doors. Our habits and practices had thus as much to do as, perhaps more than, all our appeals, in leading them to glimpses of the life to which the Lord Jesus was calling them.

Another war-burst, that caused immense consternation, passed over with only two or three deaths; and I succeeded in obtaining the consent of twenty Chiefs to fight no more except on the defensive,—a covenant to which, for a considerable time, they strictly adhered, in the midst of fierce provocations. But to gain any such end, the masses of the people must be educated to the point of desiring it. The few cannot, in such circumstances, act up to it, without laying themselves open to be down-trodden and swept away by the Savages around.

About this time, several men, afraid or ashamed by day, came to me regularly by night for conversation and instruction. Having seen the doors of the Mission House made fast and the windows blinded so that they could not be observed, they continued with me for many hours, asking all strange questions about the new Religion and its laws. I remember one Chief particularly, who came often, saying to me, " I would be an Awfuaki man (*i.e.*, a Christian) were it not that all the rest would laugh at me ; that I could not stand ! "

" Almost persuaded "—before you blame him, remember how many in Christian lands and amid greater privileges live and die without ever passing beyond that stage.

The wife of one of those Chiefs died, and he resolved to imitate a Christian burial. Having purchased white calico from a Trader, he came to me for some tape which the Trader could not supply, and told me that he was going to dress the body as he had seen my dear wife's dressed, and lay her also in a similar grave. He declined my offer to attend the funeral and to pray with them, as in that case many of the villagers would not attend. He wanted all the people to be present, to see and to hear, as it was the first funeral of the kind ever celebrated among the Tannese ; and my friend Nowar the Chief had promised to conduct a Service and offer prayer to Jehovah before all the Heathen. It moved me to many strange emotions, this Christian burial, conducted by a Heathen and in the presence of Heathens, with an appeal to the true and living God by a man as yet darkly groping among idols and superstitions ! Many were the wondering questions from time to time addressed to me. The idea of a resurrection from the dead was that which most keenly interested these Natives, and called forth all their powers of inquiry and argument. Thus the waves of hope and fear swept alternately across our lives ; but we embraced every possible opportunity of telling them the story of the life and death of Jesus, in the strong hope that God would spare us yet to bring the benighted Heathen to the knowledge of the true salvation, and to love and serve the only Saviour.

Confessedly, however, it was uphill, weary, and trying work. For one thing, these Tannese were terribly dishonest; and when there was any special sickness, or excitement from any cause, their bad feeling towards the Worship was displayed by the more insolent way in which they carried off whatever they could seize. When I opposed them, the club or tomahawk, the musket or *kawas* (*i.e.*, killing stone), being instantly raised, intimated that my life would be taken, if I resisted. Their skill in stealing on the sly was phenomenal! If an article fell, or was seen on the floor, a Tanna-man would neatly cover it with his foot, while looking you frankly in the face, and, having fixed it by his toes or by bending in his great toe like a thumb to hold it, would walk off with it, assuming the most innocent look in the world. In this way, a knife, a pair of scissors, or any smaller article, would at once disappear. Another fellow would deftly stick something out of sight amongst the whip-cord plaits of his hair, another would conceal it underneath his naked arm, while yet another would shamelessly lift what he coveted and openly carry it away.

With most of them, however, the shame was not in the theft, but in doing it so clumsily that they were discovered! Once, after continuous rain and a hot damp atmosphere, when the sun shone out I put my bed-clothes on a rope to dry. I stood at hand watching, as also the wives of two Teachers, for things were mysteriously disappearing almost under our very eyes. Suddenly, Miaki, who with his war-companions had been watching us unobserved, came rushing to me breathless and alone, crying, " Missi, come in, quick, quick! I want to tell you something and to get your advice!"

He ran into my house, and I followed; but before he had got into his story, we heard the two women crying out, "Missi, Missi, come quick! Miaki's men are stealing your sheets and blankets!"

I ran at once, but all were gone into the bush, and with them my sheets and blankets. Miaki for a moment looked abashed, as I charged him with deceiving me just to give his men their opportunity. But he soon rose to the occasion. He wrought himself into a towering rage at them, flourished his huge club and smashed the bushes all around, shouting to me, " Thus will I smash these fellows, and compel them to return your clothes."

Perhaps he hoped to move me to intercede for his men, and to prevent bloodshed, as he knew that I always did, even to my own loss ; but I resisted all his tricks, and urged him to return these articles at once if there were any honour or honesty in him or his men. Of course, he left me but to share the plunder ! He kept out of my way for a considerable time, which showed a small glimmering of conscience somewhere ; and when I tackled him on the subject, at our first meeting, he declared he was unable to get the articles back, which of course showed the lying spirit, amongst them everywhere applauded,—for a lie that succeeded, or seemed to succeed, was in their esteem a crowning virtue.

One dark night, I heard them amongst my fowls. These I had purchased from them for knives and calico ; and they now stole them all away, dead or alive. Had I interfered, they would have gloried in the chance to club or shoot me in the dark, when no one could exactly say who had done the deed. Several of the few goats, which I had for milk, were also killed or driven away ; indeed, all the injury that was possible was done to me, short of taking away my life, and that was now frequently attempted. Having no fires or fireplaces in my Mission House, such being not required there,—though sometimes a fire would have been invaluable for drying our bed-clothes in the Rainy Season,—we had a house near by in which all our food was cooked, and there, under lock and key, we secured all our cooking utensils, pots, dishes, etc. One night, that too was broken into, and everything was stolen. In consternation, I appealed to the Chief, telling him what had been done. He also flew into a great rage, and vowed vengeance on the thieves, saying that he would compel them to return everything. But, of course, nothing was returned ; the thief could not be found ! I, unable to live without something in which to boil water, at length offered a blanket to any one that would bring back my kettle. Miaki himself, after much professed difficulty, returned it *minus* the lid—that, he said, probably fishing for a higher bribe, could not be got at any price, being at the other side of the island in a tribe over which he had no control! In the circumstances, I was glad to get kettle *minus* lid—realizing how life itself may depend on so small a luxury!

Having no means of redress, and feeling ourselves entirely at their mercy, we strove quietly to bear all and to make as little of our trials as possible; indeed, we bore them all gladly for Jesus' sake. All through these sorrows, our assurance deepened rather than faded, that if God only spared us to lead them to love and serve the same Lord Jesus, they would soon learn to treat us as their friends and helpers. That, however, did not do away with the hard facts of my life— being now entirely alone amongst them, opposed by their cruelty at every turn, and deceived by their unfailing lies.

One morning, the Tannese, rushing towards me in great excitement, cried, " Missi, Missi, there is a God, or a ship on fire, or something of fear, coming over the sea! We see no flames, but it smokes like a volcano. Is it a Spirit, a God, or a ship on fire? What is it? what is it?"

One party after another followed in quick succession, shout ing the same questions in great alarm, to which I replied, " I cannot go at once; I must dress first in my best clothes; it will likely be one of Queen Victoria's Men-of-war, coming to ask of me if your conduct is good or bad, if you are stealing my property, or threatening my life, or how you are using me?"

They pled with me to go and see it; but I made much fuss about dressing, and getting ready to meet the great Chief on the vessel, and would not go with them. The two principal Chiefs now came running and asked, " Missi, will it be a ship of war?"

I called to them, "I think it will; but I have no time to speak to you now, I must get on my best clothes!"

They said, " Missi, only tell us, will he ask you if we have been stealing your things?"

I answered, " I expect he will."

They asked, " And will you tell him ? "

I said, " I must tell him the truth ; if he asks, I will tell him."

They then cried out, " Oh, Missi, tell him not ! Everything shall be brought back to you at once, and no one will be allowed again to steal from you."

Then said I, " Be quick ! Everything must be returned before he comes. Away, away ! and let me get ready to meet the great Chief on the Man-of-war."

Hitherto, no thief could ever be found, and no Chief had power to cause anything to be restored to me ; but now, in an incredibly brief space of time, one came running to the Mission House with a pot, another with a pan, another with a blanket, others with knives, forks, plates, and all sorts of stolen property. The Chiefs called me to receive these things, but I replied, " Lay them all down at the door, bring everything together quickly ; I have no time to speak with you ! "

I delayed my toilet, enjoying mischievously the magical effect of an approaching vessel that might bring penalty to thieves. At last the Chiefs, running in breathless haste, called out to me, " Missi, Missi, do tell us, is the stolen property all here ? "

Of course I could not tell, but, running out, I looked on the promiscuous heap of my belongings, and said, " I don't see the lid of the kettle there yet ! "

One Chief said, " No, Missi, for it is on the other side of the island ; but tell him not, I have sent for it, and it will be here to-morrow."

I answered, " I am glad you have brought back so much ; and now, if you three Chiefs, Nauka, Miaki, and Nowar, do not run away when he comes, he will not likely punish you ; but, if you and your people run away, he will ask me why you are afraid, and I will be forced to tell him ! Keep near me and you are all safe ; only there must be no more stealing from me."

They said, " We are in black fear, but we will keep near you, and our bad conduct to you is done."

The charm and joy of that morning are fresh to me still, when H.M.S. *Cordelia,* Captain Vernon, steamed into our lovely Harbour. The Commander, having heard rumour of my dangers on Tanna, kindly came on shore as soon as the ship cast anchor, with two boats, and a number of his officers and men, so far armed. He was dressed in splendid uniform, being a tall and handsome man, and he and his attendants made a grand and imposing show. On seeing Captain Vernon's boat nearing the shore, and the men glittering in gold lace and arms, Miaki the Chief left my side on the beach and rushed towards his village. I concluded that he had run for it through terror, but he had other and more civilized intentions in his Heathen head! Having obtained, from some trader or visitor in previous days, a soldier's old red coat, he had resolved to rise to the occasion and appear in his best before the Captain and his men. As I was shaking hands with them and welcoming them to Tanna, Miaki returned with the short red coat on, buttoned tightly round his otherwise naked body; and, surmounted by his ugly painted face and long whipcords of twisted hair, it completely spoiled any appearance that he might otherwise have had of savage freedom, and made him look a dirty and insignificant creature.

The Captain was talking to me, his men stood in order near oy—to my eyes, oh how charming a glimpse of Home life!— when Miaki marched up and took his place most consequentially at my side. He felt himself the most important personage in the scene, and with an attempt at haughty dignity he began to survey the visitors. All eyes were fixed on the impudent little man, and the Captain asked, " What sort of a character is this ? "

I replied, "This is Miaki, our great war Chief"; and whispered to the Captain to be on his guard, as this man knew a little English, and might understand or misunderstand just enough to make it afterwards dangerous to me.

The Captain only muttered, " The contemptible creature ! ' But such words were far enough beyond Miaki's vocabulary, so he looked on and grinned complacently.

At last he said, " Missi, this great Chief whom Queen Victoria has sent to visit you in her Man-of-war, cannot go over the whole of this island so as to be seen by all our people ; and I wish you to ask him if he will stand by a tree, and allow me to put a spear on the ground at his heel, and we will make a nick in it at the top of his head, and the spear will be sent round the island to let all the people see how tall this great man is!" They were delighted at the good Captain agreeing to their simple request; and that spear was exhibited to thousands, as the vessel, her Commander, officers, and men, were afterwards talked of round and round the island.

Captain Vernon was extremely kind, and offered to do anything in his power for me, thus left alone on the island amongst such Savages; but, as my main difficulties were connected with my spiritual work amongst them rousing up their cruel prejudices, I did not see how his kindness could effectually interpose. At his suggestion, however, I sent a general invitation to all the Chiefs within reach, to meet the Captain next morning at my house. True to their instincts of suspicion and fear, they despatched all their women and children to the beach on the opposite side of the island, beyond reach of danger, and next morning my house was crowded with armed men, manifestly much afraid. Punctually at the hour appointed, 10 a.m., the Captain came on shore; and soon thereafter twenty Chiefs were seated with him in my house. He very kindly spent about an hour, giving them wise counsels and warning them against outrages on strangers, all calculated to secure our safety and advance the interests of our Mission work. He then invited all the Chiefs to go on board and see his vessel. They were taken to see the Armoury, and the sight of the big guns running so easily on rails vastly astonished them. He then placed them round us on deck and showed them two shells discharged towards the Ocean, at which, as they burst and fell far off, splash—splashing into the water, the terror of the Natives visibly increased. But, when he sent a large ball crashing through a cocoa-nut grove, breaking the trees like straws and cutting its way clear and swift, they were quite dumbfoundered, and pled to be again set safely on shore. After receiving each some small gift, however, they were reconciled to the situation, and returned immensely interested in all that they had seen. Doubtless many a wild romance was spun by these savage heads, in trying to describe and hand down to others the wonders of the fire-god of the sea, and the

Captain of the great white Queen. How easily it all lends itself to the service of poetry and myth !

About this time also, the London Missionary Society's ship, the *John Williams*, visited me, having on board the Rev. Messrs. Turner, Inglis, Baker, and Macfarlan. They urged me to go with them on a three weeks' trip round the Islands, as I had lately suffered much from fever and ague, and was greatly reduced by it. But a party of Bush Natives had killed one of our Harbour people the week before, and sadly bruised several others with their clubs, and I feared a general war of revenge if I left—for my presence amongst them at least helped to keep the peace. I also was afraid that, if I left, they might not allow me to return to the island,—so I declined once more the pleasure of much-needed change and rest. Further, as the *John Williams* brought me the wood for building a Church which I had bought on Aneityum, the Tannese now plainly saw that, though their conduct had been very bad, and I had suffered much on their island, I had no intention of leaving them or of giving up the work of Jehovah.

Too much, perhaps, had I hoped for from the closely succeeding visits of the good Bishop Selwyn, the gallant Captain Vernon, and the Mission ship *John Williams*. The impressions were undoubtedly good, but evanescent ; and things soon went on as they had done before among our benighted Tannese, led by Satan at his will, and impelled to the grossest deeds of Heathen darkness. The change by Divine grace, however, we knew to be possible ; and for this we laboured and prayed incessantly, fainting not, or if fainting, only to rise again and tackle every duty in the name of the Lord who had placed us there.

Fever and ague had attacked me fourteen times severely, with slighter recurring attacks almost continuously after my first three months on the island, and I now felt the necessity of taking the hint of the Tannese Chief before referred to— " Sleep on the higher ground." Having also received medical counsel to the same effect, though indeed experience was painfully sufficient testimony, I resolved to remove my house, and began to look about for a suitable site. There rose behind my present site, a hill about two hundred feet high, surrounded on all sides by a valley, and swept by the breezes of the trade winds, being only separated from the Ocean by a narrow neck of land. On this I had set my heart; there was room for a Mission House and a Church, for which indeed Nature seemed to have adapted it. I proceeded to buy up every claim by the Natives to any portion of the hill, paying each publicly and in turn, so that there might be no trouble afterwards. I then purchased from a Trader the deck planks of a shipwrecked vessel, with which to construct a house of two apartments, a bedroom and a small store-room adjoining it, to which I purposed to transfer and add the old house as soon as I was able.

Just at this juncture, the fever smote me again more severely than ever; my weakness after this attack was so great, that I felt as if I never could rally again. With the help of my faithful Aneityumese Teacher, Abraham, and his wife, however, I made what appeared my last effort to creep—I could not climb—up the hill to get a breath of wholesome air. When about two-thirds up the hill, I became so faint that I concluded I was dying. Lying down on the ground, sloped against the root of a tree to keep me from rolling to the bottom, I took farewell of old Abraham, of my Mission work, and of everything around! In this weak state I lay, watched over by my faithful companion, and fell into a quiet sleep. When consciousness returned, I felt a little stronger, and a faint gleam of hope and life came back to my soul.

Abraham and his devoted wife Nafatu lifted me and carried me to the top of the hill. There they laid me on cocoa-nut leaves on the ground, and erected over me a shade or screen of the same; and there the two faithful souls, inspired surely by something diviner even than mere human pity, gave me the cocoa-nut juice to drink and fed me with native food and kept me living—I know not for how long. Consciousness did, however, fully return. The trade wind refreshed me day by day. The Tannese seemed to have given me up for dead; and providentially none of them looked near us for many days. Amazingly my strength returned, and I began planning about my new house on the hill. Afraid again to sleep at the old site, I slept under the tree, and sheltered by the cocoa-nut leaf screen, while preparing my new bedroom.

Here again, but for these faithful souls, the Aneityumese Teacher and his wife, I must have been baffled, and would have died in the effort. The planks of the wreck, and all other articles required, they fetched and carried; and it taxed my utmost strength to get them in some way planted together. But life depended on it. It was at length accomplished; and after that time I suffered comparatively little from anything like continuous attacks of fever and ague. That noble old soul, Abraham, stood by me as an angel of God in sickness and in danger; he went at my side wherever I had to go; he helped me willingly to the last inch of strength in all that I had to do; and it was perfectly manifest that he was doing all this not from mere human love, but for the sake of Jesus. That man had been a Cannibal in his Heathen days, but by the grace of God there he stood verily a new creature in Christ Jesus. Any trust, however sacred or valuable, could be absolutely reposed in him; and in trial or danger, I was often refreshed by that old Teacher's prayers, as I used to be by the prayers of my saintly father in my childhood's home. No white man could have been a more valuable helper to me in my perilous circumstances; and no person, white or black, could have shown more fearless and chivalrous devotion.

When I have read or heard the shallow objections of irreligious scribblers and talkers, hinting that there was no reality in conversions, and that Mission effort was but waste, oh, how my heart has yearned to plant them just one week on Tanna, with the " natural " man all around in the person of Cannibal and Heathen, and only the one " spiritual " man in the person of the converted Abraham, nursing them, feeding them, saving them " for the love of Jesus "—that I might just learn how many hours it took to convince them that Christ in man was a reality after all ! All the scepticism of Europe would hide its head in foolish shame ; and all its doubts would dissolve under one glance of the new light that Jesus, and Jesus alone, pours from the converted Cannibal's eye.

Perhaps it may surprise some unsophisticated reader to learn, though others who know more will be quite prepared for it, that this removal of our house, as also Mr. Mathieson's for a similar reason, was severely criticised by the people who try to evangelize the world while sitting in easy chairs at home. Precious nonsense appeared, for instance, in the *Nova Scotian Church Magazine,* about my house being planted on the fighting ground of the Natives, and thereby courting and provoking hostilities. As matter of fact, the hill-top was too narrow to accommodate both the Church and my house, and had to be levelled out for that purpose, and it was besides surrounded by a deep valley on three sides ; but the arm-chair critics, unwilling to believe in the heathen hatred of the Gospel, had to invent some reason out of their own brains to account for my being so persecuted and plundered. In truth, we were learning by suffering for the benefit of those who should follow us to these Islands,—that health could be found only on the higher levels, swept by the breath of the trade winds, and that fever and ague lay in wait near the shore, and especially on the leeward side. Even Mr. Inglis had his house on Aneityum removed also to the higher ground ; and no Missionary since has been located in the fever-beds by the swamp or shore. Life is God's great gift, to be preserved for His uses, not thrown away.

CHAPTER VIII.

MORE MISSION LEAVES FROM TANNA.

A.D. 1860. ÆT. 36.

The Blood-Fiend Unleashed.— In the Camp of the Enemy.—A Typical South Sea Trader.—Young Rarip's Death.—The Trader's Retribution. —Worship and War.—Saved from Strangling.—Wrath Restrained.— Under the Axe.—The Clubbing of Namuri.—Native Saint and Martyr.—Bribes Refused.—Widows Saved from Strangling.—The Sinking of the Well.—Church-Building on Tanna.—Ancient Stone-God.—Printing First Tannese Book.—A Christian Captain.— Levelled Muskets.—A French Refugee.—A Villainous Captain.— Like Master Like Men.—Wrecked on Purpose.—The Kanaka Traffic.—A Heathen Festival.—Sacrifices to Idols.—Heathen Dances and Sham Fights.—Six Native Teachers.—A Homeric Episode.— Victims for a Cannibal Feast.—The Jaws of Death.—Nahak of Sorcery.—Killing Me by Nahak.—Nahak Defied.—Protected by Jehovah.—Almost Persuaded.—Escorted to the Battlefield.—Praying for Enemies.—Our Canoe on the Reef.—A Perilous Pilgrimage.— Rocks and Waters.

THE Peace-party, my band of twenty Chiefs already spoken of, kept all the tribes around the Harbour acting only on the defensive for a season. But the Inland people murdered eight Chiefs from a distance who, after paying a friendly visit to the Harbour people, were returning to their homes. At the same time, one of the Inland Chiefs, who had pled with his people to give up war and live at peace with surrounding tribes, was overthrown and murdered by his own men, as also his brother and four wives and two children, and was supplanted by another leader more akin to their wishes and tastes. They proceeded, according to their custom of declaring war, to shoot one of the Harbour men and to break down their fences and plantations. So, once again, the blood-fiend was unleashed,—the young men of Tanna being as eager to get up a battle, as young men of the world at home seem eager to get up a concert or a ball.

The Harbour people advised me to remove a mile further away from these warriors; but the Inland Tribes sent me word not to desert my house, lest it might be burned and plundered, for that they themselves had no quarrel against me. Early next morning, I, accompanied by Abraham and another Aneityumese, started off to visit the Bush party, and if possible avert the impending war, but without informing my Harbour people. About four miles from our Station, we met the Chief of our farthest inland friendly tribe with all his fighting men under arms. Forcing me to disclose our errand, he reluctantly allowed us to pass. Praying to Jesus for guidance and protection, we pressed along the path through the thick bush four miles further still. My two attendants, sinking into silence, betrayed growing fear; and I, after trying to cheer them, had at their most earnest appeal to walk on also in silence, my heart and theirs going up to Jesus in prayer. We passed many deserted villages and plantations, but saw no living person. At last, unexpectedly, we stumbled upon the whole host assembled on the Village Common at a great feast; and at sight of us every man rushed for his weapons of war. Keeping my Teachers close beside me, I walked straight into the midst of them, unarmed of course, and cried as loud as I possibly could in their own tongue, "My love to all you men of Tanna! Fear not; I am your friend; I love you every one, and am come to tell you about Jehovah God and good conduct such as pleases Him!"

An old Chief thereon came and took me by the hand, and, after leading me about among the people, said, "Sit down beside me here and talk with me; by-and-bye the people will not be afraid."

A few ran off to the bush in terror. Others appeared to be beside themselves with delight. They danced round us frantically, striking the ground and beating a canoe with their clubs, while shouting to each other, "Missi is come! Missi is come!" The confusion grew every moment wilder, and there was a fiendish look about the whole scene. Men and boys rushed thronging around from every quarter, all painted in varied and savage devices, and some with their hair stuck full of fantastic feathers. Women and children peered through the bush, and instantaneously disappeared. Even in that anxious moment, it struck me that they had many more children amongst them than the people around the shores, where women and children are destroyed by the cruelty and vices of " civilized " visitors ! After spending about an hour, conversing and answering all questions, they apparently agreed to give up the war, and allowed me to conduct the Worship amongst them. They then made me a present of cocoa-nuts and sugarcane and two fowls, which my attendants received from them ; and I, in return, presented a red shirt to the principal Chief, and distributed a quantity of fish-hooks and pieces of red calico amongst the rest. The leading men shook hands graciously, and invited us often to come and see them, for after that visit they would harm no person connected with our Mission. Meantime, the Harbour people having learned where we had gone, had concluded that we would all be killed and feasted upon. When we returned, with a present of food, and informed them what we had heard and seen, their astonishment was beyond measure ; it had never been so seen after this manner on Tanna ! The peace continued for more than four weeks, an uncommonly prolonged truce. All hands were busy at work. Many yam-plantations were completed, and all fences were got into excellent condition for a year.

The prejudices and persecutions of Heathens were a sore enough trial, but sorer and more hopeless was the wicked and contaminating influence of, alas, my fellow-countrymen. One, for instance, a Captain Winchester, living with a native woman at the head of the bay as a Trader, a dissipated wretch, though a well-educated man, was angry forsooth at this state of peace ! Apparently there was not the usual demand for barter for the fowls, pigs, etc., in which he traded. He developed at once a wonderful interest in their affairs, presented all the Chiefs around with powder, caps, and balls, and lent among them a number of flash-muskets. He urged them not to be afraid of war, as he would supply any amount of ammunition I remonstrated, but he flatly told me that peace did not suit his purposes! Incited and encouraged thus, these poor Heathen people were goaded into a most unjust war on neighbouring tribes. The Trader immediately demanded a high price for the weapons he had lent; the price of powder, caps, and balls rose exorbitantly with every fresh demand; his yards were crowded with poultry and pigs, which he readily disposed of to passing vessels; and he might have amassed great sums of money but for his vile dissipations. Captain Winchester, now glorying in the war, charged a large hog for a wine-glass full of powder, or three or four balls, or ten gun-caps; he was boastful of his "good luck" in getting rid of all his old muskets and filling his yards with pigs and fowls. Such is the infernal depth to which we can sink, when the misery and ruin of many are thought to be more than atoned for by the wealth and prosperity of a few who trade in their doom!

Miaki the war Chief had a young brother, Rarip by name, about eighteen years of age. When this war began, he came to live with me at the Mission House. After it had raged some time, Miaki forced him to join the fighting men; but he escaped through the bush, and returned to me, saying, "Missi, I hate this fighting; it is not good to kill men; I will live with you!"

Again the war Chief came, and forced my dear young Rarip to join the hosts. Of course, I could only plead; I could not prevent him. This time, he placed him at his own side in the midst of his warriors. On coming in sight of the enemy, and hearing their first yells as they rushed from the bush, a bullet pierced young Rarip's breast, and he fell dead into the arms of Miaki. The body was carried home to his brother's village, with much wailing, and a messenger ran to tell me that Rarip was dead. On hasting thither, I found him quite dead, and the centre of a tragic ceremonial. Around him, some sitting, others lying on the ground, were assembled all the women and girls, tearing their hair, wounding themselves with split bamboos and broken bottles, dashing themselves headlong to the earth, painting all black their faces, breasts and arms, and wailing with loud lamentations! Men were also there, knocking their heads against the trees, gashing their bodies with knives till they ran with streaks of blood, and indulging in every kind of savage symbol of grief and anguish. My heart broke to see them, and to think that they knew not to look to our dear Lord Jesus for consolation.

I returned to the Mission House, and brought a white sheet and some tape, in which the body of dear young Rarip was wrapped and prepared for the grave. The Natives appeared to be gratified at this mark of respect; and all agreed that Rarip should have under my direction a Christian burial. The men prepared the grave in a spot selected near to his own house; I read the Word of God, and offered prayer to Jehovah, with a psalm of praise, amidst a scene of weeping and lamentation never to be forgotten; and the thought burned through my very soul—oh, when, when will the Tannese realize what I am now thinking and praying about, the life and immortality brought to light through Jesus?

As the war still raged on, and many more were killed, vengeance threatened the miserable Trader. Miaki attacked him thus, " You led us into this war. You deceived us, and we began it. Rarip is dead, and many others. Your life shall yet go for his."

Captain Winchester, heartless as a dog so long as pigs and fowls came to the yard at whatever cost to others' lives, now trembled like a coward for himself. He implored me to let him and his Maré wife sleep at my house for safety; but I refused to allow my Mission to be in any way identified with his crimes. The Natives from other islands, whom he kept and wrought like slaves, he now armed with muskets for his defence; but, having no faith in their protecting or even warning him, he implored me to send one of my Teachers, to assist his wife in watching till he snatched a few hours of sleep every day, and, if awake, he would sell his life as dearly as he could by aid of musket and revolver. The Teachers were both afraid and disinclined to go; and I could not honestly ask them to do so. His peril and terror became so real that by night he slept in his boat anchored out in the centre of the bay, with his arms beside him, and a crew ready to start off at the approach of danger and lose everything; while by day he kept watch on shore, armed, and also ready to fly. Thus his miserable existence dragged on, keeping watch alternately with his wife, till a trading vessel called and carried him off with all that he had rescued—for which deliverance we were unfeignedly thankful ! The war, which he had wickedly instigated, lingered on for three months ; and then, by a present given secretly to two leading Chiefs, I managed to bring it to a close. But feelings of revenge for the slain burned fiercely in many breasts ; and young men had old feuds handed on to them by the recital of their fathers' deeds of blood.

All through this war, I went to the fighting ground every Sabbath, and held worship amongst our Harbour people. Hundreds assembled around me, and listened respectfully, but they refused to give up the war. One day, I determined to go through the bush that lay between and speak and pray with the enemies also. Our Harbour folks opposed me, and one leading man said, " Missi, pray only for us, and your God will be strong to help us and we will not be afraid ! You must not pray with the enemy, lest He may help them too."

After this episode, I made it my duty always to visit both Camps, when I went to the fighting ground, and to have worship with both—teaching them that Jehovah my God was angry at all such scenes and would not fight for either, that He commanded them to live at peace.

About this time, our Sabbath audiences at the Mission numbered forty or so. Nowar and three or four more, and only they, seemed to love and serve Jesus. They were, however, changeable and doubtful, though they exerted a good influence on their villages, and were generally friendly to us and to the Worship. Events sometimes for a season greatly increased our usefulness. For instance, one of the Sacred Men when fishing on the coral reef was bitten by a poisonous fish. After great agony, he died, and his relatives were preparing to strangle his two wives, that their spirits might accompany and serve him in the other world. Usually such tragedies were completed before I ever heard of them. On this occasion, I had called at the village that very day, and succeeded in persuading them to bury him alone—his wives being saved alive at my appeal. Thus the idea got to be talked of, and

the horrible custom was being undermined—the strangling of
widows !

In connection with such poisonings, I may mention that
some of these fishes were deadly poisonous; others were unwholesome, and even poisonous, only at certain seasons; and
still others were always nutritious and good. For our own
part, we used fish sparingly and cautiously; and the doubtful
ones we boiled with a piece of silver in the water. If the
silver became discoloured, we regarded the fish as unwholesome : if the silver remained pure, we could risk it.

One morning at daybreak I found my house surrounded by
armed men, and a Chief intimated that they had assembled to
take my life. Seeing that I was entirely in their hands, I knelt
down and gave myself away body and soul to the Lord Jesus,
for what seemed the last time on earth. Rising, I went out to
them, and began calmly talking about their unkind treatment
of me and contrasting it with all my conduct towards them.
I also plainly showed them what would be the sad conse
quences, if they carried out their cruel purpose. At last some
of the Chiefs, who had attended the Worship, rose and said,
" Our conduct has been bad; but now we will fight for you,
and kill all those who hate you."

Grasping hold of their leader, I held him fast till he promised
never to kill any one on my account, for Jesus taught us to
love our enemies and always to return good for evil ! During
this scene, many of the armed men slunk away into the bush,
and those who remained entered into a bond to be friendly
and to protect us. But again their Public Assembly resolved
that we should be killed, because, as they said, they hated
Jehovah and the Worship; for it made them afraid to do as
they had always done. If I would give up visiting the villages,
and praying and talking with them about Jehovah, they intimated that they would like me to stay and trade with them,
as they liked the Traders but hated the Missionaries ! I told
them that the hope of being able to teach them the Worship
of Jehovah alone kept me living amongst them ; that I was
there, not for gain or pleasure, but because I loved them, and
pitied their estate, and sought their good continually by leading
them to know and serve the only true God.

One of the Chiefs, who had lived in Sydney and spoke English, replied for all the rest, " Missi, our fathers loved and worshipped whom you call the Devil, the Evil Spirit ; and we are determined to do the same, for we love the conduct of our fathers. Missi Turner came here and tried to break down our worship, but our fathers fought him and he left us. They fought also Peta, the Samoan Teacher, and he fled. They fought and killed some of the Samoan Teachers placed on the other side of the Harbour, and their companions left. We killed the last foreigner that lived in Tanna before you came here. We murdered the Aneityumese Teachers, and burned down their houses. After each of these acts, Tanna was good ; we all lived like our fathers, and sickness and death left us. Now, our people are determined to kill you, if you do not leave this island ; for you are changing our customs and destroying our worship, and we hate the Jehovah Worship."

Then, surrounded by a number of men, who had spent some years in the Colonies, he continued in a bitter strain to this effect : "The people of Sydney belong to your Britain ; they know what is right and wrong as well as you ; and we have ourselves seen them fishing, feasting, cooking, working, and seeking pleasure on the Sabbath as on any other day. You say, we do not here need to cook any food on Sabbaths or to toil at our ovens, but you yourself cook, for you boil your kettle on that day ! We have seen the people do all the conduct at Sydney which you call bad, but which we love. You are but one, they are many ; they are right, and you must be wrong ; you are teaching lies for Worship."

After many such speeches, I answered all the questions of the people fully, and besides I cross-questioned my assailants on several subjects, regarding which they grossly contradicted each other, till the majority of voices cried out, "They are lying ! Their words are crooked ! Missi knows all the truth about the people of Sydney ! "

Alas, I had to admit that what they reported was too true regarding the godless multitudes at home who made the Sabbath a day of pleasure, but not regarding Jehovah's servants. By this time, they were willing to remain quiet, and allowed me to talk of spiritual things and of the blessings that the

Sabbath and the Bible brought to all other lands, and to conduct in their presence and hearing the Worship of Jehovah.

But my enemies seldom slackened their hateful designs against my life, however calmed or baffled for the moment. Within a few days of the above events, when Natives in large numbers were assembled at my house, a man furiously rushed on me with his axe ; but a Kaserumini Chief snatched a spade with which I had been working, and dexterously defended me from instant death. Life in such circumstances led me to cling very near to the Lord Jesus ; I knew not, for one brief hour, when or how attack might be made; and yet, with my trembling hand clasped in the Hand once nailed on Calvary, and now swaying the sceptre of the Universe, calmness and peace and resignation abode in my soul.

Next day, a wild Chief followed me about for four hours with his loaded musket, and, though often directed towards me, God restrained his hand. I spoke kindly to him, and attended to my work as if he had not been there, fully persuaded that my God had placed me there, and would protect me till my allotted task was finished. Looking up in unceasing prayer to our dear Lord Jesus, I left all in His hands, and felt immortal till my work was done. Trials and hairbreadth escapes strengthened my faith, and seemed only to nerve me for more to follow ; and they did tread swiftly upon each other's heels. Without that abiding consciousness of the presence and power of my dear Lord and Saviour, nothing else in all the world could have preserved me from losing my reason and perishing miserably. His words, " Lo, I am with you alway, even unto the end of the world," became to me so real that it would not have startled me to behold Him, as Stephen did, gazing down upon the scene. I felt His supporting power, as did St. Paul, when he cried, " I can do all things through Christ which strengtheneth me." It is the sober truth, and it comes back to me sweetly after twenty years, that I had my nearest and dearest glimpses of the face and smile of my blessed Lord in those dread moments when musket, club, or spear was being levelled at my life. Oh the bliss of living and enduring, as seeing " Him who is invisible " !

One evening, I awoke three times to hear a Chief and his

men trying to force the door of my house. Though armed with muskets, they had some sense of doing wrong, and were wholesomely afraid of a little retriever dog which had often stood betwixt me and death. God restrained them again ; and next morning the report went all round the Harbour, that those who tried to shoot me were "smitten weak with fear," and that shooting would not do. A plan was therefore deliberately set on foot to fire the premises, and club us if we attempted to escape. But our Aneityumese Teacher heard of it, and God helped us to frustrate their designs. When they knew that their plots were revealed to us, they seemed to lose faith in themselves, and cast about to circumvent us in some more secret way. Their evil was overruled for good.

Namuri, one of my Aneityumese Teachers, was placed at our nearest village. There he had built a house for himself and his wife, and there he led amongst the Heathen a pure and humble Christian life. Almost every morning, he came and reported on the state of affairs to me. Without books or a school, he yet instructed the Natives in Divine things, conducted the Worship, and taught them much by his good example. His influence was increasing, when one morning a Sacred Man threw at him the kawas or killing stone, a deadly weapon like a scythe stone in shape and thickness, usually round but sometimes angular, and from eighteen to twenty inches long. They throw it from a great distance and with fatal precision. The Teacher, with great agility, warded his head and received the deep cut from it in his left hand, reserving his right hand to guard against the club that was certain to follow swiftly. The Priest sprang upon him with his club and with savage yells. He evaded, yet also received, many blows; and, rushing out of their hands, actually reached the Mission House, bleeding, fainting, and pursued by howling murderers. I had been anxiously expecting him, and hearing the noise I ran out with all possible speed.

On seeing me, he sank down by a tree, and cried, "Missi, Missi, quick ! and escape for your life ! They are coming to kill you ; they say, they must kill us all to-day, and they have begun with me ; for they hate Jehovah and the Worship !"

I hastened to the good Teacher where he lay; I bound up, washed, and dressed his wounds; and God, by the mystery of His own working, kept the infuriated Tannese watching at bay. Gradually they began to disappear into the bush, and we conveyed the dear Teacher to the Mission House. In three or four weeks, he so far recovered by careful nursing that he was able to walk about again. Some petitioned for him to return to the village; but I insisted, as a preliminary, that the Harbour Chiefs should unitedly punish him who had abused the Teacher; and this to test them, for he had only carried out their own wishes,—Nowar excepted, and perhaps one or two others. They made a pretence of atoning by presenting the Teacher with a pig and some yams as a peace-offering; but I said, "No! such bad conduct must be punished, or we would leave their island by the first opportunity."

Now that Sacred Man, a Chief too, had gone on fighting with other tribes, till his followers had all died or been slain; and, after three weeks' palaver, the other Chiefs seized him, tied him with a rope, and sent me word to come and see him punished, as they did not want us after all to leave the island. I had to go, for fear of more bloody work, and after talk with them, followed by many fair promises, he was loosed.

All appearing friendly for some time, and willing to listen and learn, the Teacher earnestly desired to return to his post. I pled with him to remain at the Mission House till we felt more assured, but he replied, "Missi, when I see them thirsting for my blood, I just see myself when the Missionary first came to my island. I desired to murder him, as they now desire to kill me. Had he stayed away for such danger, I would have remained Heathen; but he came, and continued coming to teach us, till, by the grace of God, I was changed to what I am. Now the same God that changed me to this, can change these poor Tannese to love and serve Him. I cannot stay away from them; but I will sleep at the Mission House, and do all I can by day to bring them to Jesus."

It was not in me to keep such a man, under such motives, from what he felt to be his post of duty. He returned to his village work, and for several weeks things appeared most encouraging. The inhabitants showed growing interest in us and our work, and less fear of the pretensions of their Heathen Priest, which, alas! fed his jealousy and anger. One morning during worship, when the good Teacher knelt in prayer, the same savage Priest sprang upon him with his great club and left him for dead, wounded and bleeding and unconscious. The people fled and left him in his blood, afraid of being mixed up with the murder. The Teacher, recovering a little, crawled to the Mission House, and reached it about mid-day in a dying condition. On seeing him, I ran to meet him, but he fell near the Teacher's house, saying, "Missi, I am dying! They will kill you also. Escape for your life."

Trying to console him, I sat down beside him, dressing his wounds and nursing him. He was quite resigned; he was looking up to Jesus, and rejoicing that he would soon be with Him in Glory. His pain and suffering were great, but he bore all very quietly, as he said and kept saying, "For the sake of Jesus! For Jesu's sake!" He was constantly praying for his persecutors, "O Lord Jesus, forgive them, for they know not what they are doing. Oh, take not away all Thy servants from Tanna! Take not away Thy Worship from this dark island! O God, bring all the Tannese to love and follow Jesus!"

To him, Jesus was all and in all; and there were no bands in his death. He passed from us, in the assured hope of entering into the Glory of his Lord. Humble though he may appear in the world's esteem, I knew that a great man had fallen there in the service of Christ, and that he would take rank in the glorious Army of the Martyrs. I made for him a coffin, and dug his grave near the Mission House. With prayers, and many tears, we consigned his remains to the dust in the certainty of a happy resurrection. Even one such convert was surely a triumphant reward for Dr. and Mrs. Geddie, whom God had honoured in bringing him to Jesus. May they have many like Namuri for their crown of joy and rejoicing in the great day!

Immediately after this, a number of Chiefs and followers called on me at the Mission House, professing great friendliness, and said, "Mr. Turner gave our fathers great quantities of calico, axes, and knives, and they became his friends. If you would give the people some just now they would be pleased. They would stop fighting against the Worship."

I retorted, "How was it then, if they were pleased, that they persecuted Messrs. Turner and Nisbet till they had to leave the island? Your conduct is deceitful and bad. I never will reward you for bad actions and for murder! No present will be given by me."

They withdrew sullenly, and seemed deeply disappointed and offended.

On one occasion, when a Chief had died, the Harbour people were all being assembled to strangle his widow. One of my Aneityumese Teachers, hearing of it, hastened to tell me. I ran to the village, and, with much persuasion, saved her life. A few weeks thereafter she gave birth to a young chieftain, who prospered well. If our Harbour people told the truth, the widows of all who fell in war were saved by our pleading. Immediately after the foregoing incident, a Sacred Man was dying, and a crowd of people were assembled awaiting the event in order to strangle his three wives. I spoke to them of the horrid wickedness of such conduct. I further reasoned with them, that God had made us male and female, the sexes so balanced, that for every man that had three or a dozen wives, as many men generally had none, and that this caused great jealousy and quarrelling. I showed them further, that these widows being spared would make happy and useful wives for other kind and loving husbands. After the Worship, I appealed to the Chief, and he replied, " Missi, it was a practice introduced to Tanna from the island of Aneityum. It was not the custom of our fathers here to strangle widows. And, as the Aneityumese have given it up since they became worshippers of Jehovah, it is good that we now should give it up on Tanna too."

Thus these three widows were saved; and we had great hope in Christ that the ghastly practice would soon disappear from Tanna.

An incident of this time created great wonder amongst the Natives ; namely, the Sinking of a Well. We had, heretofore, a boiling spring to drink from, the water of which literally required in that climate days to cool down ; we had, also, a stagnant pool at the lower end of a swamp in which the Natives habitually bathed, the only available fresh water bath! Beyond that, no drinking water could be had for four or five miles. I managed to sink a well, near the Mission House, and got about twelve feet deep a good supply of excellent fresh water, though, strange to say, the surface of the well rose and fell regularly with every tide! This became the universal supply for us and for the Natives all round the Harbour and for miles inland. Hundreds of Natives from all parts of Tanna flocked to examine this greatest wonder they had ever seen—rain rising up out of the earth. I built it round with a kind of stone brought in my boat from the other side of the bay; and for many years it was the only fresh water supply for the Natives all around. Some years later a native Chief sank another well about a mile nearer the entrance to the Harbour at his own village, and built it round with the bricks that I had purchased for house-building; these he grabbed and thus appropriated! Many a vessel, calling at the Harbour, was glad to get her casks refilled at my well, and all were apparently more friendly because of it; but the Sinking of this Well produced no such revolution as on Aniwa,—to be hereafter related.

For fully three months, all our available time, with all the native help which I could hire, was spent in erecting a building to serve for Church and School. It was fifty feet long, by twenty-one feet six inches broad. The studs were three feet apart, and all fixed by tenon and mortise into upper and lower wall plates. The beautiful roof of iron-wood and sugar-cane leaf was supported by three massive pillars of wood, sunk deeply into the ground. The roof extended about three feet over the wall plates, both to form a verandah and to carry the rain-drop free beyond the walls. It was made of sugar-cane leaf and cocoa-nut leaves all around. The floor was laid with white coral, broken small, and covered with cocoa-nut leaf mats, such as those on which the Natives sat. Indeed, it was as comfortable a House of Prayer as any man need wish for in the tropics, though having only open spaces for doors and windows! I bought the heavy wood for it on Aneityum—price, fifty pairs of trousers for Natives; and these again were the gift of my Bible Class in Glasgow, all cut and sewed by their own hands. I gave also one hundred and thirty yards of cloth, along with other things, for other needful wood.

My Tannese people at first opposed the erection of a Church. They did not wish Jehovah to secure a House on their island. On the opening day, only five men, three women, and three children were present, besides our Aneityumese Teachers. But after the morning service, on that day, I visited ten villages, and had worship in each. The people were generally shy and unfriendly. They said that we were the cause of the prevailing sickness and fever. They had no idea of any sickness or death being natural, but believed that all such events were caused by some one *nahaking,* *i.e.,* bewitching them. Hence their incessant feuds; and many were murdered in blind revenge.

As we were preparing a foundation for the Church, a huge and singular-looking round stone was dug up, at sight of which the Tannese stood aghast. The eldest Chief said, " Missi, that stone was either brought there by Karapanamun (the Evil Spirit), or hid there by our great Chief who is dead. That is the Stone God to which our forefathers offered human sacrifices ; these holes held the blood of the victim till drunk up by the Spirit. The Spirit of that stone eats up men and women and drinks their blood, as our fathers taught us. We are in greatest fear ! "

A Sacred Man claimed possession, and was exceedingly desirous to carry it off; but I managed to keep it, and did everything in my power to show them the absurdity of these foolish notions. Idolatry had not indeed yet fallen throughout Tanna ; but one cruel idol, at least, had to give way for the erection of God's House on that benighted land.

An ever-memorable event was the printing of my first book in Tannese. Thomas Binnie, Jun., Glasgow, gave me a printing-press and a font of type. Printing was one of the things I had never tried, but having now prepared a booklet in Tannese, I got my press into order, and began fingering the type. But book-printing turned out to be for me a much more difficult affair than house-building had been. Yet by dogged perseverance I succeeded at last. My biggest difficulty was how to arrange the pages properly ! After many failures, I folded a piece of paper into the number of leaves wanted, cut the corners, folding them back, and numbering as they would be when correctly placed in the book ; then folding all back without cutting up the sheet, I found now by these numbers how to arrange the pages in the frame or case for printing, as indicated on each side. And do you think me foolish, when I confess that I shouted in an ecstasy of joy when the first sheet came from the press all correct ? It was about one o'clock in the morning. I was the only white man then on the island, and all the Natives had been fast asleep for hours ! Yet I literally pitched my hat into the air, and danced like a schoolboy round and round that printing-press ; till I began to think, Am I losing my reason ? Would it not be liker a Missionary to be upon my knees, adoring God for this first portion of His blessed Word ever printed in this new language ? Friend, bear with me, and believe me—that was as true worship as ever was David's dancing before the Ark of his God ! Nor think that I did not, over that first sheet of God's Word ever printed in the Tannese tongue, go upon my knees too, and then, and every day since, plead with the mighty Lord to carry the light and joy of His own Holy Bible into every dark heart and benighted home on Tanna ! But the Tannese had a superstitious dread of books, and especially of God's Book. I afterwards heard that Dr. Turner had printed a small primer in Tannese, translated by the help of the Samoan Teachers ; but this I never saw till near the close of my work on Tanna. Dr. Geddie sent me a copy, but it was more Samoan than Tannese, especially in its spelling, and I could make little or nothing of it.

Shortly after this, I was greatly refreshed by the visit of an American whaler, the *Camden Packet*, under Captain Allan. He, his chief officer, and many of his double company of seamen, were decided Christians—a great contrast to most of the Traders that had called at Port Resolution. The Captain cordially invited me on board to preach and conduct a religious service. That evening I enjoyed exceedingly— wells in the desert ! The Captain introduced me, saying, " This is my ship's company. My first officer and most of my men are real Christians, trying to love and serve Jesus Christ. We have been three years out on this voyage, and are very happy with each other. You would never hear or see worse on board of this vessel than you see now. And God has given us gratifying success."

He afterwards told me that he had a very valuable cargo of sperm oil on board, the vessel being nearly filled up with it. He was eager to leave supplies, or do something for me, but I needed nothing that he could give. His mate, on examining my boat, found a hole in her, and several planks split and bulged in, as I had gone down on a reef with her when out on Mission work, and narrowly escaped drowning. Next morning, the Captain, of his own accord, set his carpenter to repair the boat, and left it as good as new. Not one farthing of recompense would any of them take from me; theii own Christian love rewarded them, in the circumstances. I had been longing for a chance to send it to Sydney for repairs, and felt deeply thankful for such unexpected and generous aid. The Captain would not admit that the delay was any loss to him,—his boats spending the day in purchasing cocoa-nuts and provisions from the Natives for his own ship. Oh, how the Christlike spirit knits together all true followers of Christ! What other earthly or human tie could have so bound that stranger to me? In the heart of Christ we met as brothers.

Dangers again darkened round me. One day, while toiling away at my house, the war Chief and his brother, and a large party of armed men, surrounded the plot where I was working. They all had muskets, besides their own native weapons. They watched me for some time in silence, and then every man levelled a musket straight at my head. Escape was impossible. Speech would only have increased my danger. My eyesight came and went for a few moments. I prayed to my Lord Jesus, either Himself to protect me or to take me home to His Glory. I tried to keep working on at my task, as if no one was near me. In that moment, as never before, the words came to me,—"Whatsoever ye shall ask in My Name, I will do it"; and I knew that I was safe. Retiring a little from their first position, no word having been spoken, they took up the same attitude somewhat farther off, and seemed to be urging one another to fire the first shot. But my dear Lord restrained them once again, and they withdrew, leaving me with a new reason for trusting Him with all that concerned me for Time and Eternity. Perils seemed, however, to enclose me on every hand, and my life was frequently attempted. I had to move about more cautiously than ever, some days scarcely daring to appear outside my Mission premises. For I have ever most firmly believed, and do believe, that only when we use every lawful and possible means for the preservation of our life, which is God's second greatest gift to man (life eternal through His Son being the first), can we expect God to protect us, or have we the right to plead His precious promises.

The vessel of one calling himself Prince de Jean Beuve, a French refugee, who had become a naturalized American, visited Port Resolution. He said, he had to escape from his own country for political offences. His large and beautiful ship was fitted up and armed like a Man-of-war. She was manned chiefly by slaves, whom he ruled with an iron hand. What a contrast to Captain Allan's whaler! Yet he also was very sympathetic and kind to me. Having heard rumour of my trials and dangers, he came on shore, as soon as his ship cast anchor, with a body of armed men. He was effusively polite, with all a Frenchman's gush and gesticulation, and offered to do anything possible for me. He would take me to Aneityum or Sydney or wherever I wished. The ship was his own ; he was sailing chiefly for pleasure, and he had called at our Islands to see if sufficient trade could be opened up to justify his laying on a line of steamers to call here in their transit. He urged me, I believe sincerely, to give him the pleasure of taking me and my belongings to some place of safety. But I was restrained from leaving, through the fear that I would never be permitted to return, and that Christ's work would suffer. In the still burning hope of being able to lead the Tannese to love and serve Jesus, I declined with much gratitude his genuine kindness. He looked truly sorry to leave me in the circumstances wherein I was placed. After two hours on shore, he returned to his ship towards evening.

Knowing that the Tannese were threatening to burn my former house, which I wished to remove to higher ground and add to the room I now occupied on the hill, I took advantage of the presence of the Prince's vessel, and set my Aneityumese Teachers and some friendly Natives to prepare for the task ; but unfortunately, I forgot to send word to the Frenchman regarding my plans and aims. We removed the sugar-cane leaf thatch from the roof of the house, and began burning it on cleared ground, so that I might be able to save the heavy wood, which could not be replaced on Tanna. Our French friend, on seeing the flames rising up furiously, at once loaded his heavy guns, and prepared his men for action. Under great excitement, he came ashore with a large number of armed men, leaving the rest on board ready at a given signal to protect them with shot and shell. Leaving one half of those brought on shore to guard the boats, he came running towards my house, followed by the other half, wet with perspiration, and crying, " Fer are dey ? fer are dey ? De scoundrels ! I vill do for dem, and protect you. I sall punish dem, de scoundrels."

He was so excited, he could scarcely compose himself to hear my explanations, which, when understood, he laughed at heartily. He again urged me to leave in his vessel ; he could not bear me to lead such a life amongst Savages. I explained to him my reasons for not leaving the island, but these he seemed unable to understand. He put his men through drill on shore, and left them under officers, ready for action at a moment's warning, saying they would all be the better for a day on shore. He wished to take pot luck with me at our Mission House of one room for all purposes ! My humble dinner and tea must have been anything but a treat for him, but he seemed to relish the deliverance for once from all the conventionalisms of the world. Before he left, he sent of his own accord for all the Chiefs within reach, and warned them that if they hurt me or took my life he would return with his Man-of-war and punish them, by killing themselves and firing their villages ; and that a British Man-of-war would also come and set their island on fire. They promised all possible good conduct, being undoubtedly put into great terror. The kind-hearted Frenchman left, with profuse expressions of admiration for my courage and of pity for my lot. No doubt he thought me a foolish dreamer of dreams.

A miserable contrast befell us in the bad impression produced by the conduct of one of Captain T——'s vessels in the Sydney sandal-wood trade. Whale-boats had been sent out with Mr. Copeland and myself from Glasgow, as part of the necessary equipment of every Missionary on these Islands. Mine being rather large and heavy, I had sold it to one of T——'s Captains; but the other had also been left to my care. After having used my boat for about twelve months—the best boat in that trade only being expected to last two years—the Captain called on Mr. Copeland, and got a note from him to me regarding the sale of his boat too. He declared, when calling on me, that Mr. Copeland had authorized him to get his boat from me in exchange for mine, which he had now been using for a year. I asked for the letter, and found it to be authority for me to sell his boat for cash only and at the same price as mine. Captain V—— then raged at me and stormed, declaring that he would return my old boat, and take the other in defiance of me. Swearing dreadfully, he made for his ship, and returned with a large party of men whom he had picked up amongst the Islands. Collecting also a company of Tannese, and offering them tobacco, he broke down the fence, burst into the boat-house, and began to draw out the boat.

I now reached the spot and sternly opposed them. He swore and foamed at me, and before the Natives knocked and pulled me about, even kicking at me, though I evaded his blows. Standing by, I said in Tannese, " You are helping that man to steal my boat; he is stealing it as you see."

On hearing this, the Tannese ran away, and his own party alone could not do it. In great wrath, he went off again to his vessel, and brought on shore as much tobacco as could be held in a large handkerchief tied by the four corners; but even for that, our own Natives refused to help him. He offered it then to a crowd of Inland Savages, gathered at the head of the bay, who, regardless of my remonstrances, launched the boat, he raging at and all but striking me. Instead of returning, however, the other boat to the house, he merely set it adrift from his vessel, and it was carried on to the reef, where it remained fast, and was knocked about by the waves. After his vessel left, I, with much difficulty, got it off and brought it to the boat-house. Imagine, when such was their tyrannical treatment of a Missionary and a British fellow-subject, how they would act towards these poor native Islanders.

By the earliest opportunity, I wrote all the facts of the case to his employer, Captain T—— of Sydney, but got not even a reply, while Captain V—— continued in their trade, a scourge to these Islands, and a dishonour to his country and to humanity. Unfriendly Tannese now said, "When a white man from his own country can so pull and knock the Missionary about, and steal his boat and chain without being punished for it, we also may do as we please!"

I hesitate not to record my conviction that that man's conduct had a very bad effect, emboldening them in acts of dishonesty and in attempts upon my life, till the Mission Station was ultimately broken up. After I had to escape from Tanna, with bare life in my hand, one of the same Captain's vessels called at Port Resolution and gave the Natives about three pounds' weight of useless tobacco, purchasable at Sydney for less than one shilling per pound, to allow them to take away my boat, with oars, sails, mast, and all other belongings. They also purchased all the plunder from my house. Both boats were so large and so strongly built, that by adding a plank or two they turned them into small-decked schooners, admirably suited for the sandal-wood traffic round the shores, while larger vessels lay at safe anchorage to receive what they collected. Once, when Dr. Inglis and I met in Sydney, we called on Captain T—— and stated the whole case, asking reasonable payment at least for the boats. He admitted that the boats had been taken and were in his service, and agreed to pay us for the boats if we would repay the large sum invested therein by his Captains. Calling one of his clerks, he instructed him to trace in the office record how much had been paid to the Tannese for the Missionary's boat. The young man innocently returned the reply, "Three pounds of tobacco."

In anger, he said, "I understood that a larger value had

9

been given !" The clerk assured him, "That is the only record."

Captain T——, after discussing the worth of the boat as being about £80, agreed to give us £60, but in writing out the check, threw down the pen and shouted, "I'll see you —— first ! "

Offering £50, to which we agreed, he again resiled, and declared he would not give a penny above £30. We appealed to him to regard this as a debt of honour, and to cease haggling over the price, as he well knew how we had been wronged in the matter. Finally he declared, " I am building similar boats just now at £25 apiece ; I will send you one of them, and you may either take that or want ! "

We left, glad to get away on any terms from such a character ; and, though next year he did send one of his promised boats for me to Aneityum, yet the conduct of his degraded servants engaged in the sandal-wood trade had a great share in the guilt of breaking up and ruining our Mission. Thousands upon thousands of money were made in it yearly, so long as it lasted ; but it was a trade steeped in human blood and indescribable vice, nor could God's blessing rest on the Traders and their ill-gotten gains. Oh, how often did we pray at that time to be delivered from the hands of unreasonable and wicked men ! Sandal-wood Traders murdered many of the Islanders when robbing them of their wood, and the Islanders murdered many of them and their servants in revenge. White men, engaged in the trade, also shot dead and murdered each other in vicious and drunken quarrels, and not a few put end to their own lives. I have scarcely known one of them who did not come to ruin and poverty ; the money that came even to the shipowners was a conspicuous curse. Fools there made a mock at sin, thinking that no one cared for these poor Savages, but their sin did find them out, and God made good in their experience His own irrepealable law, " The wages of sin is death."

Ships, highly insured, were said to be sent into this Island trade to be deliberately wrecked. One Sabbath evening, towards dark, the notorious Captain H——, in command of a large ship, allowed her to drift ashore and be wrecked without any apparent effort to save her. Next morning, the whole company were wading about in the water and pretending to have lost everything ! The Captain, put in prison when he returned to Sydney for running away with another man's wife and property, imposed on Mr. Copeland and myself, getting all the biscuits, flour, and blankets we could spare for his destitute and shipwrecked company. We discovered afterwards that she was lying on a beautiful bank of sand, only a few yards from the shore, and that everything contained in her could be easily rescued without danger to life or limb ! What we parted with was almost necessary for our life and health ; of course he gave us an order on Captain T—— for everything, but not one farthing was ever repaid. At first he made a pretence of paying the Natives for food received ; but afterwards, an armed band went inland night by night and robbed and plundered whatever came to hand. The Natives, though seeing the food of their children ruthlessly stolen, were shot down without mercy when they dared to interfere ; and the life of every white man was therefore marked for speedy revenge. Glad were we when a vessel called, and carried away these white-skinned Savages.

The same Captain T—— also began the shocking Kanaka labour-traffic to the Colonies, after the sandal-wood trade was exhausted, which has since destroyed so many thousands of the Natives in what was nothing less than Colonial slavery, and has largely depopulated the Islands either directly or indirectly. And yet he wrote, and published in Sydney, a pamphlet declaring that he and his Sandal-wooders and Kanaka-labour collectors had done more to civilize the Islanders than all our Mission efforts combined. Civilize them, indeed ! By spreading disease and vice, misery and death amongst them, even at the best ; at the worst, slaving many of them till they perished at their toils, shooting down others under one or other guilty pretence, and positively sweeping thousands into an untimely grave. A common cry on their lips was, " Let them perish and let the white men occupy these Isles."

It was such conduct as this, that made the Islanders suspect all foreigners and hate the white man and seek revenge in robbery and murder. One Trader, for instance, a Sandal-wooder and collector of Kanakas, living at Port Resolution, abominably ill-used a party of Natives. They determined in revenge to plunder his store. The cellar was underneath his house, and he himself slept above the trap-door by which alone it could be entered. Night and day he was guarded by armed men, Natives of adjoining islands, and all approaches to his premises were watched by savage dogs that gave timely warning. He felt himself secure. But the Tannese actually constructed a tunnel underground from the bush, through which they rolled away tobacco, ammunition, etc., and nearly emptied his cellar! My heart bled to see men so capable and clever thus brutally abused and demoralized and swept away. By the Gospel, and the civilization which it brings, they were capable of learning anything and being trained to a useful and even noble manhood. But all influence that ever I witnessed from these Traders was degrading, and dead against the work of our Missions.

The Chief, Nowar Noukamara, usually known as Nowar, was my best and most-to-be-trusted friend. He was one of the nine or ten who were most favourable to the Mission work, attending the Worship pretty regularly, conducting it also in their own houses and villages, and making generally a some-what unstable profession of Christianity. One or more of them often accompanied me on Sabbath, when going to conduct the Worship at inland villages; and sometimes they protected me from personal injury. This Nowar influenced the Harbour Chiefs and their people for eight or ten miles around to get up a great feast in favour of the Worship of Jehovah. All were personally and specially invited, and it was the largest Assembly of any kind that I ever witnessed on the Islands.

When all was ready, Nowar sent a party of Chiefs to escort me and my Aneityumese Teachers to the feast. Fourteen Chiefs, in turn, made speeches to the assembled multitude; the drift of all being, that war and fighting be given up on Tanna,—that no more people be killed by Nahak, for witchcraft and sorcery were lies,—that Sacred Men no longer profess to make wind and rain, famine and plenty, disease and death,— that the dark Heathen talk of Tanna should cease,—that all here present should adopt the Worship of Jehovah as taught to them by the Missionary and the Aneityumese,—and that all

the banished Tribes should be invited to their own lands to
live in peace! These strange speeches did not draw forth a
single opposing voice. Doubtless these men were in earnest,
and had there been one master mind to rule and mould them,
their regeneration had then dawned. Though for the moment
a feeling of friendliness prevailed, the Tannese were unstable
as water and easily swayed one way or the other. They are
born talkers, and can and will speechify on all occasions; but
most of it means nothing, bears no fruit.

After these speeches, a scene followed which gradually assumed shape as an idolatrous ceremonial and greatly horrified
me. It was in connection with the immense quantity of food
that had been prepared for the feast, especially pigs and fowls.
A great heap had been piled up for each Tribe represented,
and a handsome portion also set apart for the Missionary and
his Teachers. The ceremony was this, as nearly as I could
follow it. One hundred or so of the leading men marched
into the large cleared space in the centre of the assembled
multitudes, and stood there facing each other in equal lines,
with a man at either end closing up the passage between. At
the middle they stood eight or ten feet apart, gradually nearing
till they almost met at either end. Amid tremendous silence
for a few moments, all stood hushed; then every man kneeled
on his right knee, extended his right hand, and bent forward
till his face nearly touched the ground. Thereon the man at
the one end began muttering something, his voice rising ever
louder as he rose to his feet, when it ended in a fearful yell as
he stood erect. Next the two long lines of men, all in a body,
went through the same ceremonial, rising gradually to their
feet, with mutterings deepening into a howl, and heightening
into a yell as they stood erect. Finally, the man at the other
end went through the same hideous forms. All this was thrice
deliberately repeated, each time with growing frenzy. And
then, all standing on their feet, they united as with one voice
in what sounded like music running mad up and down the
scale—closing with a long, deep-toned, hollow howl as of souls
in pain. With smiles of joy, the men then all shook hands
with each other. Nowar and another Chief briefly spoke;
and the food was then divided and exchanged, a principal

man of each Tribe standing by to receive and watch his portion.

At this stage, Nowar and Nerwangi, as leaders, addressed the Teachers and the Missionary to this effect : " This feast is held to move all the Chiefs and People here to give up fighting, to become friends, and to worship your Jehovah God. We wish you to remain, and to teach us all good conduct. As an evidence of our sincerity, and of our love, we have prepared this pile of food for you."

In reply, I addressed the whole multitude, saying how pleased I was with their speeches and with the resolutions and promises which they all had made. I further urged them to stick fast by these, and that grand fruits would arise to their island, to themselves, and to their children.

Having finished a brief address, I then walked forward to the very middle of the circle, and laid down before them a bundle of stripes of red calico and pieces of white calico, a number of fish-hooks, knives, etc., etc., requesting the two Chiefs to divide my offering of goodwill among the Tribes assembled, and also the pile of food presented to us, as a token of my love and friendship to them all.

Their insisting upon me taking their present of food, laid upon me an unpleasant and dangerous necessity of explaining my refusal. I again thanked them very warmly, and explained that, as they had in my presence given away all their food to an Idol-God and asked his blessing on it as a sacrifice, even to Karapanamun, the great Evil Spirit, my people and I durst not and could not eat of it, for that would be to have fellowship with their Idols and to dishonour Jehovah God. Christians could acknowledge only the one true and living God, and ask His blessing on their food, and offer it and themselves in thanksgiving unto Him, but unto no cruel or evil Spirit. Yet I explained to them how much I thanked them, and how I loved them just as much as if we had eaten all their gifts, and how it would please us to see them all, along with my own gifts, divided amongst their Tribes.

Not without some doubt, and under considerable trial, did I take this apparently unfriendly attitude. But I feared to seem even to approve of any act of devil-worship, or to confirm them in it, being there to discourage all such scenes, and to lead them to acknowledge only the true God. I felt guilty, as if the hat were rising from my head, when I heard them imprecating and appeasing their god, without being able to show them the God of Love and the better way into His presence through Jesus Christ. My opportunity to do so arose over the refusal of the food offered unto Idols, and I told them of the claims of Jehovah, the jealous God, who would not share His worship with any other. But all the time I felt this qualm,—that it were better to eat food with men who acknowledged some God and asked his blessing, than with those white Heathens at home, who asked the blessing of no God, nor thanked Him—in this worse than the dog which licks the hand that feeds it! Nowar and Nerwangi explained in great orations what I meant, and how I wished all to be divided amongst the assembled Tribes to show my love. With this, all seemed highly satisfied.

Heathen dances were now entered upon, their paint and feathers and ornaments adding to the wildness of the scene. The men seemed to dance in an inside ring, and the women in an outside ring, at a considerable distance from each other. Music was supplied by singing and clapping of hands. The order was perfect, and the figures highly intricate. But I have never been able to associate dancing with things lovely and of good report! After the dancing, all retired to the bush ; and a kind of sham fight then followed on the public cleared ground. A host of painted Savages rushed in and took possession with songs and shoutings. From the bush, on the opposite side, the chanting of women was heard in the distance, louder and louder as they approached. Snatching from a burning fire flaming sticks, they rushed on the men with these, beating them and throwing burning pieces of wood among them, till with deafening yells amongst themselves and amidst shouts of laughter from the crowd, they drove them from the space, and danced thereon and sang a song of victory. The dancing and fighting, the naked painted figures, and the constant yells and shoutings, gave one a weird sensation, and suggested strange ideas of Hell broken loose.

The final scene approached, when the men assisted their

women to fill all the allotted food into baskets, to be carried
home and eaten there; for the different Tribes do not sit
down together and eat together as we would do; their coming
together is for the purpose of exchanging and dividing the
food presented. And now they broke into friendly confusion,
and freely walked about mingling with each other; and a kind
of savage rehearsal of Jonathan and David took place. They
stripped themselves of their fantastic dresses, their handsomely
woven and twisted grass skirts, leaf skirts, grass and leaf
aprons; they gave away or exchanged all these, and their
ornaments and bows and arrows, besides their less romantic
calico and print dresses more recently acquired. The effusion
and ceremonial of the gifts and exchanges seemed to betoken
a loving people; and so they were for the feast—but that laid
not aside a single deadly feud, and streams of blood and cries
of hate would soon efface all traces of this day.

I had now six Stations, opened up and ministered to by
Aneityumese Teachers, at the leading villages along the coast,
and forming links in a chain towards the other Mission
Establishment on Tanna. And there were villages prepared
to receive as many more. These Teachers had all been
Cannibals once; yet, with one exception, they proved themselves to the best of my judgment to be a band of faithful and
devoted followers of Christ. Their names were Abraham,
Kowari, Namuri, Nerwa, Lazarus, and Eoufati. I visited
them periodically and frequently, encouraging and guiding
them, as well as trying to interest the villagers in their teaching
and work. But whenever war broke out they had all to return
to the Mission House, and sleep there for safety by night,
visiting their Stations, if practicable, by the light of day. My
poor dear Teachers, too, had to bear persecutions for Jesu's
sake, as the following incident will sorrowfully prove.

A native woman, with some murderous purpose in her heart,
pretended great friendship to the excellent wife of one of my
fellow-labourers She was specially effusive in bringing to her
dishes of food from time to time. Having thus gained
confidence, she caught a little black fish of those parts, known
to be deadly poisonous, and baked it up in a mess for the
unsuspecting Teacher's wife. On returning, she boasted of

what she had done, and thereon a friendly neighbour rushed off to warn the other, but arrived just to learn that the fatal meal had been taken. Beyond all reach of human skill, this unknown Martyr for Christ died soon after in great agony, and doubtless received her Master's reward.

In helping to open up new Stations, those dear Native Teachers often bore the greatest hardships and indignities with a noble self-denial and positively wonderful patience. Nothing known to men under Heaven could have produced their new character and disposition, except only the grace of God in Christ Jesus. Though still marred by many of the faults of Heathenism, they were at the roots of their being literally new creatures, trying, according to their best light, to live for and to please their new Master, Jesus Christ. This shone out very conspicuously in these two apostolic souls, Abraham and Kowari, as leaders among all the devoted band.

Let me recall another occasion, on which I prevented a war. Early one morning, the savage yells of warring Tribes woke me from sleep. They had broken into a quarrel about a woman, and were fiercely engaged with their clubs. According to my custom, I rushed in amongst them, and, not without much difficulty, was blessed in separating them before deadly wounds had been given or received. On this occasion, the Chiefs of both Tribes, being very friendly to me, drove their people back from each other at my earnest appeals. Sitting down at length within earshot, they had it out in a wild scolding match, a contest of lung and tongue. Meanwhile I rested on a canoe midway betwixt them, in the hope of averting a renewal of hostilities. By-and-bye an old Sacred Man, a Chief called Sapa, with some touch of savage comedy in his breast, volunteered an episode which restored good humour to the scene. Leaping up, he came dancing and singing towards me, and there, to the amusement of all, re-enacted the quarrel, and mimicked rather cleverly my attempt at separating the combatants. Smashing at the canoe with his club, he yelled and knocked down imaginary enemies; then, rushing first at one party and then at the other, he represented me as appealing and gesticulating and pushing them afar from each other, till he became quite exhausted. Thereon he came and planted himself in great glee beside me, and looked around as if to say, "You must laugh, for I have played." At this very juncture, a loud cry of "Sail O !" broke upon our ears, and all parties leapt to their feet, and prepared for a new sensation ; for in those climes, everything—war itself— is a smaller interest than a vessel from the Great Unknown Beyond sailing into your Harbour.

Not many days thereafter, a very horrible transaction occurred. Before daybreak, I heard shot after shot quickly discharged in the Harbour. One of my Teachers came running, and cried, " Missi, six or seven men have been shot dead this morning for a great feast. It is to reconcile Tribes that have been at war, and to allow a banished Tribe to return in peace."

I learned that the leading men had in council agreed upon this sacrifice, but the name of each victim was kept a secret till the last moment. The torture of suspense and uncertainty seemed to be borne by all as part of their appointed lot ; nor did they prepare as if suspecting any dread assault. Before daylight, the Sacred Men allocated a murderer to the door of each house where a victim slept. A signal shot was fired ; all rushed to their doors, and the doomed ones were shot and clubbed to death, as they attempted to escape. Their bodies were then borne to a sacred tree, and hung up there by the hands for a time, as an offering to the gods. Being taken down, they were carried ceremoniously and laid out on the shore near my house, placed under a special guard.

Information had reached me that my Teachers and I were also destined victims for this same feast ; and sure enough we espied a band of armed men, the killers, despatched towards our premises. Instantaneously I had the Teachers and their wives and myself securely locked into the Mission House ; and, cut off from all human hope, we set ourselves to pray to our dear Lord Jesus, either Himself to protect us or to take us to His glory. All through that morning and forenoon we heard them tramp-tramping round our house, whispering to each other, and hovering near window and door. They knew that there were a double-barrelled fowling-piece and a revolver on the premises, though they never had seen me use them, and that may, under God, have held them back in dread. But the thought of using them did not enter our souls even in that awful time. I had gone to save, and not to destroy. It would be easier for me at any time to die, than to kill one of them Our safety lay in our appeal to that blessed Lord who had placed us there, and to whom all power had been given in Heaven and on Earth. He that was with us was more than all that could be against us. This is strength; this is peace :—to feel, in entering on every day, that all its duties and trials have been committed to the Lord Jesus,—that, come what may, He will use us for His own glory and our real good!

All through that dreadful morning, and far into the afternoon, we thus abode together, feeling conscious that we were united to this dear Lord Jesus ; and we had sweet communion with Him, meditating on the wonders of His person and the hopes and glories of His kingdom. Oh that all my readers may learn something of this in their own experience of the Lord! I can wish them nothing more precious. Towards sundown, constrained by the Invisible One, they withdrew from our Mission House, and left us once more in peace. They bore away the slain to be cooked and distributed amongst the Tribes, and eaten in their feast of reconciliation ; a covenant sealed in blood, and soon, alas, to be buried in blood again! For many days thereafter, we had to take unusual care, and not unduly expose ourselves to danger ; for dark characters were seen prowling about in the bush near at hand, and we knew that our life was the prize. We took what care we could, and God the Lord did the rest; or rather He did all—for His wisdom guided us, and His power baffled them.

Shortly thereafter war was again declared, by the Inland people attacking our Harbour people. It was an old quarrel ; and the war was renewed and continued, long after the cause thereof had passed away. Going amongst them every day, I did my utmost to stop hostilities, setting the evils of war before them, and pleading with the leading men to renounce it. Thereon arose a characteristic incident of Island and Heathen life. One day I held a Service in the village where morning after morning their Tribes assembled, and declared that if they would believe in and follow the Jehovah God, He would deliver them from all their enemies and lead them into a happy life. There were present three Sacred Men, Chiefs, of whom the whole population lived in terror—brothers or cousins, heroes of traditional feats, professors of sorcery, and claiming the power of life and death, health and sickness, rain and drought, according to their will. On hearing me, these three stood up and declared they did not believe in Jehovah, nor did they need His help; for they had the power to kill my life by Nahak (*i.e.*, sorcery or witchcraft), if only they could get possession of any piece of the fruit or food that I had eaten. This was an essential condition of their black art; hence the peel of a banana or an orange, and every broken scrap of food, is gathered up by the Natives, lest it should fall into the hands of the Sacred Men, and be used for Nahak. This superstition was the cause of most of the bloodshed and terror upon Tanna; and being thus challenged, I asked God's help, and determined to strike a blow against it.

A woman was standing near with a bunch of native fruit in her hand, like our plums, called quonquore. I asked her to be pleased to give me some; and she, holding out a bunch, said, "Take freely what you will!"

Calling the attention of all the Assembly to what I was doing, I took three fruits from the bunch, and taking a bite out of each, I gave them one after another to the three Sacred Men, and deliberately said in the hearing of all, "You have seem me eat of this fruit, you have seen me give the remainder to your Sacred Men; they have said they can kill me by Nahak, but I challenge them to do it if they can, without arrow or spear, club or musket; for I deny that they have any power against me, or against any one, by their Sorcery."

The challenge was accepted; the Natives looked terror-struck at the position in which I was placed! The ceremony of Nahak was usually performed in secret,—the Tannese fleeing in dread, as Europeans would from the touch of the plague; but I lingered and eagerly watched their ritual. As the three Chiefs arose, and drew near to one of the Sacred Trees, to begin their ceremonial, the Natives fled in terror, crying, "Missi, Iawé! Alas Missi!"

But I held on at my post of observation. Amidst wavings and incantations, they rolled up the pieces of the fruit from which I had eaten, in certain leaves of this Sacred Tree, into a shape like a waxen candle ; then they kindled a sacred fire near the root, and continued their mutterings, gradually burning a little more and a little more of the candle-shaped things, wheeling them round their heads, blowing upon them with their breaths, waving them in the air, and glancing wildly at me as if expecting my sudden destruction. Wondering whether after all they did not believe their own lie, for they seemed to be in dead earnest, I, more eager than ever to break the chains of such vile superstition, urged them again and again, crying, " Be quick ! Stir up your gods to help you ! I am not killed yet ; I am perfectly well ! "

At last they stood up and said, " We must delay till we have called all our Sacred Men. We will kill Missi before his next Sabbath comes round. Let all watch, for he will soon die, and that without fail."

I replied, " Very good ! I challenge all your Priests to unite and kill me by Sorcery or Nahak. If on Sabbath next I come again to your village in health, you will all admit that your gods have no power over me, and that, I am protected by the true and living Jehovah God ! "

Every day throughout the remainder of that week, the Conchs were sounded ; and over that side of the island all their Sacred Men were at work trying to kill me by their arts. Now and again messengers arrived from every quarter of the island, inquiring anxiously after my health, and wondering if I was not feeling sick, and great excitement prevailed amongst the poor deluded idolaters.

Sabbath dawned upon me peacefully, and I went to that village in more than my usual health and strength. Large numbers assembled, and when I appeared they looked at each other in terror, as if it could not really be I myself still spared and well. Entering into the public ground, I saluted them to this effect, " My love to you all, my friends ! I have come again to talk to you about the Jehovah God and His Worship."

The three Sacred Men, on being asked, admitted that they

had tried to kill me by Nahak, but had failed; and on being questioned, why they had failed, they gave the acute and subtle reply, that I also was myself a Sacred Man, and that my God being the stronger had protected me from their gods. Addressing the multitude, I answered thus, " Yea, truly ; my Jehovah God is stronger than your gods. He protected me, and helped me; for He is the only living and true God, the only God that can hear or answer any prayer from the children of men. Your gods cannot hear prayers, but my God can and will hear and answer you, if you will give heart and life to Him, and love and serve Him only. This is my God, and He is also your friend if you will hear and follow His voice."

Having said this, I sat down on the trunk of a fallen tree, and addressed them : " Come and sit down all around me, and I will talk to you about the love and mercy of my God, and teach you how to worship and please Him."

Two of the Sacred Men then sat down, and all the people gathered round and seated themselves very quietly. I tried to present to them ideas of sin, and of salvation through Jesus Christ, as revealed to us in the Holy Scriptures.

The third Sacred Man, the highest in rank, a man of great stature and uncommon strength, had meantime gone off for his warrior's spear, and returned brandishing it in the air and poising it at me. I said to the people, " Of course he can kill me with his spear, but he undertook to kill me by Nahak or Sorcery, and promised not to use against me any weapons of war; and if you let him kill me now, you will kill your friend, one who lives among you and only tries to do you good, as you all know so well. I know that if you kill me thus, my God will be angry and will punish you."

Thereon I seated myself calmly in the midst of the crowd, while he leaped about in rage, scolding his brothers and all who were present for listening to me. The other Sacred Men, however, took my side, and, as many of the people also were friendly to me and stood closely packed around me, he did not throw his spear. To allay the tumult and obviate further bloodshed, I offered to leave with my Teachers at once, and, in doing so, I ardently pled with them to live at peace. Though we got safely home, that old Sacred Man seemed still to hunger after my blood. For weeks thereafter, go where I would, he would suddenly appear on the path behind me, poising in his right hand that same Goliath spear. God only kept it from being thrown, and I, using every lawful precaution, had all the same to attend to my work, as if no enemy were there, leaving all other results in the hands of Jesus. This whole incident did, doubtless, shake the prejudices of many as to Sorcery; but few even of converted Natives ever get entirely clear of the dread of Nahak.

If not truly converted, the two Priests were fast friends of mine from that day, as also another leading man in the same district. They also received an Aneityumese Teacher to their village, protecting and showing kindness to him; one of the Sacred Men who could speak his language lived almost constantly with him, and some young people were allowed daily to attend our School. These two and a number of others began to wear a kilt, and some a shirt also. Three of them especially, if not Christians, appeared to be not far from the Kingdom of God, and did all that was in their power to protect and to assist me. A few began to pray to Jehovah in their houses, offering a kind of rude Family Worship, and breathing out such prayers and desires as I had taught them for the knowledge of the true God and only Saviour. And these, as my companions, accompanied me from place to place when I visited their district.

But let us return to the war. Many Chiefs and villages were now involved in it; and a large part of the bush over the country between had been consumed by fire, to prevent surprises. Yet, our Harbour people being assembled one night for consultation, a number of the Inland warriors crept near unobserved and discharged a volley of muskets amongst them. Several were shot dead, and in the darkness and confusion the enemy got clear away. Revenge and self-preservation now united our people as one man, and every man assembled for action on the borders of the hostile Tribes. I again visited them on the fighting ground. As I was seen approaching, the two old Priests, my friends, came to receive and escort me, protected by their clubs and muskets,—the one blind of an eye lost in war marching before me, and the other behind me with poised spear and mighty club. Seating me in a central position, they assembled all the warriors, except the watchmen, and these savage men listened attentively to my message, and bowed quietly during prayer. God only knows what may have been the fruit in some dark benighted soul ! The whole host of them ceased firing, till the two friendly Priests had again conveyed me safely beyond the reach of danger.

Going among them frequently thus, they treated me with exceptional kindness, till one Sabbath I determined to go over and talk with the enemy also, in the hope of getting this sad war put an end to. Our people were sternly opposed to this, not for fear of my safety, but lest I prayed for the enemy and my God might help them in the war. But my two friends, the old Priests, persuaded them to let me go, and to cease their shooting till my return. They had an idea to buy, in this way, my intercession with Jehovah exclusively on their be- half ; but I explained to them, as on former occasions, that I was there for the good of all alike, that I loved them all and sought to lead them to give up war and bad conduct, for my God would hear and bless only those who feared and loved and obeyed Him. I had a long interview with the enemies also, arguing against the evils of war, and urging them to give it up. They were so far friendly ; they allowed me to have worship amongst them ; and I returned in safety before another musket was discharged on either side. The war still went on, though more languidly ; but after a time the leaders entered into a kind of truce, and peace reigned for a season.

The other Mission Station, on the south-west side of Tanna, had to be visited by me from time to time. Mr. and Mrs. Mathieson, there, were both in a weak state of health, having a tendency to consumption. On this account they visited Aneityum several times. They were earnestly devoted to their work, and were successful so far as health and the time allowed to them permitted. At this juncture, a message reached me that they were without European food, and a request to send them a little flour if possible. The war made the journey overland impossible. A strong wind and a high sea round the coast rendered it impracticable for my boat to go. The danger to life from the enemy was so great, that I could not hire a crew. I pled therefore with Nowar and Manuman, and a few leading men, to take one of their best canoes, and themselves to accompany me. I had a large flat-bottomed pot with a close-fitting lid, and that I pressed full of flour; and, tying the lid firmly down, I fastened it right in the centre of the canoe, and as far above water-mark as possible. All else that was required we tied around our own persons. Sea and land being as they were, it was a perilous undertaking, which only dire necessity could have justified. They were all good swimmers, but as I could not swim the strongest man was placed behind me, to seize me and swim ashore, if a crash came.

Creeping round near the shore all the way, we had to keep just outside the great breakers on the coral reef, and were all drenched through and through with the foam of an angry surf. We arrived, however, in safety within two miles of our destination, where lived the friends of my canoe's company, but where a very dangerous sea was breaking on the reef. Here they all gave in, and protested that no further could they go; and truly their toil all the way with the paddles had been severe. I appealed to them, that the canoe would for certain be smashed if they tried to get on shore, that the provisions would be lost, and some of us probably drowned. But they turned to the shore, and remained for some time thus, watch ing the sea. At last their Captain cried, " Missi, hold on ! There's a smaller wave coming; we'll ride in now."

My heart rose to the Lord in trembling prayer ! The wave came rolling on; every paddle with all their united strength struck into the sea; and next moment our canoe was flying like a sea-gull on the crest of the wave towards the shore. Another instant, and the wave had broken on the reef with a mighty roar, and rushed past us hissing in clouds of foam. My company were next seen swimming wildly about in the sea, Manuman the one-eyed Sacred Man alone holding on by the canoe, nearly full of water, with me still clinging to the seat of it, and the very next wave likely to devour us. In desperation, I sprang for the reef, and ran for a man half-wading, half-swimming to reach us; and God so ordered it, that just as

10

the next wave broke against the silvery rock of coral, the man caught me and partly swam with me through its surf, partly carried me till I was set safely ashore. Praising God, I looked up and saw all the others nearly as safe as myself, except Manuman, my friend, who was still holding on by the canoe in the face of wind and sea, and bringing it with him. Others ran and swam to his help. The paddles were picked up amid the surf. A powerful fellow came towards me with the pot of flour on his head, uninjured by water! The Chief who held on by the canoe got severely cut about the feet, and had been badly bruised and knocked about; but all the rest escaped without further harm, and everything that we had was saved. Amongst friends, at last, they resolved to await a favourable wind and tide to return to their own homes. Singing in my heart unto God, I hired a man to carry the pot of flour, and soon arrived at the Mission Station.

Supplying the wants of our dear friends, Mr. and Mrs Mathieson, whom we found as well as could be expected, we had to prepare, after a few hours of rest, to return to our own Station by walking overland through the night. I durst not remain longer away, lest my own house should be plundered and broken into. Though weak in health, my fellow-Missionaries were both full of hope, and zealous in their work, and this somewhat strange visit was a pleasant blink amidst our darkness. Before I had gone far on my return journey, the sun went down, and no Native could be hired to accompany me. They all told me that I would for certain be killed by the way. But I knew that it would be quite dark before I reached the hostile districts, and that the Heathen are great cowards in the dark and never leave their villages at night in the darkness, except in companies for fishing and such-like tasks. I skirted along the sea-shore as fast as I could, walking and running alternately; and, when I got within hearing of voices, I slunk back into the bush till they had safely passed, and then groped my way back near the shore, that being my only guide to find a path.

Having made half the journey, I came to a dangerous path, almost perpendicular, up a great rock round the base of which the sea roared deep. With my heart lifted up to Jesus, I succeeded in climbing it, cautiously grasping roots, and resting by bushes, till I reached safely to the top. There, to avoid a village, I had to keep crawling slowly along the bush near the sea, on the top of that great ledge of rock—a feat I could never have accomplished even in daylight without the excitement; but I felt that I was supported and guided in all that life or death journey by my dear Lord Jesus. I had to leave the shore, and follow up the bank of a very deep ravine to a place shallow enough for one to cross, and then through the bush away for the shore again. By holding too much to the right, I missed the point where I had intended to reach it. Small fires were now visible through the bush; I heard the voices of the people talking in one of our most Heathen villages.

Quietly drawing back, I now knew where I was, and easily found my way towards the shore; but on reaching the Great Rock, I could not in the darkness find the path down again. I groped about till I was tired. I feared that I might stumble over and be killed; or, if I delayed till daylight, that the Savages would kill me. I knew that one part of the rock was steep-sloping, with little growth or none thereon, and I searched about to find it, resolved to commend myself to Jesus and slide down thereby, that I might again reach the shore and escape for my life. Thinking I had found this spot, I hurled down several stones and listened for their splash that I might judge whether it would be safe. But the distance was too far for me to hear or judge. At high tide the sea there was deep; but at low tide I could wade out of it and be safe. The darkness made it impossible for me to see anything. I let go my umbrella, shoving it down with considerable force, but neither did it send me back any news.

Feeling sure, however, that this was the place I sought, and knowing that to await the daylight would be certain death, I prayed to my Lord Jesus for help and protection, and resolved to let myself go. First, I fastened all my clothes as tightly as I could, so as not to catch on anything; then I lay down at the top on my back, feet foremost, holding my head downwards on my breast to keep it from striking on the rock; then, after one cry to my Saviour, having let myself down as far as possible by a branch, I at last let go, throwing my arms forward and trying to keep my feet well up. A giddy swirl, as if flying through the air, took possession of me ; a few moments seemed an age ; I rushed quickly down, and felt no obstruction till my feet struck into the sea below. Adoring and praising my dear Lord Jesus, who had ordered it so, I regained my feet ; it was low tide, I had received no injury, I recovered my umbrella, and, wading through, I found the shore path easier and lighter than the bush had been. The very darkness was my safety, preventing the Natives from rambling about. I saw no person to speak to, till I reached a village quite near to my own house, fifteen or twenty miles from where I had started ; here I left the sea path and promised some young men a gift of fish-hooks to guide me the nearest way through the bush to my Mission Station, which they gladly and heartily did. I ran a narrow risk in approaching them ; they thought me an enemy, and I arrested their muskets only by a loud cry,—

" I am Missi! Don't shoot; my love to you, my friends ! "

Praising God for His preserving care, I reached home, and had a long refreshing sleep. The Natives, on hearing next day how I had come all the way in the dark, exclaimed,—

" Surely any of us would have been killed ! Your Jehovah God alone thus protects you and brings you safely home."

With all my heart, I said, " Yes! and He will be your protector and helper too, if only you will obey and trust in Him."

Certainly that night put my faith to the test. Had it not been for the assurance that I was engaged in His service, and that in every path of duty He would carry me through or dispose of me therein for His glory, I could never have undertaken either journey. St. Paul's words are true to-day and for ever,—" I can do all things through Christ which strengtheneth me."

CHAPTER IX.

DEEPENING SHADOWS.

A.D. 1860—1861.   ÆT. 36—37.

Welcome Guests.—A Fiendish Deed.—The Plague of Measles.—A
Heroic Soul.—Horrors of Epidemic.—A Memorable New Year.—A
Missionary Attacked.—In the Valley of the Shadow.—Blow from an
Adze.—A Missionary's Death.—Mrs. Johnston's Letter.—A Heavy
Loss.—The Story of Kowia.—Kowia's Soliloquy.—The Passing of
Kowia.—Mortality of Measles.—Fuel to the Fire.—Hurricanes.—A
Spate of Blood and Terror.—Nowar Vacillates.—The Anger of the
Gods.—Not Afraid to Die.—Martyrs of Erromanga.—Visit to the
Gordons.—Their Martyrdom.—Vindication of the Gordons.—Gordon's
Last Letter.—Plots of Murder.—Death by Nahak.—Nowar Halting
Again.—Old Abraham's Prayer.—Miaki at the Mission House.—
Satanic Influences.—Perplexity Deepening.—Selwyn's Testimony.—
Rotten Tracts.—Captain and Mate of *Blue Bell.*—My Precious Dog.
—Fishing Nets and Kawases.—The Taro Plant.—The Kava Drink.—
Katasian and the Club Scene.—The Yams.—Sunshine and Shadow.
—The Teachers Demoralized.—The Chief's Alphabet.—Our Evil
Genius.—Ships of Fire Again.—Commodore Seymour's Visit.—
Nouka and Queen 'Toria.—The Dog to his Vomit Again.

IN September, 1860, I had the very great pleasure of welcoming, as fellow-labourers on Tanna, the Rev. S. F.
Johnston and his wife, two able and pious young Missionaries
from Nova Scotia. Having visited the whole group of the
New Hebrides, they preferred to cast their lot on Tanna.
During the Rainy Season, and till they had acquired a little of
the language, and some preparation had been made of a Station
for themselves, I gladly received them as my guests. The
company was very sweet to me! I gave them about fourteen
Tannese words to be committed to memory every day, and
conversed with them, using the words already acquired; so
that they made very rapid progress, and almost immediately

were of some service in the Mission work.   No man could
have desired better companions in the ministry of the Gospel.

About this time I had a never-to-be-forgotten illustration of
the infernal spirit that possessed some of the Traders towards
these poor Natives.   One morning, three or four vessels entered
our Harbour and cast anchor in Port Resolution.   The
Captains called on me ; and one of them, with manifest delight,
exclaimed, " We know how to bring down your proud Tannese
now !   We'll humble them before you ! "

I answered, " Surely you don't mean to attack and destroy
these poor people ? "

He replied, not abashed but rejoicing, " We have sent the
measles to humble them !   That kills them by the score !
Four young men have been landed at different ports, ill with
measles, and these will soon thin their ranks."

Shocked above measure, I protested solemnly and denounced
their conduct and spirit ; but my remonstrances only called
forth the shameless declaration, " Our watchword is,—Sweep
these creatures away and let white men occupy the soil ! "

Their malice was further illustrated thus : they induced
Kapuku, a young Chief, to go off to one of their vessels,
promising him a present.   He was the friend and chief sup-
porter of Mr. Mathieson and of his work.   Having got him on
board, they confined him in the hold amongst Natives lying ill
with measles.   They gave him no food for about four-and-twenty
hours ; and then, without the promised present, they put him
ashore far from his own home.   Though weak and excited,
he scrambled back to his Tribe in great exhaustion and terror.
He informed the Missionary that they had put him down
amongst sick people, red and hot with fever, and that he
feared their sickness was upon him.   I am ashamed to say
that these Sandal-wood and other Traders were our own
degraded countrymen ; and that they deliberately gloried in
thus destroying the poor Heathen.   A more fiendish spirit
could scarcely be imagined ; but most of them were horrible
drunkards, and their traffic of every kind amongst these Islands
was, generally speaking, steeped in human blood.

The measles, thus introduced, became amongst our Islanders
the most deadly plague.   It spread fearfully, and was accom-

panied by sore throat and diarrhœa. In some villages, man, woman, and child were stricken, and none could give food or water to the rest. The misery, suffering, and terror were unexampled, the living being afraid sometimes even to bury the dead. Thirteen of my own Mission party died of this disease; and, so terror-stricken were the few who survived, that when the little Mission schooner *John Knox* returned to Tanna, they all packed up and left for their own Aneityum, except my own dear old Abraham.

At first, thinking that all were on the wing, he also had packed his chattels, and was standing beside the others ready to leave with them. I drew near to him, and said, " Abraham, they are all going ; are you also going to leave me here alone on Tanna, to fight the battles of the Lord ? "

He asked, " Missi, will you remain ? "

I replied, " Yes ; but, Abraham, the danger to life is now so great that I dare not plead with you to remain, for we may both be slain. Still, I cannot leave the Lord's work now."

The noble old Chief looked at the box and his bundles, and, musing, said, " Missi, our danger is very great now."

I answered, " Yes ; I once thought you would not leave me alone to it ; but, as the vessel is going to your own land, I cannot ask you to remain and face it with me ! "

He again said, " Missi, would you like me to remain alone with you, seeing my wife is dead and in her grave here ? "

I replied, "Yes, I would like you to remain; but, considering the circumstances in which we will be left alone, I cannot plead with you to do so."

He answered, " Then, Missi, I remain with you of my own free choice, and with all my heart. We will live and die together in the work of the Lord. I will never leave you while you are spared on Tanna."

So saying, and with a light that gave the fore-gleam of a Martyr's glory to his dark face, he shouldered his box and bundles back to his own house ; and thereafter, Abraham was my dear companion and constant friend, and my fellow-sufferer in all that remains still to be related of our Mission life on Tanna.

Before this plague of measles was brought amongst us, Mr

Johnston and I had sailed round in the *John Knox* to Black Beach on the opposite side of Tanna, and prepared the way for settling Teachers there. And they were placed soon after by Mr. Copeland and myself with encouraging hopes of success, and with the prospect of erecting there a Station for Mr. and Mrs. Johnston. But this dreadful imported epidemic blasted all our dreams. Mr. Johnston and his wife devoted themselves, from the very first, and assisted me in every way to alleviate the dread sufferings of the Natives. We carried medicine, food, and even water, to the surrounding villages every day, few of themselves being able to render us much assistance. Nearly all who took our medicine and followed instructions as to food, etc., recovered; but vast numbers of them would listen to no counsels, and rushed into experiments which made the attack fatal all around. When the trouble was at its height, for instance, they would plunge into the sea, and seek relief; they found it in almost instant death. Others would dig a hole into the earth, the length of the body and about two feet deep; therein they laid themselves down, the cold earth feeling agreeable to their fevered skins; and when the earth around them grew heated, they got friends to dig a few inches deeper, again and again, seeking a cooler and cooler couch. In this ghastly effort many of them died, literally in their own graves, and were buried where they lay! It need not be surprising, though we did everything in our power to relieve and save them, that the Natives associated us with the white men who had so dreadfully afflicted them, and that their blind thirst for revenge did not draw fine distinctions between the Traders and the Missionaries. Both were whites—that was enough.

The 1st January, 1861, was a New Year's Day ever to be remembered. Mr. and Mrs. Johnston, Abraham and I, had spent nearly the whole time in a kind of solemn yet happy festival. Anew in a holy covenant before God, we unitedly consecrated our lives and our all to the Lord Jesus, giving ourselves away to His blessed service for the conversion of the Heathen on the New Hebrides. After evening Family Worship, Mr. and Mrs. Johnston left my room to go to their own house, only some ten feet distant; but he returned to inform me that there were two men at the window, armed with huge clubs, and having black painted faces. Going out to them and asking them what they wanted, they replied, "Medicine for a sick boy."

With difficulty, I persuaded them to come in and get it. At once, it flashed upon me, from their agitation and their disguise of paint, that they had come to murder us. Mr. Johnston had also accompanied us into the house. Keeping my eye constantly fixed on them, I prepared the medicine and offered it. They refused to receive it, and each man grasped his killing stone. I faced them firmly and said, "You see that Mr. Johnston is now leaving, and you too must leave this room for to-night. To-morrow, you can bring the boy or come for the medicine."

Seizing their clubs, as if for action, they showed unwillingness to withdraw, but I walked deliberately forward and made as if to push them out, when both turned and began to leave.

Mr. Johnston had gone in front of them and was safely out. But he bent down to lift a little kitten that had escaped at the open door; and at that moment one of the Savages, jerking in behind, aimed a blow with his huge club, in avoiding which Mr. Johnston fell with a scream to the ground. Both men sprang towards him, but our two faithful dogs ferociously leapt in their faces and saved his life. Rushing out, but not fully aware of what had occurred, I saw Mr. Johnston trying to raise himself, and heard him cry, "Take care! these men have tried to kill me, and they will kill you!"

Facing them sternly I demanded, "What is it that you want? He does not understand your language. What do you want? Speak with me."

Both men, thereon, raised their great clubs and made to strike me; but quick as lightning these two dogs sprang at their faces and baffled their blows. One dog was badly bruised, and the ground received the other blow, that would have launched me into Eternity. The best dog was a little crossbred retriever, with terrier's blood in him, splendid for warning us of approaching dangers, and which had already been the means of saving my life several times. Seeing how matters stood, I now hounded both dogs furiously upon them, and the two Savages fled. I shouted after them, "Remember, Jehovah God sees you and will punish you for trying to murder His servants !"

In their flight, a large body of men, who had come eight or ten miles to assist in the murder and plunder, came slipping here and there from the bush and joined them, fleeing too. Verily, "the wicked flee, when no man pursueth." David's experience and assurance came home to us, that evening, as very real :—" God is our refuge and our strength, . . . therefore we will not fear." But, after the danger was all past, I had always a strange feeling of fear, more perhaps from the thought that I had been on the verge of Eternity and so near the great White Throne than from any slavish fear. During the crisis, I felt generally calm, and firm of soul, standing erect and with my whole weight on the promise, "Lo ! I am with you alway." Precious promise ! How often I adore Jesus for it, and rejoice in it ! Blessed be His name.

I, now accustomed to such scenes on Tanna, retired to rest and slept soundly ; but my dear fellow-labourer, as I afterwards learned, could not sleep for one moment. His pallor and excitement continued next day, indeed for several days ; and after that, though he was naturally lively and cheerful, I never saw him smile again. He told me next morning, " I can only keep saying to myself, Already on the verge of Eternity ! How have I spent my time ? What good have I done ? What zeal for souls have I shown ? Scarcely entered on the work of my life, and so near death ! O my friend, I never realized what death means, till last night !" So saying, he covered his face with both hands, and left me to hide himself in his own room.

For that morning, 1st January, 1861, the following entry was found in his Journal : "To-day, with a heavy heart and a feeling of dread, I know not why, I set out on my accustomed wanderings amongst the sick. I hastened back to get the Teacher and carry Mr. Paton to the scene of distress. I carried a bucket of water in one hand and medicine in the other ; and so we spent a portion of this day endeavouring to alleviate their sufferings, and our work had a happy effect also on the minds of others." In another entry, on 22nd December, he wrote: "Measles are making fearful havoc amongst the poor Tannese. As we pass through the villages, mournful scenes meet the eye ; young and old prostrated on the ground, showing all those painful symptoms which accompany loathsome and malignant diseases. In some villages few are left able to prepare food, or to carry drink to the suffering and dying. How pitiful to see the sufferers destitute of every comfort, attention, and remedy that would ameliorate their suffering or remove their disease! As I think of the tender manner in which we are nursed in sickness, the many remedies employed to give relief, with the comforts and attention bestowed upon us, my heart sickens, and I say, Oh my ingratitude and the ingratitude of Christian people! How little we value our Christian birth, education, and privileges, etc."

Having, as above recorded, consecrated our lives anew to God on the first day of January, I was, up till the sixteenth of the month, accompanied by Mr. Johnston and sometimes also by Mrs. Johnston on my rounds in the villages amongst the sick, and they greatly helped me. But by an unhappy accident, I was laid aside when most sorely needed. When adzing a tree for house-building, I observed that Mahanan the war Chief's brother had been keeping too near me, and that he carried a tomahawk in his hand ; and, in trying both to do my work and to keep an eye on him, I struck my ankle severely with the adze. He moved off quickly, saying, "I did not do that," but doubtless rejoicing at what had happened. The bone was badly hurt, and several of the blood-vessels cut. Dressing it as well as I could, and keeping it constantly soaked in cold water, I had to exercise the greatest care. In this con-dition, amidst great sufferings, I was sometimes carried to the villages to administer medicine to the sick, and to plead and pray with the dying.

On such occasions, in this mode of transit even, the conversations that I had with dear Mr. Johnston were most solemn and greatly refreshing. He had, however, scarcely ever slept since the first of January, and during the night of the sixteenth he sent for my bottle of laudanum. Being severely attacked with ague and fever, I could not go to him, but sent the bottle, specifying the proper quantity for a dose, but that he quite understood already. He took a dose for himself, and gave one also to his wife, as she too suffered from sleeplessness. This he repeated three nights in succession, and both of them obtained a long, sound, and refreshing sleep. He came to my bedside, where I lay in the ague-fever, and said with great animation, amongst other things, " I have had such a blessed sleep, and feel so refreshed ! What kindness in God to provide such remedies for suffering man ! "

At mid-day his dear wife came to me crying, " Mr. Johnston has fallen asleep, so deep that I cannot awake him."

My fever had reached the worst stage, but I struggled to my feet, got to his bedside, and found him in a state of coma, with his teeth fixed in tetanus. With great difficulty we succeeded in slightly rousing him ; with a knife, spoon, and pieces of wood, we forced his teeth open, so as to administer an emetic with good effects, and also other needful medicines. For twelve hours, we had to keep him awake by repeated cold dash in the face, by ammonia, and by vigorously moving him about. He then began to speak freely ; and next day he rose and walked about a little. For the two following days, he was sometimes better and sometimes worse ; but we managed to keep him up till the morning of the 21st, when he again fell into a state of coma, from which we failed to rouse him. At two o'clock in the afternoon, he fell asleep—another Martyr for the testimony of Jesus in those dark and trying Isles, leaving his young wife in indescribable sorrow, which she strove to bear with Christian resignation. Having made his coffin and dug his grave, we two alone at sunset laid him to rest beside my own dear wife and child, close by the Mission House.

In Mrs. Johnston's account, in a letter to friends regarding his death, she says :—

" Next morning, the 17th, he rose quite well. He slept well the night before, from having taken a dose of laudanum. He also gave some to me, as I had been ill all the day, having slept little for two or three nights. . . . Two men helped Mr. Paton to his bedside, as I found him lying very low in fever, yet he waited on Mr. Johnston affectionately. For some time, while he was in Mr. Paton's hands, I could scarcely keep myself up at all. We thought it was from the laudanum I had

taken. I had to throw myself down every few minutes. . . .
For some weeks after, I was almost constantly bedfast. I ate
little; still I felt no pain, but very stupid. . . . At times, we
have services with the Natives. For a week past, we have
scarcely gone to bed without fears. One night, our house was
surrounded with crowds of armed men, ready at any moment
to break in upon us for our lives. We have had to sit in the
house for days past, with the doors locked, to prevent any of
the Savages from entering; for every party seems to be united
against us now. The great sickness that prevails amongst them
is the cause of this rage. They say, we made the disease, and
we must be killed for it; that they never died off in this way
before the religion came amongst them, etc., etc."

Mrs. Johnston recovered gradually, returned by the first
opportunity to Aneityum, and for nearly three years taught
the girls' School at Dr. Geddie's Station. Thereafter she was
married to my dear friend the Rev. Joseph Copeland, and
spent with him the remainder of her life on Fotuna, working
devotedly in the service of the Mission, and seeking the salvation of the Heathen.

The death of Mr. Johnston was a heavy loss. From his
landing on Tanna, he appeared to enjoy excellent health, and
was always very active, bright, and happy, till after that attack
by the Savages with their clubs on New Year's Day. From
that night, he never again was the same. He never admitted
that he had got a blow; but I fear his nervous system must
have been unhinged by the shock and horror of the scene.
He was genuinely lamented by all who knew him. Our intercourse on Tanna was very sweet, and I missed him exceedingly.
Not lost to me, however; only gone before!

Another tragedy followed, with, however, much of the light
of Heaven amid its blackness, in the story of Kowia, a Tannese
Chief of the highest rank. Going to Aneityum in youth, he
had there become a true Christian. He married an Aneityumese Christian woman, with whom he lived very happily and
had two beautiful children. Some time before the measles
reached our island, he returned to live with me as a Teacher
and to help forward our work on Tanna. He proved himself
to be a decided Christian; he was a real Chief amongst them,

dignified in his whole conduct, and every way a valuable helper
to me.   Everything was tried by his own people to induce him
to leave me and to renounce the Worship, offering him every
honour and bribe in their power.   Failing these, they threatened
to take away all his lands, and to deprive him of Chieftainship,
but he answered, "Take all ! I shall still stand by Missi and
the Worship of Jehovah.

From threats, they passed to galling insults, all which he
bore patiently for Jesu's sake.   But one day, a party of his
people came and sold some fowls, and an impudent fellow
lifted them after they had been bought and offered to sell them
again to me.   Kowia shouted, "Don't purchase these, Missi;
I have just bought them for you, and paid for them!"

Thereon the fellow began to mock at him.   Kowia, gazing
round on all present and then on me, rose like a lion awaking
out of sleep, and with flashing eyes exclaimed, "Missi, they
think that because I am now a Christian I have become a
coward! a woman! to bear every abuse and insult they can
heap upon me.   But I will show them for once that I am no
coward, that I am still their Chief, and that Christianity does
not take away but gives us courage and nerve."

Springing at one man, he wrenched in a moment the mighty
club from his hands, and swinging it in air above his head like
a toy, he cried, "Come any of you, come all against your
Chief!   My Jehovah God makes my heart and arms strong.
He will help me in this battle as He helps me in other things,
for He inspires me to show you that Christians are no cowards,
though they are men of peace.   Come on, and you will yet
know that I am Kowia your Chief."

All fled as he approached them ; and he cried, " Where are
the cowards now?" and handed back to the warrior his club.
After this they left him at peace.

He lived at the Mission House, with his wife and children,
and was a great help and comfort to Abraham and myself.
He was allowed to go more freely and fearlessly amongst the
people, than any of the rest of our Mission staff.   The ague
and fever, on me at Mr. Johnston's death, so increased and
reduced me to such weakness that I had become insensible,
while Abraham and Kowia alone attended to me.   On returning

to consciousness, I heard as in a dream Kowia lamenting over me, and pleading that I might recover, so as to hear and speak with him before he died. Opening my eyes and looking at him, I heard him say, " Missi, all our Aneityumese are sick. Missi Johnston is dead. You are very sick, and I am weak and dying. Alas, when I too am dead, who will climb the trees and get you a cocoa-nut to drink? And who will bathe your lips and brow ? "

Here he broke down into deep and long weeping, and then resumed, " Missi, the Tanna-men hate us all on account of the Worship of Jehovah ; and I now fear He is going to take away all His servants from this land, and leave my people to the Evil One and his service ! "

I was too weak to speak, so he went on, bursting into a soliloquy of prayer : "O Lord Jesus, Missi Johnston is dead ; Thou hast taken him away from this land. Missi Johnston the woman and Missi Paton are very ill; I am sick, and Thy servants the Aneityumese are all sick and dying. O Lord, our Father in Heaven, art Thou going to take away all Thy servants, and Thy Worship from this dark land ? What meanest Thou to do, O Lord ? The Tannese hate Thee and Thy Worship and Thy servants ; but surely, O Lord, Thou canst not forsake Tanna and leave our people to die in the darkness ! Oh, make the hearts of this people soft to Thy Word and sweet to Thy Worship ; teach them to fear and love Jesus ; and oh, restore and spare Missi, dear Missi Paton, that Tanna may be saved ! "

Touched to the very fountains of my life by such prayers from a man once a Cannibal, I began under the breath of God's blessing to revive.

A few days thereafter, Kowia came again to me, and rousing me out of sleep, cried, " Missi, I am very weak ; I am dying. I come to bid you farewell, and go away to die. I am nearing death now, and I will soon see Jesus."

I spoke what words of consolation and cheer I could muster, but he answered, " Missi, since you became ill my dear wife and children are dead and buried. Most of our Aneityumese are dead, and I am dying. If I remain on the hill, and die here at the Mission House, there are none left to help Abraham to carry me down to the grave where my wife and children are laid. I wish to lie beside them, that we may rise together in the Great Day when Jesus comes. I am happy, looking unto Jesus ! One thing only deeply grieves me now ; I fear God is taking us all away from Tanna, and will leave my poor people dark and benighted as before, for they hate Jesus and the Worship of Jehovah. O Missi, pray for them, and pray for me once more before I go ! "

He knelt down at my side, and we prayed for each other and for Tanna. I then urged him to remain at the Mission House, but he replied, " O Missi, you do not know how near to death I am ! I am just going, and will soon be with Jesus, and see my wife and children now. While a little strength is left, I will lean on Abraham's arm, and go down to the graves of my dear ones and fall asleep there, and Abraham will dig a quiet bed and lay me beside them. Farewell, Missi, I am very near death now ; we will meet again in Jesus and with Jesus ! "

With many tears he dragged himself away ; and my heart-strings seemed all tied round that noble simple soul, and felt like breaking one by one as he left me there on my bed of fever all alone. Abraham sustained him, tottering to the place of graves ; there he lay down, and immediately gave up the ghost and slept in Jesus ; and there the faithful Abraham buried him beside his wife and children. Thus died a man who had been a cannibal Chief, but by the grace of God and the love of Jesus changed, transfigured into a character of light and beauty. What think ye of this, ye scoffers at Missions ? What think ye of this, ye sceptics as to the reality of conversion ? He died, as he had lived since Jesus came to his heart,—without a fear as to death, with an ever-brightening assurance as to salvation and glory through the blood of the Lamb of God, that blood which had cleansed him from all his sins, and had delivered him from their power. I lost, in losing him, one of my best friends and most courageous helpers ; but I knew that day, and I know now, that there is one soul at least from Tanna to sing the glories of Jesus in Heaven—and, oh, the rapture when I meet him there !

Before leaving this terrible plague of measles, I may record my belief that it swept away, with the accompanying sore throat and diarrhœa, a third of the entire population of Tanna; nay, in certain localities more than a third perished. The living declared themselves unable to bury the dead, and great want and suffering ensued. The Teacher and his wife and child, placed by us at Black Beach, were also taken away; and his companion, the other Teacher there, embraced the first opportunity to leave along with his wife for his own island, else his life would have been taken in revenge. Yet, from all accounts afterwards received, I do not think the measles were more fatal on Tanna than on the other Islands of the group. They appear to have carried off even a larger proportion on Aniwa—the future scene of many sorrows but of greater triumphs.

A new incentive was added to the already cruel superstitions of the Natives. The Sandal-wooders, our degraded fellow-countrymen, in order to divert attention from themselves, stirred the Natives with the wild faith that the Missionaries and the Worship had brought all this sickness, and that our lives should be taken in revenge. Some Captains, on calling with their ships, made a pretence of refusing to trade with the Natives as long as I was permitted to live on the island. One Trader offered to come on shore and live amongst the Tannese, and supply them with tobacco and powder, and caps and balls, on condition that the Missionary and Abraham were got out of the way! He knew that these were their greatest wants, and that they eagerly desired these things, but he refused to make any sales to them, till we were murdered or driven away. This was fuel to their savage hate, and drove them mad with revenge, and added countless troubles to our lot.

Hurricane and tempest also fought against us at that time. On the 3rd, and again on the 10th March, 1861, we had severe and destructive storms. They tore up and smashed bread-fruit, chestnut, cocoa-nut, and all kinds of fruit trees. The ground was strewn thick with half-ripe and wasted fruits. Yam plantations and bananas were riven to pieces, and fences and houses lay piled in a common ruin. My Mission House was also greatly injured; and the Church, on which I had spent many weeks of labour, was nearly levelled with the ground. Trees of forty years' growth were broken like straws, or lifted by the roots and blown away. At the other Station, all Mr. Mathieson's premises except one bedroom were swept off in the breath of the hurricane. The sea rose alarmingly and its waves rolled far inland, causing terrible destruction. Had not the merciful Lord left one bedroom at my Station and one at Mr. Mathieson's partly habitable, I know not what in the circumstances we could have done. Men of fifty years declared that never such a tempest had shaken their Islands. Canoes were shivered on the coral rocks, and Villages were left with nothing but ruins to mark where they had been. Though rain poured in torrents, I had to keep near my fallen house for hours and hours to prevent the Natives from carrying away everything I had in this world; and after the second storm, all my earthly belongings had to be secured in the one still-standing room.

Following upon this came another spate of thirst for our blood, which was increased in the following manner. Miaki the war Chief had an infant son, who had just died. They told us that four men were slain at the same time, that their spirits might serve and accompany him in the other world; and that our death also was again resolved upon. For four days they surrounded our diminished premises. We locked ourselves all up in that single bedroom, and armed Savages kept prowling about to take our lives. What but the restraining pity of the Lord kept them from breaking in upon us? They killed our fowls. They cut down and destroyed all our remaining bananas. They broke down the fence around the plantation, and tried to burn it, but failed. They speared and killed some of the few goats—my sole supply of milk. We were helpless, and kept breathing out our souls in prayer; and God did preserve us, but, oh, what a trying time!

The horror grew, when shortly thereafter we learned that our people near the Harbour had killed four men and presented their bodies to certain Chiefs, who feasted on them; and that they in return had given large fat hogs to our people, one for each of ten bodies which our people had formerly presented to them. Within a few months, thirteen or fourteen persons, nearly all refugees or prisoners of war, were reported to us as killed and feasted upon. We generally heard nothing of these murders till all was over, but in any case I would have been helpless against their bloodthirst, even had I exposed myself to their savage enmity. They sent two dead bodies to our nearest village, where we still conducted Worship every Sabbath when we durst appear amongst them ; but our people refused to receive them, saying, " Now we know that it is wrong to kill and eat our fellow-creatures." A Chief from another village, being present, eagerly received them and carried them off to a great feast for which he was preparing.

At this juncture, our friendly Chief Nowar seemed to become afraid. His life also had been threatened ; and our life had been often attempted of late. Society around was all in turmoil, and Nowar urged us to leave and take refuge in Aneityum till these dangers blew past, and he himself would accompany us. I refused, however, to leave. Indeed, there was no immediate means of escape, except my boat,—which would have been almost madness in an open sea voyage of fifty miles, with only Nowar and the Teachers, all inexperienced hands. Nowar, being angry and afraid, took his revenge by laying aside his shirt and kilt, returning to his Heathen nakedness and paint, attending the meetings of the Savages, and absenting himself from the Sabbath Worship. But after about three weeks he resumed the Christian garments ; and, feeling that the danger had for the time passed over, he returned to us as friendly as ever. Poor Nowar! if he only knew what thousands of Christians at home do every day just to save their skins ; and then if he only knew how hardly these Christians can speak against Heathen converts !

My first baptism on Tanna was that of a Teacher's child. About fifty persons were present, and Miaki the war Chief was there also. Alas, that child died in the plague of measles, and of course the Worship was blamed. Deaths, hurricanes, all seemed to be turned against us. A thunderstorm came in the wake of the last hurricane. A man and a woman were killed. Not far from my house, the hill was struck ; a large mass was dislodged from its shoulder and hurled into the valley below. This was the manifest token to them that the gods were angry and that we were the cause! God's grace alone kept us from sinking, and the hope of yet seeing them delivered from their Heathenism, and brought to love and serve Jesus Christ. For that everything could be borne; and I knew that this was the post of duty, for it was the Lord undoubtedly that placed me there.

One day, about this time, I heard an unusual bleating amongst my few remaining goats, as if they were being killed or tortured. I rushed to the goat-house, and found myself instantly surrounded by a band of armed men. The snare had caught me, their weapons were raised, and I expected next instant to die. But God moved me to talk to them firmly and kindly; I warned them of their sin and its punishment; I showed them that only my love and pity led me to remain there seeking their good, and that if they killed me they killed their best friend. I further assured them that I was not afraid to die, for at death my Saviour would take me to be with Himself in Heaven, and to be far happier than I had ever been on Earth; and that my only desire to live was to make them all as happy, by teaching them to love and serve my Lord Jesus. I then lifted up my hands and eyes to the Heavens, and prayed aloud for Jesus to bless all my dear Tannese, and either to protect me or to take me home to Glory as He saw to be for the best. One after another they slipped away from me, and Jesus restrained them once again. Did ever mother run more quickly to protect her crying child in danger's hour, than the Lord Jesus hastens to answer believing prayer and send help to His servants in His own good time and way, so far as it shall be for His glory and their good? A woman may forget her child, yet will I not forget thee, saith the Lord. Oh that all my readers knew and felt this, as in those days and ever since I have felt that His promise is a reality, and that He is with His servants to support and bless them even unto the end of the world!

May, 1861, brought with it a sorrowful and tragic event, which fell as the very shadow of doom across our path; I mean the martyrdom of the Gordons on Erromanga. Rev. G. N. Gordon was a native of Prince Edward Island, Nova Scotia, and was born in 1822. He was educated at the Free Church College, Halifax, and placed as Missionary on Erro-

manga, in June, 1857. Much troubled and opposed by the
Sandal-wooders, he had yet acquired the language and was
making progress by inroads on Heathenism. A considerable
number of young men and women embraced the Christian
Faith, lived at the Mission House, and devotedly helped him
and his excellent wife in all their work. But the hurricanes
and the measles, already referred to, caused great mortality
in Erromanga also; and the degraded Traders, who had
introduced the plague, in order to save themselves from
revenge, stimulated the superstitions of the Heathen, and
charged the Missionaries there too with causing sickness and
all other calamities. The Sandal-wooders hated him for
fearlessly denouncing and exposing their hideous atrocities.

When Mr. Copeland and I placed the Native Teachers at
Black Beach, Tanna, we ran across to Erromanga in the *John
Knox*, taking a harmonium to Mrs. Gordon, just come by
their order from Sydney. When it was opened out at the
Mission House and Mrs. Gordon began playing on it and
singing sweet hymns, the native women were in ecstasies.
They at once proposed to go off to the bush and cut each a
burden of long grass, to thatch the printing-office which Mr.
Gordon was building in order to print the Scriptures in their
own tongue, if only Mrs. Gordon would play to them at night
and teach them to sing God's praises. They joyfully did so,
and then spent a happy evening singing those hymns. Next
day being Sabbath, we had a delightful season there, about
thirty attending Church and listening eagerly. The young men
and women, living at the Mission House, were being trained
to become Teachers; they were reading a small book in their
own language, telling them the story of Joseph; and the work
every way seemed most hopeful. The Mission House had
been removed a mile or so up a hill, partly for Mrs. Gordon's
health, and partly to escape the annoying and contaminating
influence of the Sandal-wooders on the Christian Natives.

On the 20th May, 1861, he was still working at the roofing
of the printing-office, and had sent his lads to bring each a
load of the long grass to finish the thatching. Meantime, a
party of Erromangans from a district called Bunk-Hill, under
a Chief named Lovu, had been watching him. They had

been to the Mission House inquiring, and they had seen him send away his Christian lads. They then hid in the bush and sent two of their men to the Missionary to ask for calico. On a piece of wood he wrote a note to Mrs. Gordon, to give them two yards each. They asked him to go with them to the Mission House, as they needed medicine for a sick boy, and Lovu their Chief wanted to see him. He tied up in a napkin a meal of food, which had been brought to him but not eaten, and started to go with them. He requested the native Narubulet to go on before, with his companion; but they insisted upon his going in front. In crossing a streamlet, which I visited shortly afterwards, his foot slipped. A blow was aimed at him with a tomahawk, which he caught; the other man struck, but his weapon was also caught. One of the tomahawks was then wrenched out of his grasp. Next moment, a blow on the spine laid the dear Missionary low, and a second on the neck almost severed the head from the body. The other Natives then rushed from their ambush, and began dancing round him with frantic shoutings. Mrs. Gordon hearing the noise, came out and stood in front of the Mission House, looking in the direction of her husband's working place, and wondering what had happened. Ouben, one of the party, who had run towards the Station the moment that Mr. Gordon fell, now approached her. A merciful clump of trees had hid from her eyes all that had occurred, and she said to Ouben, " What's the cause of that noise ? "

He replied, " Oh, nothing! only the boys amusing themselves ! "

Saying, " Where are the boys ? " she turned round. Ouben slipped stealthily behind her, sank his tomahawk into her back, and with another blow almost severed her head !

Such was the fate of those two devoted servants of the Lord ; loving in their lives, and in their deaths not divided—their spirits, wearing the crown of martyrdom, entered Glory together, to be welcomed by Williams and Harris, whose blood was shed near the same now hallowed spot for the name and cause of Jesus. They had laboured four years on Erromanga, amidst trials and dangers manifold, and had not been without tokens of blessing in the Lord's work. Never more earnest or devoted Missionaries lived and died in the Heathen field. Other accounts, indeed, have been published, and another was reported to me by Mr. Gordon's Christian lads ; but the above combines faithfully the principal facts in the story. One young Christian lad from a distance saw Mr. Gordon murdered; and a woman saw Mrs. Gordon fall. The above facts are vouched for by a Mr. Milne, one of the few respectable Sandal-wooders, who was there at the time, and helped the Christian Natives to bury the remains—which, he says, were painfully mutilated.

Some severe criticisms, of course, were written and published by those angelic creatures who judge all things from their own safe and easy distance. Mr. Gordon's lack of prudence was sorely blamed, forsooth ! One would so like to see these people just for one week in such trying circumstances. As my near fellow-labourer and dearest friend, I know what was the whole spirit of the man's life, his watchful care, his ceaseless anxiety to do everything that in his judgment was for God's glory and the prosperity of the Mission, and my estimate of him and of his action to the last fills me with supreme regard to his memory.

The Rev. Dr. Inglis of Aneityum, best qualified of all men living * to form an opinion, wrote : " Mr. Gordon was a strong, bold, fearless, energetic, self-denying, and laborious Missionary; eager, earnest, and unwearied in seeking the salvation of the Heathen. . . . Even if Mr. Gordon was to blame for any imprudence, no blame of this kind could be attached to Mrs. Gordon. Hers was a meek, gentle, loving spirit ; quiet and uncomplaining, prudent, earnest, and devoted to Christ. She was esteemed and beloved by all who knew her."

My *Amen* follows, soft and deep, on all that he has written ; and I add, Mr. Gordon was doing what any faithful and devoted Missionary would in all probability for the Master's sake in similar circumstances have done. Those who charge

---

* While revising this page for the press, I have just received notice of the death of the Rev. Dr. John Inglis, my brother's revered and beloved friend, at Lincuan Cottage, Galloway, on July 18th, 1891, in his eighty-fifth year. Like a shock of corn fully ripe, he has been peacefully gathered into the Garner of his Lord. — *Editor.*

him with imprudence would, doubtless, grievously blame Stephen for bringing that stoning upon himself, which he could so easily have escaped!

Mr. Gordon, in his last letter to me, of date 15th February, 1861, says:

"MY DEAR BROTHER,—

"I have news of the best and of the worst character to communicate. A young man died in December, in the Lord, as we believe. We are still preserved in health at our work by the God of all grace, whose power alone could have preserved us in all our troubles, which have come upon us by the measles *per* the *Blue Bell.* Ah, this is a season which we will not soon forget. Some settlements are nearly depopulated, and the principal Chiefs are nearly all dead! And oh, the indescribable fiendish hatred that exists against us! There is quite a famine here. The distress is awful, and the cry of mourning perpetual. A few on both sides of the Island who did not flee from the Worship of God are living, which is now greatly impressing some and exciting the enmity of others. I cannot now write of perils. We feel very anxious to hear from you. If you have to flee, Aneityum of course is the nearest and best place to which you can go. Confidence in us is being restored. Mana, a native Teacher, remains with us for safety from the fury of his enemies. I cannot visit as usual. The persecution cannot be much worse on Tanna. I hope the worst is past. Mrs. G—— unites in love to you, and to Mr. and Mrs. Johnston. In great haste,

"I remain, dear Brother, Yours truly,

"G. N. GORDON."

Let every reader, in view of this epistle, like a voice from the World Unseen, judge of the spirit of the man of God who penned it, and of the causes that were even then at work and were bringing about his sorrowful death. Cruel superstition, measles, and the malignant influences of the godless Traders— these on Erromanga, as elsewhere, were the forces at work that brought hatred and murder in their train.

Immediately thereafter, a Sandal-wood Trader brought in

his boat a party of Erromangans by night to Tanna. They assembled our Harbour Chiefs and people, and urged them to kill us and Mr. and Mrs. Mathieson and the Teachers, or allow them to do so, as they had killed Mr. and Mrs. Gordon. Then they proposed to go to Aneityum and kill the Missionaries there, as the Aneityumese Natives had burned their Church, and thus they would sweep away the Worship and the servants of Jehovah from all the New Hebrides. Our Chiefs, however, refused, restrained by the Merciful One, and the Erromangans returned to their own island in a sulky mood.

Notwithstanding this refusal, as if they wished to reserve the murder and plunder for themselves, our Mission House was next day thronged with armed men, some from Inland, others from Mr. Mathieson's Station. They loudly praised the Erromangans! The leaders said again and again in my hearing, "The men of Erromanga killed Missi Williams long ago. We killed the Rarotongan and Samoan Teachers. We fought Missi Turner and Missi Nisbet, and drove them from our island. We killed the Aneityumese Teachers on Aniwa, and one of Missi Paton's Teachers too. We killed several white men, and no Man-of-war punished us. Let us talk over this, about killing Missi Paton and the Aneityumese, till we see if any Man-of-war comes to punish the Erromangans. If not, let us unite, let us kill these Missionaries, let us drive the worship of Jehovah from our land!"

An Inland Chief said or rather shouted in my hearing, "My love to the Erromangans! They are strong and brave men, the Erromangans. They have killed their Missi and his wife, while we only talk about it. They have destroyed the Worship and driven away Jehovah!"

I stood amongst them and protested, "God will yet punish the Erromangans for such wicked deeds. God has heard all your bad talk, and will punish it in His own time and way."

But they shouted me down, amidst great excitement, with the cry, "Our love to the Erromangans! Our love to the Erromangans!"

After I left them, Abraham heard them say, "Miaki is lazy. Let us meet in every village, and talk with each other. Let us all agree to kill Missi and the Aneityumese for the first of our Chiefs that dies."

On Tanna, as on Erromanga, the Natives have no idea of death coming to any one naturally, or sickness, or any disease; everything comes by Nahak, or sorcery. When one person grows sick or dies, they meet to talk over it and find out who has bewitched or killed him; and this ends in fixing upon some individual upon whom they take revenge, or whom they murder outright. Thus many wars arise on Tanna, for the friends or the tribe of the murdered man generally seek a counter-revenge; and so the blood-fiend is let loose over all the island, and from island to island throughout the whole of the New Hebrides.

The night after the visit of the Erromangan boat, and the sad news of Mr. and Mrs. Gordon's death, the Tannese met on their village dancing-grounds and held high festival in praise of the Erromangans. Our best friend, old Nowar the Chief, who had worn shirt and kilt for some time and had come regularly to the Worship, relapsed once more; he painted his face, threw off his clothing, resumed his bow and arrows, and his tomahawk, of which he boasted that it had killed very many men and at least one woman! On my shaming him for professing to worship Jehovah and yet uniting with the Heathen in rejoicing over the murder of His servants on Erromanga, he replied to this effect: "Truly, Missi, they have done well. If the people of Erromanga are severely punished for this by the Man-of-war, we will all hear of it; and our people will then fear to kill you and the other Missionaries, so as to destroy the Worship of Jehovah. Now, they say, the Erromangans killed Missi Williams and the Samoan, Rarotongan, and Aneityumese Teachers, besides other white men, and no Man-of-war has punished either them or us. If they are not punished for what has been done on Erromanga, nothing else can keep them here from killing you and me and all who worship at the Mission House!"

I answered, "Nowar, let us all be strong to love and serve Jehovah Jesus. If it be for our good and His glory, He will protect us; if not, He will take us to be with Himself. We will not be killed by their bad talk. Besides, what avails it to us, when dead and gone, if even a Man-of-war should come and punish our murderers ? "

He shrugged his shoulders, answering, " Missi, by-and-bye you will see. Mind, I tell you the truth. I know our Tannese people. How is it that Jehovah did not protect the Gordons and the Erromangan worshippers ? If the Erromangans are not punished, neither will our Tannese be punished, though they murder all Jehovah's people ! "

I felt for Nowar's struggling faith, just trembling on the verge of Cannibalism yet, and knowing so little of the true Jehovah.

Groups of Natives assembled suspiciously near us and sat whispering together. They urged old Abraham to return to Aneityum by the very first opportunity, as our lives were certain to be taken, but he replied, " I will not leave Missi."

Abraham and I were thrown much into each other's company, and he stood by me in every danger. We conducted Family Prayers alternately ; and that evening he said during the prayer in Tannese, in which language alone we understood each other :

" O Lord, our Heavenly Father, they have murdered Thy servants on Erromanga. They have banished the Aneityumese from dark Tanna. And now they want to kill Missi Paton and me ! Our great King, protect us, and make their hearts soft and sweet to Thy Worship. Or, if they are permitted to kill us, do not Thou hate us, but wash us in the blood of Thy dear Son Jesus Christ. He came down to Earth and shed His blood for sinners ; through Him forgive us our sins and take us to Heaven—that good place where Missi Gordon the man and Missi Gordon the woman and all Thy dear servants now are singing Thy praise and seeing Thy face. Our Lord, our hearts are pained just now, and we weep over the death of Thy dear servants ; but make our hearts good and strong for Thy cause, and take Thou away all our fears. Make us two and all Thy servants strong for Thee and for Thy Worship ; and if they kill us two, let us die together in Thy good work, like Thy servants Missi Gordon the man and Missi Gordon the woman."

In this manner his great simple soul poured itself out to God ; and my heart melted within me as it had never done under any prayer poured from the lips of cultured Christian men !

Under the strain of these events, Miaki came to our house, and attacked me in hearing of his men to this effect: "You and the Worship are the cause of all the sickness and death now taking place on Tanna! The Erromanga men killed Missi Gordon the man and also the woman, and they are all well long ago. The Worship is killing us all; and the Inland people will kill us for keeping you and the Worship here; for we love the conduct of Tanna, but we hate the Worship. We must kill you and it, and we shall all be well again."

I tried to reason firmly and kindly with them, showing them that their own conduct was destroying them, and that our presence and the Worship could only be a blessing to them in every way, if only they would accept of it and give up their evil ways. I referred to a poor girl, whom Miaki and his men had stolen and abused—that they knew such conduct to be bad, and that God would certainly punish them for it.

He replied, "Such is the conduct of Tanna. Our fathers loved and followed it, we love and follow it, and if the Worship condemns it, we will kill you and destroy the Worship."

I said, "The Word of the Holy God condemns all bad conduct, and I must obey my God in trying to lead you to give it up, and to love and serve His Son Jesus our Saviour. If I refuse to obey my God, He will punish me."

He replied, "Missi, we like many wives to attend us and to do our work. Three of my wives are dead and three are yet alive. The Worship killed them and my children. We hate it. It will kill us all."

I answered, "Miaki, is it good for you to have so many wives, and many of your men to have none? Who waits on them? Who works for them? They cannot get a wife, and so, having to work for themselves, they are led to hate you and all the Chiefs who have more wives than one. You do not love your wives, else you would not slave them and beat them as you do."

But he declared that his heart was good, that his conduct was good, and that he hated the teaching of the Worship. He had a party of men staying with him from the other side of the island, and he sent back a present of four large fat hogs to their Chiefs, with a message as to the killing of the Mathiesons.

If that were done, his hands would be strengthened in dealing with us.

Satan seemed to fill that man's heart. He incited his people to steal everything from us, and to annoy us in every con-ceivable way. They killed one of my precious watch-dogs, and feasted upon it. So sad was the condition of Tanna, that if a man were desperate enough in wickedness, if he killed a number of men and tyrannized over others, he was dignified with the name and rank of a Chief. This was the secret of Miaki's influence, and of his being surrounded by the outlaws and refugees, not only of his own but even other islands. It was all founded upon terror and upheld by cruelty. The Sacred Man, for instance, who murdered my Teacher, and a young man who threw three spears at me, which by God's help I avoided, were both praised and honoured for their deeds. But the moment they were laid aside by measles and unable to retaliate, their flatterers turned upon them and declared that they were punished for their bad conduct against Jehovah and His servants and His Worship!

To know what was best to be done, in such trying circum-stances, was an abiding perplexity. To have left altogether, when so surrounded by perils and enemies, at first seemed the wisest course, and was the repeated advice of many friends. But again, I had acquired the language, and had gained a considerable influence amongst the Natives, and there were a number warmly attached both to myself and to the Worship. To have left would have been to lose all, which to me was heart-rending; therefore, risking all with Jesus, I held on while the hope of being spared longer had not absolutely and entirely vanished. God only knows how deep and genuine were my pity and affection for the poor Tannese, labouring and longing to bring them from their dark idolatry and heathenism to love and serve and please Jesus Christ as their God and Saviour. True, some of the awfully wise people wrote, as in the case of Mr. Gordon, much nonsense about us and the Tanna Mission. They knew, of course, that I was to blame, and they from safe distances could see that I was not in the path of duty!

Perhaps, to people less omnisciently sure, the following

quotation from a letter of the late A. Clark, Esq., J.P., Auckland, New Zealand, will show what Bishop Selwyn thought of my standing fast on Tanna at the post of duty, and he knew what he was writing about. He says :

"In addition, Bishop Selwyn told us that he had seen the Commodore (Seymour), who told him that at Tanna the Natives were in a very insulting and hostile state of mind ; so much so that he felt it his duty to offer Mr. Paton a passage in his ship to Auckland or some other place of safety. He said, 'Talk of bravery! talk of heroism! The man who leads a forlorn hope is a coward in comparison with him, who, on Tanna, thus alone, without a sustaining look or cheering word from one of his own race, regards it as his duty to hold on in the face of such dangers. We read of the soldier, found after the lapse of ages among the ruins of Herculaneum, who stood firm at his post amid the fiery rain destroying all around him, thus manifesting the rigidity of the discipline amongst those armies of ancient Rome which conquered the World. Mr. Paton was subjected to no such iron law. He might, with honour, when offered to him, have sought a temporary asylum in Auckland, where he would have been heartily received. But he was moved by higher considerations. He chose to remain, and God knows whether at this moment he is in the land of the living !' When the Bishop told us that he declined leaving Tanna by H.M.S. *Pelorus*, he added, 'And I like him all the better for so doing !'"

For my part I feel quite confident that, in like circumstances, that noble Bishop of God would have done the same. I, born in the bosom of the Scottish Covenant, descended from those who suffered persecution for Christ's honour, would have been unworthy of them and of my Lord had I deserted my post for danger only. Yet not to me, but to the Lord who sustained me, be all the praise and the glory ! On his next visit to these Islands, the good Bishop brought a box of Mission goods to me in his ship, besides £90 for our work from Mr. Clark and other friends in Auckland. His interest in us and our work was deep and genuine, and was unmarred on either side by any consciousness of ecclesiastical distinctions. We were one in Christ ; and, when next we meet again in the glory of our

Lord, Bishop and Presbyter will be eternally one in that blessed fellowship.

The following incident illustrates the depth of native superstition. One morning two Inland Chiefs came running to the Mission House, breathless, and covered with perspiration. One of them held up a handful of half-rotten tracts, crying, "Missi, is this a part of God's Word, the sacred Book of Jehovah? or is it the work, the words, the book of man?"

I examined them and replied, "These are the work, the words, and the book of man, not of Jehovah."

He questioned me again, "Missi, are you certain that it is not the Word of Jehovah?"

I replied, "It is only man's work and man's book.'

He continued then, "Missi, some years ago, Kaipai, a sacred Chief, and certain Tannese, went on a visit to Aneityum, and Missi Geddie gave him these books. On his return, when he showed them to the Tannese, the people were all so afraid of them, for they thought they were the sacred Books of Jehovah, that they met for consultation and agreed solemnly to bury them. Yesterday, some person in digging had disinterred them, and at once our Inland people said that our dead Chief had buried a part of Jehovah's Word, which made Him angry, and that He had therefore caused the Chief's death and the plague of measles, etc. Therefore they were now assembled to kill the dead Chief's son and daughter in revenge! But, before that should be done, I persuaded them to send these books, to inquire of you if this be part of Jehovah's Book, and if the burying of it caused all these diseases and deaths."

I assured him that these books never caused either sickness or death to any human being; and that none of us can cause sickness or death by sorcery; that burying these Tracts did not make Jehovah angry, nor cause evil to any creature. "You yourselves know," I said, "the very ships that brought the measles and caused the deaths; and you killed some of the young men who were landed sick with the disease."

The Inland Chief declared, "Missi, I am quite satisfied; no person shall be put to death over these books now."

They went off, but immediately returned, saying, "Missi,

have you any books like these to show to us ?   And will you
show us the sacred Book of Jehovah beside them ? "

I showed them a Bible, and then a handful of Tracts with
pictures like those they had brought ; and I offered them the
Bible and specimens of these Tracts, that they might show
both to the people assembled.   The Tracts they received, but
the Bible they refused to touch.   They satisfied the Inland
people and prevented bloodshed; but oh, what a depth of
superstition to be raised out of! and how easily life might be
sacrificed at every turn !

On another occasion I had the joy of saving the lives of
Sandal-wood Traders, to whom neither I nor the Mission
owed anything, except for Christ's sake.   The *Blue Bell* cast
anchor in the Harbour on a beautiful morning, and the
Captain and Mate immediately came on shore.   They had
letters for me ; but, on landing, they were instantly surrounded
by the Chiefs and people, who formed a ring about them on
the beach and called for me to come.   The two white men
stood in the midst, with many weapons pointed at them, and
death if they dared to move.   The Natives shouted to me,
"This is one of the Vessels which brought the measles.   You
and they made the sickness, and destroyed our people.   Now,
if you do not leave with this vessel, we will kill you all."

Of course, their intention was to frighten me on board just
as I was, and leave my premises for plunder !   I protested,
"I will not leave you ; I cannot leave you in this way ; and if
you murder these men or me, Jehovah will punish you.   I am
here for your good ; and you know how kind I have been to
you all, in giving you medicine, knives, axes, blankets, and
clothing.   You also know well that I have never done ill to
one human being, but have constantly sought your good.   I
will not and cannot leave you thus."

In great wrath they cried, "Then will we kill you and this
Captain and Mate."

I kept reasoning with them against such conduct, standing
firmly before them and saying, "If you do kill me, Jehovah
will punish you ; the other men in that vessel will punish you
before they sail ; and a Man-of-war will come and burn your
villages and canoes and fruit trees."

I urged the two men to try and get into their boat as quickly as possible, in silence, while I kept arguing with the Natives. The letters which they had for me, the Savages forbade me to take into my hands, lest thereby some other foreign disease should come to their island. Miaki exclaimed in great wrath that my medicine had killed them all; but I replied, " My medicine with God's blessing saved many lives. You know well that all who followed my rules recovered from the measles, except only one man, and are living still. Now, you seek to kill me for saving your lives and the lives of your people ! "

I appealed to Yorian, another Chief, if the medicine had not saved his life when he appeared to be dying, which he admitted to be the truth. The men had now slipped into their boat and were preparing to leave. Miaki shouted, " Let them go ! Don't kill them to-day." Then he called to the Captain, " Come on shore and trade with us to-morrow."

Next day they foolishly came on shore and began to trade. Natives surrounded the boat with clubs and tomahawks. But Miaki's heart failed him when about to strike ; and he called out, " Missi said that, if we kill them, a Man-of-war will come and take revenge on us."

In the altercation that followed, the men thrust the boat into deep water and forced it out of the grasp of the Savages ; but they caught the Captain's large Newfoundland dog and kept it prisoner. As a compensation for this disappointment, Miaki urged that my life and Abraham's be at once taken ; but again Nowar's firm opposition and God's goodness rescued us from the jaws of the lion. The *Blue Bell* left next morning, and the dog remained behind, as no one from the vessel would venture ashore.

Revenge for the murder of the four men killed to accompany Miaki's child, threatened to originate another war ; but the Chiefs for eight miles around met, and, after much speechifying, agreed that as they were all weak for war, owing to the measles and the want of food through the hurricanes, they should delay it till they all grew stronger. Nowar was, however, greatly excited, and informed me that Miaki had urged the people of an inland district to shoot Nowar and the Teacher and me, and he pled with me again to take Abraham and

12

flee to Aneityum,—impossible except by canoe, and perhaps impossible even so. That night and the following night they tried to break into my house. On one occasion my valuable dog was let out, and cleared them away. Next night I shouted at them from inside, when they thought me asleep, and they decamped again. Indeed, our continuous danger caused me now oftentimes to sleep with my clothes on, that I might start at a moment's warning. My faithful dog Clutha would give a sharp bark and awake me. At other times, she would leap up and pull at the clothes till I awoke ; and then she turned her head quietly and indicated by a wondrous instinct where the danger lay. God made them fear this precious creature, and often used her in saving our lives. Soon after this, six Inland Chiefs came to see me. We had a long talk on the evils of war, and the blessings of the Worship of Jehovah. I gave each a knife and a fork and a tin plate, and they promised to oppose the war which Miaki was forcing on. A man came also with a severe gash in his hand, which a fish had given him ; I dressed it, and he went away very grateful, and spread everywhere the news of healing, a kind of Gospel which he and they could most readily appreciate.

Another incident made them well-disposed for a season ; namely, the use of a fishing-net. Seeing that the Natives had so little food—there being, in fact, a famine after the hurricane —I engaged an inland Tribe to make a net forty feet long and very broad. Strange to say, the Inland people who live far from the sea make the best fishing materials, which again they sell to the Harbour people for the axes, knives, blankets, and other articles obtained from vessels calling. They also make the killing stones, and trade with them amongst the shore people all round the island. This *kawas* or killing stone is made of blue whinstone, eighteen to twenty-four inches long, an inch and a half across, perfectly straight, and hewn as round and neat as any English tradesman could have done it, exactly like a large scythe-stone, such as they use on the harvest fields in Scotland. The kawas seems to be peculiar to Tanna, at least I have not seen it on any other island. The Natives, with pieces of very hard heavy wood of the same size and shape, are taught from infancy to throw it at a given mark. In warfare, it is thrown first; where it strikes it stuns or kills, and then they spring forward with their large double-handed heavy club. Every man or boy carries his killing stone and other weapons, even when moving about peaceably in his own village, war being, in fact, the only regular occupation for men!

Well, these same Inland people, the sort of artisans of the island, being mostly the women and the girls, manufactured for me this huge fishing-net. The cord was twisted from the fibre made out of the bark of their own trees, and prepared with immense toil and care ; and not without touches of skill and taste, when woven and knotted and intertwined. This net I secured, and lent about three days in turn to every village all round the Harbour and near it. One night I saw them carrying home a large hog, which they had got from an Inland Chief for a portion of the fish which they had taken. I thought it right to cause them to return the net to the Mission House every Saturday evening, that they might not be tempted to use it on Sabbath. It was a great help to them, and the Harbour yielded them much wholesome food in lieu of what the hurricane had destroyed.

When, about this time, the *John Knox* came to anchor in the bay, a Native was caught in the act of stealing from her. Angry at being discovered, he and his friends came to shoot me, pretending that it was because the *John Knox* knew they were in want of food and had not brought them a load of Taro from Aneityum. Taro is a plant of the genus *Arum*, the *Æsculentum*, or *Colocasia Æsculenta*, well known all through Polynesia. The Natives spread it in a very simple way. Cutting off the leaves, with a very little of the old bulb still attached, they fix these in the ground, and have the new Taro about a year after that. It is of several kinds and of a great variety of colours—white, yellow, blue, etc. It grows best in ground irrigated by streams of pure water, or in shallow, swampy ground, over which the water runs. The dry-ground Taro is small and inferior, compared with the water-grown roots. Nutritious and pleasant, not unlike the texture of cheese when laid in slices on the table, in size and appearance like a Swedish turnip, it can be either boiled or baked. Hurricanes may destroy all other native food, but the Taro lies uninjured below the water; hence on islands, where it will grow, it forms one of the most permanent and valuable of all their crops.

Our people also demanded that the *John Knox* should bring them kava and tobacco. Kava is the plant, *Piper Methysticum*, from which they make a highly-intoxicating drink. The girls and boys first chew it, and spit the juice into a basin; there it is mixed with water, and then strained through a fibrous cloth-like texture, which they get from the top of the cocoa-nut trees, where it surrounds the young nuts, and drops off with them when they are ripe. This they freely drink; it does not make them violent, but stupefies them and induces sleep like opium. A portion is always poured out to their gods; and the dregs in every mouth after drinking are always spit out with the exclamation, " That's for you, Kumesan! " It is sometimes offered and partaken of with very great ceremony; but its general use by the men is as a soporific, regularly after the evening meal. Women and children are not allowed to drink it. Many men have been attacked and murdered at night, when lying enfeebled and enfolded by kava. That, indeed, is their common mode of taking revenge and of declaring war. These angry men, who came to me about the *John Knox*, tried to smash in my window and kill my faithful dog; but I reasoned firmly and kindly with them, and they at last withdrew.

At that time, though my life was daily attempted, a dear lad, named Katasian, was coming six miles regularly to the Worship and to receive frequent instruction. One day, when engaged in teaching him, I caught a man stealing the blind from my window. On trying to prevent him, he aimed his great club at me, but I seized the heavy end of it with both my hands as it swung past my head, and held on with all my might. What a prayer went up from me to God at that dread moment! The man, astonished and abashed at my kind words and appeal, slunk away and left me in peace.

I had planted a few Yams, of the genus *Dioscoria;* a most valuable article of food, nearly as precious as potatoes were to the poor in Ireland, and used very much in the same way. Years after, when I went to Melbourne, I took one from Aniwa, by no means the largest, weighing seventy-two pounds, and another, forty-two. The things, however, that I planted on Tanna the Natives stole and carried away, making themselves extremely troublesome. But God never took away from me the consciousness that it was still right for me to be kind and forgiving, and to hope that I might lead them to love and imitate Jesus.

For a season thereafter, the friendly feeling grew on every side. The Natives prepared, for payment, an excellent foundation for a new Church, by levelling down the hill near to my Mission House. Any number of men offered to work for calico, knives, axes, etc. All the fences were renewed, and the Mission premises began to look nice once more—at least, in my eyes. My work became encouraging, and I had many opportunities of talking with them about the Worship and Jehovah. This state of matters displeased Miaki and his men ; and one day, having been engaged thus, I rushed back only in time to extinguish a fire which they had kindled under the verandah and close to the door of my house. Our watch had to be unrelaxing. A cousin of Miaki's, for instance, sold me a fish as good for food which he knew to be poisonous ; but Nowar saw in time and warned me of its deadly character. Miaki then threatened to shoot any of the Inland people who came to work or to receive instruction, yet larger numbers came than before, but they came fully armed !

Nouka, the high Chief of the Harbour, Miaki's uncle, came and sat beside us often, and said, " Miaki breaks my heart ! He deceives Missi. He hates the Worship of Jehovah."

For some time, Nouka and his wife and daughter—a handsome girl, his only child—and Miaki's principal wife and her two sons, and nine Chiefs attended Worship regularly at the Mission House, on Sabbaths and on the afternoon of every Wednesday. In all, about sixty persons somewhat regularly waited on our ministrations at this time ; and amidst all perils I was encouraged, and my heart was full of hope. Yet one evening, when feeling more consoled and hopeful than ever before, a musket was discharged at my very door, and I was constrained to realize that we were in the midst of death. Father, our times are in Thy hand !

As my work became more encouraging, I urgently applied

to the Missionaries on Aneityum for more Teachers, but none could be found willing to return to Tanna. The plague of measles had almost demoralized them. Even on Aneityum, where they had medicine and would follow the Missionaries' advice, no fewer than eleven hundred had been cut off; and the mortality was very much greater on such islands as Tanna, Aniwa, etc., where they were still Heathen, and either had not or would not follow medical counsels. Of my Teachers and their wives ten were swept away in the epidemic; and the few that were left were so disheartened that they escaped to their own land at the first opportunity, as before recorded, excepting only dear old faithful Abraham. But I need not wonder; smaller perils deter God's people at home from many a call of duty.

In my Mission School, I offered as a prize a red shirt for the first Chief who knew the whole Alphabet without a mistake. It was won by an Inikahi Chief, who was once a terror to the whole community. Afterwards, when trying to teach the A B C to others, he proceeded in something like this graphic style: "A is a man's legs with the body cut off; B is like two eyes; C is a three-quarters moon; D is like one eye; E is a man with one club under his feet and another over his head; F is a man with a large club and a smaller one," etc., etc.; L was like a man's foot; Q was the talk of the dove, etc. Then he would say, "Remember these things; you will soon get hold of the letters and be able to read. I have taught my little child, who can scarcely walk, the names of them all. They are not hard to hold, but soft and easy. You will soon learn to read the book, if you try it with all your heart!"

But Miaki was still our evil genius, and every incident seemed to be used by him for one settled purpose of hate. A Kaserumini Chief, for instance, and seven men took away a young girl in a canoe to Aniwa, to be sold to friends there for tobacco leaf, which the Aniwans cultivated extensively. They also prepared to take revenge there for a child's death, killed in their belief by the sorcery of an Aniwan. When within sight of the shore, the canoes were upset and all were said to have been devoured by sharks, excepting only one canoe out of six. This one returned to Tanna and reported that there you said his word was good; obey it now, else we will punish you and defend the Missi."

Miaki accepted the token, and gave good promises for the future. Ian then came to the hill-top near our house, by which passed the public path, and cried aloud in the hearing of all, "Abraham, tell Missi that you and he now live on our land. This path is the march betwixt Miaki and us. We have this day bought back the land of our fathers by a great price to prevent war. Take of our bread-fruits and also of our cocoa-nuts what you require, for you are our friends and living on our land, and we will protect you and the Worship!"

For some time things moved on quietly after this. An inland war, however, had continued for months. As many as ten men, they said, were sometimes killed in one day and feasted on by the warriors. Thousands had been thereby forced down from the mountains, and sought protection under Ian and his people. All the people claiming connection with his Tribe were called Naraimini; the people in the Volcano district were called the Kaserumini; and the Harbour Tribes were the Watarenmini; and so on all over the island. In such divisions, there might be from two to twenty Chiefs and Villages under one leader, and these stood by each other for purposes defensive and offensive. Now Nouka and Miaki had been frustrated in all their plans to get the Inland and the Harbour people involved in the war, as their own followers were opposed to it. In violation of his promises, however, Nouka invited all the men who wished to go to the war to meet him one morning, and only one appeared! Nouka, in great wrath, marched off to the war himself, but, as no one followed, he grew faint-hearted, and returned to his own village. On another morning, Miaki summoned all his fighting men; but only his own brother and six lads could be induced to accompany him, and with these he started off. But the enemy, hearing of his coming, had killed two of his principal allies the night before, and Miaki, learning this, turned and fled to his own house, and was secretly laughed at by his tribe.

Next day Nouka came to me professing great friendship, and pleading with me to accompany him and Miaki to talk with the Kaserumini, and persuade them to give up the war. He was annoyed and disappointed when I refused to go. Nowar and others informed me, two days thereafter, that three persons had died in that district, that others were sick, and that the Heathen there had resolved to kill me in revenge as the cause of all. As Nouka's wife was one of the victims, this scheme was concocted to entrap me. I was warned on no account to leave my house at night for a considerable time, but to keep it locked up and to let no one in after dark. The same two men from that district, who had tried to kill Mr. Johnston and me, were again appointed, and were watching for Abraham and me, lurking about in the evenings for that purpose. Again I saw how the Lord had preserved me from Miaki and Nouka! Truly all are safe who are in God's keeping; and nothing can befall them, except for their real good and the glory of their Lord.

Chafed at the upsetting of all their plans and full of revenge, Nouka and Miaki and their allies declared publicly that they were now going to kill Ian by sorcery, *i.e.*, by Nahak, more feared by the poor Tannese than the field of battle. Nothing but the grace of God and the enlightenment of His Spirit through the Scriptures, has ever raised these Natives above that paralyzing superstition. But, thank God, there are now, while I write this (1887), about twelve thousand in the New Hebrides who have been thus enlightened and lifted out of their terrors, for the Gospel is still, as of old, the power of God unto salvation! Strange to say, Ian became sick shortly after the Sacred Men had made the declaration about their Nahak-sorcery. I attended him, and for a time he recovered, and appeared very grateful. But he soon fell sick again. I sent him and the Chief next under him a blanket each; I also gave shirts and calico to a number of his leading men. They wore them and seemed grateful and pleased. Ian, however, gradually sank and got worse. He had every symptom of being poisoned, a thing easily accomplished, as they know and use many deadly poisons. His sufferings were very great, which prevented me from ascribing his collapse to mere superstitious terror. I did all that could be done; but all thought him dying, and of course by sorcery. His people

Miaki and Nouka said, "If you will keep Missi and his Worship, take him with you to your own land, for we will not have him to live at the Harbour."

Ian, the great Inland Chief, rose in wrath and said, "On whose land does the Missi live, yours or ours? Who fight against the Worship and all good, who are the thieves and murderers, who tell the lies, you or we? We wish peace, but you will have war. We like Missi and the Worship, but you hate them and say, 'Take him to your own land!' It is our land on which he now lives; it is his own land which he bought from you, but which our fathers sold Missi Turner long ago. The land was not yours to sell; it was really ours. Your fathers stole it from us long ago by war; but we would not have asked it back, had you not asked us to take Missi away. Now we will defend him on it, and he will teach us and our people in our own land!" So meeting after meeting broke into fiery speech, and separated with many threats.

To the next great meeting I was invited, but did not go, contenting myself with a message pleading that they should live at peace and on no account go to war with each other. But Ian himself came for me. I said, "Ian, I have told you my whole heart. Go not to that meeting. I will rather leave the island or die, than see you going to war about me!"

He answered, "Missi, come with me, come now!"

I replied, "Ian, you are surely not taking me away to kill me? If you are, my God will punish it."

His only reply was, "Follow me, follow me quickly."

I felt constrained to go. He strode on before me till we reached the great village of his ancestors. His followers, armed largely with muskets as well as native weapons, filled one half the Village Square or dancing ground. Miaki, Nouka, and their whole party sat in manifest terror upon the other half. Marching into the centre, he stood with me by his side, and proudly looking round, exclaimed, "Missi, these are my men and your friends! We are met to defend you and the Worship." Then pointing across to the other side, he cried aloud, "These are your enemies and ours! The enemies of the Worship, the disturbers of the peace on Tanna! Missi, say the word, and the muskets of my men will sweep all opposition away, and the Worship will spread and we will all be strong for it on Tanna. We will not shoot without your leave; but if you refuse they will kill you and persecute us and our children, and banish Jehovah's Worship from our land."

I said, "I love all of you alike. I am here to teach you how to turn away from all wickedness, to worship and serve Jehovah, and to live in peace. How can I approve of any person being killed for me or for the Worship? My God would be angry at me and punish me, if I did!"

He replied, "Then, Missi, you will be murdered and the Worship destroyed."

I then stood forth in the middle before them all and cried, "You may shoot or murder me, but I am your best friend. I am not afraid to die. You will only send me the sooner to my Jehovah God, whom I love and serve, and to my dear Saviour Jesus Christ, who died for me and for you, and who sent me here to tell you all His love. If you will only love and serve Him and give up your bad conduct, you will be happy. But if you kill me, His messenger, rest assured that He will in His own time and way punish you. This is my word to you all; my love to you all!"

So saying, I turned to leave; and Ian strode sullenly away and stood at the head of his men, crying, "Missi, they will kill you! they will kill us, and you will be to blame!"

Miaki and Nouka, full of deceit, now cried out, "Missi's word is good! Let us all obey it. Let us all worship."

An old man, Sirawia, one of Ian's under-chiefs, then said, "Miaki and Nouka say that the land on which Missi lives was theirs; though they sold it to him and he has paid them for it, they all know that it was ours, and is yet ours by right; but if they let Missi live on it in peace, we will all live at peace, and worship Jehovah. And if not, we will surely claim it again."

Miaki and his party hereon went off to their plantations, and brought a large present of food to Ian and his men as a peace-offering. This they accepted; and the next day Ian and his men brought Miaki a return present and said, "You know that Missi lives on our land? Take our present, be friends, and let him live quietly and teach us all. Yesterday brave marines ranked up on deck, and heard a great cannon discharged. For all such efforts to impress them and open their eyes, I felt profoundly grateful ; but too clearly I knew and saw that only the grace of God could lastingly change them ! They were soon back to their old arguments, and were heard saying to one another, " If no punishment is inflicted on the Erromangans for murdering the Missi there, we fear the bad conduct of the Tannese will continue."

No punishment was inflicted at Erromanga, and the Tannese were soon as bold and wicked as ever. For instance, while the Man-of-war lay in the Harbour, Nowar kept himself closely concealed; but no sooner had she sailed than the cowardly fellow came out, laughing at the others, and protesting that he was under no promise and was free to act as he pleased ! Yet in the hour of danger he generally proved to be our friend ; such was his vacillating character. Nor was Miaki very seriously impressed. Mr. Mathieson shortly thereafter sent his boat round to me, being again short of European food. On his crew leaving her to deliver their message to me, some of Miaki's men at once jumped into the boat and started off round the island in search of kava. I went to Miaki, to ask that the boat might be brought back soon, but on seeing me he ran for his club and aimed to strike me. I managed to seize it, and to hold on, pleading with God and talking with Miaki, till by interference of some friendly Natives his wrath was assuaged a little. Returning home, I sent food overland to keep the Mathiesons going till the boat returned, which she did in about eight days. Thus light and shadow pursued each other, the light brightening for a moment, but upon the whole the shadows deepening.

CHAPTER X.

FAREWELL SCENES.

A.D. 1861—1862.   ÆT. 37—38.

The War Fever.—Forced to the War Council.—A Truce among the Chiefs.—Chiefs and People.—The Kiss of Judas.—The Death of Ian.—The Quivering Knife.—A War of Revenge.—In the Thick of the Battle.—Tender Mercies of the Wicked.—Escape for Life.—The Loss of All.—Under the Tomahawk.—Jehovah is Hearing.—The Host Turned Back.—The War against Manuman.—Traps Laid.— House Broken Up.—War against our Friends.—A Treacherous Murderer.—On the Chestnut Tree.—Bargaining for Life.—Five Hours in a Canoe.—Kneeling on the Sands.—Faimungo's Farewell. —"Follow! Follow!"—A Race for Life.—Ringed Round with Death.—Faint yet Pursuing.—Out of the Lion's Jaws.—Brothers in Distress.—Intervening Events.—A Cannibal's Taste.—Pillars of Cloud and of Fire.—Passing by on the other Side.—Kapuku and the Idol Gods.—A Devil Chief.—In Perils Oft.—Through Fire and Water.—"Sail O! Sail O!"—Let Me Die.—In Perils on the Sea.— Tannese Visitors.—The Devil Chief of Tanna.—Speckled and Spotted. —Their Desired Haven.—"I am Left Alone."—My Earthly All.— Eternal Hope.—Australia to the Rescue.—For my Brethren's Sake.— A New Holy League.—The Uses of Adversity.—The Arm-Chair Critics Again.—Concluding Note.

A TIME of great excitement amongst the Natives now prevailed. War, war, nothing but war was spoken of! Preparations for war were being made in all the villages far and near. Fear sat on every face, and armed bands kept watching each other, as if uncertain where the war was to begin or by whom. All work was suspended, and that war spirit was let loose which rouses the worst passions of human nature. Again we found ourselves the centre of conflict, one party set for killing us or driving us away ; the other wishing to retain us, while all old bitter grievances were also dragged into their speeches.

were two white Traders living on Aniwa, that they had plenty of ammunition and tobacco, but that they would not come to Tanna as long as a Missionary lived there. Under this fresh incitement, a party of Miaki's men came to my house, praising the Erromangans for the murder of their Missionaries, and threatening me.

Even the friendly Nowar said, " Miaki will make a great wind and sink any Man-of-war that comes here. We will take the Man-of-war and kill all that are on board. If you and Abraham do not leave us we will kill you both, for we must have the Traders and the powder."

Just as they were assuming a threatening attitude, other Natives came running with the cry, " Missi, the *John Knox* is coming into the Harbour, and two great ships of fire, Men-of-war, behind her, coming very fast ! "

I retorted upon Nowar and the hostile company, "Now is your time ! Make all possible haste ! Let Miaki raise his great wind now ; get all your men ready ; I will tell them that you mean to fight, and you will find them always ready ! "

Miaki's men fled away in unconcealed terror ; but Nowar came to me and said " Missi, I know that my talk is all lies, but if I speak the truth, they will kill me ! "

I answered, " Trust in Jehovah, the same God who sent these vessels now, to protect us from being murdered." But Nowar always wavered.

And now from all parts of the island those who were most friendly flocked to us. They were clamorous to have Miaki and some others of our enemies punished by the Man-of-war in presence of the Natives ; and then they would be strong to speak in our defence and to lead the Tannese to worship Jehovah.

Commodore Seymour, Captain Hume, and Dr. Geddie came on shore. After inquiring into everything, the Commodore urged me to leave at once, and very kindly offered to remove me to Aneityum, or Auckland, or any place of safety that I preferred. Again, however, I hesitated to leave my dear benighted Tannese, knowing that both Stations would be instantly broken up, that all the influence gained would be thrown away, that the Church would lose all that had been expended, and above all, that those friendly to us would be left to persecution and destruction. For a long time I had seldom taken off my clothes at night, needing to be constantly on the alert to start at a moment's notice; yet, while hope burned within my soul I could not withdraw, so I resolved to risk all with my dear Lord Jesus, and remained at my post. At my request, however, they met and talked with all the leaders who could be assembled at the Mission House. The Natives declared frankly that they liked me, but did not like the Worship. The Commodore reminded them that they had invited me to land among them, and had pledged their word more than once to protect me; he argued with them that as they had no fault to find with me, but only with the Worship, which could do them only good, they must bind themselves to protect my life. Miaki and others promised and gave him their hands to do so. Lathella, an Aneityumese Chief, who was with Dr. Geddie, interpreted for him and them, Dr. Geddie explaining fully to Lathella in Aneityumese what the Commodore said in English, and Lathella explaining all to the Tannese in their own tongue.

At last old Nouka spoke out for all and said, "Captain Paddan and all the Traders tell us that the Worship causes all our sickness and death. They will not trade with us, nor sell us tobacco, pipes, powder, balls, caps, and muskets, till we kill our Missi like the Erromangans, but after that they will send a Trader to live among us and give us plenty of all these things. We love Missi. But when the Traders tell us that the Worship makes us sick, and when they bribe us with tobacco and powder to kill him or drive him away, some believe them and our hearts do bad conduct to Missi. Let Missi remain here, and we will try to do good conduct to Missi; but you must tell Queen 'Toria of her people's bad treatment of us, and that she must prevent her Traders from killing us with their measles, and from telling us lies to make us do bad conduct to Missi! If they come to us and talk as before, our hearts are very dark and may again lead us to bad conduct to Missi."

After this little parley, the Commodore invited us all on board, along with the Chiefs. They saw about three hundred

So he nailed up the door, and they all marched for Nowar's. We prayed as one can only pray when in the jaws of death and on the brink of Eternity. We felt that God was near, and omnipotent to do what seemed best in His sight. When the Savages were about three hundred yards off, at the foot of a hill leading up to the village, Nowar touched my knee, saying, " Missi, Jehovah is hearing! They are all standing still."

Had they come on they would have met with no opposition, for the people were scattered in terror. On gazing shorewards, and round the Harbour, as far as we could see was a dense host of warriors, but all were standing still, and apparently absolute silence prevailed. We saw a messenger or herald running along the approaching multitude, delivering some tidings as he passed, and then disappearing in the bush. To our amazement, the host began to turn, and slowly marched back in great silence, and entered the remote bush at the head of the Harbour. Nowar and his people were in ecstasies, crying out, " Jehovah has heard Missi's prayer! Jehovah has protected us and turned them away back."

We were on that day His trusting and defenceless children; would you not, had you been one of our circle, have joined with us in praising the Lord God for deliverance from the jaws of death ? I know not why they turned back; but I have no doubt it was the doing of God to save our lives.

We learned that they all assembled in a cleared part of the bush and there held a great wrangling palaver. Nouka and Miaki advised them first to fight Manuman and his people. They said, " His brother, the Sacred Man Kanini, killed Ian by Nahak. He is a friend of Missi and of the Worship. He also sent the hurricane to destroy us. They have plenty of yams and pigs. Let us fight and plunder them, and when they are out of the way, we will be strong to destroy Missi and the Worship."

On this the whole mass went and attacked Manuman s first village, where they murdered two of his men, two women, and two children. The inhabitants fled, and all the sick, the feeble, and the children who fell into their hands were reported to us to be murdered, cooked, and eaten. Led on by Miaki they plundered and burned seven villages.

About mid-day, Nouka and Miaki sent their cousin Jonas, who had always been friendly to me, to say that I might return to my house in safety, as they were now carrying the war inland. Jonas had spent some years on Samoa, and been much with Traders in Sydney, and spoke English well; but we felt they were deceiving us. That night, Abraham ventured to creep near the Mission House, to test whether we might return, and save some valuable things, and get a change of clothing. The house appeared to stand as when they nailed up the door. But a large party of Miaki's allies at once enclosed Abraham, and, after asking many questions about me, they let him go since I was not there. Had I gone there, they would certainly that night have killed me. Again, at midnight Abraham and his wife and Matthew went to the Mission House, and found Nouka, Miaki, and Karewick near by, concealed in the bush among the reeds. Once more they enclosed them, thinking I was there too, but Nouka, finding that I was not, cried out, " Don't kill them just now ! Wait till Missi comes."

Hearing this, Matthew slipped into the bush and escaped. Abraham's wife waded into the sea, and they allowed her to get away. Abraham was allowed to go to the Mission House, but he too crept into the bush, and after an anxious waiting they all came back to me in safety. We now gave up all hope of recovering anything from the house.

Towards morning, when Miaki and his men saw that I was not coming back to deliver myself into their hands, they broke up my house and stole all they could carry away. They tore my books, and scattered them about. They took away the type of my printing-press, to be made into bullets for their muskets. For similar uses they melted down the zinc lining of my boxes, and everything else that could be melted. What they could not take away, they destroyed. I lay on the ground all night, concealed in an outhouse of Nowar's, but it was a sleepless and anxious night, not only to me and my Aneityumese, but also to Nowar and his people.

Next day, the attack was renewed by the three Chiefs on the district of my dear friend Manuman. His people fled; the villages were burned; all who came in their way were killed, and all food and property carried away. At night they returned was taken there, as their portion of the plunder. Abraham, his wife, and I waited anxiously for the morning light. Miaki, the false and cruel, came to assure us that the Heathen would not return that day. Yet, as daylight came in, Miaki himselr stood and blew a great conch not far from our house. I ran out to see why this trumpet-shell had been blown, and found it was the signal for a great company of howling armed Savages to rush down the hill on the other side of the bay and make straight for the Mission House. We had not a moment to lose. To have remained would have been certain death to us all, and also to Matthew, a Teacher just arrived from Mr. Mathieson's Station. Though I am by conviction a strong Calvinist, I am no Fatalist. I held on while one gleam of hope remained. Escape for life was now the only path of duty. I called the Teachers, locked the door, and made quickly for Nowar's village. There was not a moment left to carry anything with us. In the issue, Abraham and his wife and I lost all our earthly goods, and all our clothing except what we had on. My Bible, the few translations which I had made into Tannese, and a light pair of blankets I carried with me.

To me the loss was bitter, but as God had so ordered it, I tried to bow with resignation. All my deceased wife's costly outfit, her piano, silver, cutlery, books, etc., with which her dear parents had provided her, besides all that I had in the world ; also a box worth £56, lately arrived, full of men's clothing and medicine, the gift of my dear friends, Samuel Wilson, Esq., and Mrs. Wilson, of Geelong. The Sandal-wood Traders bought all the stolen property for tobacco, powder, balls, caps, and shot. One Trader gathered together a number of my books in a sadly torn and wasted condition and took them to Aneityum, demanding £10 from Dr. Geddie for his trouble. He had to pay him £7 10s., which I repaid to him on my second return to the Islands. This, by way of digression, only to show how white and black Heathenism meet together.

Let us return to the morning of our flight. We could not take the usual path along the beach, for there our enemies would have quickly overtaken us. We entered the bush in the hope of getting away unobserved. But a cousin of Miaki, evidently secreted to watch us, sprang from behind a bread-fruit tree, and swinging his tomahawk, aimed it at my brow with a fiendish look. Avoiding it, I turned upon him and said in a firm bold voice, " If you dare to strike me, my Jehovah God will punish you.   He is here to defend me now ! "

The man, trembling, looked all round as if to see the God who was my defender, and the tomahawk gradually lowered at his side. With my eye fixed upon him, I gradually moved backwards in the track of the Teachers, and God mercifully restrained him from following me.

On reaching Nowar's village unobserved, we found the people terror-stricken, crying, rushing about in despair at such a host of armed Savages approaching. I urged them to ply their axes, cut down trees, and blockade the path. For a little they wrought vigorously at this ; but when, so far as eye could reach, they saw the shore covered with armed men rushing on towards their village, they were overwhelmed with fear, they threw away their axes and weapons of war, they cast themselves headlong on the ground, and they knocked themselves against the trees as if to court death before it came. They cried, " Missi, it's of no use ! We will all be killed and eaten to-day ! See what a host are coming against us."

Mothers snatched up little children and ran to hide in the bush. Others waded as far as they could into the sea with them, holding their heads above the water. The whole village collapsed in a condition of indescribable terror. Nowar, lame with his wounded knee, got a canoe turned upside-down and sat upon it where he could see the whole approaching multitude. He said, " Missi, sit down beside me, and pray to our Jehovah God, for if He does not send deliverance now, we are all dead men. They will kill us all on your account, and that quickly. Pray, and I will watch ! "

They had gone to the Mission House and broken in the door, and finding that we had escaped, they rushed on to Nowar's village. For, as they began to plunder the bedroom, Nouka said, " Leave everything. Missi will come back for his valuable things at night, and then we will get them and him also ! "

battle-cry, rushed in with great impetuosity and carried their wounded Chief home in triumph. The Inland people now discharged muskets at my house and beat against the walls with their clubs. They smashed in the door and window of our store-room, broke open boxes and casks, tore my books to pieces and scattered them about, and carried off everything for which they cared, including my boat, mast, oars, and sails. They broke into Abraham's house and plundered it ; after which they made a rush at the bedroom, into which we were locked, firing muskets, yelling, and trying to break it in. A Chief, professing to be sorry for us, called me to the window, but on seeing me he sent a tomahawk through it, crying, " Come on, let us kill him now ! "

I replied, " My Jehovah God will punish you ; a Man-of-war will come and punish you, if you kill Abraham, his wife, or me."

He retorted, " It's all lies about a Man-of-war ! They did not punish the Erromangans. They are afraid of us. Come on, let us kill them ! "

He raised his tomahawk and aimed to strike my forehead, many muskets were uplifted as if to shoot, so I raised a revolver in my right hand and pointed it at them. The Rev. Joseph Copeland had left it with me on a former visit. I did not wish it, but he insisted upon leaving it, saying that the very knowledge that I had such a weapon might save my life. Truly, on this occasion it did so. Though it was harmless, they fell back quickly. My immediate assailant dropped to the ground, crying, " Missi has got a short musket ! He will shoot you all ! "

After lying flat on the ground for a little, they all got up and ran to the nearest bush, where they continued yelling about and showing their muskets. Towards nightfall they left, loaded with the plunder of the store and of Abraham's house. So God once more graciously protected us from falling into their cruel hands.

In the evening, after they left, I went to Miaki and Nouka. They professed great sorrow at what had taken place, and pretended to have given them a present of food not to do us further injury. But Nowar informed us that, on the contrary,

13

they had hired them to return and kill us next morning and plunder everything on the Mission premises. Miaki, with a sneer, said, " Missi, where was Jehovah to-day ? There was no Jehovah to-day to protect you. It's all lies about Jehovah. They will come and kill you, and Abraham, and his wife, and cut your bodies into pieces to be cooked and eaten in every village upon Tanna."

I said, " Surely, when you had planned all this, and brought them to kill us and steal all our property, Jehovah did protect us, or we would not have been here ! "

He replied, " There was no Jehovah to-day ! We have no fear of any Man-of-war. They dare not punish us. They durst not punish the Erromangans for murdering the Gordons. They will talk to us and say we must not do so again, and give us a present. That is all. We fear nothing. The talk of all Tanna is that we will kill you and seize all your property to-morrow."

I warned him that the punishment of a Man-of-war can only reach the body and the land, but that Jehovah's punishment reached both body and soul in Time and in Eternity.

He replied, " Who fears Jehovah ? He was not here to protect you to-day ! "

"Yes," I said, " my Jehovah God is here now. He hears all we say, sees all we do, and will punish the wicked and protect His own people."

After this, a number of the people sat down around me, and I prayed with them. But I left with a very heavy heart, feeling that Miaki was evidently bent on our destruction.

I sent Abraham to consult Nowar, who had defended us till disabled by a spear in the right knee. He sent a canoe by Abraham, advising me to take some of my goods in it to his house by night, and he would try to protect them and us. The risk was so great, we could only take a very little. Enemies were on every hand to cut off our flight, and Miaki, the worst of all, whose village had to be passed in going to Nowar's. In the darkness of the Mission House, we durst not light a candle for fear of some one seeing and shooting us. Not one of Nowar's men durst come to help us. But in the end it made no difference, for Nowar and his men kept what were angry at me for not consenting before to their shooting of Miaki ; and Miaki's people were now rejoicing that Ian was being killed by Nahak.

One night, his brother and a party came for me to go and see Ian, but I declined to go till the morning for fear of the fever and ague. On reaching his village, I saw many people about, and feared that I had been led into a snare ; but I at once entered into his house to talk and pray with him, as he appeared to be dying. After prayer, I discovered that I was left alone with him, and that all the people had retired from the village ; and I knew that, according to their custom, this meant mischief. Ian said, " Come near me, and sit by my bedside to talk with me, Missi."

I did so, and while speaking to him he lay as if lost in a swoon of silent meditation. Suddenly he drew from the sugar-cane leaf thatch close to his bed a large butcher-like knife, and instantly feeling the edge of it with his other hand, he pointed it to within a few inches of my heart and held it quivering there, all a-tremble with excitement. I durst neither move nor speak, except that my heart kept praying to the Lord to spare me, or if my time was come to take me home to Glory with Himself. There passed a few moments of awful suspense. My sight went and came. Not a word had been spoken, except to Jesus ; and then Ian wheeled the knife around, thrust it into the sugar-cane leaf, and cried to me, " Go, go quickly ! "

Next moment I was on the road. Not a living soul was to be seen about the village. I understood then that it had been agreed that Ian was to kill me, and that they had all withdrawn so as not to witness it, so that when the Man-of-war came to inquire about me Ian would be dead, and no punishment could overtake the murderer. I walked quietly till quite free of the village, lest some hid in their houses might observe me. Thereafter, fearing that they, finding I had escaped, might overtake and murder me, I ran for my life a weary four miles till I reached the Mission House, faint, yet praising God for such a deliverance. Poor Ian died soon after, and his people strangled one of his wives and hanged another, and took out the three bodies together in a canoe and sank them in the sea.

Miaki was jubilant over having killed his enemy by Nahak ; but the Inland people now assembled in thousands to help Sirawia and his brother to avenge that death on Miaki, Nouka, and Karewick. These, on the other hand, boasted that they would kill all their enemies by Nahak-sorcery, and would call up a hurricane to destroy their houses, fruit trees, and planta- tions. Miaki and a number of his men also came to the Mission House ; but, observing his sullen countenance, I asked kindly after his wife who was about to be confined, and gave a blanket, a piece of calico, and a bit of soap as a present for the baby. He seemed greatly pleased, whispered some- thing to his men, and peaceably withdrew. Immediately after Miaki's threat about bringing a storm, one of their great hurricanes actually smote that side of the island and laid everything waste. His enemies were greatly enraged, and many of the injured people united with them in demanding revenge on Miaki. Hitherto I had done everything in my power to prevent war, but now it seemed inevitable, and both parties sent word that if Abraham and I kept to the Mission House no one would harm us. We had little faith in any of their promises, but there was no alternative for us.

On the following Saturday, 18th January, 1862, the war began. Musket after musket was discharged quite near us, and the bush all round rang with the yell of their war-cry, which if once heard will never be forgotten. It came nearer and nearer, for Miaki fled, and his people took shelter behind and around our house. We were placed in the heart of danger, and the balls flew thick all around us. In the afternoon Ian's brother and his party retired, and Miaki quickly sent mes- sengers and presents to the Inikahimini and Kaserumini districts, to assemble all their people and help him "to fight Missi and the Tannese who were friends of the Worship." He said, " Let us cook his body and Abraham's, and distribute them to every village on this side of the island ! "

Yet all the while Miaki assured me that he had sent a friendly message. The war went on, and poor Nowar the Chief protected us, till he had a spear broken into his right knee. The enemy would have carried him off to feast on his body ; but his young men, shouting wildly his name and men, all armed, and watching as outposts. Some were for shooting us, but others hesitated. Every musket was, however, raised and levelled at me. Faimungo poised his great spear and said, " No, you shall not kill Missi to-day. He is with me." Having made this flourish, he strode off after his own men, and my Aneityumese followed, leaving me face to face with a ring of levelled muskets.

Sirawia, who was in command of this party, and who once, like Nowar, had been my friend, said to me, Judas-like, " My love to you, Missi." But he also shouted after Faimungo, " Your conduct is bad in taking the Missi away; leave him to us to be killed ! " I then turned upon him, saying, " Sirawia, I love you all. You must know that I sought only your good. I gave you medicine and food when you and your people were sick and dying under measles ; I gave you the very clothing you wear. Am I not your friend ? Have we not often drunk tea and eaten together in my house ? Can you stand there and see your friend shot ? If you do, my God will punish you severely."

He then whispered something to his company which I did not hear ; and, though their muskets were still raised, I saw in their eyes that he had restrained them. I therefore began gradually to move backwards, still keeping my eyes fixed on them, till the bush hid them from my view, whereon I turned and ran after my party, and God kept the enemy from following. I would like to think that Sirawia only uttered the cruel words which I heard as a blind to save his own life ; for at this time he was joined to Miaki's party, his own people having risen against him, and had to dissemble his friendly feelings towards me. Poor Sirawia ! Well I knew that Miaki would only use him as a tool for selfish interests, and sacrifice him at last. All this showed how dangers grew around our path. Still we trusted in Jehovah Jesus, and pressed on in flight.

A second hostile party encountered us, and with great difficulty we also got away from them. Soon thereafter a friendly company crossed our path. We learned from them that the enemies had slaughtered other two of Manuman's men, and burned several villages with fire. Another party of the enemy encountered us, and were eager for our lives. But this time

Faimungo withstood them firmly, his men encircled us, and he said, " I am not afraid now, Missi ; I am feeling stronger near my own land ! "

Hurrying still onwards, we came to that village on their high ground called Aneai, *i.e.*, Heaven. The sun was oppressively hot, the path almost unshaded, and our whole party very exhausted, especially Faimungo, carrying his load of stolen goods. So here he sat down on the village dancing ground for a smoke, saying, " Missi, I am near my own land now. We can rest with safety."

In a few minutes, however, he started up, he and his men, in wild excitement. Over a mountain, behind the village and above it, there came the shoutings, and anon the tramp, tramp of a multitude making rapidly towards us. Faimungo got up and planted his back against a tree. I stood beside him, and the Aneityumese woman and the two men stood near me, while his men seemed prepared to flee. At full speed a large body of the tallest and most powerful men that I had seen on Tanna came rushing on and filled the dancing ground. They were all armed, and flushed with their success in war. A messenger had informed them of our escape, probably from Miaki, and they had crossed the country to intercept us.

Faimungo was much afraid, and said, " Missi, go on in that path, you and your Aneityumese ; and I will follow when I have had a smoke and a talk with these men."

I replied, " No, I will stand by your side till you go ; and if I am killed, it will be by your side. I will not leave you."

He implored us to go on, but that I knew would be certain death. They began urging one another to kill us, but I looked round them as calmly as possible, saying, " My Jehovah God will punish you here and hereafter, if you kill me or any of His servants."

A killing stone, thrown by one of the Savages, grazed poor old Abraham's cheek, and the dear soul gave such a look at me, and then upwards, as if to say, " Missi, I was nearly away to Jesus." A club was also raised to follow the blow of the killing stone, but God baffled the aim. They encircled us in a deadly ring, and one kept urging another to strike the first blow or fire the first shot. My heart rose up to the Lord

Dear old Abraham said, "Thank you for that, Missi. I will be strong. I pray to God and ply my paddle. God will save us!"

With much labour, and amid deadly perils, we got the canoe turned; and after four hours of a terrible struggle, we succeeded, towards daylight as the tide turned, in again reaching smooth water. With God's blessing we at last reached the shore, exactly where we had left it five hours ago!

Now drenched and weary, with the skin of our hands sticking to the paddles, we left the canoe on the reef and waded ashore. Many Natives were there, and looked sullen and disappointed at our return. Katasian, the lad who had been with us, instantly fled for his own land; and the Natives reported that he was murdered soon after. Utterly exhausted, I lay down on the sand and immediately fell into a deep sleep. By-and-bye I felt some one pulling from under my head the native bag in which I carried my Bible and the Tannese translations—the all that had been saved by me from the wreck! Grasping the bag, I sprang to my feet, and the man ran away. My Teachers had also a hedging knife, a useless revolver, and a fowling-piece, the sight of which, though they had been under the salt water for hours, God used to restrain the Savages. Calling my Aneityumese near, we now, in united prayer and kneeling on the sands, committed each other unto the Lord God, being prepared for the last and worst.

As I sat meditating on the issues, Faimungo, the friendly Inland Chief, again appeared to warn us of our danger, now very greatly increased by our being driven back from the sea. All Nowar's men had fled, and were hid in the bush and in rocks along the shore; while Miaki was holding a meeting not half a mile away, and preparing to fall upon us. Faimungo said, "Farewell, Missi, I am going home. I don't wish to see the work and the murders of this morning."

He was Nowar's son-in-law. He had always been truthful and kindly with me. His home was about half-way across the island, on the road that we wanted to go, and under sudden impulse I said, "Faimungo, will you let us follow you? Will you show us the path? When the Mission Ship arrives, I will give you three good axes, blankets, knives, fish-hooks, and many things you prize."

The late hurricanes had so destroyed and altered the paths, that only Natives who knew them well could follow them. He trembled much and said, " Missi, you will be killed. Miaki and Karewick will shoot you. I dare not let you follow. I have only about twenty men, and your following might endanger us all."

I urged him to leave at once, and we would follow of our own accord. I would not ask him to protect us ; but if he betrayed us and helped the enemy to kill us, I assured him that our God would punish him. If he spared us, he would be rewarded well ;, and if we were killed against his wishes, God would not be angry at him. He said, " Seven men are with me now, and thirteen are to follow. I will not now send for them. They are with Miaki and Nouka. I will go ; but if you follow, you will be killed on the way. You may follow me as far as you can ! "

Off he started to Nowar's, and got a large load of my stolen property, blankets, sheets, etc., which had fallen to his lot. He called his seven men, who had also shared in the plunder, and, to avoid Miaki's men, they ran away under a large cocoa-nut grove skirting the shore, calling, " Be quick ! Follow and keep as near to us as you can."

Though Nowar had got a box of my rice and appropriated many things from the plunder of the Mission House besides the goods entrusted to his care, and got two of my goats killed and cooked for himself and his people, yet now he would not give a particle of food to my starving Aneityumese or myself, but hurried us off, saying, " I will eat all your rice and keep all that has been left with me in payment for my lame knee and for my people fighting for you ! "

My three Aneityumese and I started after Faimungo and his men. We could place no confidence in any of them ; but, feeling that we were in the Lord's hands, it appeared to be our only hope of escaping instant death. We got away unobserved by the enemies. We met several small parties of friends in the Harbour, apparently glad to see us trying to get away. But about four miles on our way, we met a large party of Miaki's assembled there to see us off. Arkurat, having got a large roll of calico from me for the loan of his canoe, hid it away, and then refused the canoe, saying that if he had to escape with his family he would require it. He demanded, for the loan of his canoe, an axe, a sail for his canoe, and a pair of blankets. As Koris had the axe and another had the quilt, I gave the quilt to him for a sail, and the axe and blankets for the canoe. In fact, these few relics of our earthly all at Nowar's were coveted by the Savages and endangered our lives, and it was as well to get rid of them altogether. He cruelly proposed a small canoe for two; but I had hired the canoe for five, and insisted upon getting it, as he had been well paid for it. As he only laughed and mocked us, I prepared to start and travel overland to Mr. Mathieson's Station. He then said, " My wrath is over! You may take it and go."

We launched it, but now he refused to let us go till daylight. He had always been one of my best friends, but now appeared bent on a quarrel, so I had to exercise much patience with him and them. Having launched it, he said I had hired the canoe but not the paddles. I protested, " Surely you know we hired the paddles too. What could we do without paddles?"

But Arkurat lay down and pretended to have fallen asleep, snoring on the sand, and could not be awaked. I appealed to Nowar, who only said, " That is his conduct, Missi, our conduct!"

I replied, " As he has got the blankets which I saved to keep me from ague and fever, and I have nothing left now but the clothes I have on, surely you will give me paddles."

Nowar gave me one. Returning to the village, friends gave me one each till I got other three. Now Arkurat started up, and refused to let us go. A Chief and one of his men, who lived on the other side of the island near to where we were going, and who was hired by me to go with us and help in paddling the canoe, drew back also and refused to go. Again I offered to leave the canoe, and walk overland if possible, when Faimungo, the Chief who had refused to go with us, came forward and said, " Missi, they are all deceiving you! The sea is so rough, you cannot go by it; and if you should get round the weather point, Miaki has men appointed to shoot you as you pass the Black Rocks, while by land all the paths are guarded by armed men. I tell you the truth, having heard all their talk. Miaki and Karewick say they hate the Worship, and will kill you. They killed your goats, and stole all your property yesterday. Farewell!"

The Teachers, the boy, and I now resolved to enter the canoe and attempt it, as the only gleam of hope left to us. After Faimungo came, the man to whom the canoe belonged had withdrawn from us, it having transpired that Miaki would not attack us that night, as other game had attracted his savage eyes. My party of five now embarked in our frail canoe; Abraham first, I next, Matthew after me, the boy at the steering paddle, and Abraham's wife sitting in the bottom, where she might hold on while it continued to float. For a mile or more we got away nicely under the lee of the island, but when we turned to go south for Mr. Mathieson's Station, we met the full force of wind and sea, every wave breaking over and almost swamping our canoe. The Native lad at the helm paddle stood up crying, "Missi, this is the conduct of the sea! It swallows up all who seek its help."

I answered, "We do not seek help from it, but from Jehovah Jesus."

Our danger became very great, as the sea broke over and lashed around us. My faithful Aneityumese, overcome with terror, threw down their paddles, and Abraham said, "Missi, we are all drowned now! We are food for the sharks. We might as well be eaten by the Tannese as by fishes; but God will give us life with Jesus in heaven!"

I seized the paddle nearest me; I ordered Abraham to seize another within his reach; I enjoined Matthew to bale the canoe for life, and the lad to keep firm in his seat, and I cried, "Stand to your post, and let us return! Abraham, where is now your faith in Jesus? Remember, He is Ruler on sea as on land. Abraham, pray and ply your paddle! Keep up stroke for stroke with me, as our lives depend on it. Our God can protect us. Matthew, bale with all your might. Don't look round on the sea and fear. Let us pray to God and ply our paddles, and He will save us yet!"

to keep watch over Nowar and me. When darkness was setting in, Miaki sent for me to go and speak with him, but Nowar and the Aneityumese were all so opposed to it that I did not go. Messages were sent to Nowar, threatening to kill him and his people for protecting me, and great excitement prevailed.

Another incident added horror to the memories of this day. A Savage from Erromanga, living with Nowar, had gone to the war that day. He got near a village unobserved, climbed into a tree, and remained there watching. After mid-day, Kamkali, a true friend of mine, the Chief of his village, came home wearied from the war, got his blanket, stealthily crept into a quiet place in the bush, rolled himself up, and lay down to sleep; for, according to their custom, the leading warriors in times of conflict seldom sleep in their own houses, and seldom twice in the same place even in the bush, for fear of personal danger. The Erromangan, having watched till he was sound asleep, crept to where he lay, raised his club, and smashed in his skull. He told, when he came home, how the blood ran from nose, mouth, and ears, with a gurgling sound in his throat, and after a few convulsive struggles all was over! And the people around Nowar praised him for his deed. Cocoa-nuts were brought for him to drink, and food was presented before him in large quantities, as to one who had done something noble. For safety, he was put into the same house where I had to sit, and even Nowar honoured him. I watched for the workings of a natural man's conscience under the guilt of murder. When left alone, he shook every now and then with agitation, and started round with a terrified gaze. He looked the picture of a man who felt that he had done to his neighbour what he would not have liked another to do to him. I wonder if that consciousness ever dies out, in the lowest and worst— that last voice of God in the soul?

That very night Nowar declared that I must leave his village before morning, else he and his people would be killed for protecting me. He advised me, as the sea was good, to try for Mr. Mathieson's Station; but he objected to my taking away any of my property—he would soon follow with it himself! But how to sail? Miaki had stolen my boat, mast, sails, and oars, as also an excellent canoe made for me and paid for by me on Aneityum; and he had threatened to shoot any person that assisted me to launch either the one or the other. The danger, however, was so great that Nowar said, "You cannot remain longer in my house! My son will guide you to the large chestnut tree in my plantation in the bush. Climb up into it, and remain there till the moon rises."

Being entirely at the mercy of such doubtful and vacillating friends, I, though perplexed, felt it best to obey. I climbed into the tree, and was left there alone in the bush. The hours I spent there live all before me as if it were but of yesterday. I heard the frequent discharging of muskets, and the yells of the Savages. Yet I sat there among the branches, as safe in the arms of Jesus. Never, in all my sorrows, did my Lord draw nearer to me, and speak more soothingly in my soul, than when the moonlight flickered among these chestnut leaves, and the night air played on my throbbing brow, as I told all my heart to Jesus. Alone, yet not alone! If it be to glorify my God, I will not grudge to spend many nights alone in such a tree, to feel again my Saviour's spiritual presence, to enjoy His consoling fellowship. If thus thrown back upon your own soul, alone, all, all alone, in the midnight, in the bush, in the very embrace of death itself, have you a Friend that will not fail you then?

Gladly would I have lingered there for one night of comparative peace! But, about midnight, Nowar sent his son to call me down from the tree, and to guide me to the shore where he himself was, as it was now time to take to sea in the canoe. Pleading for my Lord's continuing presence, I had to obey. My life and the lives of my Aneityumese now hung upon a very slender thread; the risk was almost equally great from our friends so-called, or from our enemies. Had I been a stranger to Jesus and to prayer, my reason would verily have given way, but my comfort and joy sprang out of these words, "I will never leave thee, nor forsake thee; lo, I am with you alway!" Pleading these promises, I followed my guide. We reached the beach, just inside the Harbour, at a beautiful white sandy bay on Nowar's ground, from which our canoe was to start. A good number of the Natives had

On the 31st, we learned that a party of Miaki's men were going about Mr. Mathieson's district inciting the people to kill us. Faimungo also came to inform us that Miaki was exerting all his artifice to get us and the Worship destroyed. Manuman even sent, from inland, Raki, his adopted son, to tell me of the fearful sufferings that he and his people were now passing through, and that some were killed almost every day. Raki's wife was a Chief's daughter, who, when the war began, returned to her father's care. The Savages of Miaki went to her own father's house and compelled him to give her up as an enemy. She was clubbed and feasted on.

On Sabbath, 2nd February, thirty-two people attended the Morning Service. I addressed them on the Deluge, its causes and lessons. I showed them a doll, explaining that such carved and painted images could not hear our prayers or help us in our need, that the living Jehovah God only could hear and help. They were much interested, and after Worship carefully examined the doll. Mr. Mathieson and I, committing ourselves to Jesus, went inland and conducted worship at seven villages, listened to by about one hundred people in all. Nearly all appeared friendly. The people of one village had been incited to kill us on our return; but God guided us to return by another way, and so we escaped.

During the day, on 3rd February, a company of Miaki's men came to the Mission House, and forced Mrs. Mathieson to show them through the premises. Providentially, I had bolted myself that morning into a closet room, and was engrossed with writing. They went through every room in the house and did not see me, concluding I had gone inland. They discharged a musket into our Teacher's house, but afterwards left quietly, greatly disappointed at not finding me. My heart still rose in praise to God for another such deliverance, neither by man nor of man's planning!

Worn out with long watching and many fatigues, I lay down that night early, and fell into a deep sleep. About ten o'clock the Savages again surrounded the Mission House. My faithful dog Clutha, clinging still to me amid the wreck of all else on Earth, sprang quietly upon me, pulled at my clothes, and awoke me, showing danger in her eye glancing at me through the shadows. I silently awoke Mr. and Mrs. Mathieson, who had also fallen asleep. We committed ourselves in hushed prayer to God and watched them, knowing that they could not see us. Immediately a glare of light fell into the room! Men passed with flaming torches; and first they set fire to the Church all round, and then to a reed fence connecting the Church and the dwelling-house. In a few minutes the house, too, would be in flames, and armed Savages waiting to kill us on attempting an escape!

Taking my harmless revolver in the left hand and a little American tomahawk in the right, I pled with Mr. Mathieson to let me out and instantly again to lock the door on himself and wife. He very reluctantly did so, holding me back and saying, "Stop here and let us die together! You will never return!"

I said, "Be quick! Leave that to God. In a few minutes our house will be in flames, and then nothing can save us."

He did let me out, and locked the door again quickly from the inside; and, while his wife and he prayed and watched for me from within, I ran to the burning reed fence, cut it from top to bottom, and tore it up and threw it back into the flames, so that the fire could not by it be carried to our dwelling-house. I saw on the ground shadows, as if something were falling around me, and started back. Seven or eight Savages had surrounded me, and raised their great clubs in air. I heard a shout—"Kill him! kill him!" One savage tried to seize hold of me, but, leaping from his clutch, I drew the revolver from my pocket and levelled it as for use, my heart going up in prayer to my God. I said, "Dare to strike me, and my Jehovah God will punish you. He protects us, and will punish you for burning His Church, for hatred to His Worship and people, and for all your bad conduct. We love you all; and for doing you good only you want to kill us. But our God is here now to protect us and to punish you."

They yelled in rage, and urged each other to strike the first blow, but the Invisible One restrained them. I stood invulnerable beneath His invisible shield, and succeeded in rolling back the tide of flame from our dwelling-house.

At this dread moment occurred an incident, which my

many children are being killed, why do they not send one for food to me and my family? They are as tender and good as the young fowls!" A remark like this lets you see deep into the heart of a Cannibal, and he a sort of half-converted one, if I may use such an expression; certainly not one of the worst type by any means.

On the 23rd January, Mr. Mathieson sent for Taura, Kati, and Kapuku, his three principal Chiefs, to induce them to promise protection till a vessel called to take us away. They appeared friendly, and promised to do their best. Alas! the promises of the Tannese Chiefs had too often proved to be vain.

On Friday, 24th January, report reached our Station that Miaki and his party, hearing that a friendly Chief had concealed two of Manuman's young men, compelled him to produce them and club them to death before their eyes. Also, that they surrounded Manuman's party on a mountain, and hemmed them in there, dying of starvation and trying to survive on the carcasses of the dead and on bark and roots. Also, that Miaki had united all the Chiefs, friends and foes alike, in a bond of blood, to kill every one pertaining to the whole Mission on Tanna. Jesus rules!

On Sunday, the 26th January, thirty persons came to worship at the Mission House. Thereafter, at great risk, we had Worship at three of the nearest and most friendly villages. Amidst all our perils and trials, we preached the Gospel to about one hundred and sixteen persons. It was verily a sowing time of tears; but, despite all that followed, who shall say that it was vain! Twenty years have passed, and now when I am writing this, there is a Church of God singing the praises of Jesus in that very district of Tanna. On leaving the second village, a young lad affectionately took my hand to lead me to the next village; but a sulky, down-browed Savage, carrying a ponderous club, also insisted upon accompanying us. I led the way, guided by the lad. Mr. Mathieson got the man to go before him, while he himself followed, constantly watching. Coming to a place where another path branched off from ours, I asked which path we took, and, on turning to the left as instructed by the lad, the Savage, getting close behind me, swung his huge club over his shoulder to strike me on the head. Mr. Mathieson, springing forward, caught the club from behind with a great cry to me; and I, wheeling instantly, had hold of the club also, and betwixt us we wrested it out of his hands. The poor creature, craven at heart however blood-thirsty, implored us not to kill him. I raised the club threateningly, and caused him to march in front of us till we reached the next village fence. In terror lest these Villagers should kill him, he gladly received back his club, as well as the boy his bow and arrows, and they were lost in the bush in a moment.

At the village from which this man and boy had come, one Savage brought his musket while we were conducting worship, and sat sullen and scowling at us all the time. Mocking questions were also shouted at us, such as, "Who made the rains, winds, and hurricanes? Who caused all the disease? Who killed Mr. Mathieson's child?" They sneered and scoffed at our answers, and in this Taura the Chief joined the rest. They retorted that trading vessels had called at the Harbour, and that all my clothes and property had been sold for muskets, powder, caps, and balls, so that Miaki and his men had plenty of ammunition for fighting purposes now! After this, feeling that no one could be trusted, we ceased visiting these villages, and refrained from exposing ourselves at any distance from the Mission House.

On the 27th, at daylight, a vessel was seen in the offing, as if to tantalize us. The Captain had been at the Harbour, and had received my letter from Nowar. I hoisted a flag to induce him to send or come on shore, but he sailed off for Aneityum, bearing the plunder of my poor Mission House, purchased for ammunition and tobacco from the Natives. He left the news at Aneityum that I had been driven from my Station some time ago, and was believed to have been murdered.

On the 29th January, the young Chief Kapuku came and handed to Mr. Mathieson his own and his father's war-gods and household idols. They consisted chiefly of a basket of small and peculiar stones, much worn and shining with use. He said, "While many are trying to kill you and drive the worship of Jehovah from this island, I give up my gods, and will send away all Heathen idols from my land."

In the flight we passed springs and streamlets, but though parched with sickening thirst, not one of us durst stoop down to drink, as we should have been almost certainly killed in the act. Faimungo now sent his own men home by a near path, and guided us himself till we were close upon the shore. There, sitting down, he said, " Missi, I have now fulfilled my promise. I am so tired, I am so afraid, I dare not go farther. My love to you all. Now go on quickly! Three of my men will go with you to the next rocks. Go quickly! Farewell."

These men went on a little, and then said, " Missi, we dare not go! Faimungo is at war with the people of the next land. You must keep straight along this path." So they turned and ran back to their own village.

To us this district was especially perilous. Many years ago the Aneityumese had joined in a war against the Tannese of this tribe, and the thirst for revenge yet existed in their hearts, handed down from sire to son. Besides, Miaki had incited the people here to murder the Teachers and me if we attempted to escape this way. Most providentially the men were absent on a war expedition, and we saw only three lads and a great number of women and children, who ran off to the bush in terror. In the evening the enraged Savages of another district assaulted the people of the shore villages for allowing us to pass, and, though sparing their lives, broke in pieces their weapons of war—a very grievous penalty. In the next district, as we hasted along the shore, two young men came running after us, poising their quivering spears. I took the useless revolver out of my little native basket, and raising it cried, "Beware! Lay down your spears at once on the sand, and carry my basket to the next landing at the Black Rocks."

They threw their spears on the sand, lifted the bag, and ran on before us to the rocks which formed the march betwixt them and their enemies. Laying it down, they said appealingly, " Missi, let us return to our home!" And how they did run, fearing the pursuit of their foes!

In the next land we saw none. After that we saw crowds all along, some friendly, others unfriendly, but they let us pass on, and with the blessing of Almighty God we drew near to Mr. Mathieson's Station in safety. Here a man gave me a

14

cocoa-nut for each of our party, which we greatly required, having tasted nothing all that day, and very little for several days before. We were so weak that only the struggle for life enabled us to keep our feet; yet my poor Aneityumese never complained and never halted, not even the woman. The danger and excitement kept us up in the race for life ; and by the blessing of God we were now approaching the Mission House, praising God for His wonderful deliverances.

Hearing of our coming, Mr. Mathieson came running to meet me. They had heard of our leaving my own Station, and they thought I was dead ! They were themselves both very weak ; their only child had just been laid in the grave, and they were in great grief and in greater peril. We praised the Lord for permitting us to meet ; we prayed for support, guidance, and protection ; and resolved now, in all events, to stand by each other till the last.

Before I left the Harbour I wrote and left with Nowar letters to be given to the Captains of any vessels which called, for the first, and the next, and the next, telling them of our great danger, that Mr. Mathieson was almost without food, and that I would reward them handsomely if they would call at the Station and remove any of us who might be spared thence to Aneityum. Two or three vessels called, and, as I afterwards learned, got my letters; but, while buying my stolen property from the Natives for tobacco, powder, and balls, they took no further notice of my appeals, and sailed past Mr. Mathieson's straight on to Aneityum. "The tender mercies of the wicked are cruel ! "

Let me now cull the leading events from my Journal, that intervened betwixt this date and the final break-up of the Mission on Tanna—at least for a season—though, blessed be God ! I have lived to see the light rekindled by my dear friends Mr. and Mrs. Watt, and shining more brightly and hopefully than ever. The candle was quenched, but the candlestick was not removed !

On Wednesday, 22nd January, 1862, we heard that other there of Manuman's people had been killed and a district burned with fire. Though this poor man was one of Nowar's chief friends, yet I heard him say before my flight, "When so

Jesus ; I saw Him watching all the scene. My peace came back to me like a wave from God. I realized that I was immortal till my Master's work with me was done. The assurance came to me, as if a voice out of Heaven had spoken, that not a musket would be fired to wound us, not a club prevail to strike us, not a spear leave the hand in which it was held vibrating to be thrown, not an arrow leave the bow, or a killing stone the fingers, without the permission of Jesus Christ, whose is all power in Heaven and on Earth. He rules all Nature, animate and inanimate, and restrains even the Savage of the South Seas. In that awful hour I saw His own words, as if carved in letters of fire upon the clouds of Heaven : "Seek, and ye shall find. Whatsoever ye shall ask in My Name, that will I do, that the Father may be glorified in the Son." I could understand how Stephen and John saw the glorified Saviour as they gazed up through suffering and perse-cution to the Heavenly Throne !

Yet I never could say that on such occasions I was entirely without fear. Nay, I have felt my reason reeling, my sight coming and going, and my knees smiting together when thus brought close to a violent death, but mostly under the solemn thought of being ushered into Eternity and appearing before God. Still, I was never left without hearing that promise in all its consoling and supporting power coming up through the darkness and the anguish, " Lo, I am with you alway." And with Paul I could say, even in this dread moment and crisis of being, " I am persuaded that neither death nor life, . . . nor any other creature, shall be able to separate us from the love of God which is in Christ Jesus our Lord."

Faimungo and others now urged us to go on in the path. I said, " Faimungo, why are we to leave you ? My God heard your promise not to betray me. He knows now what is in your heart and in mine. I will not leave you ; and if I am to die, I will die by your side."

He replied, " Now, I go on before ; Missi, keep close to me."

His men had gone, and I persuaded my Aneityumese to follow them. At last, with a bound, Faimungo started after them. I followed, keeping as near him as I could, pleading with Jesus to protect me or to take me home to Glory. The host of armed men also ran along on each side with their weapons ready ; but leaving everything to Jesus, I ran on as if they were my escort, or as if I saw them not. If any reader wonders how they were restrained, much more would I, unless I believed that the same Hand that restrained the lions from touching Daniel held back these Savages from hurting me ! We came to a stream crossing our path. With a bound all my party cleared it, ran up the bank opposite, and disappeared in the bush. " Faint yet pursuing," I also tried the leap, but I struck the bank and slid back on my hands and knees towards the stream. At this moment I heard a crash above my head amongst the branches of an overhanging tree, and I knew that a killing stone had been thrown, and that that branch had saved me. Praising my God, I scrambled up on the other side, and followed the track of my party into the bush. The Savages gazed after me for a little in silence, but no one crossed the stream ; and I saw them separate into two, one portion returning to the village and another pressing inland. With what gratitude did I recognise the Invisible One who brought their counsels to confusion !

I found my party resting in the bush, and amazed to see me escaped alive from men who were thirsting for my blood. Faimungo and his men received me with demonstrations of joy, perhaps feeling a little ashamed of their own cowardice. He now ascended the mountain and kept away from the common path to avoid other Native bands. At every village enemies to the Worship were ready to shoot us. But I kept close to our guide, knowing that the fear of shooting him would prevent their shooting at me, as he was the most influential Chief in all that section of the island.

One party said, " Miaki and Karewick said that Missi made the sickness and the hurricanes, and we ought to kill him."

Faimungo replied, " They lie about Missi ! It is our own bad conduct that makes us sick."

They answered, " We don't know who makes the sickness ; but our fathers have taught us to kill all foreign men."

Faimungo, clutching club and spear, exclaimed, standing betwixt them and us, " You won't kill Missi to-day ! "

readers may explain as they like, but which I trace directly to the interposition of my God. A rushing and roaring sound came from the South, like the noise of a mighty engine or of muttering thunder. Every head was instinctively turned in that direction, and they knew, from previous hard experience, that it was one of their awful tornadoes of wind and rain. Now, mark, the wind bore the flames *away* from our dwelling-house; had it come in the opposite direction, no power on Earth could have saved us from being all consumed! It made the work of destroying the Church only that of a few minutes; but it brought with it a heavy and murky cloud, which poured out a perfect torrent of tropical rain. Now, mark again, the flames of the burning Church were thereby cut off from extending to and seizing upon the reeds and the bush; and, besides, it had become almost impossible now to set fire to our dwelling-house. The stars in their courses were fighting against Sisera !

The mighty roaring of the wind, the black cloud pouring down unceasing torrents, and the whole surroundings, awed those Savages into silence. Some began to withdraw from the scene, all lowered their weapons of war, and several, terror-struck, exclaimed, "That is Jehovah's rain! Truly their Jehovah God is fighting for them and helping them. Let us away !"

A panic seized upon them; they threw away their remaining torches; in a few moments they had all disappeared in the bush; and I was left alone, praising God for His marvellous works. "O taste and see that God is good ! Blessed is the man that trusteth in Him !"

Returning to the door of the Mission House, I cried, "Open and let me in. I am now all alone."

Mr. Mathieson let me in, and exclaimed, "If ever, in time of need, God sent help and protection to His servants in answer to prayer, He has done so to-night ! Blessed be His holy Name !"

In fear and in joy we united our praises. Truly our Jesus has all power, not less in the elements of Nature than in the savage hearts of the Tannese. Precious Jesus ! Does He not chide us, saying, "Hitherto ye have asked nothing in

My Name. Ask and ye shall receive, that your joy may be full?" How much help, blessing, and joy we lose every day, because we do not take all to Jesus as we ought! Often since have I wept over His love and mercy in that deliverance, and prayed that every moment of my remaining life may be con- secrated to the service of my precious Friend and Saviour!

All through the remainder of that night I lay wide awake keeping watch, my noble little dog lying near me with ears alert. Early in the morning friends came weeping around us. Our enemies were loudly rejoicing. It had been finally resolved to kill us at once, to plunder our house and then to burn it. The noise of the shouting was distinctly heard as they neared the Mission premises, and our weeping, friendly Natives looked terror-struck, and seemed anxious to flee for the bush. But just when the excitement rose to the highest pitch, we heard, or dreamed that we heard, a cry higher still, "Sail O!"

We were by this time beginning to distrust almost our very senses; but again and again that cry came rolling up from the shore, and was repeated from crowd to crowd all along the beach, "Sail O! Sail O!"

The shouts of those approaching us gradually ceased, and the whole multitude seemed to have melted away from our view. I feared some cruel deception, and at first peered out very cautiously to spy the land. But yonder in very truth a vessel came sailing into view. It was the *Blue Bell*, Captain Hastings. I set fire to the reeds on the side of the hill to attract his attention. I put a black shawl as a flag on one end of the Mission House and a white sheet on the other.

This was one of the vessels that had been to Port Resolu- tion, and had sailed past to Aneityum some time ago. I after- wards saw the mate and some of the men wearing my shirts, which they had bought from the Tannese on their former visit. At the earnest request of Messrs. Geddie and Copeland, Mr. Underwood, the owner, had sent Captain Hastings to Tanna to rescue us if yet alive. For this purpose he had brought twenty armed men from Aneityum, who came on shore in two boats in charge of the mate, the notorious Ross Lewin. He returned to the ship with a boat-load of Mr. Mathieson's things, leaving ten of the Natives to help us to pack more and carry them down to the beach, especially what the Missionary thought most valuable.

The two boats were now loaded and ready to start. It was about two o'clock in the afternoon, when a strange and painful trial befell us. Poor dear Mr. Mathieson, apparently unhinged, locked himself all alone into what had been his study, telling Mrs. Mathieson and me to go, for he had resolved to remain and die on Tanna. We tried to show him the inconsistency of praying to God to protect us or grant us means of escape, and then refusing to accept a rescue sent to us in our last extremity. We argued that it was surely better to live and work for Jesus than to die as a self-made martyr, who, in God's sight, was guilty of self-murder. His wife wept aloud and pled with him, but all in vain ! He refused to leave or to unlock his door. I then said, " It is now getting dark. Your wife must go with the vessel, but I will not leave you alone. I shall send a note explaining why I am forced to remain ; and as it is certain that we shall be murdered whenever the vessel leaves, I tell you God will charge you with the guilt of our murder."

At this he relented, unlocked the door, and accompanied us to the boats, in which we all immediately left.

Meantime, having lost several hours, the vessel had drifted leeward ; darkness suddenly settled upon us, and when we were out at sea we lost sight of her and she of us. After drifting about for some hours in a heavy sea and unable to find her, those in charge of the boats came near for consultation, and, if possible, to save the lives of all. We advised that they should steer for Port Resolution by the flame of the Volcano —a never-failing lighthouse, seen fifty miles away—and there await the vessel. The boats were to keep within hearing of each other by constant calling ; but this was soon lost to the ear, though on arriving in the bay we found they had got to anchor before us. There we sat in the boats and waited for the coming day. As the light appeared, we anchored as far out as possible, beyond the reach of musket shots ; and there without water or food we sat under a tropical sun till mid-day came, and still there was no sign of the vessel. The mate at last put all the passengers and the poorest seamen into one boat and left her to swing at anchor; while, with a strong crew in the other, he started off in search of the vessel.

In the afternoon, Nowar and Miaki came off in a canoe to visit us. Nowar had on a shirt, but Miaki was naked and frowning. He urged me to go and see the Mission House, but as we had seen a body of men near it, I refused to go. Miaki declared that everything remained as I had left it, but we knew that he lied. Old Abraham and a party had slipped on shore in a canoe, and had found the windows smashed and everything gone except my books, which were scattered about and torn in pieces. The armed men there wanted to kill the Aneityumese, but others said, " Not till we get Missi killed too ! " They learned that Miaki had sold everything that he could sell to the Traders. The mate and men of the *Blue Bell* had on my very clothes. They boasted that they had bought them for a few figs of tobacco and for powder, caps, and balls. But they would not return a single shirt to me, though I was without a change ! We had all been without food in the boat since the morning before, so Nowar brought us off a cocoa-nut each, and two very small roasted yams for the ladies. Those, however, only seemed to make our thirst the more severe, and we spent a trying day in that boat under a burning sun.

Miaki said, " As our fathers did not destroy Missi Turner's house, we will not destroy yours." But after a time, failing to persuade me to accompany him and fall into a trap, he muttered, " We have taken everything your house contained, and would take you too if we could; for we hate the Worship, it causes all our diseases and deaths; it goes against our customs, and it condemns the things we delight in."

Nowar informed me that only a few nights before this, Miaki and his followers went inland to a village where last year they had killed ten men. Having secretly placed a Savage at the door of every house, at a given signal they yelled, and when the terrified inmates tried to escape, they killed almost every man, woman, and child. Some fled into the bush, others rushed to the shore. A number of men got into a canoe to escape, but hearing women and children crying after them they returned, and taking those they could with them, they killed the rest, lest they should fall alive into Miaki's hands. These are surely " they who through fear of death are all their lifetime subject to bondage." The Chief and nearly his whole village were cut off in one night ! Not an uncommon thing in those Islands, where war becomes chronic, and the thirst for blood becomes insatiable. The dark places of the Earth are "full of the habitations of horrid. cruelty." To have actually lived amongst the Heathen and seen their life gives a man a new appreciation of the power and blessings of the Gospel, even where its influence is only very imperfectly allowed to guide and restrain the passions of men. Oh, what will it be when all men in all nations love and serve the glorious Redeemer !

This Miaki and his followers were a scourge and terror to the whole island of Tanna. They intensely hated Nowar, because he would not join in their cruelties. Yet he and Manuman and Sirawia and Faimungo continued to survive long after war and death had swept all the others away. The first three lived to be very old men ; and to the last they made a profession of being Christians, though their knowledge was very limited and their inconsistencies very grave and very numerous. Happy is it for us that we are not the judges, for souls either of the white or the dark skin, as to how many and grievous things may be forgiven, and whether there be or be not that spark of love, that grain of faith which the Lord the Pitiful will graciously accept and increase ! *

About five o'clock in the evening the vessel hove in sight. Before dark we were all on board, and were sailing for Aneityum. Though both Mr. and Mrs. Mathieson had become very weak, they stood the voyage wonderfully. Next day we were safely landed. We had offered Captain Hastings £20 to take us to Aneityum, but he declined any fare. However, we divided it amongst the mate and crew, for they had every one shown great kindness to us on the voyage.

After arriving on Aneityum, Mrs. Mathieson gradually sank under consumption, and fell asleep in Jesus on 11th March, 1862, and was interred there in the full assurance of a glorious

* See Appendix C, " The Prayer of the Tannese," etc.

resurrection. Mr. Mathieson, becoming more and more de-
pressed after her death, went over to Mr. Creagh's Station, on
Maré, and there died on 14th June, 1862, still trusting in
Jesus, and assured that he would soon be with Him in Glory.
Never more earnest or more faithful souls entered the Mission
field; but they both suffered from weakness and ill-health
during all their time on Tanna, and had frequently to seek
change by removal for a short period from the island. Their
memory is very fragrant to me as follow-labourers in the Gospel
of Jesus.

After their death, I was the only one left alive in all the New
Hebrides Mission north of Aneityum to tell the story of those
pioneer years, during which were sown the seeds of what is
now fast becoming a glorious harvest. Twenty-five years ago,
all these dear brethren and sisters who were associated with
me in the work of the Mission were called home to Glory,
to cast their crowns at the feet of Jesus and enjoy the bliss of
the redeemed; while I am privileged still to toil and pray for
the salvation of the poor Islanders, and plead the cause of
the Mission both in the Colonies and at home, in which work
the Lord has graciously given me undreamt-of success. My
constant desire and prayer are that I may be spared to see at
least one Missionary on every island of the group, or trained
Native Teachers under the superintendence of a Missionary,
to unfold the riches of redeeming love and to lead the poor
Islanders to Jesus for salvation.

What could be taken in three boats was saved out of the
wreck of Mr. Mathieson's property; but my earthly all
perished, except the Bible and the translations into Tannese.
Along with the goods pertaining to the Mission, the property
which I had to leave behind would be under-estimated at £600,
besides the value of the Mission House, etc. Often since
have I thought that the Lord stripped me thus bare of all
these interests, that I might with undistracted mind devote my
entire energy to the special work soon to be carved out for me,
and of which at this moment neither I nor any one had ever
dreamed. At any rate, the loss of my little Earthly All, though
doubtless costing me several pangs, was not an abiding sorrow
like that which sprang from the thought that the Lord's work

was now broken up at both Stations, and that the Gospel was for the time driven from Tanna.

In the darkest moment, I never doubted that ultimately the victory there, as elsewhere, would be on the side of Jesus, believing that the whole Earth would yet be filled with the glory of the Lord. But I sometimes sorely feared that I might never live to see or hear of that happy day ! By the goodness of the Ever-merciful One I have lived to see and hear of a Gospel Church on Tanna, and to read about my dear fellow-Missionaries, Mr. and Mrs. Watt, celebrating the Holy Supper to a Native Congregation of Tannese, amid the very scenes and people where the seeds of faith and hope were planted not only in tears, but tears of blood,—" in deaths oft."

My own intention was to remain on Aneityum, go on with my work of translating the Gospels, and watch the earliest opportunity, as God opened up my way, to return to Tanna. I had, however, got very weak and thin; my health was undoubtedly much shaken by the continued trials and dangers through which we had passed ; and therefore, as Dr. and Mrs. Inglis were at home carrying the New Testament through the press in the language of Aneityum, and as Tanna was closed for a season—Dr. Geddie, the Rev. Joseph Copeland, and Mr. Mathieson all urged me to go to Australia by a vessel then in the Harbour and leaving in a few days. My commission was to awaken an interest among the Presbyterian Churches of our Colonies in this New Hebrides Mission which lay at their doors, up till this time sustained by Scotland and Nova Scotia alone. And further, and very specially, to raise money there, if possible, to purchase a new Mission Ship for the work of God in the New Hebrides,—a clamant necessity, which would save all future Missionaries some of the more terrible of the privations and risk of which a few examples have in these pages already been recorded.

After much prayerful deliberation with my brethren and with my own heart before God, I somewhat reluctantly felt constrained to undertake the task. If my story was to be the means of providing more Missionaries for the Islands, and of providing a commodious Ship for the service of the Mission alone, to keep open their communications with the

outer world and with Christian influences, not to speak of
carrying their provisions at fixed periods, or rescuing them
when in troubles and perils from the jaws of death, I was not
unwilling to tell it again and again, if the Lord would open up
my path.   God knows my heart, and any one who really knows
me will easily admit, that no selfish or egotistical motive has
influenced me in reciting through all the Australasian Colonies,
New Zealand, Scotland, and latterly in many parts of England
and Ireland, the incidents of my career and experience, first
of all on Tanna, and thereafter for nearly twenty years—as the
Second Part of my biography will relate—on the neighbouring
island of Aniwa ; an island entirely given to me by the Lord,
the whole population of which, in course of time, became
Christian ; and they and their race will be my crown of joy
and rejoicing in the day of the Lord Jesus.

   With regrets, and yet with unquenchable hope for these
Islands, I embarked for Australia, having received the solemn
promise of my brethren, that in entering upon this great effort
I was to be left absolutely free of all control, and empowered
to carry out the work as God might seem to guide me and
open up my way.   I had only spoken to one man in Sydney ;
all the doors to influence had therefore to be unlocked ; and I
had no helper, no leader, but the Spirit of my Lord.   The
Second Part of this Autobiography, should God spare me to
write it, will record His marvellous goodness in using my
humble voice and pen, and the story of my life, for interesting
thousands and tens of thousands in the work of Missions ; and
especially for binding together the children of the Sabbath
Schools of Australasia in a Holy League of help to the New
Hebrides, which has already borne precious fruit to His glory,
and will continue to do so for ages to come.

   Oftentimes, while passing through the perils and defeats of
my first four years in the Mission-field on Tanna, I wondered,
and perhaps the reader hereof has wondered, why God permitted
such things.   But on looking back now, I already clearly
perceive, and the reader of my future pages will, I think,
perceive, that the Lord was thereby preparing me for doing,
and providing me materials wherewith to accomplish, the best
work of all my life, namely, the kindling of the heart of

Australian Presbyterianism with a living affection for these Islanders of their own Southern Seas—the binding of all their children into a happy league of shareholders, first in one Mission Ship, and finally in a larger and more commodious Steam-Auxiliary—and, last of all, in being the instrument under God of sending out Missionary after Missionary to the New Hebrides, to claim another island and still another for Jesus. That work, and all that may spring from it in Time and Eternity, never could have been accomplished by me, but for first the sufferings and then the story of my Tanna enterprise !

Some unsophisticated souls who read these pages will be astonished to learn, but others who know more of the heartless selfishness of human creatures will be quite prepared to hear, that my leaving Tanna was not a little criticised, and a great deal of nonsense was written, even in Church Magazines, about the breaking up of the Mission. All such criticism came, of course, from men who were themselves destitute of sympathy, and who, probably, never endured one pang for Jesus in all their comfortable lives. Conscious that I had, to the last inch of life, tried to do my duty, I left all results in the hands of my only Lord, and all criticisms to His unerring judgment. Hard things also were occasionally spoken to my face. One dear friend, for instance, said, "You should not have left. You should have stood at the post of duty till you fell. It would have been to your honour, and better for the cause of the Mission, had you been killed at the post of duty like the Gordons and others."

I replied, "I regard it as a greater honour to live and to work for Jesus, than to be a self-made martyr. God knows that I did not refuse to die ; for I stood at the post of duty, amid difficulty and danger, till all hope had fled, till everything I had was lost, and till God in answer to prayer sent a means of escape. I left with a clear conscience, knowing that in doing so I was following God's leading, and serving the Mission too. To have remained longer would have been to incur the guilt of self-murder in the sight of God."

Never for one moment have I had occasion to regret the step then taken. The Lord has so used me, during the five-

and twenty years that have passed over me since my farewell to Tanna, as to stamp the event with His own most gracious approval. Oh to see a Missionary, and Christian Teachers, planted on every island of the New Hebrides! For this I labour, and wait, and pray. To help on the fulfilment thereof is the sacred work of my life, under God. When I see that accomplished, or in a fair way of being so, through the organization that will provide the money and call forth the men, I can lay down my head as peacefully and gratefully as ever warrior did, with the shout of victory in his ears—" Lord, now lettest Thou Thy servant depart in peace ! "

CONCLUDING NOTE.

I N the original issue, the first volume of this *Autobiography* closed with these words: "For the present, my pen is here laid aside. I shall wait to see what use the Lord makes of Part First of my Autobiography before I prosecute the theme. If the Christian Public seems not to find in it the help and quickening that some friends think it likely to bestow on those who read, the remainder need not be written. Part Second, if called for, will contain a record, in many respects, an utter contrast to all that has gone before, and yet directly springing therefrom, as will be seen by all who look beneath the surface. I am penning these words in 1887, and five-and-twenty years lie betwixt this date and my farewell to Tanna. . . . The Lord whom I serve in the Gospel knows my motive and my hope, and I very calmly leave this book to His disposal—and the succeeding volume to His guidance, if such there shall ever be—as the reader well knows I have had to leave heavier and darker issues in the same blessed Hands. I offer every one, who has done me the favour to read or to listen, my kindly greeting. May you and I meet in the glory of Jesus, and continue our fellowship there! Good-bye."

PART SECOND.

CHAPTERS I.—IX.

A.D. 1862—1885.

ÆT. 38—61.

PRELIMINARY NOTE.

A S originally published, the First Chapter of the second volume opened with the following sentences :

"Strange yet gratifying news has reached me. Part First of my Autobiography has met with a wonderful response from the Public. Within three weeks of its appearance, a second edition has been called for.

"At the Editor's urgent appeal, therefore, and assured also that the finger of God is guiding me, I take up my pen to write Part Second, feeling that I am bound to do so by my promise at the close of the first volume, and by loyalty to the Lord, who seems thus to use my humble life-story to promote the glory of His Name both at home and abroad.

"But, oh, surely never any man was called upon to write a book amid such distracting circumstances! Ceaselessly travelling from Church to Church and from town to town from one end of Australia to the other,—addressing a meeting almost every evening of the week, often also during the afternoons, and several Congregations and Sabbath Schools every Lord's Day,—the following pages are the outpourings of a heart saturated with the subject, but bereft of all opportunity for quiet thought or studious hours.

"Having thus far done my part, I leave all else to the careful Editorship of my dear brother, whose loving hand will put everything into shape for the public eyes. This only I can sincerely testify,—The Lord has called for it, and I lay on His altar the only gift of this kind that I have to offer, believing that He will both accept it and use it as He sees to be for the best."

CHAPTER I.

THE FLOATING OF THE "DAYSPRING."

A.D. 1862—1863.   ÆT. 38—39.

Call for a Mission Ship.—A Brutal Captain.—Sun-Worshippers or Slaves?—The Lights of Sydney.—Thrown upon the Lord.—Mr. Foss's Open Door.—Climbing into Pulpits.—Shipping Company for Jesus.—The Golden Shower.—Wanted More Missionaries.—Commissioned to Scotland.—Wayside Incidents of Australian Travel.—Lost in the Bush.—Sinking in the Swamp.—Put through My Catechism.—"Do for the Parson!"—Crossing the Colony on Novel Conditions.—Pay-Day at a Squatter's.—Three Days in a Public House.—A Meeting among the Diggers.—Camping Out.—A Squatter Rescued.—John Gilpin's Ride through the Bush.

RESCUED from Tanna by the *Blue Bell* in the Spring of 1862, I was landed on Aneityum, leaving behind me all that I owned on Earth, save the clothes upon my back, my precious Bible, and a few translations that I had made from it into the Tannese language. The Missionaries on Aneityum —Messrs. Geddie and Copeland—united, after repeated deliberations, in urging me to go to Australia in the interests of our Mission. In this appeal they were joined now by my companions in tribulation, Mr. and Mrs. Mathieson. A Mission Ship was sorely needed—was absolutely required— to prevent the needless sacrifice of devoted lives. More Missionaries were called for, and must somehow be brought into the field, unless the hope of claiming these fair Islands for Jesus was to be for ever abandoned.

With unaffected reluctance, I at last felt constrained to undertake this unwelcome but apparently inevitable task. It meant the leaving of my dear Islanders for a season; but it embraced within it the hope of returning to them again, with perhaps every power of blessing amongst them tenfold increased.

A *Sandal-wooder*, then lying at Aneityum, was to sail in a few days direct for Sydney. My passage was secured for £10. And, as if to make me realize how bare the Lord had stripped me in my late trials, the first thing that occupied me on board was the making with my own hands, from a piece of cloth obtained on Aneityum, another shirt for the voyage, to change with that which I wore—the only one that had been left to me.

The Captain proved to be a profane and brutal fellow. He professed to be a Roman Catholic, but he was typical of the coarse and godless Traders in those Seas. If he had exerted himself to make the voyage disagreeable, and even disgusting, he could scarcely have had better success. He frequently fought with the mate and steward, and his tyrannical bearing made every one wretched. He and his Native wife (a Heathen —but not more so than himself!) occupied the Cabin. I had to sleep on boards, without a bed, in a place where they stored the sandal-wood ; and never could take off my clothes by night or day during that voyage of nearly fourteen hundred miles. The vessel was miserably supplied. Any food I got was scarcely eatable, and was sent to me in a plate on deck. There I spent all my time, except at night or in heavy rain, when I crept in and lay upon my planks.

The poor steward often came rushing on deck from the cabin with blood streaming from his face, struck by the passionate Captain with whatever came to his hand. Yet he appeared to be a smart and obliging lad, and I pitied him exceedingly. Seeing no hope for redress, I took careful notes of his shocking treatment, and resolved to bide my time for exposing this base and cruel inhumanity.

On reaching Sydney, the steward was dismissed without wages,—the Captain having accused him to his employers of refusing to work on board. He found me out, and told me, weeping, that he cared more for his poor aged mother than himself, as his pay was all her support. On my advice, he informed the Captain that he would summon him, and that I had consented to appear in Court and produce my notes of what I had seen, day by day, on the voyage. He was immediately paid in full, and came to me big with gratitude.

One hesitates to dwell further on this miserable episode. But I must relate how my heart bled for some poor Islanders also, whom that Captain had on board. They knew not a word of English, and no one in the vessel knew a sound of their language. They were made to work, and to understand what was expected of them, only by hard knocks and blows, being pushed and pulled hither and thither. They were kept quite naked on the voyage up; but, when nearing Sydney, each received two yards of calico to be twisted as a kilt around his loins. A most pathetic spectacle it was to watch these poor Natives,—when they had leisure to sit on deck,—gazing, gazing, intently and imploringly, upon the face of the Sun! This they did every day, and at all hours, and I wept much to look on them, and not be able to tell them of the Son of God, the Light of the world, for I knew no word of their language. Perhaps they were worshippers of the Sun; and perhaps, amid all their misery—oh, *perhaps*, some ray of truth from the great Father of Lights may have streamed into those darkened souls!

When we arrived at Sydney, the Inspecting Officer of the Government, coming on board, asked how these Islanders came to be there. The Captain impudently replied that they were "passengers." No further question was put. No other evidence was sought. Yet all who knew anything of our South-Sea Island Traders were perfectly aware that the moral certainty was that these Natives were there practically as Slaves. They would be privately disposed of by the Captain to the highest bidder; and that, forsooth, is to be called the *Labour* Traffic.*

About midnight we came to anchor in Sydney harbour. The Captain condescended to say, " I will not drive you ashore to-night, but you must be off by daylight." His orders might have been spared. It was too great a relief to get away from such coarseness and profanity.

As we came to anchorage, I anxiously paced the deck,

---

* See Appendix D, "The Kanaka Traffic."

gazing towards the gas-lighted city, and pleading with God to open up my way, and give success in the work before me, on which the salvation of thousands of the Heathen might depend. Still I saw them perishing, still heard their wailing cry on the Islands behind me. I saw them groaning under blinding superstitions, and imbruing their hands in each other's blood, and I felt as if crushed by the awful responsibility of my work and by the thought of all that hung upon its success or failure. But I felt also that there must be many of God's dear people in Sydney who would sympathize with such work and help me, if only I could get access to them. At the same time, I knew not a soul in that great city; though I had a note of introduction to one person, which, as experience proved, I would have been better without.

Unfortunately, I had not with me a copy of the Resolution of the Missionaries, commissioning me to plead their cause and to raise funds for the new Mission Ship. Again and again I had earnestly requested it, but the Clerk of the meeting, pressed by correspondence, or for some other reason, gave me instead that note of introduction, which proved more of a hindrance than a help in launching my work; except that it threw me more exclusively on the guidance of my Lord, and taught me to trust in Him, and in the resources He had given me, rather than in any human aid, from that day till the present hour.

That friend, however, did his best. He kindly called with me on a number of Ministers and others. They heard my story, sympathized with me, shook hands, and wished me success; but, strangely enough, something "very special" prevented every one of them from giving me access to his pulpit or Sabbath School. At length, I felt so disappointed, so miserable, that I wished I had been in my grave with my dear departed and my brethren on the Islands who had fallen around me, in order that the work on which so much now appeared to depend might have been entrusted to some one better fitted to accomplish it. The heart seemed to keep repeating, "All these things are against thee."

Finding out at last the Rev. A. Buzacott, then retired, but formerly the successful and honoured representative of the

London Missionary Society on Rarotonga, considerable light was let in upon the mystery of my last week's experiences. He informed me that the highly esteemed friend, who had kindly been introducing me all round, was at that moment immersed in a keen Newspaper war with Presbyterians and Independents. He had published statements and changes of view, which charged them with being unscriptural in belief and practice. They, of course, were vigorously defending themselves. This made it painfully manifest that, in order to succeed, I must strike out a new course for myself, and one clear from all local entanglement.

Paying a fortnight in advance, I withdrew even from the lodging I had taken, and turned to the Lord more absolutely for guidance. He brought me into contact with good and generous-souled servants of His, the open-hearted Mr. and Mrs. Foss. Though entire strangers, they kindly invited me to be their guest while in Sydney, assuring me that I would meet with many Ministers and other Christians at their house who could help me in my work. God had opened the door ; I entered with a grateful heart ; they will not miss their recompense.

A letter and appeal had been already printed on behalf of our Mission. I now re-cast and reprinted it, adding a postscript, and appending my own name and new address. This was widely circulated among Ministers and others engaged in Christian work ; and by this means, and by letters in the Newspapers, I did everything in my power to make our Mission known. But one week had passed, and no response came. One Lord's Day had gone by, and no pulpit had been opened to me. I was perplexed beyond measure, how to get access to Congregations and Sabbath Schools ; though a Something deep in my soul assured me, that if once my lips were opened, the Word of the Lord would not return void.

On my second Sabbath in Sydney, I wandered out with a great yearning at heart to get telling my message to any soul that would listen. It was the afternoon ; and children were flocking into a Church that I passed. I followed them—that yearning growing stronger every moment. My God so ordered it, that I was guided thus to the Chalmers Presbyterian Church.

The Minister, the Rev. Mr. McSkimming, addressed the children. At the close I went up and pleaded with him to allow me ten minutes to speak to them. After a little hesitation, and having consulted together, they gave me fifteen minutes. Becoming deeply interested, the good man invited me to preach to his Congregation in the evening. This was duly intimated in the Sabbath School ; and thus my little boat was at last launched—surely by the hand of the dear Lord, with the help of His little children.

The kindly Minister, now very deeply interested, offered to spend the next day in introducing me to his clerical brethren. For his sake, I was most cordially received by them all, but especially by Dr. Dunmore Lang, who greatly helped me ; and now access was granted me to almost every Church and Sabbath School, both Presbyterian and Independent. In Sabbath Schools, I got a collection in connection with my address, and distributed, with the sanction of Superintendents, Collecting Cards amongst the children, to be returned through the teachers within a specified date. In Congregations, I received for the Mission the surplus over and above the ordinary collection when I preached on Sabbaths, and the full collection at all week-night meetings for which I could arrange.

I now appealed to a few of the most friendly Ministers to form themselves into an Honorary Committee of advice ; and, at my earnest request, they got J. Goodlet, Esq., an excellent elder, to become Honorary Treasurer, and to take charge of all funds raised for the Mission Ship. For the Public knew nothing of me ; but all knew my good Treasurer and these faithful Ministers, and had confidence in the work. They knew that every penny went direct to the Mission ; and they saw that my one object was to promote God's glory in the conversion of the Heathen. Our dear Lord Jesus thus opened up my way ; and now I had invitations from more Schools and Congregations than I knew how to overtake—the response in money being also gratifying beyond almost all expectation.

It was now that I began a little plan of interesting the children, that attracted them from the first, and has since had an amazing development. I made them shareholders in the new Mission Ship—each child receiving a printed form, in acknowledgment of the number of shares, at sixpence each, of which he was the owner. Thousands of these shares were taken out, were shown about amongst families, and were greatly prized. The Ship was to be their very own! They were to be a great Shipping Company for Jesus. In hundreds of homes, these receipt-forms have been preserved; and their owners, now in middle years, are training *their* children of to-day to give their pennies to support the white-winged Angel of the Seas, that bears the Gospel and the Missionary to the Heathen Isles.

Let no one think me ungrateful to my good Treasurer and his wife, to Dr. and Mrs. Moon, and to other dear friends who generously helped me, when I trace step by step how the Lord opened up my way. The Angel of His Presence went before me, and wonderfully moved His people to contribute in answer to my poor appeals. I had indeed to make all my own arrangements, and correspond regarding all engagements and details,—to me, always a slow and laborious writer, a very burdensome task. But it was all necessary in order to the fulfilment of the Lord's purposes; and, to one who realizes that he is a fellow-labourer with Jesus, every yoke that He lays on becomes easy and every burden light.

Having done all that could at that time be accomplished in New South Wales, and as rapidly as possible—my Committee gave me a Letter of Commendation to Victoria. But there I had no difficulty. The ministers had heard of our work in Sydney. They received me most cordially, and at my request formed themselves into a Committee of Advice. Our dear friend, James McBain, Esq., now Sir James, became Honorary Treasurer. All moneys from this Colony, raised by my pleading for the Ship, were entrusted to him; and, ultimately, the acknowledging of every individual sum cost much time and labour. Dr. Cairns, and many others now gone to their rest, along with two or three honoured Ministers yet living, formed my Committee. The Lord richly reward them all in that Day!

As in New South Wales, I made, chiefly by correspondence, all my own engagements, and arranged for Churches and Sabbath Schools as best I could. Few in the other Denomi-

nations of Victoria gave any help, but the Presbyterians rose
to our appeal as with one heart. God moved them by
one impulse; and Ministers, Superintendents, Teachers, and
Children heartily embraced the scheme as their own. I
addressed three or four meetings every Sabbath, and one or
more every week-day ; and thus travelled over the length and
breadth of Victoria, Tasmania, and South Australia. Wheresoever a few of the Lord's people could be gathered together,
thither I gladly went, and told the story of our Mission, setting
forth its needs and claims.

The contributions and collections were nearly all in very
small sums. I recall only one exception,—a gift of £250
from the late Hon. G. F. Angus, South Australia, whose heart
the Lord had touched. Yet gently and steadily the required
money began to come pouring in ; and my personal outlays
were reduced to a minimum by the hospitality of Christian
friends and their kindly conveying of me from place to place.
For all this I felt deeply grateful ; it saved money for the
Lord's work.

Each of my Treasurers, to whom all contributions were sent
direct, kept me duly posted as to sums received from time
to time. The progress made soon led on to the resolution
to aim at a Ship three times the size of that originally proposed.
We set apart the sum of £3,000 as necessary for it ; and I
vowed, in my solitude, that if God sent an additional £800
within a given time, that would be my Gideon's fleece, and
would warrant me in going home to Scotland to secure more
Missionaries for the Islands. By this time, I had heard of
the death of my dear fellow-labourers, Mrs. Mathieson on
Aneityum, and shortly thereafter Mr. Mathieson on Maré. I
alone north of Aneityum was now left to tell the story of the
planting of the Standard on Tanna—our Mission numbered
then only four agents in the field—and the thought arose,
Why keep a Mission Vessel for so few? The resolution was,
therefore, taken in God's Name to get more Missionaries too.
But this, as yet, was betwixt my own soul and the Lord.

The work was unceasingly prosecuted. Meetings were
urged upon me now from every quarter. Money flowed in
so freely that, at the close of my tour, the fund had risen to

£5,000, including special Donations of £300 for the support of Native Teachers. Many Sabbath Schools, and many ladies and gentlemen, had individually promised the sum of £5 yearly to keep a Native Teacher on one or other of the New Hebrides Islands. This happy custom prevails still, and is largely developed; the sum required being now £6 per annum at least—for which you may have your own personal representative toiling among the Heathen and telling them of Jesus.

Returning to Melbourne, the whole matter was laid before my Committee. I reported how God had blessed the undertaking, and what sums were now in the hands of the several Treasurers, indicating also what larger hopes and plans had been put into my soul. Dear Dr. Cairns rose and said, " Sir, it is of the Lord. This whole enterprise is of God, and not of us. Go home, and He will give you more Missionaries for the Islands." My ever-honoured friends, Dr. and Mrs. Inglis, had just returned to Melbourne from Britain, where they had been carrying the complete New Testament in Aneityumese through the press. Dr. Inglis was present at that meeting, and approved warmly of my going home for more Missionaries, especially as from want of time and opportunity he had not himself succeeded in getting any additions to our Missionary staff.

Melbourne held a Farewell meeting. The Governor, Sir Henry Barkley, took the chair. The Hall was crowded ; and the Governor's sympathetic utterances arrested public attention and deepened the interest in our Mission. The fact was emphasized that this work, lying at their very doors in the Pacific Seas, had peculiar claims on the heart and conscience of Australia.

Thence I hasted to Sydney, and reported myself also there. The New South Wales Committee gave their cordial approval to our larger plans. A Farewell was held there too ; and the Governor, Sir John Young, took the chair. The meeting was a great success. His presence, and his excellent speech, again helped to fix the eyes of all Australians on the peculiar claims of the New Hebrides. This was *their* work, more than that of any other people on the face of the Earth. The awakening of this consciousness, and intensifying it into a practical and burning faith, was a great and far-reaching achievement for Australia and for the Islanders. It is one of the purest joys of my life, that in this work I was honoured to have some share, along with many other dear servants of the Lord.

Of the money which I had raised, £3,000 were sent to Nova Scotia, to pay for the building of our new Mission Ship, the *Dayspring*. The Church which began the Mission on the New Hebrides was granted the honour of building our new Mission Ship. The remainder was set apart to pay for the outfit and passage of additional Missionaries for the field, and I was commissioned to return home to Scotland in quest of them. Dr. Inglis wrote, in vindication of this enterprise, to the friends whom he had just left, "From first to last, Mr. Paton's mission here has been a great success; and it has been followed up with such energy and promptitude in Nova Scotia, both in regard to the Ship and the Missionaries, that Mr. Paton's pledge to the Australian Churches has been fully redeemed. The hand of the Lord has been very visible in the whole movement from beginning to end, and we trust He has yet great blessing in store for the long and deeply-degraded Islanders."

Here let me turn aside from the current of Missionary toils, and record a few wayside incidents that marked some of my wanderings to and fro in connection with the Floating of the *Dayspring*. Travelling in the Colonies in 1862-63 was vastly less developed than it is to-day; and a few of my experiences then will, for many reasons, be not unwelcome to most readers of this book. Besides, these incidents, one and all, will be felt to have a vital connection with the main purpose of writing this Autobiography, namely, to show that the Finger of God is as visible still, to those who have eyes to see, as when the fire-cloud Pillar led His People through the wilderness.

Twenty-six years ago, the roads of Australia, except those in and around the principal towns, were mere tracks over unfenced plains and hills, and on many of them packhorses only could be used in slushy weather. During long journeys through the bush, the traveller could find his road only by following the deep notches, gashed by friendly precursors into the larger trees, and all pointing in one direction. If he lost his way, he had to struggle back to the last indented tree, and try to interpret more correctly its pilgrim notch. Experienced bush-travellers seldom miss the path ; yet many others, losing the track, have wandered round and round till they sank and died. For then it was easy to walk thirty or forty miles, and see neither a person nor a house. The more intelligent do sometimes guide their steps by sun, moon, and stars, or by glimpses of mountain peaks or natural features on the far and high horizon, or by the needle of the compass ; but the perils are not illusory, and occasionally the most experienced have miscalculated and perished.

An intelligent gentleman, a sheep farmer, who knew the country well, once kindly volunteered to lift me in an out-of-the-way place, and drive me to a meeting at his Station. Having a long spell before us, we started at mid-day in a buggy drawn by a pair of splendid horses, in the hope of reaching our destination before dusk. He turned into the usual bush-track through the forests, saying, " I know this road well ; and we must drive steadily, as we have not a moment to lose."

Our conversation became absorbingly interesting. After we had driven about three hours, he remarked, "We must soon emerge into the open plain."

I doubtfully replied, "Surely we cannot have turned back ! These trees and bushes are wonderfully like those we passed at starting."

He laughed, and made me feel rather vexed that I had spoken, when he said, "I am too old a hand in the bush for that ! I have gone this road many a time before."

But my courage immediately revived, for I got what appeared to me a glint of the roof of the Inn beyond the bush, from which we had started at noon, and I repeated, " I am certain we have wheeled, and are back at the beginning of our journey ; but there comes a Chinaman ; let us wait and inquire."

My dear friend learned, to his utter amazement, that he had erred. The bush-track was entered upon once more, and followed with painful care, as he murmured, half to himself, " Well, this beats all reckoning ! I could have staked my life that this was impossible."

Turning to me, he said, with manifest grief, "Our meeting is done for ! It will be midnight before we can arrive."

The sun was beginning to set, as we reached the thinly-timbered ground. Ere dusk fell, he took his bearings with the greatest possible care. Beyond the wood, a vast plain stretched before us, where neither fence nor house was visible, far as the eye could reach. He drove steadily towards a far-distant point, which was in the direction of his home. At last we struck upon the wire fence that bounded his property. The horses were now getting badly fagged ; and, in order to save them a long roundabout drive, he lifted and laid low a portion of the fence, led his horses cautiously over it, and, leaving it to be re-erected by a servant next day, he started direct for the Station. That seemed a long journey too ; but it was for him familiar ground ; and through amongst great patriarchal trees here and there, and safely past dangerous water-holes, we swung steadily on, reached his home in safety, and had a joyous welcome. The household had by this time got into great excitement over our non-appearance. The expected meeting had, of course, been abandoned hours ago ; and the people were all gone, wondering in their hearts "whereto this would grow ! "

At that time, in the depth of winter, the roads were often wrought into rivers of mire, and at many points almost impassable even for well-appointed conveyances. In connection therewith, I had one very perilous experience. I had to go from Clunes to a farm in the Learmouth district. The dear old Minister there, Mr. Downes, went with me to every place where a horse could be hired ; but the owners positively refused—they would sell, but they would not hire, for the conveyance would be broken, and the horse would never return alive ! Now, I was advertised to preach at Learmouth, and must somehow get over the nine miles that lay between. This would have been comparatively practicable, were it not that I carried with me an indispensable bag of " curios," and a heavy bundle of clubs, arrows, dresses, etc., from the Islands, wherewith to illustrate my lectures and enforce my appeals. No one could be hired to carry my luggage nor could I get it sent after me by coach on that particular way. Therefore, seeing no alternative opening up my path, I committed myself once more to the Lord, as in harder trials before, shouldered my bundle of clubs, lifted my heavy bag, and started off on foot. They urged me fervently to desist; but I heard a voice repeating, " As thy days, so shall thy strength be." There came back to me also the old adage that had in youthful difficulties spurred me on, " Where there's a will, there's a way." And I thought that, with these two in his heart, a Scotchman and a Christian would not be easily·beaten.

When I found the road wrought into mire, and dangerous, or impassable, I climbed the fence, and waded along in the ploughed fields—though they were nearly as bad. My bundle was changed from shoulder to shoulder, and my bag from hand to hand, till I became thoroughly tired of both. Pressing on, however, I arrived at a wayside Public House, where several roads met, and there I inquired the way to Learmouth, and how far it was. The Innkeeper, pointing, answered,—

" This is the road. If you are on horseback, it might be three to four miles just now, as your horse is able to take it. If you are in a conveyance, with a good horse, it might be six miles. And if you are walking, it might be eight or ten miles, or even more."

I said, " I am walking. How many English miles is it to Mr. Baird's farm ? "

He laughingly replied, " You will find it a long way indeed this dark night, considering the state of the road, fenced in on both sides so that you cannot get off."

I passed on, leaving my Job's comforter ; but a surly watchdog got upon my track, and I had much difficulty in keeping it from biting me. Its attacks, renewed upon me again and again, had one good effect,—they stirred up my spirits and made me hasten on.

Having persevered along the Learmouth road, I next met a company of men hastening on with a bundle of ropes. They were on their way to relieve a poor bullock, which by this time had almost disappeared, sinking in the mire on the public highway ! They kindly pointed me to a light, visible through the dusk. That was the farm at which I was to stay, and they advised me to clear the fence, and make straight for that light, as the way was good.

With thankful heart, I did so. The light was soon lost to me, but I walked steadily on in the direction thereof, to the best of my judgment. Immediately I began to feel the ground all floating under me. Then at every step I took, or tried to take, I sank deeper and deeper, till at last I durst not move either backward or forward. I was floundering in a deadly swamp. I called out again and again, and "coo-eed" with all my strength, but there came no reply. It grew extremely dark, while I kept praying to God for deliverance. About midnight, I heard two men conversing, apparently at no very great distance. I began "coo-eeing" again, but my strength was failing. Fortunately, the night was perfectly calm. The conversation ceased for a while; but I kept on crying for help. At length, I heard one voice remark to the other, "Some one is in the swamp." And then a question came, "Who's there?"

I answered, "A stranger. Oh, do help me!"

Again a voice came through the darkness, "How did you get in there?"

And I feebly replied, "I have lost my way."

I heard the one say to the other, "I will go and get him out, whoever he may be. We must not leave him there; he'll be dead before the morning. As you pass by our door, tell my wife that I'm helping some poor creature out of the swamp, and will be home immediately."

He kept calling to me, and I answering his call through the darkness, till, not without peril, he managed to reach and aid me. Once I was safely dragged out, he got my bag in his hand and slung my clubs on his shoulder, and in a very short time landed me at the farm, dripping and dirty and cold. Had God not sent that man to save me, I must have perished there, as many others have similarly perished before. The farmer's wife heartily welcomed me and kindly ministered to all my needs. Though not yet gone to rest, they had given up all hope of seeing me. I heard the kind servant say to his mistress, "I don't know where he came from, or how far he has carried his bundles; but I got him stuck fast in the swamp, and my shoulder is already sore from carrying his clubs ! "

A cup of warm tea restored me. The Lord gave me a sound and blessed sleep. I rose next morning wonderfully refreshed, though arms and shoulders were rather sore with the burdens of yesterday. I conducted three Services, and told the story of my Mission, not without comfort and blessing; and with gratifying results in money. The people gave liberally to the work.

One day, after this, I was driving a long distance on the outside of a crowded coach. A grave and sensible-looking Scotchman sat next me. He had inquiringly marked me reading in silence, while all around were conversing on matters of common interest. At last, he queried, " Are you a Minister ? " I answered, " Yes."

" Where is your Church ? "

" I have no Church."

" Where are you placed ? "

" I am not placed in any charge now."

" Where is your home ? "

" I have no home."

" Where have you come from ? '

" The South Sea Islands."

" What are you doing in Australia ? "

" Pleading the cause of the Mission.'

" Are you a Presbyterian ? "

" I am."

Having gone through this Catechism to his satisfaction, a most interesting and profitable conversation followed. When the time came for the payment of fares, nothing would please but that I must allow him to pay for me—some twenty-two shillings—which he did with all his heart, protesting, " A joy to me, Sir, a great joy ; I honour you for your work's sake ! "

Thereafter, a Schoolmaster drove me a long distance across the country to Violet Town, where for the night we had to stay at an Inn. We had a taste of what Australian life really was, when the land was being broken in. A company of wild and reckless men were carousing there at the time, and our arrival was the signal for an outbreak of malicious mischief.

A powerful fellow, who turned out to be a young Medical, rushed upon me as I left the conveyance, seized me by the throat, and shook me roughly, shouting, "A parson, a parson! I will do for the parson!"

Others with great difficulty relieved me from his grips, and dragged him away, cursing as if at his mortal enemy.

After tea, we got into the only bedroom in the house, available for two. The Teacher and I locked ourselves in and barricaded the door, hearing in the next room a large party of drunken men gambling and roaring over their cards. By-and-bye they quarrelled and fought; they smashed in and out of their room, and seemed to be murdering each other; every moment we expected our door to come crashing in, as they were thrown or lurched against it. Their very language made us tremble. One man in particular seemed to be badly abused; he shouted that they were robbing him of his money; and he groaned and cried for protection, all in vain. We spent a sleepless and most miserable night. At four in the morning I arose, and was glad to get away by the early coach. My friend also left in his own conveyance, and reached his home in safety. At that period, it was not only painful but dangerous for any decent traveller to stay at many of these wayside Inns, in the new and rough country. Every man lived and acted just as he pleased, doing that which was right in his own eyes; and Might was Right.

After this, I made a Mission tour, in a somewhat mixed and original fashion, right across the Colony of Victoria, from Albury in New South Wales to Mount Gambier in South Australia. I conducted Mission Services almost every day, and three or more every Sabbath, besides visiting all Sunday Schools that could be touched on the way. When I reached a gold-digging or township, where I had been unable to get any one to announce a meeting, the first thing I did on arriving was to secure some Church or Hall, and, failing that, to fix on some suitable spot in the open air. Then, I was always able to hire some one to go round with the bell, and announce the meeting. Few will believe how large were the audiences in this way gathered together, and how very substantial was the help that thereby came to the Mission fund. Besides, I know that much good was done to many of those addressed ; for I have always, to this hour, combined the Evangelist's appeal with the Missionary's story, in all public addresses, whether on Sabbath or other days. I tried to bring every soul to feel personal duty and responsibility to the Lord Jesus, for I knew that then they would rightly understand the claims of the Heathen.

Wheresoever railway, steamboat, and coach were available, I always used them ; but failing these, I hired, or was obliged to friends of Missions for driving me from place to place. On this tour, having reached a certain place, from which my way lay for many miles across the country, where there was no public conveyance, I walked to the nearest squatter's Station and frankly informed the owner how I was situated ; that I could not hire, and that I would like to stay at his house all night, if he would kindly send me on in the morning by any sort of trap to the next Station on my list. He happened to be a good Christian and a Presbyterian, and gave me a right cordial welcome. A meeting of his servants was called, which I had the pleasure of addressing. Next morning, he gave me £20, and sent me forward with his own conveyance, telling me to retain it all day, if necessary.

On reaching the next squatter's Station, I found the master also at home, and said, " I am a Missionary from the South Sea Islands. I am crossing Victoria to plead the cause of the Mission. I would like to rest here for an hour or two. Could you kindly send me on to the next Station by your conveyance ? If not, I am to keep the last squatter s buggy, until I reach it."

Looking with a queer smile at me, he replied, " You propose a rather novel condition on which to rest at my house ! My horses are so employed to-day, I fear that I may have difficulty in sending you on. But come in ; both you and your horses need rest ; and my wife will be glad to see you."

I immediately discovered that the good lady came from Glasgow, from a street in which I had lodged when a student at the Free Normal College. I even knew some of her friends. All the places of her youthful associations were equally familiar to me. We launched out into deeply-interesting conversation, which finally led up, of course, to the story of our Mission.

The gentleman, by this time, had so far been won, that he slipped out and sent my conveyance and horses back to their owner, and ordered his own to be ready to take me to the next Station, or, if need be, to the next again. At parting, the lady said to her husband, "The Missionary has asked no money, though he sees we have been deeply interested; yet clearly that is the object of his tour. He is the first Missionary from the Heathen that ever visited us here; and you must contribute something to his Mission fund."

I thanked her, explaining, "I never ask money directly from any person for the Lord's work. My part is done when I have told my story and shown the needs of the Heathen and the claims of Christ; but I gratefully receive all that the Lord moves His people to give for the Mission."

Her husband replied, rather sharply, "You know I don't keep money here." To which she retorted with ready tact and with a resistless smile, "But you keep a cheque book; and your cheque is as good as gold! This is the first donation we ever gave to such a cause, and let it be a good one." He made it indeed handsome, and I went on my way, thanking them very sincerely, and thanking God.

At the next Station, the owner turned out to be a gruff Irishman, forbidding and insolent. Stating my case to him as to the others, he shouted at me, "Go on! I don't want to be troubled with the loikes o' you here."

I answered, "I am sorry if my coming troubles you; but I wish you every blessing in Christ Jesus. Good-bye!"

As we drove off, he kept growling after us. On leaving his door, I heard a lady calling to him from the window, "Don't let that Missionary go away! Make haste and call him back. I want the children to see the idols and the South Sea curios."

At first he drowned her appeal in his own shoutings. But she must have persisted effectually; for shortly we heard him "coo-eeing," and stopped. When he came up to us, he explained, "That lady in my house heard you speaking in Melbourne. The ladies and children are very anxious to see your idols, dresses, and weapons. Will you please come back?"

We did so. I spent fifteen minutes or so, giving them

information about the Natives and our Mission. As I left, our boisterous friend handed me a cheque for £5, and wished me great success !

The next Station at which we arrived was one of the largest of all. It happened to be a sort of pay-day, and men were assembled from all parts of the "run," and were to remain there over night. The squatter and his family were from home ; but Mr. Todd, the overseer, being a good Christian and a Scotchman, was glad to receive us, arranged to hold a meeting that evening in the men's hut, and promised to set me forward on my journey next day. The meeting was very enthusiastic ; and they subscribed £20 to the Mission—every man being determined to have so many shares in the new Mission Ship. With earnest personal dealing, I urged the claims of the Lord Jesus upon all who were present, seeking the salvation of every hearer. I ever found even the rough digger, and the lowest of the hands about far-away Stations, most attentive and perfectly respectful.

To the honour of Australia I must here record, that anything like uncivil treatment was a rare exception in all my travels. Sometimes, indeed, I have suspected that people were acting as if to say, Let us treat him kindly, do as little for his cause as we can, and get rid of him as quickly as possible ! But, as a rule, almost without an exception, I have met with remarkable kindness, hospitality, and help from all the Ministers and people of Australia. Scarcely ever, at any place visited, was I without one or more invitations to be guest of some of the Lord's people ; and I was there treated as a dear friend of the family, rather than a passing stranger. Colonials, indeed, are proverbial for the open door and the generous hand to pilgrims by the way. May the Divine Master grant them evermore of His own Spirit, with His ever-enriching blessings on their Souls and in their homes !

Disappointments and successes were strangely intermingled. Once I travelled a very long way to conduct a meeting at a certain township. I had written pleading with the Minister to make due intimation ; but he had informed no person of my intended visit, neither had he written to me, which he could easily have done. When I arrived, he met me on horseback, said, "I have arranged no meeting here," and instantly rode away. Only two coaches weekly passed that way, so I had to remain there at a Public House for the next three days. Drinking and noise, of course, abounded; but they kindly gave me a small back room, as far away as possible, and looking out into a quiet garden. It was to cost me thirteen shillings and sixpence per day; and there I sat patiently and somewhat sadly working up my heavy correspondence. The district was rich, and I knew that there were pious as well as wealthy people there, who could have been interested in our Mission and would have helped me,— hence my keen disappointment.

On the afternoon of the second day, I saw a beautiful garden from my bedroom window, wherein a considerable party of ladies, gentlemen, and handsomely-dressed children were disporting in happy amusements. Thinking that they were growing tired, and might not object to a little variety, I summoned courage to walk up and ask for the gentleman of the house. I told him that I was a Missionary from the South Sea Islands and had come here to address a meeting, and how I had been disappointed; that I was staying at the Public House till the next Mail passed inland; and that I had there some Heathen idols, clubs, dresses, and "curios," which perhaps the ladies and children would like to see, and to hear a little about the Lord's work on the Islands. I explained also that I asked no money and received no reward, but only wished an opportunity of interesting them in this work of God. He consulted the company. They were eager to see what I had got, and to hear what I had to say.

On returning with my bundle of "curios," I found them all arranged under the verandah, and a chair placed in front for me and my articles of mystery. They eagerly examined everything, and listened to my description of its uses. I gave them a short account of the Islanders, and of our efforts to carry to them the Gospel of Jesus. I pressed on them the blessings and the advantages of the great Redemption, and the peace and joy of living for and walking daily with God here, in the assured hope of eternal glory with Him hereafter; and I urged one and all to love and serve the Lord Jesus.

Having stated how I came to be there, and how I had been disappointed, knowing that many would have sympathized with and helped my Mission if only I could have addressed them, I intimated that I would not ask any contributions, but I would leave a few of the Collecting Cards for the new Mission Ship ; and if, after what they had heard, they chose to do anything, all money was to be sent to the Treasurer at Melbourne.

Some offered me donations, but I declined, saying, " I am a stranger to you all. The Minister has cast suspicion on me by refusing to intimate any meeting. In the circumstances, I can in this case receive nothing. But I will rejoice if you all do whatever you can for the precious work of our Lord Jesus among the Heathen, and send it on to Melbourne, whence every penny will be acknowledged in due time."

Many took cards and became eager collectors for the Mission ; and I knew, ere I returned to the Public House that day, that the Lord's finger was here also, and that the trial of disappointment through the Minister was being already overruled for good.

This was even more remarkably manifested on the evening of that same day, and within the said Public House itself. A very large number of men were assembled there, some at tea, and others drinking noisily, on their return from a great cattle market and show. I tried to get into conversation with some of the quieter spirits, and produced and explained to them the idols, clubs, and dresses, till nearly all crowded eagerly around me. Then I told them the story of our Mission, in process of which I managed to urge the Gospel message on their own hearts also ; and invited them to ask questions at the close. The rough fellows became wonderfully interested. Several took Collecting Cards for the *Dayspring* fund. And the publican and his wife were thereafter very kind, declining to take anything from me either for bed or meals—another gleam out of the darkness !

It is my conviction that in these ways the Lord helped me to gain as much, if not more, for the Mission than all that was lost through lack of a meeting ; and it is certain that I thus had opportunity of speaking of sin and salvation, and of setting forth the claims of Jesus, before many souls that never could have been reached through any ordinary Congregation. Again I learned to praise the Lord in all circumstances—" Bless the Lord *at all times*, O my soul."

A lively and memorable extemporized meeting on this tour is associated in memory with one of my dearest friends. The district was very remote. He, the squatter, and his beloved wife were sterling Christians, and have been ever since warmly devoted to me. On my arrival, he invited the people from all the surrounding Stations, as well as his own numerous servants, to hear the story of our Mission. Next day he volunteered to drive me a long distance over the plains of St. Arnaud, his dear wife accompanying us. At that time there were few fences in such districts in Australia. The drive was long, but the day had been lovely, and the fellowship was so sweet that it still shines a sunny spot in the fields of memory.

Having reached our destination about seven o'clock, he ordered tea at the Inn for the whole party ; and we sallied out meantime and took the only Hall in the place, for an extemporized meeting to be held that evening at eight o'clock. I then hired a man to go through the township with a bell, announcing the same ; while I myself went up one side of the main street, and my friend up the other, inviting all who would listen to us to attend the Mission meeting, where South Sea Island idols, weapons, and dresses would be exhibited, and stories of the Natives told.

Running back for a hurried cup of tea, I then hasted to the Hall, and found it crowded to excess with rough and boisterous diggers. The hour struck as I was getting my articles arranged and spread out upon the table, and they began shouting, "Where's the Missionary ?"—"Another hoax !"—indicating that they were not unwilling for a row. I learned that, only a few nights ago, a so-called Professor had advertised a lecture, lifted entrance money till the Hall was crowded, and then quietly slipped off the scene. In our case, though there was no charge, they seemed disposed to gratify themselves by some sort of promiscuous revenge.

Amidst the noisy chaff and rising uproar, I stepped up on the table, and said, "Gentlemen, I am the Missionary. If you will now be silent, the lecture will proceed. According to my usual custom, let us open the meeting with prayer."

The hush that fell was such a contrast to the preceding hubbub, that I heard my heart throbbing aloud! Then they listened to me for an hour, in perfect silence and with ever-increasing interest. At the close I intimated that I asked no collection ; but if, after what they had heard, they would take a Collecting Card for the new Mission Ship, and send any contributions to the Treasurer at Melbourne, I would praise God for sending me amongst them. Many were heartily taken, and doubtless some souls felt the " constraining love " who had till then been living without God. Next morning, I mounted the Mail Coach, and started on a three days' run, while my dear friend returned safely to his home.

It was really very seldom, however, that I found myself thus driven to extemporize my meetings. Some Christian friend, if not the Minister of the place, arranged all, and advertised my coming. And the Lord greatly helped me in carrying on the burdensome correspondence thereanent, and keeping it always three weeks ahead.

I travelled thus over the length and breadth of New South Wales, Victoria, Tasmania, and South Australia, telling the story of our Mission, and delivering the Lord's message, not only in great centres of population, but in almost every smaller township ; and not only thereby Floating the *Dayspring*, but sowing, by God's help, seeds of far-reaching blessing, whose fruits will ripen through the years to come. Blessed be His holy Name !

And here let me recall what happened at Penola, a border town between Victoria and South Australia. In the flooded, swampy country and bad bush-track between it and Mount Gambier the roads were impassable, and the coach broke down. The Mail was sent forward on horseback. I had waited for nearly a week, in the hope of getting to the Mount for the Sabbath Services that had been arranged. At length I succeeded in engaging a man, with a pair of horses and a light spring cart, to drive me there for £4 10s. He declared the horses to be fresh, and able for the journey. We started about mid-day ; but, ere many miles had been covered, he began to whip them severely. The horses looked utterly exhausted, and the truth at once flashed on me. I was pleading with him not to flog them so, when, on reaching a higher piece of ground, he pulled up, and said :

" I am ashamed to tell you that my horses are done ! They had just come off a journey of forty miles when we started. I have told you a lie ; but I hope you will forgive me. I was sorely in need of the hire, and I deceived you. There is no help for it now. We must camp out for the night on this dry ground. I do hope you won't catch cold. You shall sleep in the cart ; I can rest under it. I will set fire to this large fallen tree to keep us warm. I have brought a loaf of bread, and a billy (= a bushman's can for boiling water). We can have some tea ; and, rest assured, I shall land you there in time for the Sabbath Morning Service."

So saying, while I listened dumbfounded, he turned aside, unyoked the horses, " hobbled " them, and let them go upon the grass. He made the black tea which bushmen drink, and appeared to enjoy it. The conveyance was drawn near to that burning tree, and I got located into it, and was expected to rest. I sat there wide-awake during weary hours ! Time passed at a dreadfully slow pace, and sleep refused to come near me. Kangaroos, wallabies, with other nameless wild creatures and screaming birds, kept loud festival all around ; and mosquitoes tortured me, apparently in thousands. Towards midnight I saw a light in the distant bush, and, awaking my companion, inquired if he could say what it might be. He had heard that a Wesleyan farmer from near Adelaide had come into that region to take up a sheep and cattle Station there, as in that swampy country the grass was excellent. It might be their light, or it might be that of some benighted party camping out like ourselves. He assured me that he could find our way to that light, and back again to our burning tree, and, partly to pass the time, I resolved to try.

We found the Wesleyan farmer there, living in a large bush-shed, surrounded by a still larger enclosure, wherein horses, cattle, and sheep were kept for the night all together upon the dry ground, awaiting the erection of houses and fencing, with which they were busily engaged. Unseemly as was our hour of call, the dogs had loudly announced our approach, and we got a cordial greeting, being immediately surrounded by all the family. They eagerly listened to everything about the Mission. We had worship together. They gave us a hearty tea, besides a loaf of bread and a jug of milk for our breakfast next morning—the jug to be left by us beside the burning tree, whither they could send for it after we departed. Their regrets were genuine and profuse that their circumstances prevented them from offering us a bed, but we exceedingly enjoyed our intercourse with them, and felt them to be dear Christian friends. How delightful and responsive is the communion of those who love he Lord Jesus, wherever they meet; and oh, what will it be in Glory, when, made like unto the Saviour, we shall " see Him as He is "! At daybreak we were off again on our weary journey, and reached the destination safely and in good time. A hearty welcome awaited us from dear Mr. and Mrs. Caldwell, who had long since despaired of my appearing. All the Services were largely attended, and the Lord led the people to take a deep interest in our Mission, many generous and devoted friends to it arising there, where the Minister and his wife struck the right key-note, and were so highly and justly esteemed.

Returning to Penola, we found that the Mail Coach would not try to run for some time. I had to reconcile myself to wait there for several days. Every day I beheld a certain man staggering about at all hours under the influence of drink. I learned that he had been a wealthy and open-handed squatter, had lost everything, had recently laid his wife in the grave, and now, followed about by his three little girls, was trying to drown his sorrows in whisky. Overcome with irresistible pity, I followed him day after day, and again and again remonstrated with him on the madness of his conduct, especially appeali ng to him for his children's sake. At last he turned upon me, with an earnest gaze, and said, "If you take the pledge with me, God helping me, I will keep it for life."

We entered the house together, signed a pledge, and solemnly invoked God in prayer to enable us to keep it till death. For his sake, I renewed the vow of my youthful days and he, by my sympathy, took this vow for the fi rst time, and.

by God's help, he kept it. He left Penola next day, shaking off old associates, and started a humble business where he had once owned much of the land. He became a Christian out and out, and has been an Elder of the Church for many years. I have often been laughed at by whisky drinkers, and also by so-called "temperance" men, for being a Total Abstainer; but even one case like that (and, thank God, there are many) is an eternal reward, and can sustain us to smile down all ridicule.

Dear reader, can you measure the effect of the example which you are setting? Are you to-day amongst the ranks of the moderate drinkers? Remember that from that class all drunkards have come; and ask yourself whether you would not act more nobly and unselfishly to abstain, for the interests of our common Humanity, for loyalty to our Lord Jesus Christ, and for the hope of leading a pure and unstained life yourself, as well as helping others to do so, whom Jesus died to save?

The crowning adventure of my tour came about in the following manner. I was advertised to conduct Services at Narracoort on Sabbath, and at a Station on the way on Saturday evening. But how to get from Penola was a terrible perplexity. On Saturday morning, however, a young lady offered me, out of gratitude for blessings received, the use of her riding horse for the journey. "Garibaldi" was his name; and, though bred for a race-horse, I was assured that if I kept him firmly in hand, he would easily carry me over the two-and-twenty miles. He was to be left at the journey's end, and the lady herself would fetch him back. I shrank from the undertaking, knowing little of horses, and having vague recollections of being dreadfully punished for more than a week after my last and almost only ride. But every one in that country is quite at ease on the back of a horse. They saw no risk; and, as there appeared no other way of getting there to fulfil my engagements, I, for my part, began to think that God had unexpectedly provided the means, and that He would carry me safely through.

I accepted the lady's kind offer, and started on my pilgrimage. A friend showed me the road, and gave me ample directions. In the bush, I was to keep my eye on the notches in the trees, and follow them. He agreed kindly to bring my luggage to the Station, and leave it there for me by-and-bye. After I had walked very quietly for some distance, three gentlemen on horseback overtook me. We entered into conversation. They inquired how far I was going, and advised me to sit a little " freer " in the saddle, as it would be so much easier for me. They seemed greatly amused at my awkward riding ! Dark clouds were now gathering ahead, and the atmosphere prophesied a severe storm ; therefore they urged that I should ride a little faster, as they, for a considerable distance, could guide me on the right way. I explained to them my plight through inexperience, said that I could only creep on slowly with safety, and bade them Good-bye. As the sky was getting darker every minute, they consented, wishing me a safe journey, and started off at a smart pace.

I struggled to hold in my horse ; but seizing the bit with his teeth, laying back his ears, and stretching out his eager neck, he manifestly felt that his honour was at stake ; and in less time than I take to write it, the three friends cleared a way for us, and he tore past them all at an appalling speed. They tried for a time to keep within reach of us, but that sound only put fire into his blood ; and in an incredibly short time I heard them not ; nor, from the moment that he bore me swinging past them, durst I turn my head by one inch to look for them again. In vain I tried to hold him in ; he tore on, with what appeared to me the speed of the wind. Then the thunderstorm broke around us, with flash of lightning and flood of rain, and at every fresh peal my " Garibaldi " dashed more wildly onward.

To me, it was a vast surprise to discover that I could sit more easily on this wild flying thing, than when at a canter or a trot. At every turn I expected that he would dash himself and me against the great forest trees ; but instinct rather than my hand guided him miraculously. Sometimes I had a glimpse of the road, but as for the " notches," I never saw one of them ; we passed them with lightning speed. Indeed, I durst not lift my eyes for one moment from watching the horse's head and the trees on our track. My high-crowned hat was now drenched, and battered out of shape ; for whenever we came to a rather clear space, I seized the chance and gave it another knock down over my head. I was spattered and covered with mud and mire.

Crash, crash, went the thunder, and on, on, went " Garibaldi " through the gloom of the forest, emerging at length upon a clearer ground with a more visible pathway. Reaching the top of the slope, a large house stood out far in front of us to the left; and the horse had apparently determined to make straight for that, as if it were his home. He skirted along the hill, and took the track as his own familiar ground, all my effort to hold him in or guide him having no more effect than that of a child. By this time, I suspect, I really had lost all power. " Garibaldi " had been at that house, probably, frequently before; he knew those stables; and my fate seemed to be instant death against door or wall.

Some members of the family, on the outlook for the Missionary, saw us come tearing along as if mad or drunk; and now all rushed to the verandah, expecting some dread catastrophe. A tall and stout young groom, amazed at our wild career, throwing wide open the gate, seized the bridle at great risk to himself, and ran full speed, yet holding back with all his might, and shouting at me to do the same. We succeeded—" Garibaldi " having probably attained his purpose —in bringing him to a halt within a few paces of the door. Staring at me with open mouth, the man exclaimed, " I have saved your life. What madness to ride like that ! " Thanking him, though I could scarcely by this time articulate a word, I told him that the horse had run away, and that I had lost all control.

Truly I was in a sorry plight, drenched, covered with mud, and my hat battered down over my eyes ; little wonder they thought me drunk or mad ! Finally, as if to confirm every suspicion, and amuse them all,—for master, mistress, governess, and children now looked on from the verandah,—when I was helped off the horse, I could not stand on my feet ! My head still went rushing on in the race; I staggered, and down I tumbled into the mud, feeling chagrin and mortification ; yet there I had to sit for some time, before I recovered myself, so as either to rise or to speak a word. When I did get to my feet, I had to stand holding by the verandah for some time, my head still rushing on in the race. At length the master said, " Will you not come in ? "

I knew that he was treating me for a drunken man ; and the giddiness was so dreadful still, that my attempts at speech seemed more drunken than even my gait.

As soon as I could stand, I went into the house, and drew near to an excellent fire in my dripping clothes. The squatter sat opposite me in silence, reading the newspapers, and taking a look at me now and again over his spectacles. By-and-bye he remarked, " Wouldn't it be worth while to change your clothes ? "

Speech was now returning to me. I replied, "Yes, but my bag is coming on in the cart, and may not be here to-night."

He began to relent. He took me into a room, and laid out for me a suit of his own. I being then very slender, and he a big-framed farmer, my new dress, though greatly adding to my comfort, enhanced the singularity of my appearance !

Returning to him, washed and dressed, I inquired if he had arranged for a meeting ? My tongue, I fear, was still unsteady, for the squatter looked at me rather reproachfully, and said, " Do you really consider yourself fit to appear before a meeting to-night ? "

I assured him that he was quite wrong in his suspicions, that I was a life-long Abstainer, and that my nerves had been so unhinged by the terrible ride and runaway horse. He smiled rather suggestively, and said we would see how I felt after tea.

We went to the table. All that had occurred was now consummated by my appearing in the lusty farmer's clothes ; and the lady and other friends had infinite difficulty in keeping their amusement within decent bounds. I again took speech in hand, but I suspect my words had still the thickness of the tippler's utterance, for they seemed not to carry much conviction. " Dear friends, I quite understand your feelings ; appearances are so strangely against me. But I am not drunken, as ye suppose. I have tasted no intoxicating drink, I am a life-long Total Abstainer ! "

This fairly broke down their reserve. They laughed aloud,

looking at each other and at me, as if to say, " Man, you're drunk at this very moment."

Before tea was over they appeared, however, to begin to entertain the idea that I *might* address the meeting ; and so I was informed of the arrangements that had been made. At the meeting, my incredulous friends became very deeply interested. Manifestly their better thoughts were gaining the ascendency. And they heaped thereafter every kindness upon me, as if to make amends for harder suspicions.

Next morning the master drove me about ten miles further on to the Church. A groom rode the race-horse, who took no scathe from his thundering gallop of the day before. It left deeper traces upon me. I got through the Services, however, and with good returns for the Mission. Twice since, on my Mission tours, I have found myself at that same memorable house ; and on each occasion, a large company of friends were regaled by the good lady there with very comical descriptions of my first arrival at her door.

CHAPTER II.

THE AUSTRALIAN ABORIGINES.

A.D. 1863. ÆT. 39.

A Fire-Water Festival.—At Tea with the Aborigines.—"Black Fellow all Gone!"—The Poison-Gift and Civilization.—The "Scattering" of the Blacks.—The "Brute-in-human-shape" Theory.—The Testimony of Nora.—Nathaniel Pepper and their "Gods."—Smooth Stone Idols.—Rites and Ceremonies.—"Too much Devil-Devil."—The Quest for Idols.—Visit to Nora in the Camp.—Independent Testimonies.—Nora's own Letters.—The Aborigines in Settlements.

DETAINED for nearly a week at Balmoral by the breakdown of the coach on these dreadful roads, I telegraphed to Hamilton for a conveyance; and the Superintendent of the Sunday School, dear Mr. Laidlaw, volunteered, in order to reduce expenses, to spend one day of his precious time coming for me, and another driving me down. While awaiting him, I came into painful and memorable contact with the Aborigines of Australia. The Publicans had organized a day of sports, horse-racing, and circus exhibitions. Immense crowds assembled, and, amongst the rest, tribe after tribe of the Aborigines from all the surrounding country. Despite the law prohibiting the giving of strong drinks to these poor creatures, foolish and unprincipled dealers supplied them with the same, and the very blankets which the Government had given them were freely exchanged for the fire-water which kindled them to madness.

Next day was Sabbath. The morning was hideous with the yells of the fighting Savages. They tore about on the Common in front of the Church, leading gentlemen having tried in vain to quiet them, and their wild voices without jarred upon the Morning Service. About two o'clock, I tried to get into conversation with them. I appealed to them whether they were not all tired and hungry? They replied that they had had no food all that day; they had fought since the morning! I said, " I love you, black fellows. I go Missionary black fellows far away. I love you, want you rest, get food. Come all of you, rest, sit round me, and we will talk, till the *jins* (= women) get ready tea. They boil water, I take tea with you, and then you will be strong!"

By broken English and by many symbols, I won their ear. They produced tea and *damper*, *i.e.*, a rather forbidding-looking bread, without yeast, baked on the coals. Their wives hasted to boil water. I kept incessantly talking, to interest them, and told them how Jesus, God's dear Son, came and died to make them happy, and how He grieved to see them beating and fighting and killing each other.

When the tea was ready, we squatted on the green grass, their tins were filled, the " damper " was broken into lumps, and I asked the blessing of God on the meal. To me it was unpleasant eating! Many of them looked strong and healthy ; but not a few were weak and dying creatures. The strong, devouring all they could get, urged me to be done, and let them finish their fighting, eager for the fray. But having gained their confidence, I prayed with them, and thereafter said, " Now, before I leave, I will ask of you to do one thing for my sake, which you can all easily do."

With one voice they replied, "Yes, we all do whatever you say."

I got their leaders to promise to me one by one. I then said, " Now you have got your tea ; and I ask every man and boy among you to lie down in the bush and take a sleep, and your wives will sit by and watch over your safety ! "

In glum silence, their war weapons still grasped in their hands, they stood looking intently at me, doubting whether I could be in earnest. I urged them, " You all promised to do what I asked. If you break your promise, these white men will laugh at me, and say that black fellows only lie and deceive. Let them see that you can be trusted. I wait here till I see you all asleep."

One said that his head was cut, and he must have revenge before he could lie down. Others filed past showing their wounds, and declaring that it was too bad to request them to go to sleep. I praised them as far as I could, but urged them for once to be men and to keep their word. Finally they all agreed to lie down, I waiting till the last man had disappeared ; and, being doubly exhausted with the debauch and the fighting, they were soon all fast asleep. I prayed that the blessed Sleep might lull their savage passions.

Before daylight next morning, the Minister and I were hastening to the scene to prevent further fighting ; but as the sun was rising we saw the last tribe of the distant Natives disappearing over the brow of a hill. A small party belonging to the district alone remained. They shouted to us, " Black fellow all gone ! No more fight. You too much like black fellow ! "

For three days afterwards I had still to linger there ; and if their dogs ran or barked at me, the women chased them with sticks and stones, and protected me. One little touch of kindness and sympathy had unlocked their darkened hearts.

The Aborigines of Australia have been regarded as perhaps the most degraded portion of the human race, at least in the Southern Hemisphere. Like the Papuans of our Islands, they rank betwixt Malay and Negro in colour and appearance. Their hair, coarse, black, curly, but not woolly ; eyes, dark and yellowish, with very heavy eyebrows ; nose flat, with hole bored through septum, in which ornament is hung ; small chin, thick lips, large mouth, and lustrous teeth ; high cheek bones, with sunken eyes and well-developed brow. Like all Savages in their natural state, they were nearly nude, and altogether filthy, and wretched ; especially in winter, when covered with kangaroo and opossum skins, which they hung around themselves loosely by day, and under which they slept at night. They sometimes daubed their bodies all over with paint, mud, charcoal, or ashes. Their women are generally of a slender build. All these features and notes are true of many of our South Sea Islanders too ; but they, again, are decidedly of a higher type. On many of the Islands, faces, though dark, are as pleasant and as well formed as amongst Europeans. Besides, the Islanders are not nomadic ; they live in settled villages, and cultivate the land for their support.

Having read very strong statements for and against the Aborigines, in my many journeys twenty-four years ago I resolved to embrace every opportunity of learning their customs and beliefs directly from themselves. I have also seen their disgusting "Corrobbarees," and know by facts how demoralizing these Heathen dances are. I know also what strong drink has done amongst them.

Who wonders that the *dark* races melt away before the *whites ?* The pioneers of Civilization *will* carry with them this demon of strong drink, the fruitful parent of every other vice. The black people drink, and become unmanageable ; and through the white man's own poison-gift an excuse is found for sweeping the poor creatures off the face of the earth. Marsden's writings show how our Australian blacks are destroyed. But I have myself been on the track of such butcheries again and again. A Victorian lady told me the following incident. She heard a child's pitiful cry in the bush. On tracing it, she found a little girl weeping over her younger brother. She said, " The white men poisoned our father and mother. They threaten to shoot me, so that I dare not go near them. I am here, weeping over my brother till we die ! "

The compassionate lady promised to be a mother to the little sufferers, and to protect them. They instantly clung to her, and have proved themselves to be loving and dutiful ever since.

In Queensland itself, the Native Police, armed and mounted, —accompanied by only *one* white officer, that no tales might be told,—were reported to be regularly sent out to " scatter " the blacks ! That meant, in many a case, wholesale murder. But in 1887, the humane Sir Samuel Griffiths, Premier, had these blood-stained forces disbanded for ever. The *Sydney Morning Herald*, 21st March, 1883, contains stronger things than were ever penned or uttered by me as to the wholesale destruction of the Aborigines. The watchword of the white settlers, practically if not theoretically, has been, " Clear them out of the way, and give us the soil ! "

Though amongst the lower types of the human race, the Aborigines have made excellent stock riders, bullock drivers, fencers, and servants in every department. And they have proved honest and faithful, especially when kindly treated.

Australians are sometimes bitter against them, for a reason that ought rather to awaken sympathy. They take Aboriginal boys or girls into their service, they train them just till they are beginning to be useful, and lo ! they go back to their own people. But in almost every case of that kind, the reason is perfectly clear. They were only taught so far as to make them useful tools. Their minds were not instructed, nor their hearts enlightened in the fear of God and the love of Jesus. They were not on an equality, in any way, either with children or with servants. They grew up without equals and without associates. They saw their parents and tribesmen treated with contempt and abuse. They instinctively felt that the moment they were unable to serve the self-interest of their employers, they themselves would be thrust out. They had not the spirit of the slave, though kept in the rank of a slave ; and they yearned for satisfaction of these instincts, which the supply of their mere animal necessities could not assuage. Among the whites, they felt degraded and outcast ; amongst their own people, they had the honour and esteem that were within reach of their kindred ; and they might weave around their poor lot the mysterious and ever-blessed ties of family and home. And here and there, doubtless, flashed in the heart of some Native boy a gleam of that patriotism that led Moses to escape from Pharaoh's court, and refuse to be identified with the despisers and oppressors of his own enslaved race,— divine in the Australian Aboriginal as in the Hebrew, though each might give a very different account of its origin !

A book once fell into my hands, entitled, " Sermons on Public Subjects," by Charles Kingsley. I knew him to be a man greatly gifted and greatly beloved ; and hence my positive distress on reading from the eighth sermon, page 234, " On the Fall," the following awful words : * " The Black People of

* See the whole context in "Sermons on National Subjects" (*Macmillan & Co.*, 1880), pp. 414—17, where it is numbered as Sermon XLI. ; particularly this regulative declaration regarding "what Original Sin may bring man to":—" What is to my mind the most awful part of the matter remains to be told—that man may actually fall by Original Sin too low to receive the Gospel of Jesus Christ and to be recovered again by it."—(*Editor.*)

Australia, exactly the same race as the African Negro, cannot take in the Gospel. . . . All attempts to bring them to a knowledge of the true God have as yet failed utterly. . . . Poor brutes in human shape . . . they must perish off the face of the earth like brute beasts."

I will not blame this great preacher for boldly uttering and publishing what multitudes of others show by their conduct that they believe, but dare not say so. Nor need any one blame me, if, knowing facts and details which Kingsley could never know, I turn aside for a few moments, and let the light of practical knowledge stream in on this and all similar teaching, come from whatsoever quarter it may.

While I was pondering over Kingsley's words, the story of Nora, an Aboriginal Christian woman, whom, as hereafter related, I myself actually visited and corresponded with, was brought under my notice, as if to shatter to pieces everything that the famous preacher had proclaimed. A dear friend told me how he had seen Nora encamped with the blacks near Hexham in Victoria. Her husband had lost, through drink, their once comfortable home at a Station where he was employed. The change back to life in camp had broken her health, and she lay sick on the ground within a miserable hut. The visitors found her reading a Bible, and explaining to a number of her own poor people the wonders of redeeming love. My friend, Roderick Urquhart, Esq., overcome by the sight, said, "Nora, I am grieved to see you here, and deprived of every comfort in your sickness."

She answered, not without tears, "The change has indeed made me unwell ; but I am beginning to think that this too is for the best; it has at last brought my poor husband to his senses, and I will grudge nothing if God thereby brings him to the Saviour's feet ! "

She further explained, that she had found wonderful joy in telling her own people about the true God and His Son Jesus, and was quite assured that the Lord in His own way would send her relief. The visitors who accompanied Mr. Urquhart showed themselves to be greatly affected by the true and pure Christian spirit of this poor Aboriginal, and on parting she said, " Do not think that I like this miserable hut, or the food,

or the company ; but I am and have been happy in trying to
do good amongst my people."

For my part, let that dear Christlike soul look out on me
from her Aboriginal hut, and I will trample under foot all
teachings or theorizings that dare to say that she or her kind
are but poor brutes, as mere blasphemies against Human
Nature ! "I thank thee, O Father, Lord of Heaven and Earth,
that Thou hast hid these things from the wise and prudent,
and hast revealed them unto babes."

Recall, ere you read further, what the Gospel has done for
the near kindred of these same Aboriginals. On our own
Aneityum 3,500 Cannibals have been led to renounce their
heathenism, and are leading a civilized and a Christian life.
In Fiji, 70,000 Cannibals have been brought under the influence of the Gospel ; and 13,000 members of the Churches are
professing to live and work for Jesus. In Samoa, 34,000 Cannibals have professed Christianity ; and, in nineteen years, its
College has sent forth 206 Native teachers and evangelists.
On our New Hebrides, more than 12,000 Cannibals have been
brought to sit at the feet of Christ, though I mean not to say that
they are all model Christians ; and 133 of the Natives have been
trained and sent forth as teachers and preachers of the Gospel.
Had Christ been brought in the same way into the heart and
life of the Aborigines by the Christians of Australia and of Britain
—equally blessed results would as surely have followed, for He
is " the same yesterday, to-day, and for ever."

It is easy to understand, moreover, how even experienced
travellers may be deluded to believe that the Aborigines have
no idols and no religion. One must have lived amongst them
or their kindred ere he can authoritatively decide these questions. Before I left Melbourne, for instance, I had met
Nathaniel Pepper, a converted Aboriginal from Wimmera.
I asked him if his people had any " Doctors," *i.e.*, Sacred Men
or priests. He said they had. I inquired if they had any
objects of Worship, or any belief in God ? He said, " No !
None whatever."

But on taking from my pocket some four small stone idols,
his expression showed at once that he recognised them as
objects of Worship. He had seen the Sacred Men use them ;

but he refused to answer any more questions. I resolved now, if possible, to secure some of their idols, and set this whole problem once for all at rest.

At Newstead, on another occasion, I persuaded a whole camp of the Aborigines to come to my meeting. After the address, they waited to examine the idols and stone gods which I had shown. Some of the young men admitted that their "doctors" had things like these, which they and the old people prayed to; but they added jauntily, "We young fellows don't worship; we know too much for that!"

No "doctors" were, however, in that camp; so I could not meet with them; but I already felt that the testimony of nearly all white people that the "blacks" had "no idols and no worship" was quickly crumbling away. Besides, my ever-dear friend, Andrew Scott, Esq., had informed me that when he first went out among the blacks,—almost alone, and one of the first white men they had ever seen,—he saw them handling and going through ceremonials with just such "smooth stones" as I had brought from the Islands, without for a moment dreaming that they were idols. Yet such is the actual fact; very much as it was in the ancient days when Isaiah (ch. lvii. 6) denounced thus the "sons of the sorceress," who were "en-flaming themselves with idols under every green tree, and slaying the children in the valleys." Then follow these suggestive words: "Among *the smooth stones* of the stream (or valley) is thy portion; they, they are thy lot; even to them hast thou poured a drink offering, thou hast offered a meat offering (or oblation)."

Yet again, R. Urquhart, Esq., Yangery, informed me that he also had seen the Aborigines engaged in religious observances. First of all, a vast multitude of men and women joined in a great Corrobbarree, or Heathen festival and dance. Thereafter each marched individually towards the centre of a huge ring, and, after certain ceremonies, bowed as if in worship towards two manlike figures cut in the ground. Our life amongst the Heathen had taught us that Worship was there.

The rite of Circumcision was also practised amongst the blacks of Australia as well as amongst our New Hebrideans.

Boys, on attaining what was looked upon as early manhood, were thus initiated into their privileges as men; and the occasion was accompanied with feasting, dancing, and what they regarded as religious ceremonies.

Some tribes in Australia, as on our Islands also, indicate the rank or class to which a man belongs by the barbarous custom of knocking out the two front teeth! This is done on reaching a certain age; with feast and dancings held at midnight, and during full moon, in connection with sacred spots, which no one but a priest will be found daring enough to approach.

Hence there is no doubt in my mind as to the character and meaning of such "mysterious figures" as those so much discussed, carved on the flat rocks at Middle Harbour, or on the South Reef promontory at Cape Cove. They are found also at Point Piper, at Mossmans, at Lane Cove, and at many other places throughout Australia, representing the human figure in almost every attitude, the kangaroo, the flying squirrel, the shark, the whale, etc., etc.,—all of which I believe to be sacred objects, and these rocks and cliffs to be sacred places. Some of the fish carved there are twenty-seven feet long. The Aborigines would give no explanation of their origin, except that they were "made by black fellows long, long ago"; and that the blacks would not live near them, for "too much devil-devil walk about there." The Balmoral blacks informed me that their sacred men carried about such objects as I showed them, and "that they were devil-devil,"— which is their only word for God or Spirit, when they talk to you in broken English.

The 18th of February, 1863, was a day worthy of being chronicled and remembered. I visited the Wonwondah Station in the Wimmera district of Victoria, and there beheld a great camp of the Aborigines on the plain near by. Securing the company of the following witnesses, I proceeded to the camp, and found that part of them had already seen me at Balmoral. Two of them spoke English fairly well. I managed to break through their reticence, and in course of time they told us freely about the customs and traditions of their people. They took us to their "doctor," or Sacred Man, who was lying sick in his hut. Half concealed among the skins and

clothes behind him, I observed several curious bags, which I
knew at once would probably contain the little idols of which
I was in quest.   I urged the witnesses to take special notice
of everything that occurred, and draw up and sign a statement
for my future use.   The following is their attested report :

"Mr. Paton, having carefully explained to the blacks that he
would like to see some of the sacred objects which they said
made the people sick and well, assured them that his aim was
not to mock at them, but to prove to white people that the
blacks had objects of worship and were not like pigs and dogs.
He offered them a number of small pieces of silver to get
bread and tea for the 'doctor,' if they would open these little
bags and let us see what was in them.   After a good deal of
talk amongst themselves, he took some of the Island stone-gods
from his pocket, saying, 'I know that these bags have such
things in them.'   An Aboriginal woman exclaimed, 'You can't
hide them from that fellow !   He knows all about us.'   Mrs.
Rutherford offered to kill a sheep, and give them sugar and
tea to feast on, if they would open the little bags, but they
refused.   After consulting the Sacred Man, however, he took
the silver pieces and allowed them to be opened before us.
They were full of exactly such stones and other things as Mr.
Paton had brought from the Islands, to prove to white people
in Melbourne that they were not like dogs, but had gods ; he
offered the Sacred Man more money for four of the objects he
had seen.   After much talk among themselves, he took the
money ; and in our presence Mr. Paton selected a stone idol,
a piece of painted wood of conical shape, a piece of bone of
human leg with seven rings carved round it, which they said had
the power of restoring sick people to health, and another piece
of painted wood which made people sick ; but they made him
solemnly promise that he would tell no other black fellows
where he got them.   They were much interested in Mr.
Paton's conversation, and said, ' No Missionary teach black
fellow.'   They then showed us square rugs, thread and grass
bags, etc., all neatly made by themselves, as proofs that if they
were taught they and their wives could learn to do things and
to work just like white people ; but they said, ' White man no
care for black fellow.'   All this, we, whose names follow, were

eye-witnesses of :—G. Rutherford, (Mrs.) A. Sutherland, (Mrs.) Martha Rutherford, Jemima Rutherford, Ben. B. Bentock, tutor of the Rutherford family."

On returning to Horsham, I informed my dear friends, Rev. P. Simpson and his excellent lady, of my exploits and possessions. He replied, "There is a black 'doctor' gone round our house just now to see one of his people who is washing here to-day. Let us go and test them, whether they know these objects."

Carrying them in his hand, we went to them. The woman instantly on perceiving them dropped what she was washing, and turned away in instinctive terror. Mr. Simpson asked, " Have you ever before seen stones like these ? "

The wily " doctor " replied, " Plenty on the plains, where I kick them out of my way."

Taking others out of my pocket, I said, " These make people sick and well, don't they ? "

His rage overcame his duplicity, and he exclaimed, "What black fellow give you these ? If I know him I do for him ! "

The woman, looking the picture of terror, and pointing to one of the objects, cried, " That fellow no good ! he kill men. No good, no good ! Me too much afraid."

Then, looking at me, she said, pointing with her finger, " That fellow savvy (knows) too much ! No white man see them. He no good."

There was more in this scene and in all its surroundings, than in many arguments ; and Mr. Simpson thoroughly believed that these were objects of idolatrous worship.

On a later occasion I showed these four objects to Aborigines, with whom I got into intercourse far off in New South Wales. They at once recognised them, and showed the same superstitious dread. They told me the peculiar characteristics and the special powers ascribed to each idol or charm. This I confirmed by the testimony of five different tribes living at great distances from each other ; and it is morally certain that amongst all the blacks of Australia such objects are so worshipped and feared in the place of God.

And now let me relate the story of my visit to Nora, the converted Aboriginal referred to above. Accompanied by

Robert Hood, Esq., J.P., Victoria, I found my way to the encampment near Hexham. She did not know of our coming, nor see us till we stood at the door of her hut. She was clean and tidily dressed, as were also her dear little children, and appeared glad to see us. She had just been reading the *Presbyterian Messenger*, and the Bible was lying at her elbow. I said, " Do you read the *Messenger* ? "

She replied, " Yes ; I like to know what is going on in the Church."

We found her to be a sensible and humble Christian woman, conversing intelligently about religion and serving God devoutly. Next Sabbath she brought her husband, her children, and six blacks to Church, all decently dressed, and they all listened most attentively.

At our first meeting I said, " Nora, they tell me you are a Christian. I want to ask you a few questions about the blacks ; and I hope that as a Christian you will speak the truth." Rather hurt at my language, she raised her right hand, and replied, " I am a Christian. I fear and serve the true God. I always speak the truth."

Taking from my pocket the stone idols from the Islands, I inquired if her people had or worshipped things like these. She replied, " The ' doctors ' have them."

" Have you a ' doctor ' in your camp? " I asked. She said, " Yes, my uncle is the Sacred Man ; but he is now far away from this."

" Has he the idols with him now? " I inquired. She answered, " No ; they are left in my care."

I then said, " Could you let us see them ? "

She consulted certain representatives of the tribe who were at hand. They rose, and removed to a distance. They had consented. Mr. Hood assured me that no fault would be found with her, as she was the real, or at least virtual head of the tribe. Out of a larger bag she then drew two smaller bags, and opened them. They were filled with the very objects which I had brought from the Islands. I asked her to consult the men of her tribe whether they would agree to sell four or five of them to me, that I might by them convince the white people that they had gods of their own, and are, therefore, above the brutes of the field ; the money to be given to their Sacred Man on his return. This, also, after a time was agreed to. I selected three of the objects, and paid the stipulated price. And the under-noted independent witness attests the transaction :

"I this day visited an encampment of the Hopkins blacks, in company with Rev. Mr. Paton, Missionary, and was witness to the following. Mr. Paton being under the impression that many of the superstitions and usages common to the South Sea Islanders were similar among the Aborigines of Australia, began by showing some idols, etc., of the former, and asking if they had seen any like them. This inquiry was made of a highly-civilized woman, named Nora, who can read and write, and has great influence with her tribe. She answered : Oh yes, the 'doctors' have them.

"On Mr. Paton expressing great anxiety to see some of them, she, after consulting some time with the other blacks, said she had some belonging to King John, her uncle, who was absent, and had left them in her care. After considerable reluctance shown on the part of the other blacks, who were off when they saw Mr. Paton knew all about them, a bag was produced, in which there were kangaroo tusks or bears' tusks, pieces of human bone, stones, charred wood, etc., etc. She described the virtues attributed to the different articles. If any evil was wanted to befall one of another tribe, the 'doctor,' after muttering, threw such a stone in the direction he was supposed to be, wishing he might fall sick, or might die, etc. The spirit from the idol entered into his body, and he was sure to fall sick or die. Another piece of charred wood, that the 'doctor' rubbed on the diseased part of any sick person, made the pain come out to the spirit in the wood, and the 'doctor' carried it away. All this time the other blacks were in evident dread of the things being seen and handled, repeating, 'No white man ever see these before !' Mr. Paton got three specimens from them, viz., an evil and a good spirit, and a piece of carved bone. Robert Hood, J.P., Hexham, Victoria, Merang, 28th February, 1863."

Mr. Hood asked Nora how he had never heard of or seen these things before, living so long amongst them, and blacks constantly coming and going about his house. She replied, "Long ago white men laughed at black fellows, praying to their idols. Black fellows said, white men never see them again! Suppose this white man not know all about them, he would not now see them. No white men live now have seen what you have seen."

Thus it has been demonstrated on the spot, and in presence of the most reliable witnesses, that the Aborigines, before they saw the white invaders, were not "brutes" incapable of knowing God, but human beings, yearning after a God of some kind. Nor do I believe that any tribe of men will ever be found, who, when their language and customs are rightly interpreted, will not display their consciousness of the need of a God, and that Divine capacity of holding fellowship with the Unseen Powers, of which the brutes are without one faintest trace.

The late Mr. Hamilton, of Mortlake, wrote me in 1863 as follows :—

"During a residence of twenty-six years in New South Wales and Victoria, from constant intercourse with Australian Aborigines I am convinced that they are capable of learning anything that white people in an equally neglected condition could learn. In two instances I met with females possessing a greater amount of religious knowledge than many of our white population. The one was able to prompt the children, whom she was attending as a servant, in the answers proper to give to the questions I put to them regarding the facts and doctrines of Christianity. This was in New South Wales. The other was Nora Hood, baptized and married to an Aboriginal. I conversed with her according to the usage of the Presbyterian Church, and I believe her to be a sincere and intelligent Christian. I baptized her children without hesitation ; while I felt it to be my duty in many cases to withhold the privilege from white parents, on account of their being unable to make a credible profession of their faith in Christ and obedience to Him. Under God, she owes her instruction and conversion to Mrs. MacKenzie. William Hamilton, Minister."

William Armstrong, Esq., of Hexham Park, wrote in 1863 :—

"The Aborigines of Australia certainly believe in spirits, and that their spirit leaves the body at death and goes to some other island, and they seem to have many superstitious ideas about the dead. . . . I believe they would have been as easily influenced by the Gospel as any other Savages, if they had been taught; but intoxicating spirits, and the accompanying vices of white people, have ruined them.—William Armstrong."

But let Nora, one of the "poor brutes in human shape," who was said to be "incapable of taking in the Gospel," and must "perish like brute beasts," now speak to the heart of every reader in her own words. In February 1863 she wrote to me as follows :—

"Dear Sir,—I received your kind letter, and was glad to hear from you. I am always reading my Bible, for I believe in God the Father and in Christ Jesus our Lord, Amen. I often speak to the blacks about Jesus Christ; and some of them believe in God and in Jesus. I always teach my children to pray to God our Father in Heaven. . . . Colin will try not to drink any more. He is always praying to God. Them blacks that come with me, I will tell about God and about their sins ; but they are so very wicked, they won't listen to me teaching them. Sir, I shall always pray for you, that God may bless and guide you. O Sir, pray for me, my husband, and my children ! Your obedient servant, Nora Hood."

In her second letter, she says : "Your kind letter gave me great comfort. I thank God that I am able to read and write. Mrs. and Miss MacKenzie taught me ; and through them I came to know Jesus Christ my Saviour. Our Lord says, 'Come unto Me, all ye that labour and are heavy laden, and I will give you rest.' 'Ho, every one that thirsteth, come ye to the waters!' Sir, I will tell Joe and King John, and I have been always telling Katy and all the rest of them about Jesus Christ our Saviour. Please, Sir, I would like you to write to me, that I may show them your letters," etc., etc.

In a third letter, also dated 1863, she says : "Dear Sir, Colin and I were glad to hear from you. I am telling the blacks always about God our Saviour and the salvation of their souls. They are so very wicked. They go from place

18

to place, and don't stop long with me. I am always teaching
my children to pray, and would like to send them to School
if I could. . . . I hope you will go home to England safely,
get more Missionaries, and then go back to your poor blacks
on the Islands. I will be glad to hear from you. May the
Lord God bless you, wherever you go! Your affectionate,
Nora Hood."

Poor, dear, Christian-hearted Nora! The Christ-spirit
shines forth unmistakably through thee,—praying for and seeking to save husband and children, enduring trials and miseries
by the aid of communion with thy Lord, weeping over the degradation of thy people, and seeking to lift them up by telling
them of the true God and of His love to Mankind through
Jesus Christ. Would that all white Christians manifested
forth as much of the Divine Master's Spirit!

Alas, in reading Marsden's "Life," and other authorities,
one shrinks with a sickening feeling at the description of the
butcheries of the poor blacks! Imagine 1830, when the
inhabitants were called out to join the troops, and nearly
three thousand armed men gloated in the work of destruction
from the 4th of October till the 26th November. Read of
one boasting that he had killed seven blacks with his own
hand; another, that he had slain, and piled up in a heap,
thirty men, women, and children; and a third, a *gentleman*,
of whom Lieutenant Laidlaw tells, exhibiting as a trophy over
his bookcase the skull of a poor black, pierced by the bullet
with which he had shot him! And their sin, their crime?
Oh, only seizing a sheep, in the frenzy of hunger, which
fattened on the lands where once grew their food, and from
which the white man had pitilessly hunted them. Retribution
comes, but sometimes slowly, and is not recognised by some
when she appears; but Australia suffers to-day from the
passions then let loose against the blacks. The demons have
come home to roost.

During my last Mission tour, in 1888, through Victoria and
part of New South Wales, I visited all Stations of the Aborigines that could be conveniently reached. There the few
remnants of a once numerous race are now assembled together.
They try hard to constrain themselves to live in houses.

But the spirit of the wanderer is in them. They start forth, every now and again, for an occasional ramble over their old hunting grounds, and to taste the sweets of freedom. In Victoria, the Government now provide food and clothing for the Aborigines who will remain at the appointed Stations, so that in regard to temporals the survivors are not badly off. Their religious training and spiritual interests are left entirely to the Churches. The Government provides a Superintendent at each Station ; and, where he is a Christian man and takes any interest in the religion and morals of the tribes, contentment reigns. At Ramayeuk, for instance, the Superintendent is Rev. F. A. Haganeur ; and he and his excellent wife regularly instruct the blacks. Nothing can be more delightful than the results. The faces of the people were shining with happiness. Their rows of clean and neat cottages were a picture and an emblem. In their Church, a Native woman played the harmonium and led the praise. I never had more attentive Congregations. On two occasions they handed me £5, collected at their own free will, for our Island Mission. Their School received from the Government examiners one of the highest percentages. Many at this Station have, after a consistent Christian life, died in the full hope of Glory together with Jesus.

At all the other Stations in Victoria the outward comforts of the Natives are attended to ; but Superintendents ought to be appointed, in every case, to care for their souls as well as their bodies. For strong drink and other vices are rapidly sweeping the Aborigines away ; and Australia has but short time to atone for the cruelties of the past, and to snatch a few more jewels from amongst them for the Crown of Jesus our Lord.

At my farewell meeting in Melbourne, Sir Henry Barkley presiding, I pleaded that the Colony should put forth greater efforts to give the Gospel to the Aborigines ; I showed the idols which I had discovered amongst them ; I read Nora's letters ; and, I may, without presumption, say, the " brute-in-human-shape " theory has been pretty effectually buried ever since.

CHAPTER III.

TO SCOTLAND AND BACK.

A.D. 1863—1865. ÆT. 39—41.

Dr. Inglis on the Mission Crisis.—Casting Lots before the Lord.—Struck by Lightning.—A Peep at London.—A Heavenly Welcome.—The Moderator's Chair.—Reformed Presbyterian Church and Free Church. —Tour through Scotland.—A Frosted Foot.—The Children's Holy League.—Missionary Volunteers.— A God-provided Help-Mate.— Farewell to the Old Family Altar.—First Peep at the *Dayspring*.— The *Dayspring* in a Dead-Lock.—Tokens of Deliverance.—The *John Williams* and the *Dayspring*.—Australia's Special Call.

EACH of my Australian Committees strongly urged my return to Scotland, chiefly to secure, if possible, more Missionaries for the New Hebrides. Dr. Inglis, just arrived from Britain, where he had the Aneityumese New Testament carried through the press, zealously enforced this appeal. " Before I left home," he wrote back to the Church in Scotland, " I thought this would be inexpedient ; but since I returned here, and have seen the sympathy, interest, and liberality displayed through the blessing of God on Mr. Paton's instrumentality, and the altered aspect of the Mission, I feel that a crisis has been reached when a special effort must be made to procure more men, for which I had neither the time, nor had I the means to employ them, but which may now be appropriately done by Mr. Paton ; and my prayer and hope are that he may be as successful in securing men at home as he has been in securing money in these Colonies."

Yet my path was far from clear, notwithstanding my Gideon's fleece referred to already. To lose time in going home to do work that others ought to do, while I still heard the wail of the perishing Heathen on the Islands, could scarcely be my duty.

276

Amidst overwhelming perplexity, and finding no light from any human counsel, I took a step, to which only once before in all my chequered career I have felt constrained. Some will mock when they read it, but others will perhaps more profoundly say, "To whomsoever this faith is given, let him obey it." After many prayers, and wrestlings, and tears, I went alone before the Lord, and, on my knees, cast lots with a solemn appeal to God, and the answer came, "Go home!" In my heart, I sincerely believe that on both these occasions the Lord condescended to decide for me the path of duty, otherwise unknown; and I believe it the more truly now, in view of the aftercome of thirty years of service to Christ that flowed out of the steps then deliberately and devoutly taken. In this, and in many other matters, I am no law to others, though I obeyed my then highest light. Nor can I refrain from adding that, for the very reasons indicated above, I regard so-called "lotteries" and "raffles" as a mockery of God, and little if at all short of blasphemy. "Ye cannot drink at the Lord's Table, and at the table of devils."

I sailed for London in the *Kosciusko*, an Aberdeen clipper, on 16th May, 1863. Captain Stewart made the voyage most enjoyable to all. The Rev. Mr. Stafford, friend of the good Bishop Selwyn and tutor to his son, conducted along with myself, alternately, an Anglican and a Presbyterian Service. We passed through a memorable thunder-burst in rounding the Cape. Our good ship was perilously struck by lightning. The men on deck were thrown violently down. The copper on the bulwarks was twisted and melted—a specimen of which the Captain gave me and I still retain. When the ball of fire struck the ship, those of us sitting on chairs, screwed to the floor around the Cabin table, felt as if she were plunging to the bottom. When she sprang aloft again, a military man and a medical officer were thrown heavily into the back passage between the Cabins, the screws that held their seats having snapped asunder. I, in grasping the table, got my leg severely bruised, being jammed betwixt the seat and the table, and had to be carried to my berth. All the men were attended to, and quickly recovered consciousness; and immediately the good Captain, an elder of the Church, came to me, and said,

" Lead us in prayer, and let us thank the Lord for this most merciful deliverance ; the ship is not on fire, and no one is seriously injured ! "

Poor fellow ! whether hastened on by this event I know not, but he struggled for three weeks thereafter in a fever, and it took our united care and love to pull him through.   The Lord, however, restored him ; and we cast anchor safely in the East India Docks, at London, on 26th August, 1863, having been three months and ten days at sea from port to port.

It was 5.30 p.m. when we cast anchor, and the gates closed at 6 o'clock.   My little box was ready on deck.   The Custom House officers kindly passed me, and I was immediately on my way to Euston Square.   Never before had I been within the Great City, and doubtless I could have enjoyed its palaces and memorials.   But the King's business, entrusted to me, "required haste," and I felt constrained to press forward, looking neither to the right hand nor to the left.   The streets through which I was driven seemed to be dirty and narrow ; many of the people had a squalid and vicious look ; and, fresh from Australia, my disappointment was keen as to the smoky and miserable appearance of what I saw.   No doubt other visitors will behold only the grandeur and the wealth ; they will see exactly what they come to see, and London will shine before them accordingly.

At nine o'clock, that evening, I left for Scotland by train. Next morning, about the same hour, I reported myself at the manse of the Rev. John Kay, Castle Douglas, the Convener of the Foreign Mission Committee of the Reformed Presbyterian Church, to which I then belonged.   We arranged for a meeting of said Committee, at earliest practicable date, that my scheme and plans might at once be laid before them.

By the next train I was on my way to Dumfries, and thence by conveyance to my dear old home at Torthorwald.   There I had a Heavenly Welcome from my saintly parents, yet not unmixed with many fast-falling tears.   Five brief years only had elapsed, since I went forth from their Sanctuary, with my young bride ; and now, alas ! alas ! that grave on Tanna held mother and son locked in each other's embrace till the Resurrection Day.

Not less glowing, but more terribly agonizing, was my reception, a few days thereafter, at Coldstream, when I first gazed on the bereaved father and mother of my beloved ; who, though godly people, were conscious of a heart-break under that stroke, from which through their remaining years they never fully rallied. They murmured not against the Lord ; but all the same, heart and flesh began to faint and fail, even as our Divine Exemplar Himself fainted under the Cross, which yet He so uncomplainingly bore.

The Foreign Mission Committee of the Reformed Presbyterian Church met in Edinburgh, and welcomed me kindly, nay, warmly. A full report of all my doings for the past, and of all my plans and hopes, was laid before them. They at once agreed to my visiting and addressing every Congregation and Sabbath School in the Church. They opened to me their Divinity Hall, that I might appeal to the Students. My Address there was published and largely circulated, under the motto—" Come over and help us." It was used of God to deepen vastly the interest in our Mission.

The Committee generously and enthusiastically did everything in their power to help me. By their influence, the Church in 1864 conferred on me the undesired and undeserved honour, the highest which they could confer—the honour of being the Moderator of their Supreme Court. No one can understand how much I shrank from all this ; but, in hope of the Lord's using it and me to promote His work amongst the Heathen, I accepted the Chair, though, I fear, only to occupy it most unworthily, for Tanna gave me little training for work like that !

The Church, as there represented, passed a Resolution, declaring—" It is with feelings of no ordinary pleasure that we behold present at this meeting one of our most devoted Missionaries. The result of Mr. Paton's appeals in Australia has been unprecedented in the history of this Mission. It appears in the shape of £4,500 added to the funds of the New Hebrides Mission, besides over £300 for Native Teachers, to be paid yearly in £5 contributions, and all expenses met. The Spirit of God must have been poured out upon the inhabitants of the Colonies, in leading them to make such a noble offering as this to the cause of Missions, and in making our Missionary the honoured instrument God employed in drawing forth the sympathy and liberality of the Colonists. Now, by the good hand of God upon him, he holds the most honoured position of Moderator of the Church," etc., etc.

The Synod also placed on record its gratitude for what God had thus done; and its cordial recognition of the many and fruitful services rendered by Ministers and Sabbath Schools, both in Scotland and Australia, in standing by me and helping on the *Floating of the " Dayspring."*

I have ever regarded it as a privilege and honour that I was born and trained within the old covenanting Reformed Presbyterian Church of Scotland. As a separate Communion, that Church was small amongst the thousands of Israel; but the principles of Civil and Religious Liberty for which her founders suffered and died are, at this moment, the heart and soul of all that is best and divinest in the Constitution of our British Empire. I am more proud that the blood of Martyrs is in my veins, and their truths in my heart, than other men can be of noble pedigree or royal names. And I was—in that day of the Church's honour so distinguished for her Missionary zeal—filled with a high passion of gratitude to be able to proclaim, at the close of my tour, and after the addition of new names to our staff, that of all her ordained Ministers, one in every six was a Missionary of the Cross.

Nor did the dear old Church thus cripple herself; on the contrary, her zeal for Missions accompanied, if not caused, unwonted prosperity at home. New waves of liberality passed over the heart of her people. Debts that had burdened many of the Churches and Manses were swept away. Additional Congregations were organized. And in May, 1876, the Reformed Presbyterian Church entered into an honourable and independent Union with her larger, wealthier, and more progressive sister, the Free Church of Scotland,—only one Minister and a few of the brethren, doubtless with perfect loyalty to what they regarded as duty to Christ, holding aloof and standing firmly in the old paths, as they appeared to them.

In the Deed of incorporating Union the Church took itself legally and formally bound to maintain the New Hebrides

Mission staff, and also the *Dayspring*, committing herself never to withdraw, as it were, till these Islands were all occupied for Jesus. Now that the French have been constrained to abandon the scene, the field is open, and the Islands wail aloud for eight or ten Missionaries more than we at present have (1889); and then the Standard of the Cross might speedily be planted on every separate Isle, and a true sense might at last come into the foolish name given to these regions by their Spanish discoverer, when he called the part at which he touched, thinking it the fabled Southern Continent, *the Land of the Holy Ghost.*

When the aforesaid Union took place, all the Missionaries of their own free accord cast in their lot with the incorporating Church ; not only those directly supported by the old Reformed Presbyterians themselves, but also the several Missionaries sent forth by them, though supported by one or other of the Australian Colonies. And, beyond question, one feature in the Free Church that drew them and bound them to her heart was her noble zeal for and sacrifices in connection with the work of Missions, both at home and abroad. For it is a fixed point in the faith of every Missionary, that the more any Church or Congregation interests itself in the Heathen, the more will it be blessed and prospered at Home.

"One of the surest signs of life," wrote the Victorian *Christian Review,* "is the effort of a Church to spread the Gospel beyond its own bounds, and especially to send the knowledge of Jesus amongst the Heathen. The Missions to the Aborigines, to the Chinese in this Colony, and to the New Hebrides, came to this Church from God. In a great crisis of the New Hebrides, they sent one of their number to Australia for help, and his appeal was largely owned by the Head of the Church. The Children, and especially the Sabbath Scholars of the Presbyterian Churches, became alive with Missionary enthusiasm. Large sums were raised for a Mission Ship. The Congregations were roused to see their duty to God and their fellow-men beyond these Colonies, and a new Missionary Spirit took possession of the whole Church. Their deputy from the Islands agreed to become the Missionary from this Church. Many circumstances indeed combined to show that it was the will of the Master, that this Church should join the other Presbyterian Churches in taking possession of this field of usefulness; and already the results are very important both to the Church and to the Mission. The Missionaries feel much encouraged in receiving substantial support from the largest Presbyterian Church in the Australian Colonies; while the Presbyterian Church in Victoria is largely blessed in her own spirit through the Missionary zeal awakened in her midst. Thus, there is that scattereth and yet increaseth; bringing out anew the words of the Lord Jesus, how He said, 'It is more blessed to give than to receive.' "

But, in all this, I am rather anticipating. My tour through Scotland brought me into contact with every Minister, Congregation, and Sabbath School in the Church of my fathers. They were never at any time a rich people, but they were always liberal. At this time they contributed beyond all previous experience, both in money and in boxes of useful articles for the Islanders.

Unfortunately, my visit to the far North, to our Congregations at Wick and Stromness, had been arranged for the month of January; and thereby a sore trial befell me in my pilgrimages. The roads were covered with snow and ice. I reached Aberdeen and Wick by steamer from Edinburgh, and had to find my way thence to Thurso. The inside seats on the Mail Coach being all occupied, I had to take my place outside. The cold was intense, and one of my feet got bitten by the frost. The storm detained me nearly a week at Thurso, but feeling did not return to the foot.

We started, in a lull, by steamer for Stromness; but the storm burst again, all were ordered below, and hatches and doors made fast. The passengers were mostly very rough, the place was foul with whisky and tobacco. I appealed to the Captain to let me crouch somewhere on deck, and hold on as best I could. He shouted, "I dare not! You'll be washed overboard."

On seeing my appealing look, he relented, directed his men to fasten a tarpaulin over me, and lash it and me to the mast, and there I lay till we reached Stromness. The sea broke heavily and dangerously over the vessel. But the Captain finding shelter for several hours under the lee of a headland, saved both the ship and the passengers. When at last we landed, my foot was so benumbed and painful that I could move a step only with greatest agony. Two meetings, however, were in some kind of way conducted; but the projected visit to Dingwall and other places had to be renounced, the snow lying too deep for any conveyance to carry me, and my foot crying aloud for treatment and skill.

On returning Southwards, I was confined for about two months, and placed under the best medical advice. All feeling seemed gradually to have departed from my foot; and amputation was seriously proposed both in Edinburgh and in Glasgow. Having somehow managed to reach Liverpool, my dear friend, the Rev. Dr. Graham, took me there to a Doctor who had wrought many wonderful recoveries by galvanism. Time after time he applied the battery, but I felt nothing. He declared that the power used would "have killed six ordinary men," and that he had never seen any part of the human body so dead to feeling on a live and healthy person. Finally, he covered it all over with a dark plaster, and told me to return in three days. But next day, the throbbing feeling of insufferable coldness in the foot compelled me to return at once. After my persistent appeals, he removed the plaster; and, to his great astonishment, the whole of the frosted part adhered to it! Again, dressing the remaining parts, he covered it with plaster as before, and assured me that with care and rest it would now completely recover. By the blessing of the Lord it did, though it was a bitter trial to me amidst all these growing plans to be thus crippled by the way; and to this day I am sometimes warned in over-walking that the part is capable of many a painful twinge. And humbly I feel myself crooning over the graphic words of the Greatest Missionary, "I bear about in my body the *marks* of the Lord Jesus."

On that tour, the Sabbath Schools joyfully adopted my scheme, and became "Shareholders" in the Mission Ship. It was thereafter ably developed by an elder of the Church. A *Dayspring* collecting box found its way into almost every family; and the returns from Scotland have yielded ever since about £250 per annum, as their proportion for the expenses

of the Children's Mission Ship to the New Hebrides. The
Church in Nova Scotia heartily accepted the same idea, and
their Sabbath School children. have regularly contributed their
£250 per annum too. The Colonial children have contributed
the rest, throughout all these years, with unfailing interest.
And whensoever the true and full history of the South Sea
Islands Mission is written for the edification of the Universal
Church, let it not be forgotten that the children of Australasia,
and Nova Scotia, and Scotland did by their united pennies
keep the *Dayspring* floating in the New Hebrides ; that the
Missionaries and their families were thereby supplied with the
necessaries of life, and that the Islanders were thus taught to
clothe themselves and to sit at the feet of Jesus. This was
the Children's Holy League, erewhile referred to ; and one
knows that on such a Union the Divine Master smiles well
pleased.

The Lord also crowned this tour with another precious fruit
of blessing, though not all by any means due to my influence.
Four new Missionaries volunteered from Scotland, and three
from Nova Scotia. By their aid we not only re-claimed for Jesus
the posts that had been abandoned, but we took possession of
other Islands in His most blessed Name. But I did not wait
and take them out with me. They had matters to look into
and to learn about, that would be infinitely helpful to them in
the Mission field. Especially, and far above everything else
in addition to their regular Clerical course, some Medical instruction was an almost absolute pre-requisite. I myself had
attended several Medical Classes at the Andersonian College,
when a student in Glasgow, and had had personal training
from an experienced physician. This had proved invaluable,
not only on the Islands, but in the remote bush during Australian tours, and indeed on many private occasions, when
other medical help was unavailable. Every future Missionary
was therefore urged to obtain all insight and instruction that
was practicable at Medical Mission Dispensary, and otherwise,
especially on lines known to be most requisite for these Islands.
For this, and similar objects, all that I raised over and above
what was required for the *Dayspring* was entrusted to the
Foreign Mission Committee, that the new Missionaries might

be fully equipped, and their outfit and travelling expenses be provided for without burdening the Church at home. Her responsibilities were already large enough for her resources. But she could give men, God's own greatest gift, and His people elsewhere gave the money,—the Colonies and the Home Country thus binding themselves to each other in this Holy Mission of the Cross.

But I did not return alone. The dear Lord had brought to me one prepared, all unknown to either of us, by special culture, by godly training, by many gifts and accomplishments, and even by family associations, to share my lot on the New Hebrides. Her brother had been an honoured Missionary in the Foreign field, and had fallen asleep while the dew of youth was yet upon him; her sister was the wife of a devoted Minister of our Church in Adelaide, both she and her husband being zealous promoters of our work; and her father had left behind him a fragrant memory through his many Christian works at Edinburgh, Kenneth, and Alloa, besides being not unknown to fame as the author of those still popular books, *Whitecross's Anecdotes*, illustrative of the Shorter Catechism and of the Holy Scriptures. Ere I left Scotland in 1864, I was married to Margaret Whitecross, and God spares us to each other still; and the family which He has been pleased in His love to grant unto us we have dedicated to His service, with the prayer and hope that He may use every one of them in spreading the Gospel throughout the Heathen World.

Our marriage was celebrated at her sister's house in Edinburgh; and I may be pardoned for recalling a little event that characterized the occasion. My youngest brother, then tutor to a gentleman studying at the University, stepped forth at the close of the ceremony and recited an *Epithalamium* composed for the day. For many a month and year the refrain, a play upon the Bride's name, kept singing itself through my memory :—

> " Long may the *Whitecross* banner wave,
> By the battle blasts unriven ;
> Long may our Brother and Sister brave
> Rejoice in the light of Heaven."

He described the Bride as hearing a "Voice from the far

Pacific Seas"; and turning to us both, he sang of an Angel "beckoning us to the Tanna-land," to gather a harvest of souls :—

> " The warfare is brief, the crown is bright,
> The pledge is the souls of men ;
> Go, may the Lord defend the Right,
> And restore you safe again ! "

But the verse which my dear wife thought most beautiful for a bridal day, and which her memory cherishes still, was this :—

> " May the ruddy Joys, and the Graces fair,
> Wait fondly around you now ;
> Sweet angel Hopes and young Loves, repair
> To your home and bless your vow ! "

My last scene in Scotland was kneeling at the family altar in the old Sanctuary Cottage at Torthorwald, while my venerable father, with his high-priestly locks of snow-white hair streaming over his shoulders, commended us once again to " the care and keeping of the Lord God of the families of Israel." It was the last time that ever on this Earth those accents of intercession, loaded with a pathos of deathless love, would fall upon my ears. I knew to a certainty that when we rose from our knees and said farewell, our eyes would never meet again till they were flooded with the lights of the Resurrection Day. But he and my darling mother gave us away once again with a free heart, not unpierced with the sword of human anguish, to the service of our common Lord and to the Salvation of the Heathen. And we went forth, praying that a double portion of their spirit, along with their precious blessing, might rest upon us in all the way that we had to go.

Our beloved mother, always more self-restrained, and less demonstrative in the presence of others, held back her heart till we were fairly gone from the door ; and then, as my dear brother afterwards informed me, she fell back into his arms with a great cry, as if all the heart-strings had broken, and lay for long in a death-like swoon. Oh, all ye that read this page, think most tenderly of the cries of Nature, even where Grace and Faith are in perfect triumph. Read, through scenes like these, a fuller meaning into the words addressed to that blessed

Mother, whose Son was given for us all, "Yea, a sword shall pierce through thine own soul also."

Here, in passing, I may mention that my mother, ever beloved, "fell on sleep," after a short agony of affliction, in 1865; and my "priest-like father" passed peacefully and joyfully into the presence of his Lord in 1868; * both cradled and cherished to the last in the arms of their own affectionate children, and both in the assured hope of a blessed immortality, where all their sons and daughters firmly expect to meet them again in the Home prepared by their blessed Saviour.

We embarked at Liverpool for Australia in *The Crest of the Wave*, Captain Ellis; and after what was then considered a fast passage of ninety-five days, we landed at Sydney on 17th January, 1865. Within an hour we had to grapple with a new and amazing perplexity. The Captain of our *Dayspring* came to inform me that his ship had arrived three days ago and now lay in the stream,—that she had been to the Islands, and had settled the Gordons, McCullaghs, and Morrisons on their several Stations,—that she had left Halifax in Nova Scotia fourteen months ago, and that now, on arriving at Sydney, he could not get one penny of money, and that the crew were clamouring for their pay, etc., etc. He continued, "Where shall I get money for current expenses? No one will lend unless we mortgage the *Dayspring*. I fear there is nothing before us but to sell her!" I gave him £50 of my own to meet clamant demands, and besought him to secure me a day or two of delay that something might be done.

Having landed, and been heartily welcomed by dear Dr. and Mrs. Moon and other friends, I went with a kind of trembling joy to have my first look at the *Dayspring*, like a sailor getting a first peep at the child born to him whilst far away on the sea. Some of the irritated ship's company stopped us by the way, and threatened prosecution and all sorts of annoyance. I could only urge again for a few days' patience. I found her to be a beautiful two-masted Brigantine, with a deck-house (added when she first arrived at Melbourne), and every way suitable for our necessities,—a thing of beauty, a

---

* See Appendix A.

white-winged Angel set a-floating by the pennies of the children
to bear the Gospel to these sin-darkened but sun-lit Southern
Isles.   To me she became a sort of living thing, the imper-
sonation of a living and throbbing love in the hearts of
thousands of "shareholders"; and I said, with a deep,
indestructible faith,—"The Lord *has* provided—the Lord *will*
provide."

Since she sailed, £1,400 had been expended; for present
liabilities at least £700 more were instantly required; and, at
any rate, as large a sum to pay her way and meet expenses of
next trip to the Islands.   Having laid our perplexing circumstances before our dear Lord Jesus, having "spread out" all the
details in His sympathetic presence, pleading that the Ship itself
and the new Missionaries were all His own, not mine, I told
Him that this money was needed to do His own blessed work.

On Friday morning, I consulted friends of the Mission, but
no help was visible.   I tried to borrow, but found that the
lender demanded twenty per cent. for interest, besides the
title deeds of the ship for security.   I applied for a loan from
the agent of the London Missionary Society (then agent for
us too) on the credit of the Reformed Presbyterian Church's
Foreign Committee, but he could not give it without a written
order from Scotland.   There were some who seemed rather
to enjoy our perplexity !

Driven thus to the wall, I advertised for a meeting of
Ministers and other friends, next morning at 11 o'clock, to
receive my report and to consult *re* the *Dayspring.*   I related
my journeyings since leaving them, and the results, and then
asked for advice about the Ship.

"Sell her," said some, "and have done with it."   "What,"
said others, "have the Sabbath Schools given you the *Dayspring*
and can you not support her yourselves?"

I pointed out to them that the salary of each Missionary
was then only £120 per annum, that they gave their lives for
the Heathen, and that surely the Colonial Christians would
undertake the up-keep of the Ship, which was necessary to the
very existence of the Mission.   I appealed to them that, as my
own Church in Scotland had now one Missionary abroad for
every six Ministers at home, and the small Presbyterian

Church of Nova Scotia had actually three Missionaries now on our Islands, it would be a blessed privilege for the Australian Churches and Sabbath Schools to keep the *Dayspring* afloat, without whose services the Missionaries could not live nor the Islanders be evangelized.

Being Saturday, the morning Services for Sabbath were all arranged for, or advertised ; but Dr. McGibbon offered me a meeting for the evening, and Dr. Steel an afternoon Service at three o'clock, combined with his Sabbath School. Rev. Mr. Patterson, of Piermont, offered me a Morning Service ; but, as his was only a Mission Church, he could not give me a collection. These openings I accepted, as from the Lord, however much they fell short of what I desired.

At the Morning Service I informed the Congregation how we were situated, and expressed the hope that under God and their devoted pastor they would greatly prosper, and would yet be able to help in supporting our Mission to their South Sea neighbours. Returning to the vestry, a lady and gentleman waited to be introduced to me. They were from Launceston, Tasmania.

"I am," said he, "Captain and owner of that vessel lying at anchor opposite the *Dayspring*. My wife and I, being too late to get on shore to attend any Church in the city, heard this little Chapel bell ringing, and followed, when we saw you going up the hill. We have so enjoyed the Service. We do heartily sympathize with you. This cheque for £50 will be a beginning to help you out of your difficulties."

The reader knows how warmly I would thank them ; and how in my own heart I knew *Who* it was that made them arrive too late for *their* plans, but not for *His*, and led them up that hill, and opened their hearts. Jehovah-Jireh !

At three o'clock, Dr. Steel's Church was filled with children and others. I told them in my appeal what had happened in the Mission Chapel, and how God had led Captain Frith and his wife, entire strangers, to sound the first note of our deliverance. One man stood up and said, "I will give £10." Another, "I will give £5." A third, "I shall send you £20 to-morrow morning." Several others followed their example, and the general collection was greatly encouraging.

19

In the evening, I had a very large as well as sympathetic Congregation. I fully explained the difficulty about the *Dayspring*, and told them what God had already done for us, announcing an address to which contributions might be sent. Almost every Mail brought me the free-will offerings of God's people ; and on Wednesday, when the adjourned meeting was held, the sum had reached in all £456. Believing that the Lord thus intervened at a vital crisis in our Mission, I dwell on it to the praise of His blessed Name. Trust in Him, obey Him, and He will not suffer you to be put to shame.

At a public meeting, held immediately thereafter, an attempt was made to organize the *first* Australian Auxiliary to the New Hebrides Mission ; but it needed an enthusiastic secretary, and for lack thereof came to nothing at that time. At another meeting, the first elements of a brooding strife appeared. The then Agent of the noble and generous London Missionary Society intimated that he had just issued Collecting Cards for the *John Williams*, and that it would be unbrotherly to urge collections for the *Dayspring* at the same time throughout New South Wales. He suggested that I should first visit Tasmania and South Australia, and that, on our return, they would help us as we would now help them. The most cordial feelings had always prevailed betwixt the Societies, and we accepted the proposal, though our circumstances were peculiarly trying, and I personally believed that no harm, but good, would have come from both of us doing everything possible to fan the Missionary spirit.

Clearing out from her sister ships, then in harbour, the *John Williams* and the *John Wesley*, our little *Dayspring* sailed for Tasmania. At Hobart we were visited by thousands of children and parents, and afterwards at Launceston, who were proud to see their own Ship, in which they were " shareholders " for Jesus. Daily, all over the Colony, I preached in Churches, and addressed public meetings, and got collections, and gave out Collecting Cards to be returned within two weeks. But here also the little rift began to show itself. At a public meeting in Hobart, the Congregational Minister said, " We support the *John Williams* for the London Missionary Society. Let the Presbyterians do as much for the *Dayspring* /"

I replied, that I was there by special invitation from those who had called the meeting, and that, rather than have any unseemly wrangling, my friend, Dr. Nicolson, and I would quietly retire.   But the Chairman intervened, and insisted that the meeting should go forward in a Christian spirit, and without any word of recrimination.   To find ourselves, even by a misunderstanding, regarded as inimical to the London Missionary Society, one of the most Catholic-spirited and Christlike Societies in the world, was peculiarly painful.   Still the little rift seemed to widen at every turn, and we found ourselves thrown more and more exclusively on Presbyterians alone.   But thus also the hearts of *two* great Communions were concentrated on Heathendom, where one only or chiefly had been bearing the burden heretofore.   And the Lord hath need of all.

We received many tokens of interest and sympathy.   The steam tug was granted to us free, and the harbour dues were remitted.   Many presents were also sent on board the *Dayspring.*   Still, after meeting all necessary outlays, the trip to Tasmania gave us only £227 8s. 11d. clear for the Mission fund.

Sailing now for South Australia, we arrived at Adelaide. Many friends there showed the deepest interest in our plans. Thousands of children and parents came to visit their own Mission Ship by several special trips.   Daily and nightly I addressed meetings, and God's people were moved greatly in the cause.   After meeting all expenses while in port, there remained a sum of £634 9s. 2d. for the up-keep of the vessel. The Honourable George Fife Angus gave me £241—a dear friend belonging to the Baptist Church.   But there was still a deficit of £400 before the *Dayspring* could sail free of debt, and my heart was sore as I cried for it to the Lord.

Leaving the ship to sail direct for Sydney, I took steamer to Melbourne; but, on arriving there, sickness and anxiety laid me aside for three days.   Under great weakness, I crept along to my dear friends at the Scotch College, Dr. and Mrs. Morrison, and Miss Fraser, and threw myself on their advice.

"Come along," said the Doctor cheerily, "and I'll introduce

you to Mr. Butchart and one or two friends in East Melbourne, and we'll see what can be done!"

I gave all information, being led on in conversation by the Doctor, and tried to interest them in our work, but no sub-scriptions were asked or received. Ere I sailed for Sydney, however, the whole deficiency was sent to me. I received in all, on this tour, the sum of £1,726 9s. 10d. Our *Dayspring* once more sailed free, and our hearts overflowed with gratitude to the Lord and to His stewards!

On my return to Sydney, and before sailing to the Islands, I called, by advertisement, a public meeting of Ministers and other friends to report success, and to take counsel for the future.

My report was received with hearty thanksgiving to Almighty God. And a resolution was unanimously adopted, in view of all that had transpired, urging that a scheme must be organized, whereby the Presbyterian Churches and Sabbath Schools of Australia should be banded together for the support of the *Dayspring*, and so prevent the necessity of such spasmodic efforts for all future time.

From that day, practically, the *Dayspring* was supported by the Presbyterians alone. At the first, all helped in the original purchase of the Mission Ship, and she was to do all needful work on the Loyalty Islands for the London Society's Mis-sionaries, as well as on the New Hebrides for us. This was the agreement; and, despite little misunderstandings with the Agents, the *Dayspring* was for some years placed heartily at their service. When the *John Williams* was wrecked, our ship, at great loss and expense, accompanied her to Sydney, and spent four months of the following year for them entirely amongst the Eastern Islands. The brethren on the Loyalty Islands sent up their Mr. Macfarland to the Colonies to secure that the promised support should be given by their friends to the *Dayspring;* but, this failing, they in 1870 declined finally to have her doing their work, when no longer paid for by their Churches. This little rift, however, amongst the contributing Churches never affected us in the Mission field; they and we have ever wrought together there in most perfect cordiality of brotherhood.

Perhaps the true way to look upon the whole series of events is this : the Australian Presbyterian Churches had been led to hear from God a special call, and must necessarily organize themselves to answer it. In this blessed work of converting the Heathen, we can all loyally rejoice, whether the instruments in the Lord's hand be Episcopal, Presbyterian, or Congregational ! I glory in the success of every Protestant Mission, and daily pray for them all. It was God's own wise Providence, and not my zeal, wise or intrusive, that matured these arrangements, and gave the Australian Presbyterian Churches a Mission Ship of their own, and a Mission field at their doors. The Ministers and the Sabbath Schools felt constrained as by one impulse to undertake this gracious work. The Presbyterian Churches in all these Colonies received this duty as from God ; and the organizing of Missionary Societies in Congregations and Sabbath Schools, for the effective accomplishment of the same, has been a principal means in the hands of the Lord of promoting and uplifting the cause of Christ throughout Australasia. It is worth while to re-travel that old road once again, were it for no other purpose than to show how, despite apparent checks and reverses, the mighty tide of Divine Love moves resistlessly onward, covers up temporary obstructions, and claims everything for Jesus.

CHAPTER IV.

CONCERNING FRIENDS AND FOES.

A.D. 1865—1866. ÆT. 41—42.

First of Missionary Duties.—Maré and Noumea.—The French in the Pacific.—The *Curaçoa* Affair.—The "Gospel and Gunpowder" Cry. —The Missionaries on their Defence.—The Mission Synod's Report. —The Shelling of the Tannese Villages.—Public Meeting and Presbytery.—Fighting at Bay.—Federal Union in Missions.—A Fiery Furnace at Geelong.—Results of Australian Tour. - New Hebrides Mission Adopted by Colonies.

WE went down to the Islands with the *Dayspring* in 1865. The full story of the years that had passed was laid before my Missionary brethren at their Annual Synod. They resolved that permanent arrangements must now be made for the Vessel's support, and that I must return to the Colonies and see these matured. This, meantime, appeared to all of them the most clamant of all Missionary duties,—their very lives, and the existence of the Mission itself, depending thereon. The Lord seemed to leave me no alternative; and, with great reluctance, my back was again turned away from the Islands. The *Dayspring*, doing duty among the Loyalty Islands, left me, along with my dear wife, on Maré, there to await an opportunity of getting to New Caledonia, and thence to Sydney.

Detained there for some time, we saw the noble work done by Messrs. Jones and Creagh, of the London Missionary Society, all being cruelly undone by the tyranny and Popery of the French. One day, in an inland walk, Mrs. Paton and I came on a large Conventicle in the bush. They were teaching each other, and reading the Scriptures which the Missionaries had translated into their own language, and which the French had forbidden them to use. They cried to God for deliverance from their oppressors! Missionaries were prohibited from teaching the Gospel to the Natives without the permission of France; their books were suppressed, and they themselves placed under military guard on the island of Lifu. Even when, by Britain's protest, the Missionaries were allowed to resume their work, the French language was alone to be used by them; and some, like Rev. J. Jones (as far down as 1888), were marched on board a Man-of-war, at half an hour's notice, and, without crime laid to their charge, forbidden ever to return to the Islands. While, on the other hand, the French Popish Missionaries were everywhere fostered and protected, presenting to the Natives as many objects of idolatry as their own, and following, as is the custom of the Romish Church in those Seas, in the wake of every Protestant Mission, to pollute and to destroy.

Being detained also for two weeks on Noumea, we saw the state of affairs under military rule. English Protestant residents, few in number, appealed to me to conduct worship, but liberty could not be obtained from the authorities, who hated everything English. Again a number of Protestant parents, some French, others English and German, applied to me to baptize their children at their own houses. To have asked permission would have been to court refusal, and to falsify my position. I laid the matter before the Lord, and baptized them all. Within two days the Private Secretary of the Governor arrived with an interpreter, and began to inquire of me, " Is it true that you have been baptizing here ? "

I replied quite frankly, " It is."

" We are sent to demand on whose authority."

" On the authority of my Great Master."

" When did you get that authority ? "

" When I was licensed and ordained to preach the Gospel, I got that authority from my Great Master."

Here a spirited conversation followed betwixt the two in French, and they politely bowed, and left me.

Very shortly they returned, saying, " The Governor sends his compliments, and he wishes the honour of a visit from you at Government House at three o'clock, if convenient for you."

I returned my greeting, and said that I would have pleasure in waiting upon his Excellency at the appointed hour. I thought to myself that I was in for it now, and I earnestly cried for Divine guidance.

He saluted me graciously as "de great Missionary of de New Hebrides." He conversed in a very friendly manner about the work there, and seemed anxious to find any indication as to the English designs. I had to deal very cautiously. He spoke chiefly through the interpreter; but, sometimes dismissing him, he talked to me as good, if not better English himself. He was eager to get my opinions as to how Britain got and retained her power over the Natives. After a very prolonged interview, we parted without a single reference to the baptisms or to religious services!

That evening the Secretary and interpreter waited upon us at our Inn, saying, "The Governor will have pleasure in placing his yacht and crew at your disposal to-morrow. Mrs. Paton and you can sail all around, and visit the Convict Island, and the Government Gardens, where lunch will be prepared for you."

It was a great treat to us indeed. The crew were in prison garments, but all so kind to us. By Convict labour all the public works seemed to be carried on, and the Gardens were most beautiful. The carved work in bone, ivory, cocoa-nuts, shells, etc., was indeed very wonderful. We bought a few specimens, but the prices were beyond our purse. It was a strange spectacle—these things of beauty and joy, and beside them the chained gangs of fierce and savage Convicts, kept down only by bullet and sword!

Thanking the Governor for his exceeding kindness, I referred to their Man-of-war about to go to Sydney, and offered to pay full passage money if they would take me, instead of leaving me to wait for a "trader." He at once granted my request, and arranged that we should be charged only at the daily cost for the sailors. At his suggestion, however, I took a number of things on board with me, and presented them to be used at the Cabin table. We were most generously treated—

the Captain giving up his own room to my wife and myself, as they had no special accommodation for passengers.

Noumea appeared to me at that time to be wholly given over to drunkenness and vice, supported as a great Convict Settlement by the Government of France, and showing every extreme of reckless, worldly pleasure, and of cruel, slavish toil. When I saw it again, three-and-twenty years thereafter, it showed no signs of progress for the better. In his book on the French Colonies, J. Bonwick, F.R.G.S., says that even yet Noumea and its dependencies contain only 1,068 Colonists from France. If there be a God of justice and of love, His blight cannot but rest on a nation whose pathway is stained with corruption and steeped in blood, as is undeniably the case with France in the Pacific Isles.

Arriving at Sydney, I was at once plunged into a whirlpool of horrors. H.M.S. *Curaçoa* had just returned from her official trip to the Islands, in which the Commodore, Sir William Wiseman, had thought it his duty to inflict punishment on the Natives for murder and robbery of Traders and others. On these Islands, as in all similar cases, the Missionaries had acted as interpreters, and of course always used their influence on the side of mercy, and in the interests of peace. But Sydney, and indeed Australia and the Christian World, were thrown into a ferment just a few days before our arrival, by certain articles in a leading publication there, and by the pictorial illustrations of the same. They were professedly from an officer on board Her Majesty's ship, and the sensation was increased by their apparent truthfulness and reality. Tanna was the scene of the first event, and a series was to follow in succeeding numbers. The *Curaçoa* was pictured lying at anchor off the shore, having the *Dayspring* astern. The Tannese warriors were being blown to pieces by shot and shell, and lay in heaps on the bloody coast. And the Missionaries were represented as safe in the lee of the Man-of-war, directing the onslaught, and gloating over the carnage.

Without a question being asked or a doubt suggested, without a voice being raised in fierce denial that such men as these Missionaries were known to be could be guilty of such conduct,—men who had jeoparded their lives for years on end rather than hurt one hair on a Native's head,—a cry of execration, loud and deep and even savage, arose from the Press, and was apparently joined in by the Church itself. The common witticism about the " Gospel and Gunpowder " headed hundreds of bitter and scoffing articles in the journals ; and, as we afterwards learned, the shocking news had been telegraphed to Britain and America, losing nothing in force by the way, and, while filling friends of Missions with dismay, was dished up day after day with every imaginable enhancement of horror for the readers of the secular and infidel Press. As I stepped ashore at Sydney, I found myself probably the best-abused man in all Australia, and the very name of the New Hebrides Mission stinking in the nostrils of the People.

The gage of battle had been thrown and fell at my feet. Without one moment's delay, I lifted it in the name of my Lord and of my maligned brethren. That evening my reply was in the hands of the editor, denying that such battles ever took place, detailing the actual facts of which I had been myself an eye-witness, and intimating legal prosecution unless the most ample and unequivocal withdrawal and apology were at once published. The Newspaper printed my rejoinder, and made satisfactory amends for having been imposed upon and deceived. I waited upon the Commodore, and·appealed for his help in redressing this terrible injury to our Mission. He informed me that he had already called his officers to account, but that all denied any connection with the articles or the pictures. He had little doubt, all the same, that some one on board was the prompter, who gloried in the evil that was being done to the cause of Christ. He offered every possible assistance, by testimony or otherwise, to place all the facts before the Christian public and to vindicate our Missionaries.

The outstanding facts are best presented in the following extract from the official report of the Mission Synod :

" When the New Hebrides Missionaries were assembled at their annual meeting on Aneityum, H.M.S. *Curaçoa*, Sir Wm. Wiseman, Bart., C.B., arrived in the harbour to investigate many grievances of white men and trading vessels among the Islands. A petition having been previously presented to the Governor in Sydney, as drawn out by the Revs. Messrs. Geddie and Copeland, after the murder of Mr. and Mrs. Gordon on Erromanga, requesting an investigation into the sad event, and the removal of a Sandal-wood Trader, a British subject, who had incited the Natives to it,—the Missionaries gave the Commodore a memorandum on the loss of life and property that had been sustained by the Mission on Tanna, Erromanga, and Efatè. He requested the Missionaries to supply him with interpreters, and requested the *Dayspring* to accompany him with them. The request was at once acceded to. Mr. Paton was appointed to act as interpreter for Tanna, Mr. Gordon for Erromanga, and Mr. Morrison for Efatè.

" At each of these Islands, the Commodore summoned the principal Chiefs near the harbours to appear before him, and explained to them that his visit was to inquire into the complaints British subjects had made against them, and to see if they had any against British subjects ; and when he had found out the truth he would punish those who had done the wrong and protect those who had suffered wrong. The Queen did not send him to compel them to become Christians, or to punish them for not becoming Christians. She left them to do as they liked in this matter ; but she was very angry at them because they had encouraged her subjects to live amongst them, sold them land, and promised to protect them, and afterwards murdered some of them and attempted to murder others, and stolen and destroyed their property ; that the inhabitants of these islands were talked of over the whole world for their treachery, cruelty, and murders ; and that the Queen would no longer allow them to murder or injure her subjects, who were living peaceably among them either as Missionaries or Traders. She would send a Ship of War every year to inquire into their conduct, and if any white man injured any Native they were to tell the Captain of the Man-of-war, and the white man would be punished as fast as the black man."

After spending much time, and using peaceably every means in his power in trying to get the guilty parties on Tanna, and not succeeding, he shelled two villages,—having the day before informed the Natives that he would do so, and advising to have all women, children, and sick removed, which in fact they did. He also sent a party on shore to destroy canoes, houses, etc.

The Tannese were astonished, beyond all precedent, by the terrific display of destructive power that was exhibited in the harbour. It was found impossible to reach the actual murderers; in these circumstances the Commodore's object was to save life and limit himself to the destruction of property, and so impress the Natives with some idea of those tremendous powers of destruction, which lie slumbering in a Man-of-war, and which can be awakened and brought into action at any moment.

On Erromanga no lives were lost. On Tanna one man was wounded; but, it was reported, three persons were afterwards killed by the bursting of a shell, when the Natives were stripping off its lead to make balls. It is matter of deep regret that one man of the party sent on shore was shot by a Native, concealed in a tree. Against orders he had wandered from his party, and was in a plantation standing eating a stick of sugar-cane when he was shot.

As I had orders to act as interpreter for the Commodore on Tanna, I will relate what happened there. From day to day, for three continuous days, he besought the Natives to comply with his wishes. He warned them that if they did not, he would shell the two villages of the Chief who murdered the last white man at Port Resolution, and destroy his canoes. He also explained to them, that all who retired to a large bay in the land of Nowar, the Christian Chief (if Christian he can be called), would be safe, as he had protected white men from being murdered; and now he would protect his property and all under his care on this land. The whole of these inhabitants, young and old, went to Nowar's land and were safe, while they witnessed what a Man-of-war could do in punishing murderers. But, before the hour approached, multitudes of Tannese warriors had assembled on the beach, painted and armed and determined to fight the Man-of-war! When the Commodore gave orders to prepare for action, I approached him and said with tears, "O Commodore, surely you are not going to shell these poor and foolish Tannese!"

Sharply, but not unkindly, he replied, "You are here as interpreter, not as my adviser. I alone am responsible. You see their defiant attitude. If I leave without punishing them now, no vessel or white man will be safe at this harbour. You can go on board your own ship, till I require your services again."

Indeed he had many counts against them, and his instructions were explicit. Shortly before that, Nouka, the Chief of one of the villages, had murdered a trader with a bar of iron, and another was murdered at his instigation. Miaki, the Chief of another, had for many years been ringleader of all mischief and murder on that side of the island. The Chief of a village on the other side of the bay was at that moment assembled with his men on the high ground within our view, and dancing to a war song in defiance !

The Commodore caused a shell to strike the hill and explode with terrific fury just underneath the dancers. The earth and the bush were torn and thrown into the air above and around them ; and next moment the whole host were seen disappearing over the brow of the hill. Two shots were sent over the heads of the warriors on the shore, with terrific noise and uproar ; in an instant, every man was making haste for Nowar's land, the place of refuge. The Commodore then shelled the villages, and destroyed their property. Beyond what I have here recorded, absolutely nothing was done.

We return then for a moment to Sydney. The public excitement made it impossible for me to open my lips in the promotion of our Mission. The Revs. Drs. Dunmore Lang and Steel, along with Professor Smith of the University, waited on the Commodore, and got an independent version of the facts. They then called a meeting on the affair by public advertisement. Without being made acquainted with the results of their investigations, I was called upon to give my own account of the *Curaçoa's* visit and of the connection of the Missionaries therewith. They then submitted the Commodore's statement, given by him in writing. He exonerated the Missionaries from every shadow of blame and from all responsibility. In the interests of mercy as well as justice, and to save life, they had acted as his interpreters ; and there all that they had to do with the *Curaçoa* began and ended. All this was published in the Newspapers next day, along with the speeches of the three deputies. The excitement began to subside. But the poison had been lodged in many hearts, and the ejectment of it was a slow and difficult process.

The Presbytery of Sydney held a special meeting, and I was summoned to appear before it. Dr. Geddie of Aneityum was also present, being then in the Colonies. Whether the tide of abuse had turned my dear fellow-Missionary's head, I cannot tell; but, on being asked to make a statement, he condemned the Missionaries for acting as interpreters, and wound up with a dramatic exclamation that "rather than have had anything to do with the *Curaçoa's* visit, he would have had his hand burned off in the fire."

The Court applauded. The Moderator then said: "Mr. Paton has heard the noble speech of Dr. Geddie. Let him now solemnly promise that, under no circumstances, will he have anything to do with a Man-of-war. Then we may see our way again to stand by him, and help him in his Mission." And in this spirit, he appealed to me.

On rising, I explained that I appeared before them only out of brotherly courtesy, as their Presbytery had no jurisdiction over me, and I spoke to the following effect:

"I am indeed a Missionary to the Heathen, but also a British subject. I have never requested redress from Man-of-war, or any civil power; but, like Paul, I reserve my full rights, if need be, to appeal unto Cæsar. If any member of this Presbytery has his house robbed, as a good citizen he seeks redress and protection. But on Tanna I lost my earthly all and sought no redress from man. The Tannese Chiefs, indeed, who were friendly, sent a petition by me to the Governor of Sydney; which, however, was never presented to him at all, fearing that thereby indirectly I might bring punishment upon my poor deluded Tannese. Others were more convinced as to the path of duty, or less considerate of the Natives. Their Petition I now take from my pocket and submit it to you. It was presented to the Governor, Sir John Young, after the death of the Gordons, and prayed for a judicial investigation as to their murders. As soon as it was known of, a counter Petition in the interests of the Traders was immediately got up and signed by many of the great merchants of Sydney, protesting against any such visit to the Islands by a Man-of-war. This

Petition, then, the original and only one ever presented in favour of a visit from Her Majesty's Commodore, was drawn up and is signed—by whom ? "

On Dr. Geddie acknowledging that he had written and signed that Petition, but that it prayed only for an *investigation*, I proceeded :

" Surely a judicial investigation like this implied all the after consequences, if once undertaken ! At any rate, this is the *only* Petition sent from the Missionaries, and it was sent unknown to me. Finally, I must respectfully inform the Presbytery that I will never make such a promise as the Moderator has indicated. I shall remain free to act in the interests of humanity and justice, as God and conscience guide me. I believe I saved both life and property by interpreting for the Commodore, and making things mutually intelligible to him and to the Natives. I have done as clear a Christian duty as I ever did in my life. I am not ashamed. I offer no apology. I do not believe that in the long run, when all facts are known, my conduct in this affair can possibly injure either myself, or, what is more, the Name of my Lord."

Perhaps my words were not too conciliatory. But excitement so blinded many friends, that I had to fight as if at bay, or get no hearing and no justice. The Presbytery hesitated, and closed without coming to any resolution. But all the members of it showed me thereafter the same respect as ever before. It was gratifying to learn in due course that all the Churches supporting our Mission, after having independently investigated the facts, justified the course adopted by us— Nova Scotia alone excepted. Yet two of her own Missionaries had also to interpret for that Man-of-war, exactly as I had done, nor did I ever hear that any rebuke was administered to them. Feeling absolutely conscious that I had only done my Christian duty, I left all results in the hands of my Lord Jesus, and pressed forward in His blessed work.

More than one dear personal friend had to be sacrificed over this painful affair. A Presbyterian Minister, and a godly elder and his wife, all most excellent and well-beloved, at whose houses I had been received as a brother, intimated to me that owing to this case of the *Curaçoa* their friendship and mine must entirely cease in this world. And it did cease; but my esteem never changed. I had learned not to think unkindly of friends, even when they manifestly misunderstood my actions. Nor would these things merit being recorded here, were it not that they may be at once a beacon and a guide. God's people are still belied. And the multitude are still as ready as ever to cry, " Crucify ! Crucify ! "

The scheme for meeting the yearly cost of the *Dayspring*, that had already been tentatively set a-going, had now to be matured and permanently organized. In this my dear friend Dr. J. Dunmore Lang, well acquainted with the resources of all the Churches, was our judicious counsellor. We proposed that Victoria should raise £500 ; New South Wales and New Zealand, £200 each ; Tasmania, Queensland, and South Australia, £100 each ; and £250 each from Nova Scotia and Scotland. Tasmania, South Australia, and Queensland fell a little short of their proportion ; Sydney, Scotland, and Nova Scotia met their claims ; and Victoria and New Zealand exceeded them, and made up for deficiency in others. This has ever since been done in great measure, though not exclusively, by the Sabbath Scholars of the Churches, through their *Dayspring* " Mission-boxes." In organizing and maturing this scheme, I visited and addressed almost every Presbyterian Congregation and Sabbath School in New South Wales and Victoria, South Australia and Tasmania ; and Ministers and Superintendents, with scarcely an exception, came to be bound together in a true federal union in support of our Mission and our Ship.

For the first three years, when everything was new, the *Dayspring* cost us about £1,400 per annum ; but since then she has cost on an average little short of £2,000 over all. There has too often been a floating deficiency of £300 or more, which has given us great anxiety ; but the Lord has sent what was required, and enabled us to keep her sailing with the Gospel and His servants amongst these Islands, free of any actual burden,—His own pure messenger of Good Tidings, unstained with the polluting and bloody associations of the foul-winged trading Ships !

Another fiery furnace awaited me on this tour, when I

reached Geelong. One of the prominent Ministers refused to shake hands. An agent of the London Missionary Society had informed them that "the £3,000 paid for the *Dayspring* had been thrown away, that the Vessel was useless, fitted only for carrying stores, and having no accommodation for passengers; and that on her second trip to the Islands our Missionaries had to wait and go down by the *John Williams.*" It was an abiding sorrow to me, that local misrepresentations gave the Societies an appearance of conflict, whereof the parent organizations knew nothing whatever. But, for all the interests at stake, facts *had* to be made known. Several Congregations had resolved to withdraw from the support of our Mission; and several Ministers at Ballarat, and elsewhere, were by similar accounts prejudiced against us.

I demanded an opportunity of stating the facts, and vindicating myself and others, in a public meeting duly called for the purpose. They at once agreed. I wrote once and a second time to the Agent, but got no answer, only an evasive note. I went by rail and saw him. He would give no explanation, or authority for his statements, but practically put me out, on a pretence of there being sickness at the house. Nevertheless, in a spirit of determined brotherhood, I resolved only to explain facts about the *Dayspring*, and not to drag in the name of that great sister Society which he so poorly served.

There was a crowded meeting. The Minister who refused to shake hands was voted to the chair. I was called upon to explain my position. By this time I had communicated with the *Dayspring* officials, and, producing the log-book, I read from it, regarding the voyage referred to, the following:

"When the *Dayspring* sailed from Sydney for the Islands, she had as passengers on board, Rev. Mr. Paton, Mrs. Paton, and child, Rev. Mr. McNair and Mrs. McNair, Rev. Mr. Niven and Mrs. Niven, Mrs. Ella and child, of the London Missionary Society, Captain Fraser, Mrs. Fraser, child, and servant, besides all the year's Mission supplies for both the New Hebrides and the Loyalty Islands. And on reaching these Islands, as the French Government had ordered the removal of all the Eastern Teachers of the London Missionary Society from that group, the *Dayspring* had to undertake an

20

unexpected voyage of three months from the Loyalties to Samoa, Rarotonga, etc., with Rev. Mr. and Mrs. Sleigh of the London Missionary Society, and sixty-one of their Native Teachers, who, along with their families, were all in health landed safely on their respective islands, as passengers by the *Dayspring*."

I also read a corroborative narrative from Captain Fraser, written from memory, as he was at that time far inland in the country, and had not access to the records of his vessel. And my statement closed to this effect :

" It must now be manifest to all, that the damaging reports circulated in Geelong are more than replied to. By the Captain, and from the log, they are proved to be false, both as to capacity for goods and passengers. At present the *Dayspring* is everything that could be desired for the furtherance of our Mission. If *you* are satisfied, I wish to leave this painful subject, and proceed with my proper work. But I am prepared to answer any question from the Chairman or the meeting, and to give the fullest information."

The round of applause that followed was my complete vindication. The Chairman gave me his hand, and pledged his utmost support. He proposed the following resolution, which was carried with acclamation :

" That this meeting, having heard Mr. Paton with satisfaction, pledges the Churches, Sabbath Schools, and friends in Geelong, henceforth to support the *Dayspring* and the New Hebrides Mission to the utmost of their power, and to receive and encourage him as much as ever in his work on behalf of the Mission."

The special object of my visit was then explained, and several Ministers and others spoke heartily in furtherance of the proposals for the permanent support of the *Dayspring* through the Sabbath Schools.

All battles through mere misunderstandings are painful, but especially those amongst Christian brethren. Still they had to be fought, never laying aside the weapons of the Cross ; and God has overruled them for the promotion of His Kingdom in a way which makes all Catholic-spirited followers of the Lord Jesus equally rejoice.

On this tour, in Victoria alone, I spent 250 days, and addressed 265 meetings, representing 180 Congregations and their Sabbath Schools. The proportion was on the same scale in the other Colonies visited. And all these arrangements I had to make for myself, by painful and laborious correspondence night and day. But the Lord's blessing was abundantly vouchsafed. Victoria gave £1,954 19s. 3d.; Tasmania, £76 12s. 7d.; South Australia, £222 16s.; New South Wales, £249; being a total of £2,503 7s. 10d., besides £220 in yearly donations of £5, promised for the maintenance of the Native Teachers.

In 1862 I appealed to the Victorian General Assembly to take up the New Hebrides Mission as their own. The appeal was followed by Rev. J. Clark, Convener of Heathen Missions Committee in 1863, getting the Assembly to accept the proposal. And in 1865 the Rev. Dr. A. J. Campbell carried our scheme, and the Assembly pledged itself to give £500 per annum for the support of the *Dayspring*, from the offerings of the Sabbath Schools. New Zealand and other Colonies soon followed Victoria's example, until all were pledged to uphold the New Hebrides Mission. For my dear friend and old College companion, Rev. Joseph Copeland, had visited at the same time Queensland and New Zealand, and had received from them respectively £101 2s. 4d. and £580; so that all the Churches adopted our scheme for the permanent support of the *Dayspring*, and the Mission fund had now a fair balance on the right side.

At the General Assembly of the Presbyterian Church of Victoria in 1866, I was adopted—being officially transferred from the Church in Scotland—as the first Missionary from the Presbyterian Churches of Australia to the New Hebrides. Dr. Geddie would also have been adopted at the same time, but Nova Scotia could not agree to part with its first and most highly honoured Missionary. The Victorian Church therefore engaged the Rev. James Cosh, M.A., on his way out from Scotland, as its other agent, in the hope that we two might be able to re-open and carry on the Tanna Mission. In their *Christian Review* of 1867, they said:

" The idea which we in Victoria had, when the Missionaries

left us in July last, was, that Messrs. Paton and Cosh would be associated on Tanna, and labour for its evangelization, under the special auspices as well as at the cost of the Presbyterian Church of Victoria ; but Mr. Cosh, having chosen the station at Pango on Efatè, where the Natives were more prepared for the Gospel, and where life and property were safe, went to spend a year's novitiateship with Mr. and Mrs. Morrison on Efatè. Mr. Paton would have fain gone back to Tanna, but the Missionaries generally feared that no one European life would have been safe at the time on Tanna. They therefore, and no doubt wisely, sent Mr. Paton to the small and less savage, but not less Heathen, Island of Aniwa."

It was indeed one of the bitterest trials of my life, not to be able ·to return and settle down at once on dear old Tanna; but I could not go alone, against the decided opposition of all the other Missionaries—Dr. Inglis, however, at last sympathizing most strongly with my views. I went, as will appear hereafter, to Aniwa, the nearest island to the scene of my former woes and perils, in the hope that God would soon open up my way and enable me to return to blood-stained Tanna.

My heart bleeds for the Heathen, and I long to see a Teacher for every tribe and a Missionary for every island of the New Hebrides. The hope still burns that I may witness it; and then I could gladly rest.

CHAPTER V.

SETTLEMENT ON ANIWA.

A.D. 1866—1867. ÆT. 42—43.

The *John Williams* on the Reef.—A Native's Soliloquy.—Nowar Pleading for Tanna.—The White Shells of Nowar.—The Island of Aniwa. —First Landing on Aniwa.—The Site of our New Home.—"Me no Steal!"—House-Building for God.—Native Expectations.—Tafigeitu or Sorcery.—The Miracle of Speaking Wood. —Perils through Superstitions.—The Mission Premises.—A City of God.—Builders and their Wages.—Great Swimming Feat.—Stronger than the "Gods" of Aniwa.

EVERYTHING being now arranged for in the Colonies, in connection with the Mission and *Dayspring*, as far as could possibly be, we sailed for the Islands on the 8th August, 1866. Besides my wife and child, the following accompanied us to the field: Revs. Copeland, Cosh, and McNair, along with their respective wives. On August 20th we reached Aneityum; and, having landed some of our friends, we sailed Northwards, as far as Efatè, to let the new Missionaries see all the Islands open for occupation, and to bring all our Missionaries back to the annual meeting, where the permanent settlements would be finally agreed upon.

On our return, we found that the beautiful new *John Williams*, reaching Aneityum on 5th of September, had stuck fast on the coral reef and swung there for three days. By the unceasing efforts of the Natives, working in hundreds, she was saved, though badly damaged. At a united meeting of all the Missionaries, representing the London Missionary Society and our own, it was resolved that she must be taken to Sydney for repairs. Twenty stout Aneityumese were placed on board to keep her pumps going by day and night, and the *Dayspring* was sent to keep her company in case of any dire emergency. Missionaries were waiting to be settled, and the season was stealing away. But the cause of humanity and the claims of a sister Mission were paramount. We remained at Aneityum for five weeks, and awaited the return of the *Dayspring*.

While staying here, I learned with as deep emotion as man ever felt for man, that noble old Abraham, the sharer of my Tannese trials, had during the interval peacefully fallen asleep in Jesus. He left for me his silver watch—one which I had myself sent to the dear soul from Sydney, and which he greatly prized. In his dying hour he said, " Give it to Missi, my own Missi Paton; and tell him that I go to Jesus, where Time is dead."

I learned also, and truly human-hearted readers will need no apology for introducing this news in so grave a story—that my faithful dog *Clutha*, entrusted to the care of a kindly Native to be kept for my return, had, despite all coaxing, grown weary of heart amongst all these dark faces, and fallen asleep too, truly not unworthy of a grateful tear !

At our annual Synod, after much prayerful deliberation and the careful weighing of every vital circumstance, I was constrained by the united voice of my brethren not to return to Tanna, but to settle on the adjoining island of Aniwa (= A-neé-wa). It was even hoped that thereby Tanna might eventually be the more surely reached and evangelized.

By the new Missionaries all the other old Stations were re-occupied, and some fresh Islands were entered upon in the name of Jesus. As we moved about with our *Dayspring*, and planted the Missionaries here and there, nothing could repress the wonder of Natives.

" How is this ? " they cried; " we slew or drove them all away ! We plundered their houses and robbed them. Had we been so treated, nothing would have made us return. But they come back with a beautiful new ship, and with more and more Missionaries. And is it to trade and to get money, like the other white men ? No! no! But to tell us of their Jehovah God and of His Son Jesus. If their God makes them do all that, we may well worship Him too."

In this way, island after island was opened up to receive the

Missionary, and their Chiefs bound themselves to protect and cherish him, before they knew anything whatever of the Gospel, beyond what they saw in the disposition and character of its Preachers or heard rumoured regarding its fruits on other Islands. Imagine *Cannibals* found thus prepared to welcome the Missionary, and to make not only his property but his life comparatively safe. The Isles "wait" for Christ.

On our way to Aniwa, the *Dayspring* had to call at Tanna. By stress of weather we lay several days in Port Resolution. And there many memories were again revived—wounds that after five-and-twenty years, when I now write, still bleed afresh! Nowar, the old Chief, unstable but friendly, was determined to keep us there by force or by fraud. The Captain told him that the council of the Missionaries had forbidden him to land our boxes at Tanna.

"Don't land them," said the wily Chief, "just throw them over; my men and I will catch everything before it reaches the water, and carry them all safely ashore!"

The Captain said he durst not. "Then," persisted Nowar, "just point them out to us; you will have no further trouble; we will manage everything for Missi."

They were in distress when he refused; and poor old Nowar tried another tack. Suspecting that my dear wife was afraid of them, he got us on shore to see his extensive plantations. Turning eagerly to her, he said, leaving me to interpret, "Plenty of food! While I have a yam or a banana, you shall not want."

She answered, "I fear not any lack of food."

Pointing to his warriors, he cried, "We are many! We are strong! We can always protect you."

"I am not afraid," she calmly replied.

He then led us to that chestnut-tree, in the branches of which I had sat during a lonely and memorable night, when all hope had perished of any earthly deliverance, and said to her with a manifest touch of genuine emotion, "The God who protected Missi there will always protect you."

She told him that she had no fear of that kind, but explained to him that we must for the present go to Aniwa, but would return to Tanna, if the Lord opened up our way. Nowar,

Arkurat, and the rest, seemed to be genuinely grieved, and it touched my soul to the quick.

A beautiful incident was the outcome, as we learned only in long after years. There was at that time an Aniwan Chief on Tanna, visiting friends. He was one of their great Sacred Men. He and his people had been promised a passage home in the *Dayspring*, with their canoes in tow. When old Nowar saw that he could not keep us with himself, he went to this Aniwan Chief, and took the white shells, the insignia of Chieftainship, from his own arm, and bound them on the Sacred Man, saying, " By these you promise to protect my Missi and his wife and child on Aniwa. Let no evil befall them ; or, by this pledge, I and my people will revenge it."

In a future crisis, this probably saved our lives, and shall be afterwards related. After all, a bit of the Christ-Spirit had found its way into that old Cannibal's soul ! And the same Christ-Spirit in me yearned more strongly still, and made it a positive pain to pass on to another Island, and leave him in that dim-groping twilight of the soul.

Aniwa became my Mission Home in November 1866 ; and for the next fifteen years it was the heart and centre of my personal labours in the Heathen World. Since 1881, alas ! my too frequent deputation pilgrimages among Churches in Great Britain and in the Colonies have rendered my visits to Aniwa but few and far between. God never guided me back to Tanna ; but others, my dear friends, have seen His Kingdom planted and beginning to grow amongst that slowly relenting race. Aniwa was to be the land wherein my past years of toil and patience and faith were to see their fruits ripening at length. I claimed Aniwa for Jesus, and by the grace of God Aniwa now worships at the Saviour's feet.

The Island of Aniwa is one of the smaller isles of the New Hebrides. It measures scarcely seven miles by two, and is everywhere girt round with a belt of coral reef. The sea breaks thereon heavily, with thundering roar, and the white surf rolls in furious and far. But there are days of calm, when all the sea is glass, and the spray on the reef is only a fringe of silver.

The ledges of coral rock indicate that Aniwa has been

heaved up from its ocean bed, at three or four separate bursts of mighty volcanic power. No stone or other rock anywhere appears, but only and always the coral, in its beautiful and mysterious variety. The highest land is less than three hundred feet above the level of the sea ; and though the soil is generally light, there are patches good and deep, mostly towards the southern end of the island, and near the crater of an extinct volcano, where excellent plantations are found, and which, if carefully cultivated, might support ten times the present population.

Aniwa, having no hills to attract and condense the clouds, suffers badly for lack of genial rains ; and the heavy rains of hurricane and tempest seem to disappear as if by magic through the light soil and porous rock. The moist atmosphere and the heavy dews, however, keep the Island covered with green, while large and fruitful trees draw wondrous nourishment from their rocky beds. The Natives suffer from a species of Elephantiasis, in all probability produced by their bad drinking water, and from the hot and humid climate of their isle.

Aniwa has no harbour, or safe anchorage of any kind for ships ; though, in certain winds, they have been seen at anchor on the outer edge of the reef, always a perilous haven ! There is one crack in the coral belt, through which a boat can safely run to shore ; but the little wharf, built there of the largest coral blocks that could be rolled together, has been once and again swept clean off by the hurricane, leaving " not a wrack behind."

I had had a glimpse of Aniwa before, in the *John Knox*, when Mr. Johnston accompanied me ; and again with my dear friend Gordon, who was murdered on Erromanga ; besides, I had seen Aniwans in their canoes at Tanna in search of food. They had pleaded with us to remain amongst them, arguing against there being two Missionaries on Tanna and none on Aniwa. Their " orator," a very subtle man, who spoke Tannese well, informed us that the white Traders told them that if they killed or drove away the Missionaries they would get plenty of ammunition and tobacco. This was why our life had been so often attempted. Beyond this all was strange. Everything had to be learned afresh on Aniwa, as on Tanna.

When we landed, the Natives received us kindly. They and the Aneityumese Teachers led us to a temporary home, prepared for our abode. It was a large Native Hut. Walls and roof consisted of sugar-cane leaf and reeds, intertwisted on a strong wooden frame. It had neither doors nor windows, but open spaces instead of these. The earthen floor alone looked beautiful, covered thick with white coral broken small. It had only one Apartment; and that, meantime, had to serve also for Church and School and Public Hall. We screened off a little portion, and behind that screen planted our bed, and stored our valuables. All the Natives within reach assembled to watch us taking our food! A box at first served for a chair, the lid of another box was our table, our cooking was all done in the open air under a large tree, and we got along with amazing comfort. But the house was under the shelter of a coral rock, and we saw at a glance that at certain seasons it would prove a very hotbed of fever and ague. We were, however, only too thankful to enter it, till a better could be built, and on a breezier site.

The Aniwans were not so violently dishonourable as the Tannese. But they had the knack of asking in a rather menacing manner whatever they coveted; and the tomahawk was sometimes swung to enforce an appeal. For losses and annoyance, we had of course no redress. But we tried to keep things well out of their way, knowing that the opportunity there, as elsewhere, sometimes develops the thief. We strove to get along quietly and kindly, in the hope that when we knew their language, and could teach them the principles of Jesus, they would be saved, and life and property would be secure. But the rumour of the *Curaçoa's* visit and her punishment of murder and robbery did more, by God's blessing, to protect us during those Heathen days than all other influences combined. The savage Cannibal was heard to whisper to his bloodthirsty mates, " not to murder or to steal, for the Man-of-war that punished Tanna would blow up their little Island ! "

Sorrowful experience on Tanna had taught us to seek the site for our Aniwan house on the highest ground, and away from the malarial influences near the shore. There was one charming mound, covered with trees whose roots ran down into the crevices of coral, and from which Tanna and Erromanga are clearly seen. But there the Natives for some superstitious reason forbade us to build, and we were constrained to take another rising ground somewhat nearer the shore. In the end, this turned out to be the very best site on the island for us, central and suitable every way. But we afterwards learned that perhaps superstition also led them to sell us this site, in the malicious hope that it would prove our ruin. The mounds on the top, which had to be cleared away, contained the bones and refuse of their Cannibal feasts for ages. None but their Sacred Men durst touch them; and the Natives watched us hewing and digging, certain that their gods would strike us dead! That failing, their thoughts may probably have been turned to reflect that after all the Jehovah God was stronger than they.

In levelling the site, and gently sloping the sides of the ground for good drainage purposes, I had gathered together two large baskets of human bones. I said to a Chief in Tannese, "How do these bones come to be here?"

And he replied, with a shrug worthy of a cynical Frenchman, " Ah, we are not Tanna-men ! We don't eat the bones ! "

While I was away building the house, Mrs. Paton had one dreadful fright. She generally remained about half a mile off, in charge of the Native Hut in which our property had been stored, with one or two of the friendly Natives around her, though as yet she could not speak their language. One day she sat alone, the baby playing at her feet. A rustling commenced amongst the boxes behind the curtain. She had been there all the morning, and no one had entered. Horror-smitten, her eyes were fastened towards the noise. Suddenly the blanket-screen was thrown aside, and a black face, with blood-red eyes and milk-white teeth, peered out, and cried in broken English, " Me no steal ! Me no steal ! "

Then, with a bound like that of a deer, the man sprang out and ran for the village. My dear wife, fearing his sudden return, snatched up her child and rushed to the place where I was working, never feeling the ground beneath her till she sank down almost fainting at my feet. Thanking God for her escape, we thought it wiser to remain where we were and finish our task for the day. We learned that, since we did not return, his wrath had cooled down and he had withdrawn. This man was a sort of wild beast in his passionate moods. His body became convulsed and his muscles twitched with rage. He had lately murdered a neighbour, a man of his own tribe, in his frenzy. We believe that the Lord baffled his rage on that memorable day, and said to his tumultuous soul— " Peace ! be still."

The site being now cleared, we questioned whether to build only a temporary home, hoping to return to dear old Tanna as soon as possible, or, though the labour would be vastly greater, a substantial house—for the comfort of our successors, if not of ourselves. We decided that, as this was work for God, we would make it the very best we could. We planned two central rooms, sixteen feet by sixteen, with a five-feet-wide lobby between, so that other rooms could be added when required. About a quarter of a mile from the sea, and thirty-five feet above its level, I laid the foundations of the house. Coral blocks raised the wall about three feet high all round. Air passages carried sweeping currents underneath each room, and greatly lessened the risk of fever and ague. A wide trench was dug all round, and filled up as a drain with broken coral. At back and front, the verandah stretched five feet wide ; and pantry, bath-room, and tool-house were partitioned off under the verandah behind. The windows sent to me had hinges ; I added two feet to each, with wood from Mission-boxes, and made them French door-windows, opening from each room to the verandah. And so we had, by God's blessing, a healthy spot to live in, if not exactly a thing of beauty !

The Mission House, as ultimately finished, had six rooms, three on each side of the lobby, and measured ninety feet in length, surrounded by a verandah, one hundred feet by five, which kept everything shaded and cool. Underneath two rooms, a cellar was dug eight feet deep, and shelved all round for a store. In more than one terrific hurricane that cellar saved our lives,—all crushing into it when trees and houses were being tossed like feathers on the wings of the wind.

Altogether, the house at Aniwa has proved one of the healthiest and most commodious of any that have been planted by Christian hands on the New Hebrides. In selecting site and in building " the good hand of our God was upon us for good."

I built also two small Orphanages, almost as inevitably necessary as the Missionary's own house. They stood on a line with the front of my own dwelling, one for girls, the other for boys, and we had them constantly under our own eyes. The orphans were practically boarded at the Mission premises, and adopted by the Missionaries. Their clothing was a heavy drain upon our resources ; and every odd and curious article that came in any of the boxes or parcels was utilized. We trained these young people for Jesus. And at this day many of the best of our Native Teachers, and most devoted Christian helpers, are amongst those who would probably have perished but for these Orphanages.

A grievous accident deprived me of special help in house-building. I cut my ankle badly with an adze, as I had done before on Tanna, through a knot in the tree. Binding my handkerchief tightly round it, I appealed to the Natives to carry me back to our hut. They stipulated for payment. My vest pocket being filled with fish-hooks, a current coin on all these Islands, I got a fellow to understand the bribe. He carried me a little, got some hooks, and then called another, who did the same, and then called a third, and so on, each man earning his hooks, and passing on the burden and the pay to another, while I suffered terribly and bled profusely. Being my own doctor, I dressed the wound for weeks, kept it constantly in cold water bandages, and by the kindness of the Lord it recovered, though it left me lame for many a day.

But the greatest sorrow was this : the good and kind Aneityumese, who had been hired to come and help me with all the unskilled parts of the labour, could do nothing without me ; and when the *Dayspring* came round at the appointed time, I had to pay them in full and let them return, deprived of their valuable aid. Even to keep them in food would have exhausted our limited stores, and some months must elapse before our next supplies could arrive from Sydney.

The Aniwans themselves could scarcely be induced to work at all, even for payment. Their personal wants were few, and were supplied by their own plantations. They replied to my appeals with all the unction of philosophers, and told me, "The conduct of the men of Aniwa is to stand by, or sit and look on, while their women do the work ! "

On Aniwa we soon found ourselves face to face with blank Heathenism. The Natives at first expected that the Missionary's *Biritania tavai* (= British Medicine) would cure at once all their complaints. Disappointment led to resentment in their ignorant and childish minds. They also expected to get for the asking, or for any trifle, an endless supply of knives, calico, fish-hooks, blankets, etc. Every refusal irritated them. Again, our Medicines relieved or cured them, so they blamed us also for their diseases,—all their Sacred Men not only curing but also *causing* sickness. Further, they generally came to us only after exhausting every resource of their own witchcraft and superstition, and when it was probably too late. I had often to taste the Medicine in their sight (or even take the first dose myself!) before the sufferers would touch it ; and if one dose did not cure them, it was almost impossible to get them to persevere. But time taught them its value, and the yearly expenditure for Medicine soon became a very heavy tax on our modest salary.

Still we set our bell a-ringing every day after dinner— intimating our readiness to give advice or medicine to all who were sick. We spoke to them, so soon as we had learned, a few words about Jesus. The weak received a cup of tea and a piece of bread. The demand was sometimes great, especially when epidemics befell them. But some rather fled from us as the cause of their sickness, and sought refuge from our presence in remotest corners, or rushed off at our approach and concealed themselves in the bush. They were but children, and full of superstition ; and we had to win them by kindly patience, never losing faith in them and hope for them, any more than the Lord did with us !

As on Tanna, all sicknesses and deaths were supposed to be caused by sorcery, there called *Nahak*, on Aniwa called *Tafigeitu*. Some Sacred Man burned the remains of food, such as the skin of a banana, or a hair from the head, or something that the person had even touched, and he was the disease-maker. Hence they were kept in a state of constant terror, and breathed the very atmosphere of revenge. When one became sick, all the people of his village met day after day, and made long speeches and tried to find out the enemy who was causing it. Having fixed on some one, they first sent presents of mats, baskets, and food to the supposed disease-makers ; if the person recovered, they took credit for it ; if the person died, his friends sought revenge on the supposed murderers. And such revenge took a wide sweep, satisfying itself with the suspected enemy, or any of his family, or of his village, or even of his tribe. Thus endless bloodshed and unceasing inter-tribal wars kept the people from one end of the island to the other in one long-drawn broil and turmoil.

Our learning the language on Aniwa was marked by similar incidents to those of Tanna, related in Part First ; though a few of them could understand my Tannese, and that greatly helped me. One day a man, after carefully examining some article, turned to his neighbour and said, " Taha tinei ? "

I inferred that he was asking, " What is this ? " Pointing to another article, I repeated their words ; they smiled at each other, and gave me its name.

On another occasion, a man said to his companion, looking toward me, " Taha neigo ? " Concluding that he was asking my name, I pointed towards him, and repeated the words, and they at once gave me their names.

Readers would be surprised to discover how much you can readily learn of any language, with these two short questions constantly on your lips, and with people ready at every turn to answer — " What's this ? " " What's your name ? " Every word was at once written down, spelled phonetically and arranged in alphabetic order, and a note appended as to the circumstances in which it was used. By frequent comparison of these notes, and by careful daily and even hourly imitation of all their sounds, we were able in a measure to understand each other before we had gone far in the house-building operations, during which some of them were constantly beside me.

One incident of that time was very memorable, and God turned it to good account for higher ends. I often tell it as "the miracle of the speaking bit of wood"; and it has happened to other Missionaries exactly as to myself. While working at the house, I required some nails and tools. Lifting a piece of planed wood, I pencilled a few words on it, and requested our old Chief to carry it to Mrs. Paton, and she would send what I wanted. In blank wonder, he innocently stared at me, and said, "But what do you want?"

I replied, "The wood will tell her." He looked rather angry, thinking that I befooled him, and retorted, "Who ever heard of wood speaking?"

By hard pleading I succeeded in persuading him to go. He was amazed to see her looking at the wood and then fetching the needed articles. He brought back the bit of wood, and eagerly made signs for an explanation. Chiefly in broken Tannese I read to him the words, and informed him that in the same way God spoke to us through His Book. The will of God was written there, and by-and-bye, when he learned to read, he would hear God *speaking* to him from its page, as Mrs. Paton heard me from the bit of wood.

A great desire was thus awakened in the poor man's soul to see the very Word of God printed in his own language. He helped me to learn words and master ideas with growing enthusiasm. And when my work of translating portions of Holy Scripture began, his delight was unbounded and his help invaluable. The miracle of a speaking page was not less wonderful than that of speaking wood!

One day, while building the house, an old Inland Chief and his three sons came to see us. Everything was to them full of wonder. After returning home one of the sons fell sick, and the father at once blamed us and the Worship, declaring that if the lad died we all should be murdered in revenge. By God's blessing, and by our careful nursing and suitable medicine, he recovered and was spared. The old Chief superstitiously wheeled round almost to another extreme. He became not only friendly, but devoted to us. He attended the Sabbath Services, and listened to the Aneityumese Teachers, and to my first attempts, partly in Tannese, translated by the orator Taia or the chief Namakei, and explained in our hearing to the people in their mother tongue.

But on the heels of this, another calamity overtook us. So soon as two rooms of the Mission House were roofed in, I hired the stoutest of the young men to carry our boxes thither. Two of them started off with a heavy box suspended on a pole from shoulder to shoulder, their usual custom. They were shortly after attacked with vomiting of blood; and one of them, an Erromangan, actually died. The father of the other swore that, if his son did not get better, every soul at the Mission House should be slain in revenge. But God mercifully restored him.

As the boat-landing was nearly three-quarters of a mile distant, and such a calamity recurring would be not only sorrowful in itself but perilous in the extreme for us all, I steeped my wits, and with such crude materials as were at hand, I manufactured not only a hand-barrow, but a wheel-barrow, for the pressing emergencies of the time. In due course, I procured a more orthodox hand-cart from the Colonies, and coaxed and bribed the Natives to assist me in making a road for it. Perhaps the ghost of *Macadam* would shudder at the appearance of that road, but it has proved immensely useful ever since.

Our Mission House was once and again threatened with fire, and we ourselves with musket, before its completion. The threats to set fire to our premises stirred up Namakei, however, to befriend us; and we learned that he and his people had us under a guard by night and by day. But a savage Erromangan lurked about for ten days, watching for us with tomahawk and musket, and we knew that our peril was extreme. Looking up to God for protection, I went on with my daily toils, having a small American tomahawk beside me, and showing no fear. The main thing was to take every precaution against surprise, for these murderers are all cowards, and will attempt nothing when observed. I sent for the old Chief, whose guest the Erromangan was, and warned him that God would hold him guilty too if our blood was shed.

"Missi," he warmly replied, "I knew not, I knew not !

21

But by the first favourable wind he shall go, and you will see him no more."

He kept his word, and we were rescued from the enemy and the avenger.

The site was excellent and very suitable for our Mission Station. The ground sloped away nearly all round us, and the pathway up to it was adorned on each side with beautiful crotons and island plants, and behind these a row of orange trees. A cocoa-nut grove skirted the shore for nearly three miles, and shaded the principal public road. Near our premises were many leafy chestnuts and wide-spreading bread-fruit trees. When, in the course of years, everything had been completed to our taste, we lived practically in the midst of a beautiful Village,—the Church, the School, the Orphanage, the Smithy and Joiner's Shop, the Printing Office, the Banana and Yam House, the Cook House, etc.; all very humble indeed, but all standing sturdily up there among the orange trees, and preaching the Gospel of a higher civilization and of a better life for Aniwa. The little road leading to each door was laid with the white coral broken small. The fence around all shone fresh and clean with new paint. Order and taste were seen to be laws in the white man's New Life; and several of the Natives began diligently to follow our example.

Many and strange were the arts which I had to try to practise, such as handling the adze, the mysteries of tenon and mortise, and other feats of skill. If a Native wanted a fish-hook, or a piece of red calico to bind his long whip-cord hair, he would carry me a block of coral or fetch me a beam; but continuous daily toil seemed to him a mean exist-ence. The women were tempted, by calico and beads for pay, to assist in preparing the sugar-cane leaf for thatch, gathering it in the plantations, and tying it over reeds four or six feet long with strips of bark or pandanus leaf, leaving a long fringe hanging over on one side. How differently they acted when the Gospel began to touch their hearts! They built their Church and their School then, by their own free toil, rejoicing to labour without money or price; and they have ever since kept them in good repair for the service of the Lord, by their voluntary offerings of wood and sugar-cane leaf and coral-lime.

The roof was firmly tied on and nailed; thereon were laid the reeds, fringed with sugar-cane leaf, row after row tied firmly to the wood; the ridge was bound down by cocoa-nut leaves, dexterously plaited from side to side and skewered to the ridge pole with hard wooden pins; and over all, a fresh storm-roof was laid on yearly for the hurricane months, composed of folded cocoa-nut leaves, held down with planks of wood, and bound to the frame-work below—which, however, had to be removed again in April to save the sugar-cane leaf from rotting beneath it. There you were snugly covered in, and your thatching good to last from eight years to ten; that is, provided you were not caught in the sweep of the hurricane, before which trees went flying like straws, huts disappeared like autumn leaves, and your Mission House, if left standing at all, was probably swept bare alike of roof and thatch at a single stroke! Well for you at such times if you have a good barometer indicating the approach of the storm; and better still, a large cellar like ours, four-and-twenty feet by sixteen, built round with solid coral blocks,—where goods may be stored, and whereinto also all your household may creep for safety, while the tornado tosses your dwelling about, and sets huge trees dancing around you!

We had also to invent a lime-kiln, and this proved one of the hardest nuts of all that had to be cracked. The kind of coral required could be obtained only at one spot, about three miles distant. Lying at anchor in my boat, the Natives dived into the sea, broke off with hammer and crowbar piece after piece, and brought it up to me, till I had my load. We then carried it ashore, and spread it out in the sun to be blistered there for two weeks or so. Having thus secured twenty or thirty boat-loads, and had it duly conveyed round to the Mission Station, a huge pit was dug in the ground, dry wood piled in below, and green wood above to a height of several feet, and on the top of all the coral blocks were orderly laid When this pile had burned for seven or ten days, the coral had been reduced to excellent lime, and the plaster work made therefrom shone like marble.

On one of these trips the Natives performed an extraordinary feat. The boat with full load was struck heavily by
a wave, and the reef drove a hole in her side. Quick as
thought the crew were all in the sea, and, to my amazement,
bearing up the boat with their shoulder and one hand, while
swimming and guiding us ashore with the other! There on
the land we were hauled up, and four weary days were spent
fetching and carrying from the Mission Station every plank,
tool, and nail, necessary for her repair. Every boat for these
seas ought to be built of cedar wood and copper-fastened,
which is by far the most economical in the end. And all
houses should be built of wood which is as full as possible of
gum or resin, since the large white ants devour not only all
other soft woods, but even Colonial blue gum trees, the hard
cocoa-nut, and window sashes, chairs, and tables!

Glancing back on all these toils, I rejoice that such exhausting demands are no longer made on our newly-arrived
Missionaries. Houses, all ready for being set up, are now
brought down from the Colonies. Zinc roofs and other im-
provements have been introduced. The Synod appoints a
deputation to accompany the young Missionary, and plant the
house along with himself at the Station committed to his care.
Precious strength is thus saved for higher uses ; and not only
property but life itself is oftentimes preserved.

I will close this chapter with an incident which, though it
came to our knowledge only years afterwards, closely bears
upon our Settlement on Aniwa. At first we had no idea
why they so determinedly refused us one site, and fixed us to
another of their own choice. But after the old Chief, Namakei,
became a Christian, he one day addressed the Aniwan people
in our hearing to this effect :

"When Missi came we saw his boxes. We knew he had
blankets and calico, axes and knives, fish-hooks and all such
things. We said, ' Don't drive him off, else we will lose all
these things. We will let him land. But we will force him
to live on the Sacred Plot. Our gods will kill him, and we
will divide all that he has amongst the men of Aniwa.' But
Missi built his house on our most sacred spot. He and his
people lived there, and the gods did not strike. He planted

bananas there, and we said, 'Now when they eat of these they will all drop down dead, as our fathers assured us, if any one ate fruit from that ground, except only our Sacred Men them-selves.' These bananas ripened. They did eat them. We kept watching for days and days, but no one died! Therefore what we say, and what our fathers have said, is not true. Our gods cannot kill them. Their Jehovah God is stronger than the gods of Aniwa."

I enforced old Namakei's appeal, telling them that, though they knew it not, it was the living and true and only God who had sent them every blessing which they possessed, and had at last sent us to teach them how to serve and love and please Him. In wonder and silence they listened, while I tried to explain to them that Jesus, the Son of this God, had lived and died and gone to the Father to save them, and that He was now willing to take them by the hand and lead them through this life to glory and immortality together with Himself.

The old Chief led them in prayer—a strange, dark, groping prayer, with streaks of Heathenism colouring every thought and sentence ; but still a heart-breaking prayer, as the cry of a soul once Cannibal, but now being thrilled through and through with the first conscious pulsations of the Christ-Spirit throbbing into the words—" Father, Father ; our Father."

When these poor creatures began to wear a bit of calico or a kilt, it was an outward sign of a change, though yet far from civilization. And when they began to look up and pray to One whom they called " Father, our Father," though they might be far, very far, from the type of Christian that dubs itself "respectable," my heart broke over them in tears of joy ; and nothing will ever persuade me that there was not a Divine Heart in the Heavens rejoicing too.

CHAPTER VI.

FACE TO FACE WITH HEATHENISM.

A.D. 1867—1869.   ÆT. 43—45.

Navalak and Nemeyan on Aniwa.—Taia the " Orator."—The Two next Aneityumese Teachers.—In the Arms of Murderers.—Our First Aniwan Converts.—Litsi Soré.—Surrounded by Torches.—Traditions of Creation, Fall, and Deluge.—Infanticide and Wife-Murder.—Last Heathen Dance.—Nelwang's Elopement.—Yakin's Bridal Attire.— Christ-Spirit *versus* War-Spirit.—Heathenism in Death-Grips.—A Great Aniwan Palaver.—The Sinking of the Well.—" Missi's Head Gone Wrong."—"Water! Living Water!"—Old Chief's Sermon on " Rain from Below."—The Idols Cast Away.—The New Social Order.—Back of Heathenism Broken.

ON landing in November 1866, we found the Natives of Aniwa, some very shy and distrustful, and others forward and imperious. No clothing was worn ; but the wives and elder women had grass aprons or girdles like our first Parents in Eden. The old Chief interested himself in us and our work ; but the greater number showed a far deeper interest in the axes, knives, fish-hooks, stripes of red calico, and blankets, received in payment for work or for bananas. Even for payment they would scarcely work at first, and they were most unreasonable, easily offended, and started off in a moment at any imaginable slight.

For instance, a Chief once came for Medicine. I was so engaged that I could not attend to him for a few minutes. So off he went, in a great rage, threatening revenge, and muttering, " I must be attended to ! I won't wait on *him*." Such were the exactions of a naked Savage !

Shortly before our arrival, an Aneityumese Teacher was sacrificed on Aniwa. The circumstances are illustrative of what may be almost called their worship of revenge. Many long years ago, a party of Aniwans had gone to Aneityum on a friendly visit ; but the Aneityumese, then all Savages, murdered and ate every man of them save one, who escaped into the bush. Living on cocoa-nuts, he awaited a favourable wind, and, launching his canoe by night, he arrived in safety. The bereaved Aniwans, hearing his terrible story, were furious for revenge; but the forty-five miles of sea between proving too hard an obstacle, they made a deep cut in the earth and vowed to renew that cut from year to year till the day of revenge came round. Thus the memory of the event was kept alive for nearly eighty years.

At length the people of Aneityum came to the knowledge of Jesus Christ. They strongly yearned to spread that saving Gospel to the Heathen Islands all around. Amid prayers and strong cryings to God they, like the Church at Antioch, designated two of their leading men to go as Native Teachers and evangelize Aniwa, viz., Navalak and Nemeyan; whilst others went forth to Fotuna, Tanna, and Erromanga, as opportunity arose. Namakei, the principal Chief of Aniwa, had promised to protect and be kind to them. But as time went on, it was discovered that the Teachers belonged to the Tribe on Aneityum, and one of them to the very land, where long ago the Aniwans had been murdered. The Teachers had from the first known their danger, but were eager to make known the Gospel to Aniwa. It was resolved that they should die. But the Aniwans, having promised to protect them, shrank from doing it themselves ; so they hired two Tanna-men and an Aniwan Chief, one of whose parents had belonged to Tanna, to waylay and shoot the Teachers as they returned from their tour of Evangelism among the villages on Sabbath afternoon. Their muskets did not go off, but the murderers rushed upon them with clubs and left them for dead.

Nemeyan was dead, and entered that day amongst the noble army of the Martyrs. Poor Navalak was still breathing, and the Chief Namakei carried him to his village and kindly nursed him. He pled with the people that the claims of revenge had been satisfied, and that Navalak should be cherished and sent home,—the Christ-Spirit beginning to work in that darkened soul ! Navalak was restored to his people, and is yet living (1888)—a high-class Chief on Aneityum and an honour to the Church of God, bearing on his body " the marks of the Lord Jesus." And often since has he visited Aniwa, in later years, and praised the Lord amongst the very people who once thirsted for his blood and left him by the wayside as good as dead !

For a time, Aniwa was left without any witness for Jesus, —the London Missionary Society Teachers, having suffered dreadfully for lack of food and from fever and ague, being also removed. But on a visit of a Mission vessel, Namakei sent his orator Taia to Aneityum, to tell them that now revenge was satisfied, the cut in the earth filled up, and a cocoa-nut tree planted and flourishing where the blood of the Teachers had been shed, and that no person from Aneityum would ever be injured by Aniwans. Further, he was to plead for more Teachers, and to pledge his Chief's word that they would be kindly received and protected. They knew not the Gospel, and had no desire for it ; but they wanted friendly intercourse with Aneityum, where trading vessels called, and whence they might obtain mats, baskets, blankets, and iron tools. At length two Aneityumese again volunteered to go, Kangaru and Nelmai, one from each side of the Island, and were located by the Missionaries, along with their families, on Aniwa, one with Namakei, and the other at the south end, to lift up the Standard of a Christlike life among their Heathen neighbours.

Taia, who went on the Mission to Aneityum, was a great speaker and also a very cunning man. He was the old Chief's appointed " Orator " on all state occasions, being tall and stately in appearance, of great bodily strength, and possessed of a winning manner. On the voyage to Aneityum, he was constantly smoking and making things disagreeable to all around him. Being advised not to smoke while on board, he pled with the Missionary just to let him take a whiff now and again till he finished the tobacco he had in his pipe, and then he would lay it aside. But, like the widow's meal, it lasted all the way to Aneityum, and never appeared to get less—at which the innocent Taia expressed much astonishment !

The two Teachers and their wives on Aniwa were little

better than slaves when we landed there, toiling in the service of their masters and living in constant fear of being murdered. They conducted the Worship in Aneityumese, while the Aniwans lay smoking and talking all round till it was over. The language of Aniwa had never yet been reduced to a written form, and consequently no book had been printed in it. The Teachers and their wives were kept hard at work on Friday and Saturday, cooking and preparing food for the Aniwans, who, after the so-called Worship, feasted together and had a friendly talk. We immediately put an end to this Sabbath feasting. That made them angry and revengeful. They even demanded food, etc., in payment for coming to the Worship (!), which we always resolutely refused. Doubtless, however, the mighty contrast presented by the life, character, and disposition of these godly Teachers was the sowing of the seed that bore fruit in other days,—though as yet no single Aniwan had begun to wear clothing out of respect to Civilization, much less been brought to know and love the Saviour.

I could now speak a little to them in their own language ; and so, accompanied generally by my dear wife and by an Aneityumese Teacher, and often by some friendly Native, I began to visit regularly at their villages and to talk to them about Jesus and His love. We tried also to get them to come to our Church under the shade of the banyan tree. Nasi and some of the worst characters would sit scowling not far off, or follow us with loaded muskets. Using every precaution, we still held on doing our work ; sometimes giving fish-hooks or beads to the boys and girls, showing them that our objects were kind and not selfish. Such visits gained their confidence.

And however our hearts sometimes trembled in the presence of imminent death and sank within us, we stood fearless in their presence, and left all results in the hands of Jesus. Often have I had to run into the arms of some Savage, when his club was swung or his musket levelled at my head, and, praying to Jesus, so clung round him that he could neither strike nor shoot me till his wrath cooled down and I managed to slip away. Often have I seized the pointed barrel and directed it upwards, or, pleading with my assailant, uncapped his musket in the struggle. At other times, nothing could be

said, nothing done, but stand still in silent prayer, asking God
to protect us or to prepare us for going home to His Glory.
He fulfilled His own promise,—"I will not fail thee nor
forsake thee."

The first Aniwan that ever came to the knowledge and love
of Jesus was the old Chief Namakei. We came to live on his
land, as it was near our diminutive harbour ; and upon the
whole, he and his people were the most friendly ; though his
only brother, the Sacred Man of the tribe, on two occasions
tried to shoot me. Namakei came a good deal about us at
the Mission House, and helped us to acquire the language.
He discovered that we took tea evening and morning. When
we gave him a cup and a piece of bread, he liked it well, and
gave a sip to all around him. At first he came for the tea,
perhaps, and disappeared suspiciously soon thereafter ; but his
interest manifestly grew, till he showed great delight in helping
us in every possible way. Along with him and as his associates
came also the Chief Naswai and his wife Katua. These three
grew into the knowledge of the Saviour together. From being
savage Cannibals they rose before our eyes, under the influence
of the Gospel, into noble and beloved characters ; and they
and we loved each other exceedingly.

Namakei brought his little daughter, his only child, the
Queen of her race, called Litsi Soré (= Litsi the Great), and
said, "I want to leave my Litsi with you. I want you to train
her for Jesus."

She was a very intelligent child, learned things like any
white girl, and soon became quite a help to Mrs. Paton. On
seeing his niece dressed and so smart-looking, the old Chief's
only brother, the Sacred Man that had attempted to shoot me,
also brought his child, Litsi Sisi (= the Little) to be trained
like her cousin. The mothers of both were dead. The
children reported all they saw, and all we taught them, and
so their fathers became more deeply interested in our work,
and the news of the Gospel spread far and wide. Soon we
had all the Orphans committed to us, whose guardians were
willing to part with them, and our Home became literally *the
School of Christ*,—the boys growing up to help all my plans,
and the girls to help my wife and to be civilized and trained

by her, and many of them developing into devoted Teachers and Evangelists.

Our earlier Sabbath Services were sad affairs. Every man came armed—indeed, every man slept with his weapons of war at his side—and bow and arrow, spear and tomahawk, club and musket, were always ready for action. On fair days we assembled under the banyan tree, on rainy days in a Native hut partly built for the purpose. One or two seemed to listen, but the most lay about on their backs or sides, smoking, talking, sleeping! When we stopped the feast at the close, for which they were always ready, the audiences at first went down to two or three; but these actually came to learn, and a better tone began immediately to pervade the Service. We informed them that it was for their good that we taught them, and that they would get no "pay" for attending Church or School, and the greater number departed in high dudgeon as very ill-used persons! Others of a more commercial turn came offering to sell their "idols," and when we would not purchase them, but urged them to give them up and cast them away for love to Jesus, they carried them off, saying they would have nothing to do with this new Worship.

Amidst our frequent trials and dangers in those earlier times on Aniwa, our little Orphans often warned us privately and saved our lives from cruel plots. When, in baffled rage, our enemies demanded who had revealed things to us, I always said, "It was a little bird from the bush." So, the dear children grew to have perfect confidence in us. They knew we would not betray them; and they considered themselves the guardians of our lives.

The excitement increased on both sides, when a few men openly gave up their idols. Morning after morning, I noticed green cocoa-nut leaves piled at the end of our house, and wondered if it were through some Heathen superstition. But one night the old Chief knocked me up and said, " Rise, Missi, and help ! The Heathen are trying to burn your house. All night we have kept them off, but they are many and we are few. Rise quickly, and light a lamp at every window. Let us pray to Jehovah, and talk loud as if we were many. God will make us strong."

I found that they had the buckets and pails from all my Premises full of water—that the surrounding bush was swarming with Savages, torch in hand—that the Teachers and other friendly Natives had been protecting themselves from the dews under the large cocoa-nut leaves which I saw, while they kept watch over us. After that I took my turn with them in watching, each guard being changed after so many hours. But they held a meeting and said amongst each other, "If our Missi is shot or killed in the dark, what will we have to watch for then? We must compel Missi to remain indoors at night!"

I yielded so far to their counsel; but still went amongst them, watch after watch, to encourage them.

What a suggestive tradition of the Fall came to me in one of those early days on Aniwa! Upon our leaving the hut and removing to our new house, it was seized upon by Tupa for his sleeping place; though still continuing to be used by the Natives, as club-house, court of law, etc. One morning at daylight this Tupa came running to us in great excitement, wielding his club furiously, and crying, "Missi, I have killed the Tebil. I have killed Teapolo. He came to catch me last night. I raised all the people, and we fought him round the house with our clubs. At daybreak he came out and I killed him dead. We will have no more bad conduct or trouble now. Teapolo is dead!"

I said, "What nonsense! Teapolo is a spirit, and cannot be seen."

But in mad excitement he persisted that he had killed him. And at Mrs. Paton's advice, I went with the man, and he led me to a great Sacred Rock of coral near our old hut, over which hung the dead body of a huge and beautiful sea-serpent, and exclaimed, "There he lies! Truly I killed him."

I protested, "That is not the Devil; it is only the body of a serpent."

The man quickly answered, "Well, but it is all the same! He is Teapolo. He makes us bad, and causes all our troubles."

Following up this hint by many inquiries, then and afterwards, I found that they clearly associated man's troubles and sufferings somehow with the serpent. They worshipped the

Serpent, as a spirit of evil, under the name of Matshiktshiki ; that is to say, they lived in abject terror of his influence, and all their worship was directed towards propitiating his rage against men.

Their story of Creation, at least of the origin of their own Aniwa and the adjacent Islands, is much more an outcome of the unaided Native mind. They say that Matshiktshiki fished up these lands out of the sea. And they show the deep print of his foot on the coral rocks, opposite each island, whereon he stood as he strained and lifted them up above the waters. He then threw his great fishing-line round Fotuna, thirty-six miles distant, to draw it close to Aniwa and make them one land ; but, as he pulled, the line broke and he fell, where his mark may still be seen upon the rocks—so the Islands remain separated unto this day.

Matshiktshiki placed men and women on Aniwa. On the southern end of the Island, there was a beautiful spring and a fresh-water river, with rich lands all around for plantations. But the people would not do what Matshiktshiki wanted them ; so he got angry, and split off the richer part of Aniwa, with the spring and river, and sailed with them across to Aneityum,— leaving them where Dr. Inglis has since built his beautiful Mission Station. To this day, the river there is called "the water of Aniwa" by the inhabitants of both Islands ; and it is the ambition of all Aniwans to visit Aneityum and drink of that spring and river, as they sigh to each other, "Alas for the waters of Aniwa !"

Their picture of the Flood is equally grotesque. Far back, when the volcano, now on Tanna, was part of Aniwa, the rain fell and fell from day to day, and the sea rose till it threatened to cover everything. All were drowned except the few who climbed up on the volcano mountain. The sea had already put out the volcano at the southern end of Aniwa ; and Mat-shiktshiki, who dwelt in the greater volcano, becoming afraid of the extinction of his big fire too, split it off from Aniwa with all the land on the south-eastern side, and sailed it across to Tanna on the top of the flood. There, by his mighty strength, he heaved the volcano to the top of a high mountain in Tanna, where it remains to this day. For, on the subsiding of the sea, he was unable to transfer his big fire to Aniwa ; and so it was reduced to a very small island, without a volcano, and without a river, for the sins of the people long ago.

Even where there are no snakes they apply the superstitions about the serpent to a large, black, poisonous lizard called *kekvau.* They call it Teapolo ; and women or children scream wildly at the sight of one. The Natives of several of our Islands have the form of the lizard, as also of snakes and birds and the face of man, cut deep into the flesh to represent their gods. When the cuts begin to heal, they tear open the figures and press back the skin and force out the flesh, till the forms stand out above the skin and abide there as a visible horror for all their remaining days. But when they become Christians and put on clothing, they are very anxious to cover these reminders of Heathenism from public view.

One of the darkest and most hideous blots on Heathenism is the practice of Infanticide. Only three cases came to our knowledge on Aniwa ; but we publicly denounced them at all hazards, and awoke not only natural feeling, but the selfish interests of the community for the protection of the children. These three were the last that died there by parents' hands. A young husband, who had been jealous of his wife, buried their male child alive as soon as born. An old Tanna-woman, who had no children living, having at last a fine healthy boy born to her, threw him into the sea before any one could interfere to save. And a Savage, in anger with his wife, snatched her baby from her arms, hid himself in the bush till night, and returned without the child, refusing to give any explanation, except that he was dead and buried. Praise be to God, these three murderers of their own children were by-and-bye touched with the story of Jesus, became members of the Church, and each adopted little orphan children, towards whom they continued to show the most tender affection and care.

Wife murder was also considered quite legitimate. In one of our inland villages dwelt a young couple, happy in every respect except that they had no children. The man, being a Heathen, resolved to take home another wife, a widow with two children. This was naturally opposed by his young wife.

And, without the slightest warning, while she sat plaiting a basket, he discharged a ball into her from his loaded musket. It crashed through her arm and lodged in her side. Everything was done that was in my power to save her life; but on the tenth day tetanus came on, and she soon after passed away. The man appeared very attentive to her all the time; but, being a Heathen, he insisted that she had no right to oppose his wishes! He was not in any way punished or disrespected by the people of his village, but went out and in amongst them as usual, and took home the other woman as his wife a few weeks thereafter. His second wife began to attend Church and School regularly with her children; and at last he also came along with them, changing very manifestly from his sullen and savage former self. They have a large family; they are avowedly trying to train them all for the Lord Jesus; and they take their places meekly at the Lord's Table.

It would give a wonderful shock, I suppose, to many namby-pamby Christians to whom the title " Mighty to Save " conveys no ideas of reality, to be told that nine or ten converted murderers were partaking with them the Holy Communion of Jesus! But the Lord who reads the heart, and weighs every motive and circumstance, has perhaps much more reason to be shocked by the presence of some of themselves. Penitence opens all the heart of God—" To-day shalt thou be with Me in Paradise."

Amongst the Heathen, a murderer was often honoured; and if he succeeded in terrifying those who ought to take revenge, he was sometimes even promoted to be a Chief. One who had thus risen to tyrannize over his village was so feared and obeyed, that one of the lads there said to me, " Missi, I wish I had lived long ago! I could have murdered some great man, and come to honour. As Christians, we have no prospects; where are your warriors? Are we always to remain common men ? "

I told him of greatness in the service of Jesus, of glory and honour with our Lord. That lad afterwards became a Native Teacher, first in his own village, and then on a Heathen Island—the Lord the Spirit having opened up for his ambition the nobler path.

The last Heathen Dance on Aniwa was intended, strange to say, in honour of our work. We had finished the burning of a large lime-kiln for our buildings, and the event was regarded as worthy of a festival. To our surprise, loud bursts of song were followed by the tramp, tramp of many feet. Men and women and children poured past us, painted, decorated with feathers and bush twigs, and dressed in their own wildest form, though almost entirely nude so far as regards the clothing of civilization. They marched into the village Public Ground, and with song and shout and dance made the air hideous to me. They danced in inner and outer circles, men with men and women with women ; but I do not know that the thing looked more irrational to an outsider than do the balls at home ! Our Islanders, on becoming followers of Jesus, have always *voluntarily* withdrawn from all these scenes, and regard such dancings as inconsistent with the presence and fellowship of the Saviour.

On calling one of their leading men and asking him what it all meant, he said, " Missi, we are rejoicing for you, singing and dancing to our gods for you and your works."

I told him that my Jehovah God would be angry at His Church being so associated with Heathen gods. The poor bewildered soul look grieved and asked, " Is it not good, Missi ? Are we not helping you ? "

I said, " No ! It is not good. I am shocked to see you. I come here to teach you to give up all these ways, and to please the Jehovah God."

He went and called away his wife and all his friends, and told them that the Missi was displeased. But the others held on for hours, and were much disgusted that I would not make them a feast and pay them for dancing ! No other dance was ever held near our Station on Aniwa.

Some most absurd and preposterous experiences were forced upon us by the habits and notions of the people. Amongst these I recall very vividly the story of Nelwang's elopement with his bride. I had begun, in spare hours, to lay the foundation of two additional rooms for our house, and felt rather uneasy to see a well-known Savage hanging around every day with his tomahawk, and eagerly watching me at work. He

had killed a man, before our arrival on Aniwa ; and it was he
that startled my wife by suddenly appearing from amongst the
boxes, and causing her to run for life. On seeing him hovering
so alarmingly near, tomahawk in hand, I saluted him. "Nelwang, do you want to speak to me ? "

"Yes, Missi," he replied ; "if you will help me now, I will
be your friend for ever."

I answered, " I am your friend. That brought me here and
keeps me here."

" Yes," said he very earnestly, " but I want you to be strong
as my friend, and I will be strong for you ! "

I replied, " Well, how can I help you ? "

He quickly answered, " I want to get married, and I need
your help."

I protested—" Nelwang, you know that marriages here are
all made in infancy, by children being bought and betrothed
to their future husbands. How can I interfere? You don't
want to bring evil on me and my wife and child ? It might
cost us our lives."

"No ! no ! Missi," earnestly retorted Nelwang. " No one
hears of this, or can hear. Only help me now. You tell me,
if you were in my circumstances, how would you act ? "

"That's surely very simple," I answered. "Every man
knows how to go about that business, if he wants to be honest !
Look out for your intended, find out if she loves you, and the
rest will follow naturally,—you will marry her."

" Yes," argued Nelwang, " but just there my trouble comes
in ! "

" Do you know the woman you would like to get ? " I asked,
wishing to bring him to some closer issue.

" Yes," replied he very frankly ; " I want to marry Yakin, the
Chief's widow up at the inland village, and that will break no
infant betrothals."

" But," I persevered, " do you know if she loves you or
would take you ? "

" Yes," replied Nelwang ; " one day I met her on the path
and told her I would like to have her for my wife. She took
out her ear-rings and gave them to me, and I know thereby that
she loves me. I was one of her late husband's men ; and if

22

she had loved any of them more than she loved me, she would have given them to another. With the ear-rings she gave me her heart."

"Then why," I insisted, " don't you go and marry her ? "

" There," said Nelwang gravely, " begins my difficulty. In her village there are thirty young men for whom there are no wives. Each of them wants her, but no one has the courage to take her, for the other nine-and-twenty will shoot him ! "

" And if you take her," I suggested, " the disappointed thirty will shoot you."

" That's exactly what I see, Missi," continued Nelwang ; " but I want you just to think you are in my place, and tell me how you would carry her off. You white men can always succeed. Missi, hear my plans, and advise me."

With as serious a face as I could command, I had to listen to Nelwang, to enter into his love affair, and to make suggestions, with a view to avoiding bloodshed and other miseries. The result of the deliberations was that Nelwang was to secure the confidence of two friends, his brother and the orator Taia, to place one at each end of the coral rocks above the village as watchmen, to cut down with his American tomahawk a passage through the fence at the back, and to carry off his bride at dead of night into the seclusion and safety of the bush ! Nelwang's eyes flashed as he flourished his tomahawk about and cried, " I see it now, Missi ! I shall win her from them all. Yakin and I will be strong for you all our days."

Next morning Yakin's house was found deserted. They sent to all the villages around, but no one had seen her. The hole in the fence behind was then discovered, and the thirty whispered to each other that Yakin had been wooed and won by some daring lover. Messengers were dispatched to all the villages, and Nelwang was found to have disappeared on the same night as the widow, and neither could anywhere be found.

The usual revenge was taken—the houses of the offenders burned, their fences broken down, and all their property either destroyed or distributed. Work was suspended, and the disappointed thirty solaced themselves by feasting at Yakin's expense. On the third day I arrived at the scene. Seeing our old friend Naswai looking on at the plunderers, I signalled him, and said innocently, " Naswai, what's this your men are about ? What's all the uproar ? "

The Chief replied, " Have you not heard, Missi ? "

" Heard ? " said I. " The whole island has heard your ongoings for three days ! I can get no peace to study, or carry on my work."

" Missi," said the Chief, " Nelwang has eloped with Yakin, the wealthy widow, and all the young men are taking their revenge."

" Oh," replied I, " is that all ? Call your men, and let us speak to them."

The men were all assembled, and I said : " After all your kindness to Yakin, and all your attention to her since her husband's death, has she really run away and left you all ? Don't you feel thankful that you are free from such an un-grateful woman ? Had one of you been married to her, and she had afterwards run away with this man that she loved, that would have been far worse ! And are you really making all this noise over such a person, and destroying so much useful food ? Let these two fools go their way, and if she be all that you now say, he will have the worst of the bargain, and you will be sufficiently avenged. I advise you to spare the fruit trees—go home quietly—leave them to punish each other— and let me get on with my work ! "

Naswai repeated my appeal : " Missi's word is good ! Gather up the food. Wait till we see their conduct, how it grows. She wasn't worth all this bother and noise ! "

Three weeks passed. The runaways were nowhere to be found. It was generally believed that they had gone in a canoe to Tanna or Erromanga. But one morning, as I began my work at my house alone, the brave Nelwang appeared at my side !

" Hillo ! " I said, " where have you come from ? and where is Yakin ? "

" I must not," he replied, " tell you yet. We are hid. We have lived on cocoa-nuts gathered at night. Yakin is well and happy. I come now to fulfil my promise : I will help you, and Yakin will help Missi Paton the woman, and we shall be your friends. I have ground to be built upon and fenced, when-ever we dare; but we will come and live with you, till peace is secured. Will you let us come to-morrow morning?"

"All right!" I said. "Come to-morrow!" And, trembling with delight, he disappeared into the bush.

Thus strangely God provided us with wonderful assistance. Yakin soon learnt to wash and dress and clean everything, and Nelwang served me like a faithful disciple. They clung by us like our very shadow, partly through fear of attack, partly from affection; but as each of them could handle freely both musket and tomahawk, which, though laid aside, were never far away, it was not every enemy that cared to try issues with Nelwang and his bride. After a few weeks had thus passed by, and as both of them were really showing an interest in things pertaining to Jesus and His Gospel, I urged them strongly to appear publicly at the Church on Sabbath, to show that they were determined to stand their ground together as true husband and wife, and that the others must accept the position and become reconciled. Delay now could gain no purpose, and I wished the strife and uncertainty to be put to an end.

Nelwang knew our customs. Every worshipper has to be seated, when our Church bell ceases ringing. Aniwans would be ashamed to enter after the Service had actually begun. As the bell ceased, Nelwang, knowing that he would have a clear course, marched in, dressed in shirt and kilt, but grasping very determinedly his tomahawk! He sat down as near to me as he could conveniently get, trying hard to conceal his manifest agitation. Slightly smiling towards me, he then turned and looked eagerly at the other door through which the women entered and left the Church, as if to say, "Yakin is coming!" But his tomahawk was poised ominously on his shoulder, and his courage gave him a defiant and almost impudent air. He was evidently quite ready to sell his life at a high price, if any one was prepared to risk the consequences.

In a few seconds Yakin entered; and if Nelwang's bearing and appearance were rather inconsistent with the feeling of worship,—what on earth was I to do when the figure and costume of Yakin began to reveal itself marching in? The

first visible difference betwixt a Heathen and a Christian is,—
that the Christian wears some clothing, the Heathen wears
none. Yakin had determined to show the extent of her
Christianity by the amount of clothing she could carry upon
her person. Being a Chief's widow before she became Nelwang's bride, she had some idea of state occasions, and
appeared dressed in every article of European apparel, mostly
portions of male attire, that she could beg or borrow from
about the premises! Her bridal gown was a man's drab-
coloured great-coat, put on above her Native grass skirts, and
sweeping down to her heels, buttoned tight. Over this she
had hung on a vest, and above that again, most amazing of
all, she had superinduced a pair of men's trousers, planting the
body of them on her neck and shoulders, and leaving her head
and face looking out from between the legs—a leg from either
side streaming over her bosom and dangling down absurdly
in front! Fastened to the one shoulder also there was a red
shirt, and to the other a striped shirt, waving about her like
wings as she sailed along. Around her head a red shirt had
been twisted like a turban, and her notions of art demanded
that a sleeve thereof should hang aloft over each of her ears!
She seemed to be a moving monster loaded with a mass of
rags. The day was excessively hot, and the perspiration
poured over her face in streams. She, too, sat as near to me
as she could get on the women's side of the Church. Nelwang
looked at me and then at her, smiling quietly, as if to say,
"You never saw, in all your white world, a bride so grandly
dressed!"

I little thought what I was bringing on myself when I urged
them to come to Church. The sight of that poor creature
sweltering before me constrained me for once to make the
service very short—perhaps the shortest I ever conducted in
all my life! The day ended in peace. The two souls were
extremely happy; and I praised God that what might have been
a scene of bloodshed had closed thus, even though it were in
a kind of wild grotesquerie!

Henceforth I never lacked a body-guard, nor Mrs. Paton a
helper. Yakin learned to read and write, and became an
excellent teacher in our Sabbath School; she also learned to

sing, and led the praise in Church, when my wife was unable to be present. In fact, she could put her hand to everything about the house or the Mission, and became a great favourite amongst the people. Nelwang fulfilled his promise faithfully. He was indeed my friend. Through all my inland tours, either he or the Sacred Man, Kalangi (who first attempted twice to shoot me, and then, after his conversion, acted as if God had entrusted him with the keeping of my life), faithfully accompanied me. With tomahawk or musket, or both, in hand, they were always within reach, and instantly started to the front wherever danger seemed to threaten us. These were amongst our first and best Church members. Nelwang and the Sacred Man have both gone to their rest. But Yakin of the many garments has also had many husbands. She rejoices now in her *fourth*, and is still a devoted Christian, and a most interesting character in many ways.

The progress of God's work was most conspicuous in relation to wars and revenges among the Natives. The two high Chiefs, Namakei and Naswai, frequently declared, " We are the men of Christ now. We must not fight. We must put down murders and crimes among our people."

Two young fools, returning from Tanna with muskets, attempted twice to shoot a man in sheer wantonness and display of malice. The Islanders met, and informed them that if man or woman was injured by them, the other men would load their muskets and shoot them dead in general council. This was a mighty step towards public order, and I greatly rejoiced before the Lord. His Spirit, like leaven, was at work !

My constant custom was, in order to prevent war, to run right in between the contending parties. My faith enabled me to grasp and realize the promise, " Lo, I am with you alway." In Jesus I felt invulnerable and immortal, so long as I was doing His work. And I can truly say, that these were the moments when I felt my Saviour to be most truly and sensibly present, inspiring and empowering me.

Another scheme had an excellent educative and religious influence. I tried to interest all the villages, and to treat all the Chiefs equally. In our early days, after getting into my two-roomed house, I engaged the Chief, or representative man of each district, to put up one or other of the many outhouses required at the Station. One, along with his people, built the cook-house ; another, the store ; another, the banana and yam-house ; another, the washing-house ; another, the boys' and girls' house ; the houses for servants and teachers, the School-house, and the large shed, a kind of shelter where Natives sat and talked when not at work about the Premises. Of course these all were at first only Native huts, of larger or smaller dimensions. But they were all built by contract for articles which they highly valued, such as axes, knives, yards of prints and calico, strings of beads, blankets, etc. They served our purpose for the time, and when another party, by contract also, had fenced around our Premises, the Mission Station was really a beautiful little lively and orderly Village, and in itself no bad emblem of Christian and Civilized life. The payments, made to all irrespectively, but only for work duly done and according to reasonable bargain, distributed property and gifts amongst them on wholesome principles, and encouraged a well-conditioned rivalry which had many happy effects.

Heathenism made many desperate and some strange efforts to stamp out our Cause on Aniwa, but the Lord held the helm. One old Chief, formerly friendly, turned against us. He ostentatiously set himself to make a canoe, working at it very openly and defiantly on Sabbaths. He becoming sick and dying, his brother started, on a Sabbath morning and in contempt of the Worship, with an armed company to provoke our people to war. They refused to fight ; and one man, whom he struck with his club, said, " I will leave my revenge to Jehovah."

A few days thereafter, this brother also fell sick and suddenly died. The Heathen party made much of these incidents, and some clamoured for our death in revenge, but most feared to murder us ; so they withdrew and lived apart from our friends, as far away as they could get. By-and-bye, however, they set fire to a large district belonging to our supporters, burning cocoa-nut and bread-fruit trees and plantations. Still our people refused to fight, and kept near to protect us. Then all the leading men assembled to talk it over. Most were for peace, but some insisted upon burning our house and driving us away or killing us, that they might be left to live as they had hitherto done. At last a Sacred Man, a Chief who had been on Tanna when the *Curaçoa* punished the murderers and robbers but protected the villages of the friendly Natives there, stood up and spoke in our defence, and warned them what might happen ; and other three, who had been under my instruction on Tanna, declared themselves to be the friends of Jehovah and of His Missionary. Finally the Sacred Man rose again, and showed them rows of beautiful white shells strung round his left arm, saying :

"Nowar, the great Chief at Port Resolution on Tanna, when he saw that Missi and his wife could not be kept there, took me to his heart, and pledged me by these, the shells of his office as Chief, taken from his own arm and bound on mine, to protect them from all harm. He told me to declare to the men of Aniwa that if the Missi be injured or slain, he and his warriors will come from Tanna and take the full revenge in blood." This turned the scale. The meeting closed in our favour.

Close on the heels of this, another and a rather perplexing incident befell us. A party of Heathens assembled and made a great display of fishing on the Lord's Day, in contempt of the practice of the men on Jehovah's side, threatening also to waylay the Teachers and myself in our village circuits. A meeting was held by the Christian party, at the close of the Sabbath Services. All who wished to serve Jehovah were to come to my house next morning, unarmed, and accompany me on a visit to our enemies, that we might talk and reason together with them. By daybreak, the Chiefs and nearly eighty men assembled at the Mission House, declaring that they were on Jehovah's side, and wished to go with me. But, alas ! they refused to lay down their arms, or leave them behind ; nor would they either refrain from going or suffer me to go alone. Pledging them to peace, I was reluctantly placed at their head, and we marched off to the village of the unfriendly party.

The villagers were greatly alarmed. The Chief's two sons came forth with every available man to meet us. That whole day was consumed in talking and speechifying, sometimes chanting their replies—the Natives are all inveterate talkers !

To me the day was utterly wearisome; but it had one redeeming feature,—their rage found vent in hours of palaver, instead of blows and blood It ended in peace. The Heathen were amazed at the number of Jehovah's friends ; and they pledged themselves henceforth to leave the Worship alone, and that every one who pleased might come to it unmolested. For this, worn out and weary, we returned, praising the Lord.

But I must here record the story of the Sinking of the Well, which broke the back of Heathenism on Aniwa. Being a flat coral island, with no hills to attract the clouds, rain is scarce there as compared with the adjoining mountainous islands ; and even when it does fall heavily, with tropical profusion, it disappears, as said before, through the light soil and porous rock, and drains itself directly into the sea. Hence, because of its greater dryness, Aniwa is more healthy than many of the surrounding isles ; though, probably for the same reason, its Natives are subject to a form of Elephantiasis, known as the "Barbadoes leg." The rainy season is from December to April, and then the disease most characteristic of all these regions is apt to prevail, viz., fever and ague.

At certain seasons, the Natives drank very unwholesome water ; and, indeed, the best water they had at any time for drinking purposes was from the precious cocoa-nut, a kind of Apple of Paradise for all these Southern Isles ! They also cultivate the sugar-cane very extensively, and in great variety ; and they chew it, when we would fly to water for thirst; so it is to them both food and drink. The black fellow carries with him to the field, when he goes off for a day's work, four or five sticks of sugar-cane, and puts in his time comfortably enough on these. Besides, the sea being their universal bathing-place, in which they swattle like fish, and little water, almost none, being required for cooking purposes, and none whatever for washing clothes (!), the lack of fresh springing water was not the dreadful trial to them that it would be to us. Yet they appreciate and rejoice in it immensely too ; though the water of the green cocoa-nut is refreshing, and in appearance, taste, and colour not unlike lemonade—one nut filling a tumbler ; and though when mothers die they feed the babies on it and on the soft white pith, and they flourish on the same, yet the Natives themselves show their delight in preferring, when they can get it, the water from the well.

My household felt sadly the want of fresh water. I prepared two large casks, to be filled when the rain came. But when we attempted to do so at the water-hole near the village, the Natives forbade us, fearing that our large casks would carry all the water away, and leave none for them with their so much smaller cocoa-nut bottles. This public water-hole was on the ground of two Sacred Men, who claimed the power of emptying and filling it by rain at will. The superstitious Natives gave them presents to bring the rain. If it came soon, they took all the credit for it. If not, they demanded larger gifts to satisfy their gods. Even our Aneityumese Teachers said to me, when I protested that surely they could not believe such things, " It is hard to know, Missi. The water does come and go quickly. If you paid them well, they might bring the rain, and let us fill our casks ! "

I told them that, as followers of Jehovah, we must despise all Heathen mummeries, and trust in Him and in the laws of His Creation to help us.

Aniwa having therefore no permanent supply of fresh water, in spring or stream or lake, I resolved by the help of God to sink a well near the Mission Premises, hoping that a wisdom higher than my own would guide me to the source of some blessed spring. Of the scientific conditions of such an experiment I was comparatively ignorant ; but I counted on having to dig through earth and coral above thirty feet, and my constant fear was that, owing to our environment, the water, if water I found, could only be salt water after all my toils ! Still I resolved to sink that shaft in hope, and in faith that the Son of God would be glorified thereby.

One morning I said to the old Chief and his fellow-Chief, both now earnestly inquiring about the religion of Jehovah and of Jesus, " I am going to sink a deep well down into the earth, to see if our God will send us fresh water up from below "

They looked at me with astonishment, and said in a tone of sympathy approaching to pity, " O Missi ! Wait till the rain comes down, and we will save all we possibly can for you."

I replied, "We may all die for lack of water. If no fresh water can be got, we may be forced to leave you."

The old Chief looked imploringly, and said, "O Missi! you must not leave us for that. Rain comes only from above. How could you expect our Island to send up showers of rain from below?"

I told him, "Fresh water does come up springing from the earth in my Land at home, and I hope to see it here also."

The old Chief grew more tender in his tones, and cried, "O Missi, your head is going wrong; you are losing some, thing, or you would not talk wild like that! Don't let our people hear you talking about going down into the earth for rain, or they will never listen to your word or believe you again."

But I started upon my hazardous job, selecting a spot near the Mission Station and close to the public path, that my prospective well might be useful to all. I began to dig, with pick and spade and bucket at hand, an American axe for a hammer and crowbar, and a ladder for service by-and-bye. The good old Chief now told off his men in relays to watch me, lest I should attempt to take my own life, or do anything outrageous, saying, "Poor Missi! That's the way with all who go mad. There's no driving of a notion out of their heads. We must just watch him now. He will find it harder to work with pick and spade than with his pen, and when he's tired we'll persuade him to give it up."

I did get exhausted sooner than I expected, toiling under that tropical sun; but we never own before the Natives that we are beaten; so I went into the house and filled my vest pocket with large, beautiful English-made fish-hooks. These are very tempting to the young men, as compared with their own,—skilfully made though *they* be out of shell, and serving their purposes wonderfully. Holding up a large hook, I cried, "One of these to every man who fills and turns over three buckets out of this hole!"

A rush was made to get the first turn, and back again for another and another. I kept those on one side who had got a turn, till all the rest in order had a chance, and bucket after bucket was filled and emptied rapidly. Still the shaft seemed to lower very slowly, while my fish-hooks were disappearing very quickly. I was constantly there, and took the heavy share of everything, and was thankful one evening to find that we had cleared more than twelve feet deep,—when lo! next morning, one side had rushed in, and our work was all undone.

The old Chief and his best men now came around me more earnestly than ever. He remonstrated with me very gravely. He assured me for the fiftieth time that rain would never be seen coming up through the earth on Aniwa!

"Now," said he, "had you been in that hole last night, you would have been buried, and a Man-of-war would have come from Queen 'Toria to ask for the Missi that lived here. We would have to say, 'He is down in that hole.' The Captain would ask, 'Who killed him and put him down there?' We would have to say, 'He went down there himself!' The Captain would answer, 'Nonsense! who ever heard of a white man going down into the earth to bury himself? You killed him, you put him there; don't hide your bad conduct with lies!' Then he would bring out his big guns and shoot us, and destroy our Island in revenge. You are making your own grave, Missi, and you will make ours too. Give up this mad freak, for no rain will be found by going downwards on Aniwa. Besides, all your fish-hooks cannot tempt my men again to enter that hole; they don't want to be buried with you. Will you not give it up now?"

I said all that I could to quiet his fears, explained to them that this falling in had happened by my neglect of precautions, and finally made known that by the help of my God, even without all other help, I meant to persevere.

Steeping my poor brains over the problem, I became an extemporized engineer. Two trees were searched for, with branches on opposite sides, capable of sustaining a cross tree betwixt them. I sank them on each side firmly into the ground, passed the beam across them over the centre of the shaft, fastened thereon a rude home-made pulley and block, passed a rope over the wheel, and swung my largest bucket to the end of it. Thus equipped, I began once more sinking away at the well, but at so great an angle that the sides might not again fall in. Not a Native, however, would enter that hole, and I had to pick and dig away till I was utterly exhausted. But a Native Teacher, in whom I had confidence, took charge above, managing to hire them with axes, knives, etc., to seize the end of the rope and walk along the ground pulling it till the bucket rose to the surface, and then he himself swung it aside, emptied it, and lowered it down again. I rang a little bell which I had with me, when the bucket was loaded, and that was the signal for my brave helpers to pull their rope. And thus I toiled on from day to day, my heart almost sinking sometimes with the sinking of the well, till we reached a depth of about thirty feet. And the phrase, "living water," "living water," kept chiming through my soul like music from God, as I dug and hammered away !

At this depth the earth and coral began to be soaked with damp. I felt that we were nearing water. My soul had a faith that God would open a spring for us ; but side by side with this faith was a strange terror that the water would be salt. So perplexing and mixed are even the highest experiences of the soul ; the rose-flower of a perfect faith, set round and round with prickly thorns. One evening I said to the old Chief, " I think that Jehovah God will give us water to-morrow from that hole ! "

The Chief said, " No, Missi ; you will never see rain coming up from the earth on this Island. We wonder what is to be the end of this mad work of yours. We expect daily, if you reach water, to see you drop through into the sea, and the sharks will eat you ! That will be the end of it—death to you, and danger to us all."

I still answered, " Come to-morrow. I hope and believe that Jehovah God will send you the rain water up through the earth."

At the moment I knew I was risking much, and probably incurring sorrowful consequences, had no water been given ; but I had faith that the Lord was leading me on, and I knew that I sought His glory, not my own.

Next morning, 1 went down again at daybreak and sank a narrow hole in the centre about two feet deep. The perspiration broke over me with uncontrollable excitement, and I trembled through every limb, when the water rushed up and began to fill the hole. Muddy though it was, I eagerly tasted it, lapping it with my trembling hand, and then I almost fell upon my knees in that muddy bottom as my heart burst up in praise to the Lord. It was water! It was fresh water! It was living water from Jehovah's well! True, it was a little brackish, but nothing to speak of; and no spring in the desert, cooling the parched lips of a fevered pilgrim, ever appeared more worthy of being called a Well of God than did that water to me!

The Chiefs had assembled with their men near by. They waited on in eager expectancy. It was a rehearsal, in a small way, of the Israelites coming round, while Moses struck the rock and called for water. By-and-bye, when I had praised the Lord, and my excitement was a little calmed, the mud being also greatly settled, I filled a jug, which I had taken down empty in the sight of them all, and ascending to the top called for them to come and see the rain which Jehovah God had given us through the well. They closed around me in haste, and gazed on it in superstitious fear. The old Chief shook it to see if it would spill, and then touched it to see if it felt like water. At last he tasted it, and rolling it in his mouth with joy for a moment, he swallowed it, and shouted, "Rain! Rain! Yes, it is Rain! But how did you get it?"

I repeated, "Jehovah my God gave it out of His own Earth in answer to our labours and prayers. Go and see it springing up for yourselves!"

Now, though every man there could climb the highest tree as swiftly and as fearlessly as a squirrel or an opossum, not one of them had courage to walk to the side and gaze down into that well. To them this was miraculous! But they were not without a resource that met the emergency. They agreed to take firm hold of each other by the hand, to place themselves in a long line, the foremost man to lean cautiously forward, gaze into the well, and then pass to the rear, and so on till all had seen "Jehovah's rain" far below. It was somewhat comical, yet far more pathetic, to stand by and watch their faces, as man after man peered down into the mystery, and then looked up at me in blank bewilderment! When all had seen it with their own very eyes, and were "weak with wonder," the old Chief exclaimed:

"Missi, wonderful, wonderful is the work of your Jehovah God! No god of Aniwa ever helped us in this way. The world is turned upside down, since Jehovah came to Aniwa! But, Missi," continued he, after a pause that looked like silent worship, "will it always rain up through the earth? or, will it come and go like the rain from the clouds?"

I told them that I believed it would always continue there for our use, as a good gift from Jehovah.

"Well, but, Missi," replied the Chief, some glimmering of self-interest beginning to strike his brain, "will you or your family drink it all, or shall we also have some?"

"You and all your people," I answered, "and all the people of the Island, may come and drink and carry away as much of it as you wish. I believe there will always be plenty for us all, and the more of it we can use the fresher it will be. That is the way with many of our Jehovah's best gifts to men, and for it and for all we praise His Name!"

"Then, Missi," said the Chief, "it will be our water, and we may all use it as our very own?"

"Yes," I answered, "whenever you wish it, and as much as you need, both here and at your own houses, as far as it can possibly be made to go."

The Chief looked at me eagerly, fully convinced at length that the well contained a treasure, and exclaimed, "Missi, what can we do to help you now?"

Oh, how like is human nature all the world over! When one toils and struggles, when help is needed which many around could easily give and be the better, not the worse, for giving it, they look on in silence, or bless you with ungenerous criticism, or ban you with malicious judgment. But let them get some peep of personal advantage by helping you, or even of the empty bubble of praise for offering it, and how they rush to your aid!

I was thankful, however, to accept of the Chief's assistance, now sorely needed, and I said, "You have seen it fall in once already. If it falls again, it will conceal the rain from below which our God has given us. In order to preserve it for us and for our children in all time, we must build it round and round with great coral blocks from the bottom to the very top. I will now clear it out, and prepare the foundation for this wall of coral. Let every man and woman carry from the shore the largest blocks they can bring. It is well worth all the toil thus to preserve our great Jehovah's gift!"

Scarcely were my words uttered, when they rushed to the shore, with shoutings and songs of gladness; and soon every one was seen struggling under the biggest block of coral with which he dared to tackle. They lay like limestone rocks, broken up by the hurricanes, and rolled ashore in the arms of mighty billows; and in an incredibly short time scores of them were tumbled down for my use at the mouth of the well. Having prepared a foundation, I made ready a sort of bag-basket, into which every block was firmly tied and then let down to me by the pulley,—a Native Teacher, a faithful fellow, cautiously guiding it. I received and placed each stone in its position, doing my poor best to wedge them one against the other, building circularly, and cutting them to the needed shape with my American axe. The wall is about three feet thick, and the masonry may be guaranteed to stand till the coral itself decays. I wrought incessantly, for fear of any further collapse, till I had it raised about twenty feet; and now, feeling secure, and my hands being dreadfully cut up, I intimated that I would rest a week or two, and finish the building then. But the Chief advanced and said,—

" Missi, you have been strong to work. Your strength has fled. But rest here beside us; and just point out where each block is to be laid. We will lay them there, we will build them solidly behind like you. And no man will sleep till it is done."

With all their will and heart they started on the job; some carrying, some cutting and squaring the blocks, till the wall rose like magic, and a row of the hugest rocks lay round the top bound all together, and formed the mouth of the well. Women, boys, and all wished to have a hand in building it, and it remains to this day, a solid wall of masonry, the circle being thirty-four feet deep, eight feet wide at the top, and six at the bottom. I floored it over with wood above all, and fixed the windlass and bucket, and there it stands as one of the greatest material blessings which the Lord has given to Aniwa. It rises and falls with the tide, though a third of a mile distant from the sea ; and when, after using it, we tasted the pure fresh water on board the *Dayspring*, the latter seemed so insipid that I had to slip a little salt into my tea along with the sugar before I could enjoy it ! All visitors are taken to see the well, as one of the wonders of Aniwa ; and an Elder of the Native Church said to me lately, " But for that water, during the last two years of drought, we would all have been dead ! "

Very strangely, though the Natives themselves have since tried to sink six or seven wells in the most likely places near their different villages, they have either come to coral rock which they could not pierce, or found only water that was salt. And they say amongst themselves, " Missi not only used pick and spade, but he prayed and cried to his God. We have learned to dig, but not how to pray, and therefore Jehovah will not give us the rain from below ! "

The well was now finished. The place was neatly fenced in. And the old Chief said, " Missi, now that this is the water for all, we must take care and keep it pure."

I was so thankful that all were to use it. Had we alone drawn water therefrom, they could so easily have poisoned it, as they do the fish-pools, in caverns among the rocks by the shore, with their nuts and runners, and killed us all But there was no fear, if they themselves were to use it daily. The Chief continued, " Missi, I think I could help you next Sabbath. Will you let me preach a sermon on the well ? "

" Yes," I at once replied, " if you will try to bring all the people to hear you."

" Missi, I will try," he eagerly promised. The news spread like wildfire that the Chief Namakei was to be the Missionary on the next day for the Worship, and the people, under great expectancy, urged each other to come and hear what he had to say.

Sabbath came round. Aniwa assembled in what was for that island a great crowd. Namakei appeared dressed in shirt and kilt. He was so excited, and flourished his tomahawk about at such a rate, that it was rather lively work to be near him.

2 3

I conducted short opening devotions, and then called upon Namakei. He rose at once, with eye flashing wildly, and his limbs twitching with emotion. He spoke to the following effect, swinging his tomahawk to enforce every eloquent gesticulation :

"Friends of Namakei, men and women and children of Aniwa, listen to my words ! Since Missi came here he has talked many strange things we could not understand—things all too wonderful ; and we said regarding many of them that they must be lies. White people might believe such nonsense, but we said that the black fellow knew better than to receive it. But of all his wonderful stories, we thought the strangest was about sinking down through the earth to get rain ! Then we said to each other, The man's head is turned ; he's gone mad. But the Missi prayed on and wrought on, telling us that Jehovah God heard and saw, and that his God would give him rain. Was he mad ? Has he not got the rain deep down in the earth ? We mocked at him ; but the water was there all the same. We have laughed at other things which the Missi told us, because we could not see them. But from this day I believe that all he tells us about his Jehovah God is true. Some day our eyes will see it. For to-day we have seen the rain from the earth."

Then rising to a climax, first the one foot and then the other making the broken coral on the floor fly behind like a war-horse pawing the ground, he cried with great eloquence :

"My people, the people of Aniwa, the world is turned upside down since the word of Jehovah came to this land ! Who ever expected to see rain coming up through the earth ? It has always come from the clouds ! Wonderful is the work of this Jehovah God. No god of Aniwa ever answered prayers as the Missi's God has done. Friends of Namakei, all the powers of the world could not have forced us to believe that rain could be given from the depths of the earth, if we had not seen it with our eyes, felt it and tasted it as we here do. Now, by the help of Jehovah God, the Missi brought that invisible rain to view, which we never before heard of or saw, and,"—(beating his hand on his breast, he exclaimed),—

"Something here in my heart tells me that the Jehovah

God does exist, the Invisible One, whom we never heard of nor saw till the Missi brought Him to our knowledge. The coral has been removed, the land has been cleared away, and lo! the water rises. Invisible till this day, yet all the same it was there, though our eyes were too weak. So I, your Chief, do now firmly believe that when I die, when the bits of coral and the heaps of dust are removed which now blind my old eyes, I shall then see the Invisible Jehovah God with my soul, as Missi tells me, not less surely than I have seen the rain from the earth below. From this day, my people, I must worship the God who has opened for us the well, and who fills us with rain from below. The gods of Aniwa cannot hear, cannot help us, like the God of Missi. Henceforth I am a follower of Jehovah God. Let every man that thinks with me go now and fetch the idols of Aniwa the gods which our fathers feared, and cast them down at Missi's feet. Let us burn and bury and destroy these things of wood and stone, and let us be taught by the Missi how to serve the God who can hear, the Jehovah who gave us the well, and who will give us every other blessing, for He sent His Son Jesus to die for us and bring us to Heaven. This is what the Missi has been telling us every day since he landed on Aniwa. We laughed at him, but now we believe him. The Jehovah God has sent us rain from the earth. Why should He not also send us His Son from Heaven? Namakei stands up for Jehovah!"

This address, and the Sinking of the Well, broke, as I already said, the back of Heathenism on Aniwa. That very afternoon, the old Chief and several of his people brought their idols and cast them down at my feet beside the door of our house. Oh, the intense excitement of the weeks that followed! Company after company came to the spot, loaded with their gods of wood and stone, and piled them up in heaps, amid the tears and sobs of some, and the shoutings of others, in which was heard the oft-repeated word, "Jehovah! Jehovah!" What could be burned, we cast into the flames; others we buried in pits twelve or fifteen feet deep; and some few, more likely than the rest to feed or awaken superstition, we sank far out into the deep sea. Let no Heathen eyes ever gaze on them again!

We do not mean to indicate that, in all cases, their motives were either high or enlightened. There were not wanting some who wished to make this new movement pay, and were much disgusted when we refused to "buy" their gods! On being told that Jehovah would not be pleased unless they gave them up of their own free will, and destroyed them without pay or reward, some took them home again and held on by them for a season, and others threw them away in contempt. Meetings were held and speeches were delivered, for these New Hebrideans are irrepressible orators, florid, and amazingly graphic; much talk followed, and the destruction of idols went on apace. By-and-bye two Sacred Men and some other selected persons constituted themselves a sort of detective Committee, to search out and expose those who pretended to give them all up, but were hiding certain idols in secret, and to encourage waverers to come to a thorough decision for Jehovah. In these intensely exciting days, we "stood still" and saw the salvation of the Lord.

They flocked around us now at every meeting we held. They listened eagerly to the story of the life and death of Jesus. They voluntarily assumed one or other article of clothing. And everything transpiring was fully and faithfully submitted to us for counsel or for information. One of the very first steps in Christian discipline to which they readily and almost unanimously took was the asking of God's blessing on every meal and praising the great Jehovah for their daily bread. Whosoever did not do so was regarded as a Heathen. (Query: how many *white* Heathens are there?) The next step, and it was taken in a manner as if by some common consent, that was not less surprising than joyful, was a form of Family Worship every morning and evening. Doubtless the prayers were often very queer, and mixed up with many remaining superstitions; but they were prayers to the great Jehovah, the compassionate Father, the Invisible One—no longer to gods of stone!

Necessarily these were the conspicuous features of our life as Christians in their midst—morning and evening Family Prayer, and Grace at Meat; and hence, most naturally, their instinctive adoption and imitation of the same as the first outward tokens of Christian discipline. Every house in which there was not Prayer to God in the family was known thereby to be Heathen. This was a direct and practical evidence of the New Religion ; and, so far as it goes (and that is very far indeed, where there is any sincerity beneath it), the test was one about which there could be no mistake on either side.

A third conspicuous feature stood out distinctly and at once, —the change as to the Lord's Day. Village after village followed in this also the example of the Mission House. All ordinary occupations ceased. Sabbath was spoken of as the Day for Jehovah. Saturday came to be called "Cooking Day," referring to the extra preparations for the coming day of rest and worship. They believed that it was Jehovah's will to keep the first day holy. The reverse was a distinctive mark of Heathenism.

The first traces of a new Social Order began to rise visibly on the delighted eye. The whole inhabitants, young and old, now attended School,—three generations sometimes at the one copy or A B C book ! Thefts, quarrels, crimes, etc., were settled now, not by club law, but by fine or bonds or lash, as agreed upon by the Chiefs and their people. Everything was rapidly and surely becoming "new" under the influence of the leaven of Jesus. Industry increased. Huts and plantations were safe. Formerly every man, in travelling, carried with him all his valuables ; now they were secure, left at home.

Even a brood of fowls or a litter of pigs would be carried in bags on their persons in Heathen days. Hence at Church we had sometimes lively episodes—the chirruping of chicks, the squealing of piggies, and the barking of puppies, one gaily responding to the other, as we sang, or prayed, or preached the Gospel ! Being glad to see the Natives there, even with all their belongings, we carefully refrained from finding fault but the thread of devotion was sometimes apt to slip through one's fingers, especially when the conflict of the owner to silence a baby-pig inspired the little wretch to drown everything in a long-sustained and high-pitched scream.

The Natives, finding this state of matters troublesome to themselves and disagreeable all round, called a General Assembly, unanimously condemned dishonesty, agreed upon

severe fines and punishments for every act of theft, and cove-
nanted to stand by each other in putting it down.   The Chiefs,
however, found this a long and difficult task, but they held at
it under the inspiration of the Gospel and prevailed.   Even
the trials and difficulties with which they met were overruled
by God, in assisting them to form by the light of their own
experience a simple code of Social Laws, fitted to repress the
crimes there prevailing, and to encourage the virtues specially
needing to be cultivated there.   Heathen Worship was gradually extinguished ; and, though no one was compelled to
come to Church, every person on Aniwa, without exception,
became an avowed worshipper of Jehovah God.   Again,

"O Galilean, Thou hast conquered !"

Often since have I meditated on that old Cannibal Chief
reasoning himself and his people, from the Sinking of the Well
and the bringing of the invisible water to view, into a belief as
to the existence and power of the great Invisible God, the only
Hearer and Answerer of prayer.   And the contrasted picture
rises before my mind of the multitudes in Britain, America,
Germany, and our Colonies, all whose wisdom, science, art,
and wealth have only left them in spiritual darkness—miserable
doubters !   In their pride of heart, they deny their Creator
and Redeemer, so gloriously revealed to them alike in Nature
and in Scripture, and are like a dog barking against the sun.
They will accept nothing but what their poorly-developed
Science can demonstrate ; yet that Science, as compared with
the All-Truth of the Universe, is infinitely smaller than was
the poor Chief Namakei's knowledge as compared with mine !
They do certainly know that their very existence, at every
moment, depends on things that neither reason nor science
can fathom, any more than Namakei could understand the rain
from below.   For every reason that he and his people had to
believe in the Invisible God, who brought the water to their
view, these sons and daughters of Civilization, "the heirs of all
the ages in the foremost files of time," have ten thousand more,
from history, from science, from material progress—yet in their
pride of Intellect they refuse to acknowledge and adore that
Invisible and Inscrutable God, in whom every day they live,

and move, and have their being, and who has spoken to us by His Son from Heaven. If their own sons, daughters, or servants, who are infinitely less dependent on them than they are upon God, should treat themselves as they are treating their Creator, what would they think? How would they feel? I pity from the depth of my heart every human being, who, from whatever cause, is a stranger to the most ennobling, uplifting, and consoling experience that can come to the soul of man—blessed communion with the Father of our Spirits, through gracious union with the Lord Jesus Christ. " I thank Thee, O Father, Lord of Heaven and Earth, because Thou hast hid these things from the wise and prudent, and hast revealed them unto babes. Even so, Father : for so it seemed good in Thy sight. . . . Come unto Me, all ye that labour and are heavy laden, and I will give you rest. Take My yoke upon you, and learn of Me ; for I am meek and lowly in heart : and ye shall find rest unto your souls. For My yoke is easy, and My burden is light " (Matt. xi. 25-30).

CHAPTER VII.

THE LIGHT THAT SHINETH MORE AND MORE.

A.D. 1869—1874. ÆT. 45—50.

My first Aniwan Book.—The Power of Music.—A Pair of Glass Eyes.—
Church Building for Jesus.—The Hanging of the Bell.—Palesa and
his Bride.—An Armed Embassage.—Youwili's Taboo.—Youwili's
Conversion.—The Tobacco Idol.—First Communion on Aniwa.—
Our Village Day Schools.—New Social Laws.—A Sabbath Day's
Work on Aniwa.—Our Week-day Life.—The Orphans and their
Biscuits.—"The Wreck of the *Dayspring*."—God's Own Finger-
Posts.—God's Work our Guarantee.—Profane Swearers Rebuked.—
A Heavenly Vision.—On Wing through New Zealand.—Our Second
Dayspring.

THE printing of my first Aniwan book was a great event,
not so much for the toil and worry which it cost me,
though that was enough to have broken the heart of many
a compositor, as rather for the joy it gave to the old Chief
Namakei.

The break-up at Tanna had robbed me of my own neat
little printing-press. I had since obtained at Aneityum the
remains of one from Erromanga, that had belonged to the
murdered Gordon. But the supply of letters, in some cases,
was so deficient that I could print only four pages at a time ;
and, besides, bits of the press were wanting, and I had first
to manufacture substitutes from scraps of iron and wood. I
managed, however, to make it go, and by-and-bye it did good
service. By it I printed our Aniwan Hymn-Book, a portion
of Genesis in Aniwan, a small book in Erromangan for the
second Gordon, and some other little things.

The old chief had eagerly helped me in translating and
preparing this first book. He had a great desire "to hear it

360

speak," as he graphically expressed it.   It was made up chiefly
of short passages from the Scriptures, that might help me
to introduce them to the treasures of Divine truth and love.
Namakei came to me, morning after morning, saying, " Missi,
is it done?   Can it speak?"

At last I was able to answer, " Yes !"

The old Chief eagerly responded, " Does it speak my
words?"

I said, " It does."

With rising interest, Namakei exclaimed, " Make it speak to
me, Missi!   Let me hear it speak."

I read to him a part of the book, and the old man fairly
shouted in an ecstasy of joy, " It does speak !   It speaks my
own language, too !   Oh, give it to me !"

He grasped it hurriedly, turned it all round every way,
pressed it to his bosom, and then, closing it with a look of
great disappointment, handed it back to me, saying, " Missi,
I cannot make it speak !   It will never speak to me."

" No," said I ;   " you don't know how to read it yet, how to
make it speak to you ; but I will teach you to read, and then
it will speak to you as it does to me."

" O Missi, dear Missi, show me how to make it speak !"
persisted the bewildered Chief.   He was straining his eyes so,
that I suspected they were dim with age, and could not see
the letters.   I looked out for him a pair of spectacles, and
managed to fit him well.   He was much afraid of putting
them on at first, manifestly in dread of some sort of sorcery.
At last, when they were properly placed, he saw the letters
and everything so clearly that he exclaimed in great excitement and joy :

" I see it all now !   This is what you told us about Jesus.
He opened the eyes of a blind man.   The word of Jesus has
just come to Aniwa.   He has sent me these glass eyes.   I
have gotten back again the sight that I had when a boy.   O
Missi, make the book speak to me now !"

I walked out with him to the public Village Ground.
There I drew A B C in large characters upon the dust,
showed him the same letters in the book, and left him to
compare them, and find out how many occurred on the first

page. Fixing these in his mind, he came running to me, and said, " I have lifted up A B C. They are here in my head, and I will hold them fast. Give me other three."

This was repeated time after time. He mastered the whole Alphabet, and soon began to spell out the smaller words. Indeed, he came so often, getting me to read it over and over, that before he himself could read it freely he had it word for word committed to memory. When strangers passed him, or young people came around, he would get out the little book, and say, " Come, and I will let you hear how the book speaks our own Aniwan words. You say, it is hard to learn to read and make it speak. But be strong to try ! If an old man like me has done it, it ought to be much easier for you."

One day I heard him read to a company with wonderful fluency. Taking the book, I asked him to show me how he had learned to read so quickly. Immediately I perceived that he could recite the whole from memory ! He became our right-hand helper in the Conversion of Aniwa.

Next after God's own Word, perhaps the power of Music was most amazingly blessed in opening up our way. Amongst many other illustrations, I may mention how Namakei's wife was won. The old lady positively shuddered at coming near the Mission House, and dreaded being taught anything. One day she was induced to draw near the door, and fixing a hand on either post, and gazing inwards, she exclaimed, " Awái, Missi ! Kái, Missi ! "—the Native cry for unspeakable wonder. Mrs. Paton began to play on the harmonium, and sang a simple hymn in the old woman's language. Manifestly charmed, she drew nearer and nearer, and drank in the music, as it were, at every pore of her being. At last she ran off, and we thought it was with fright, but it was to call together all the women and girls from her village "to hear the *bokis* sing ! " (Having no *x*, the word *box* is pronounced thus.) She returned with them all at her heels. They listened with dancing eyes. And ever after the sound of a hymn, and the song of the *bokis*, made them flock freely to class or meeting.

Being myself as nearly as possible destitute of the power of singing, all my work would have been impaired and sadly hindered, and the joyous side of the Worship and Service of

Jehovah could not have been presented to the Natives, but for the gift bestowed by the Lord on my dear wife. She led our songs of praise, both in the Family and in the Church, and that was the first avenue by which the New Religion winged its way into the heart of Cannibal and Savage.

The old chief was particularly eager that this same aged lady, his wife Yauwaki, should be taught to read. But her sight was far gone. So, one day, he brought her to me, saying, "Missi, can you give my wife also a pair of new glass eyes like mine? She tries to learn, but she cannot see the letters. She tries to sew, but she pricks her finger, and throws away the needle, saying, 'The ways of the white people are not good!' If she could get a pair of glass eyes, she would be in a new world like Namakei." In my bundle I found a pair that suited her. She was in positive terror about putting them on her face, but at last she cried with delight, "Oh, my new eyes! my new eyes! I have the sight of a little girl. I will learn hard now. I will make up for lost time."

Her progress was never very great, but her influence for good on other women and girls was immense.

In all my work amongst the Natives, I have striven to train them to be self-supporting, and have never helped them where I could train to help themselves. In this respect I was exceedingly careful, when the question arose of building their Churches and Schools. At first we moved about amongst them from village to village, acquired their language, and taught them everywhere,—by the roadside, under the shade of a tree, or on the public Village Ground. Our old Native Hut, when we removed to the Mission House formerly referred to, was used for all sorts of public meetings. Feeling by-and-bye that the time had come to interest them in building a new Church, and that it would be every way helpful, I laid the proposal before them, carefully explaining that for this work no one would be paid, that the Church was for all the Islanders and for the Worship alone, and that every one must build purely for the love of Jesus.

I told them that God would be pleased with such materials as they had to give, that they must not begin till they had divided the work and counted the cost, and that for my part I

364 THE LIGHT THAT SHINETH MORE AND MORE.

would do all that I could to direct and help, and would supply
the sinnet (= cocoa-nut fibre rope) which I had brought from
Aneityum, and the nails from Sydney.

They held meeting after meeting throughout the Island.
Chiefs made long speeches; orators chanted their palavers;
and warriors acted their part by waving of club and tomahawk.
An unprecedented friendliness sprang up amongst them. They
agreed to sink every quarrel, and unite in building the first
Church on Aniwa,—one Chief only holding back. Women
and children began to gather and prepare the sugar-cane leaf
for thatch. Men searched for and cut down suitable trees.

The Church measured sixty-two feet by twenty-four. The
wall was twelve feet high. The studs were of hard iron-wood,
and were each by tenon and mortise fastened into six iron-
wood trees forming the upper wall plates. All were not only
nailed, but strongly tied together by sinnet-rope, so as to resist
the hurricanes. The roof was supported by four huge iron-
wood trees, and a fifth of equally hard wood, sunk about eight
feet into the ground, surrounded by building at the base, and
forming massive pillars. There were two doorways and eight
window spaces; the floor was laid with white coral, broken
small, and covered with cocoa-nut tree leaf-mats, on which
the people sat. I had a small platform, floored and surrounded with reeds; and Mrs. Paton had a seat enclosing
the harmonium, also made of reeds, and in keeping. Great
harmony prevailed all the time, and no mishap marred the
work. One hearty fellow fell from the roof-tree to the ground,
and was badly stunned. But, jumping up, he shook himself,
and saying—" I was working for Jehovah! He has saved me
from being hurt"—he mounted the roof again and went on
cheerily with his work.

Our pride in the New Church soon met with a dreadful
blow. That very season a terrific hurricane levelled it with
the ground. After much wailing, the principal Chief, in a
public Assembly, said, " Let us not weep, like boys over their
broken bows and arrows! Let us be strong, and build a yet
stronger Church for Jehovah."

By our counsel, ten days were spent first in repairing houses
and fences, and saving food from the plantations, many of

which had been swept into utter ruin. Then they assembled on the appointed day. A hymn was sung. God's blessing was invoked, and all the work was dedicated afresh to Him. Days were spent in taking the iron-wood roof to pieces, and saving everything that could be saved. The work was allocated equally amongst the villages, and a wholesome emulation was created. One Chief still held back. After a while, I visited him and personally invited his help,—telling him that it was God's House, andf or all the people of Aniwa; and that if he and his people did not do their part, the others would cast it in their teeth that they had no share in the House of God. He yielded to my appeal, and entered vigorously upon the work.

One large tree was still needed to complete the couples, and could nowhere be found. The work was at a standstill; for, though the size was now reduced to fifty feet by twenty-two, the roof lowered by four feet, and there was still plenty of smaller wood on Aniwa, the larger trees were apparently exhausted. One morning, however, we were awoke at early daybreak by the shouting and singing of a company of men, carrying a great black tree to the Church, with this same Chief dancing before them, leading the singing, and beating time with the flourish of his tomahawk. Determined not to be beaten, though late in the field, he had lifted the roof-tree out of his own house, as black as soot could make it, and was carrying it to complete the couplings. The rest of the builders shouted against this. All the other wood of the Church was white and clean, and they would not have this black tree, conspicuous in the very centre of all. But I praised the old Chief for what he had done, and hoped he and his people would come and worship Jehovah under his own roof-tree. At this all were delighted; and the work went on apace, with many songs and shoutings.

Whenever the Church was roofed in, we met in it for Public Worship. Coral was being got and burned, and preparations made for plastering the walls. The Natives were sharp enough to notice that I was not putting up the bell; and suspicions arose that I kept it back in order to take it with me when I returned to Tanna. It was a beautiful Church bell, cast and sent out by our dear friend, James Taylor, Esq.,

Birkenhead. The Aniwans, therefore, gave me no rest till I agreed to have it hung on their new Church. They found a large iron-wood tree near the shore, cut a road for half a mile through the bush, tied poles across it every few feet, and with shouts lifted it bodily on their shoulders—six men or so at each pole—and never set it down again till they reached the Church; for as one party got exhausted, others were ready to rush in and relieve them at every stage of the journey. The two old Chiefs, flourishing their tomahawks, went capering in front of all the rest, and led the song to which they marched, joyfully bearing their load. They dug a deep hole, into which to sink it; I squared the top and screwed on the bell; then we raised the tree by ropes, letting it sink into the hole, and built it round eight feet deep with coral blocks and lime; and there from its top swings and rings ever since the Church bell of Aniwa.

A fortnight's cessation of labour at the Church now followed. Their own plantations were attended to, and other needful duties performed. Our resumption of operations at the Church gave the opportunity for a deed of horrid cruelty. The Chief's son, Palesa, had just been married to a youthful widow, whom Nasi, a Tanna-man living on Aniwa, had also desired. The people of the young bridegroom's village agreed to sleep over-night near the Mission Premises, in order to be ready for the work early next morning; and they deputed the young couple to return to the village and sleep there, watching over their property. Nasi and his half-brother, Nouka, knowing they were alone, crept stealthily towards their hut at earliest day-break, and removed the door without awakening either of the sleepers. Next moment a ball struck the young husband dead. The wife sprang up and implored Nasi to spare her; but he sent a ball through her heart, and she fell dead upon her dead spouse! Their people, hearing the double shot, rushed to the scene, and found the hut flowing with blood. Early that same forenoon the bride and bridegroom were laid in the same grave, in the sleep of love and death.

For a week all our work was suspended. Men and boys went about fully armed, and all their talk was for revenge. Nasi had a number of desperate fellows at his back, all armed with muskets, and I feared the loss of many lives. I implored them for once to leave the vengeance in the hands of God, and to stand by each other in carrying forward the work of Jehovah. But I solemnly forbade the murderers to come near the Mission House, or to help us with the Church. My counsel was so far accepted. But every man came to the work armed with musket, tomahawk, spear, and club, and the boys with bows and arrows ; and these were piled up round the fence at hand, with watchmen stationed for alarm. Thus literally with sword in one hand and trowel in the other, the House of the Lord was reared again on Aniwa.

Coral was secured, as described in a preceding chapter ; lime was prepared therefrom by burning it in extemporized kilns ; and each village vied with all the rest in plastering beautifully its own allocated portion—the first job of the kind they had ever done. The floor was covered with broken coral and mats, but the natives are now (1889) laying a concrete floor, and furnishing it with white men's seats. Originally they had a row of seats all round it inside, made of bamboo cane and reeds. The women and girls enter by one door, and the men and boys by another ; and they sit on separate sides,—except at the Lord's Table, when all sit together as one family. It was a Church perfectly suitable for their circumstances, and it cost the Home Committees not a single penny. It has withstood many a hurricane. A large number of the original builders are gone to their rest ; but their work abides, and witnesses for God amongst their children. On its rude walls I could see the glorious motto—" Jehovah Shammah."

One of the last attempts ever made on my life resulted, by God's blessing, in great good to us all and to the work of the Lord. It was when Nourai, one of Nasi's men, struck at me again and again with the barrel of his musket ; but I evaded the blows, till rescued by the women—the men looking on stupefied. After he escaped into the bush, I assembled our people, and said, " If you do not now try to stop this bad conduct, I shall leave Aniwa, and go to some island where my life will be protected."

Next morning at daybreak, about one hundred men arrived at my house, and in answer to my query why they came armed they replied, "We are now going to that village, where the men of wicked conduct are gathered together. We will find out why they sought your life, and we will rebuke their Sacred Man for pretending to cause hurricanes and diseases. We cannot go unarmed. We will not suffer you to go alone. We are your friends and the friends of the Worship. And we are resolved to stand by you, and you must go at our head to-day!"

In great perplexity, yet believing that my presence might prevent bloodshed, I allowed myself to be placed at their head. The old Chief followed next, then a number of fiery young men; then all the rest, single file, along the narrow path. At a sudden turn, as we neared their village, Nourai, who had attacked me the Sabbath day before, and his brother were seen lurking with their muskets; but our young men made a rush in front, and they disappeared into the bush.

We took possession of the Village Public Ground; and the Chief, the Sacred Man, and others soon assembled. A most characteristic Native Palaver followed. Speeches, endless speeches, were fired by them at each other. My friends declared, in every conceivable form of language and of graphic illustration, that they were resolved at any cost to defend me and the worship of Jehovah, and that they would as one man punish every attempt to injure me or take my life. The orator, Taia, exclaimed, "You think that Missi is here alone, and that you can do with him as you please! No! We are now all Missi's men. We will fight for him and his rather than see him injured. Every one that attacks him attacks us. That is finished to-day!"

In the general scolding, the Sacred Man had special attention, for pretending to cause hurricanes. One pointed out that he had himself a stiff knee, and argued, "If he can make a hurricane, why can't he restore the joint of his own knee? It is surely easier to do the one than the other!"

The Natives laughed heartily, and taunted him. Meantime he sat looking down to the earth in sullen silence; and a ludicrous episode ensued. His wife, a big, strong woman, scolded him roundly for the trouble he had brought them all into; and then, getting indignant as well as angry, she seized a huge cocoa-nut leaf out of the bush, and with the butt end thereof began thrashing his shoulders vigorously, as she poured out the vials of her wrath in torrents of words, always winding up with the cry, " I'll knock the Tevil out of him! He'll not try hurricanes again ! "

The woman was a Malay, as all the Aniwans were. Had a Papuan woman on Tanna or Erromanga dared such a thing, she would have been killed on the spot. But even on Aniwa, the unwonted spectacle of a wife beating her husband created uproarious amusement. At length I remonstrated, saying, "You had better stop now! You don't want to kill him, do you? You seem to have knocked 'the Tevil' pretty well out of him now! You see how he receives it all in silence, and repents of all his bad talk and bad conduct."

They exacted from him a solemn promise as to the making of no more diseases or hurricanes, and that he would live at peace with his neighbours. The offending villagers at length presented a large quantity of sugar-cane and food to us as a peace-offering; and we returned, praising God that the whole day's scolding had ended in talk, not blood. The result was every way most helpful. Our friends knew their strength and took courage. Our enemies were disheartened and afraid. We saw the balance growing heavier every day on the side of Jesus ; and our souls blessed the Lord.

These events suggest to me another incident of those days full at once of trial and of joy. It pertains to the story of our young Chief, Youwili. From the first, and for long, he was most audacious and troublesome. Observing that for several days no Natives had come near the Mission House, I asked the old Chief if he knew why, and he answered, "Youwili has *tabooed* the paths, and threatens death to any one who breaks through it."

I at once replied, " Then I conclude that you all agree with him, and wish me to leave. We are here only to teach you and your people. If he has power to prevent that we shall leave with the *Dayspring*."

The old Chief called the people together, and they came to me, saying, "Our anger is strong against Youwili. Go with us and break down the *taboo*. We will assist and protect you."

24

I went at their head and removed it. It consisted simply of reeds stuck into the ground, with twigs and leaves and fibre tied to each in a peculiar way, in a circle round the Mission House. The Natives had an extraordinary dread of violating the *taboo*, and believed that it meant death to the offender or to some one of his family. All present entered into a bond to punish on the spot any man who attempted to replace the *taboo*, or to revenge its removal. Thus a mortal blow was publicly struck at this most miserable superstition, which had caused bloodshed and misery untold.

One day, thereafter, I was engaged in clearing away the bush around the Mission House, having purchased and paid for the land for the very purpose of opening it up, when suddenly Youwili appeared and menacingly forbade me to proceed. For the sake of peace I for the time desisted. But he went straight to my fence, and with his tomahawk cut down the portion in front of our house, also some bananas planted there—the usual declaration of war, intimating that he only awaited his opportunity similarly to cut down me and mine. We saw the old Chief and his men planting themselves here and there to guard us, and the Natives prowling about armed and excited. On calling them, they explained the meaning of what Youwili had done, and that they were determined to protect us. I said, "This must not continue. Are you to permit one young fool to defy us all, and break up the Lord's work on Aniwa? If you cannot righteously punish him, I will shut myself up in my House and withdraw from all attempts to teach or help you, till the Vessel comes, and then I can leave the Island."

Now that they had begun really to love us, and to be anxious to learn more, this was always my most powerful argument. We retired into the Mission House. The people surrounded our doors and windows and pleaded with us. After long silence, we replied, "You know our resolution. It is for you now to decide. Either you must control that foolish young man, or we must go!"

Much speech-making, as usual, followed. The people resolved to seize and punish Youwili; but he fled, and had hid himself in the bush. Coming to me, the Chief said, "It

is left to you to say what shall be Youwili's punishment. Shall
we kill him?"

I replied firmly, "Certainly not! Only for murder can life
be lawfully taken away."

"What then?" they continued. "Shall we burn his houses
and destroy his plantations?"

I answered, "No."

"Shall we bind him and beat him?"

"No."

"Shall we place him in a canoe, thrust him out to sea, and
let him drown or escape as he may?"

"No! by no means."

"Then, Missi," said they, "these are our ways of punishing.
What other punishment remains that Youwili cares for?"

I replied, "Make him with his own hands, and alone, put
up a new fence, and restore all that he has destroyed; and
make him promise publicly that he will cease all evil conduct
towards us. That will satisfy me."

This idea of punishment seemed to tickle them greatly.
The Chiefs reported our words to the Assembly; and the
Natives laughed and cheered, as if it were a capital joke!
They cried aloud, "It is good! It is good! Obey the word
of the Missi."

After considerable hunting, the young Chief was found.
They brought him to the Assembly and scolded him severely
and told him their sentence. He was surprised by the nature
of the punishment, and cowed by the determination of the
people.

"To-morrow," said he, "I will fully repair the fence. Never
again will I oppose the Missi. His word is good."

By daybreak next morning Youwili was diligently repairing
what he had broken down, and before evening he had everything made right, better than it was before. While he toiled
away, some fellows of his own rank twitted him, saying,
"Youwili, you found it easier to cut down Missi's fence than
to repair it again. You will not repeat that in a hurry!"

But he heard all in silence. Others passed with averted
heads, and he knew they were laughing at him. He made
everything tight, and then left without uttering a single word.

My heart yearned after the poor fellow, but I thought it better to let his own mind work away, on its new ideas as to punishment and revenge, for a little longer by itself alone. I instinctively felt that Youwili was beginning to turn, that the Christ-Spirit had touched his darkly-groping soul. My doors were now thrown open, and every good work went on as before. We resolved to leave Youwili entirely to Jesus, setting apart a portion of our prayer every day for the enlightenment and conversion of the young Chief, on whom all other means had been exhausted apparently in vain.

A considerable time elapsed. No sign came, and our prayers seemed to fail. But one day, I was toiling between the shafts of a hand-cart, assisted by two boys, drawing it along from the shore loaded with coral blocks. Youwili came rushing from his house, three hundred yards or so off the path, and said, " Missi, that is too hard for you. Let me be your helper ! "

Without waiting for a reply, he ordered the two boys to seize one rope, while he grasped the other, threw it over his shoulder and started off, pulling with the strength of a horse. My heart rose in gratitude, and I wept with joy as I followed him. I knew that that yoke was but a symbol of the yoke of Christ, which Youwili with his change of heart was beginning to carry ! Truly there is only one way of regeneration, being born again by the power of the Spirit of God, the new heart ; but there are many ways of conversion, of outwardly turning to the Lord, of taking the actual first step that shows on whose side we are. Regeneration is the sole work of the Holy Spirit in the human heart and soul, and is in every case one and the same. Conversion, on the other hand, bringing into play the action also of the human will, is never absolutely the same perhaps in even two souls—as like and yet as different as are the faces of men.

Like those of old praying for the deliverance of Peter, and who could not believe their ears and eyes when Peter knocked and walked in amongst them, so we could scarcely believe our eyes and ears when Youwili became a disciple of Jesus, though we had been praying for his conversion every day. His once sullen countenance became literally bright with inner light.

His wife came immediately for a book and a dress, saying, "Youwili sent me. His opposition to the Worship is over now. I am to attend Church and School. He is coming too. He wants to learn how to be strong, like you, for Jehovah and for Jesus."

Oh, Jesus! to Thee alone be all the glory. Thou hast the key to unlock every heart that Thou hast created.

Youwili proved to be slow at learning to read, but he had perseverance, and his wife greatly helped him. The two attended the Communicants' Class together, and ultimately both sat down at the Lord's Table. After his first Communion, he waited for me under an orange-tree near the Mission House, and said, " Missi, I've given up everything for Jesus, *except one*. I want to know if it is bad, if it will make Jesus angry ; for if so, I am willing to give it up. I want to live so as to please Jesus now."

We feared that it was some of their Heathenish immoralities, and were in a measure greatly relieved when he proceeded, "Missi, I have not yet given up my pipe and tobacco ! Oh, Missi, I have used it so long, and I do like it so well ; but if you say that it makes Jesus angry with me, I will smash my pipe now, and never smoke again ! "

The man's soul was aflame. He was in tremendous earnest, and would have done anything for me. But I was more anxious to instruct his conscience than to dominate it. I therefore replied in effect thus, " I rejoice, Youwili, that you are ready to give up anything to please Jesus. He well deserves it, for He gave up His life for you. For my part, you know that I do not smoke ; and from my point of view I would think it wrong in me to waste time and money and perhaps health in blowing tobacco smoke into the air. It would do me no good. It could not possibly help me to serve or please Jesus better. I think I am happier and healthier without it. And I am certain that I can use the time and money, spent on this selfish and rather filthy habit, far more for God's glory in many other ways. But I must be true to you, Youwili, and admit that many of God's dear people differ from me in these opinions. They spend time and money, and sometimes injure health, in smoking, besides setting a wasteful

374 THE LIGHT THAT SHINETH MORE AND MORE.

example to lads and young men, and do not regard it as sinful. I will not therefore condemn these, our fellow-Christians, by calling smoking a *sin* like drunkenness ; but I will say to you that I regard it as a foolish and wasteful indulgence, a bad habit, and that though you may serve and please Jesus with it, you might serve and please Jesus very much better without it."

He looked very anxious, as if weighing his habit against his resolution, and then said, " Missi, I give up everything else. If it won't make Jesus angry, I will keep the pipe. I have used it so long, and oh, I do like it ! "

Renewing our advice and counsel, but leaving him free to do in that matter so as to please Jesus according to his own best light, Youwili departed with a conscience so far greatly relieved, and we had many meditations upon the incident. Most of our Natives, on their conversion, have voluntarily renounced the Tobacco Idol ; but what more could I say to Youwili, with thousands of white Christians at my back burning incense to that same idol every day of their lives ?   Marvellous to me, in this connection, has often been the working of a tender conscience, asking itself how to serve and please Jesus, or how to do more for Jesus. Some years ago, for instance, I met a State School Teacher in Victoria, who had been lately brought under the power of the Gospel.   In his fresh love, he wanted to do something to show his gratitude to Jesus.   He had a young family, and the way was barred to the Mission-field.   His dear wife and he calculated over all their expenditure, to find out how much they could save to support the work of Jesus at home and abroad.   Little or nothing could be spared from what appeared necessary claims. He fell upon his knees, and in tears implored God to show him how he could do something more to save the perishing. A voice came to him like a flash, " If you so care for Me and My work, you can easily sacrifice your pipe."

He instantly took up his pipe, and laid it before the Lord, saying, " There it is, O my Lord, and whatsoever it may have cost me, shall now from year to year be Thine ! "

He was not what is called a heavy smoker—anything under one shilling per week being considered " moderate," as I am informed.   But he found that he had been spending fifty shillings per annum on tobacco ; and every year since he has laid that money upon the altar to Jesus, and prayed Him to use it in sending His Gospel to Heathen lands. I wonder which soul is the richer at the end of a year—he who lays his money, saved from a selfish indulgence, at the feet of Jesus, or he ·ho blows it away in filthy smoke ?

And this leads me to relate the story of our First Communion on Aniwa. It was Sabbath, 24th October, 1869 ; and surely the Angels of God and the Church of the Redeemed in Glory were amongst the " great cloud of witnesses " who eagerly " peered " down upon the scene,—when we sat around the Lord's Table and partook the memorials of His body and blood with those few souls rescued out of the Heathen World. My Communicants' Class had occupied me now a considerable time. The conditions of attendance at this early stage were explicit, and had to be made very severe, and only twenty were admitted to the roll. At the final examination only twelve gave evidence of understanding what they were doing, and of having given their hearts to the service of the Lord Jesus. At their own urgent desire, and after every care in examining and instructing, they were solemnly dedicated in prayer to be baptized and admitted to the Holy Table. On that Lord's Day, after the usual opening Service, I gave a short and careful exposition of the Ten Commandments and of the Way of Salvation according to the Gospel. The twelve Candidates then stood up before all the inhabitants there assembled ; and, after a brief exhortation to them as Converts, I put to them the two questions that follow, and each gave an affirmative reply, " Do you, in accordance with your profession of the Christian Faith, and your promises before God and the people, wish me now to baptize you ?

And—" Will you live henceforth for Jesus only, hating all sin and trying to love and serve your Saviour ? "

Then, beginning with the old Chief, the twelve came forward, and I baptized them one by one according to the Presbyterian usage. Two of them had also little children, and they were at the same time baptized, and received as the lambs of the flock. Solemn prayer was then offered, and in the name of the Holy Trinity the Church of Christ on Aniwa was formally constituted. I addressed them on the words of the Holy Institution—1 Corinthians xi. 23—and then, after the prayer of Thanksgiving and Consecration, administered the Lord's Supper,—the first time since the Island of Aniwa was heaved out of its coral depths! Mrs. McNair, my wife, and myself, along with six Aneityumese Teachers, communicated with the newly baptized twelve. And I think, if ever in all my earthly experience, on that day I might truly add the blessed words— " Jesus in the midst."

The whole Service occupied nearly three hours. The Islanders looked on with a wonder whose unwonted silence was almost painful to bear. Many were led to inquire carefully about everything they saw, so new and strange. For the first time the Dorcas Street Sabbath School Teachers' gift from South Melbourne Presbyterian Church was put to use—a new Communion Service of silver. They gave it in faith that we would require it, and in such we received it. And now the day had come and gone! For three years we had toiled and prayed and taught for this. At the moment when I put the bread and wine into those dark hands, once stained with the blood of Cannibalism, but now stretched out to receive and partake the emblems and seals of the Redeemer's love, I had a foretaste of the joy of Glory that well nigh broke my heart to pieces. I shall never taste a deeper bliss, till I gaze on the glorified face of Jesus Himself.

On the afternoon of that Communion Day, an open-air Prayer Meeting was held under the shade of the great banyan tree in front of our Church. Seven of the new Church members there led the people in prayer to Jesus, a hymn being sung after each. My heart was so full of joy that I could do little else but weep. Oh, I wonder, I *wonder*, when I see so many good Ministers at home, crowding each other and treading on each other's heels, whether they would not part with all their home privileges, and go out to the Heathen World and reap a joy like this—".the joy of the Lord."

Having now our little Aniwan book, we set about establishing Schools at every village on the Island. Mrs. Paton and I had been diligently instructing those around us, and had now a number prepared to act as helpers. Experience has proved that, for the early stages, their own fellow-Islanders are the most successful instructors. Each village built its own School, which on Sabbath served as a district Church. For the two most advanced Schools I had our good Aneityumese Teachers, and for the others I took the best readers that could be found. These I changed frequently, returning them to our own School for a season, which was held for them in the afternoon; and to encourage them, a small salary was granted to each of them yearly, drawn from what is now known throughout the Churches as the Native Teachers' Fund.

These village Schools have all to be conducted at daybreak, while the heavy dews still drench the bush; for so soon as the dews are lifted by the rising sun, the Natives are off to their plantations, on which they depend for their food almost exclusively. I had a large School at the Mission Station, also at daybreak, besides the afternoon School at three o'clock for the training of Teachers. At first they made very little progress; but they began to form habits of attention; and they learned the fruitful habit of acknowledging God always, for all our Schools were opened and closed with prayer. As their knowledge and faith increased, we saw their Heathen practices rapidly passing away, and a new life shaping itself around us. Mrs. Paton taught a class of about fifty women and girls. They became experts at sewing, singing, plaiting hats, and reading. Nearly all the girls could at length cut out and make their own dresses, as well as shirts or kilts for the men and clothing for the children. Yet, three short years before, men and women alike were running about naked and savage. The Christ-Spirit is the true civilizing power.

The new Social Order, referred to already in its dim beginnings, rose around us like a sweet-scented flower. I never interfered directly, unless expressly called upon or appealed to. The two principal Chiefs were impressed with the idea that there was but one law—the Will of God; and one rule for them and their people as Christians—to please the Lord Jesus. In every difficulty they consulted me. I explained to them and read in their hearing the very words of Holy Scripture, showing what appeared to me to be the will of God and what would please the Saviour; and then sent them away to talk it over with their people, and to apply these principles of the word of God as wisely as they could according to their circumstances. Our own part of the work went on very joyfully, notwithstanding occasional trying and painful incidents. Individual cases of greed and selfishness and vice brought us many a bitter pang. But the Lord never lost patience with us, and we durst not therefore lose patience with them! We trained the Teachers, we translated and printed and expounded the Scriptures, we ministered to the sick and dying; we dispensed medicines every day, we taught them the use of tools, we advised them as to laws and penalties; and the New Society grew and developed, and bore amidst all its imperfections some traces of the fair Kingdom of God amongst men.

Our life and work will reveal itself to the reader, if I briefly outline a Sabbath Day on Aniwa. Breakfast is partaken of immediately after daylight. The Church bell then rings, and ere it stops every worshipper is seated. The Natives are guided in starting by the sunrise, and are forward from farthest corners at this early hour. The first Service is over in about an hour; there is an interval of twenty minutes; the bell is again rung, and the second Service begins. We follow the ordinary Presbyterian ritual; but in every Service I call upon an Elder or a Church Member to lead in one of the prayers, which they do with great alacrity and with much benefit to all concerned.

As the last worshipper leaves, at close of second Service, the bell is sounded twice very deliberately, and that is the signal for the opening of my Communicants' Class. I carefully expound the Church's Shorter Catechism and show how its teachings are built upon Holy Scripture, applying each truth to the conscience and the life. This Class is conducted all the year round; and from it, step by step, our Church Members are drawn as the Lord opens up their way, the most of them attending two full years at least before being admitted to the Lord's Table. This discipline accounts for the fact that so very few of our baptized converts have ever fallen away—as few in proportion, I verily believe, as in Churches at home. Meantime, many of the Church members have been holding a prayer-meeting amongst themselves in the adjoining School,—a thing started of their own free accord,— in which they invoke God's blessing on all the work and worship of the day.

Having snatched a brief meal of tea, or a cold dinner cooked on Saturday, the bell rings within an hour, and our Sabbath School assembles,—in which the whole inhabitants, young and old, take part, myself superintending and giving the address, as well as questioning on the lesson, Mrs. Paton teaching a large class of adult women, and the Elders and best readers instructing the ordinary classes for about half-an-hour or so.

About one o'clock the School is closed, and we then start off on our village tours. An experienced Elder, with several Teachers, takes one side of the Island this Sabbath, I with another company taking the other side, and next Sabbath we reverse the order. A short Service is conducted in the open air, or in Schoolrooms, at every village that can be reached; and on their return they report to me cases of sickness, or any signs of progress in the work of the Lord. The whole Island is thus steadily and methodically evangelized.

As the sun is setting I am creeping home from my village tour; and when darkness begins to approach, the canoe drum is beat at every village, and the people assemble under the banyan-tree for evening village prayers. The Elder or Teacher presides. Five or six hymns are joyously sung, and five or six short prayers offered between, and thus the evening hour passes happily in the fellowship of God. On a calm evening, after Christianity had fairly taken hold of the people, and they loved to sing over and over again their favourite hymns, these village prayer-meetings formed a most blessed close to every day, and set the far-distant bush echoing with the praises of God.

At the Mission House, before retiring to rest, we assembled all the young people and any of our villagers who chose to join them. They sat round the dining-room floor in rows, sang hymns, read verses of the Bible, and asked and answered questions about the teaching of the day. About nine o'clock we dismissed them, but they pled to remain and hear our Family Worship in English:

"Missi, we like the singing! We understand a little. And we like to be where prayer is rising!"

Thus Sabbath after Sabbath flowed on in incessant service and fellowship. I was often wearied enough, but it was not a "weary" day to me, nor what some would call Puritanical and dull. Our hearts were in it, and the people made it a weekly festival. They had few other distractions; and amongst them "The Worship" was an unfailing sensation and delight. As long as you gave them a chance to sing, they knew not what weariness was. When I returned to so-called civilization, and saw how the Lord's Day was abused in *white* Christendom, my soul longed after the holy Sabbaths of Aniwa!

Nor is our week-day life less crowded or busy, though in different ways. At grey dawn on Monday, and every morning, the *Tavaka* (=the canoe drum) is struck in every village on Aniwa. The whole inhabitants turn in to the early School, which lasts about an hour and a half, and then the Natives are off to their plantations. Having partaken breakfast, I then spend my forenoon in translating or printing, or visiting the sick, or whatever else is most urgent. About two o'clock the Natives return from their work, bathe in the sea, and dine off cocoa-nut, bread-fruit, or anything else that comes handily in the way. At three o'clock the bell rings, and the afternoon School for the Teachers and the more advanced learners then occupies my wife and myself for about an hour and a half. After this, the Natives spend their time in fishing or lounging or preparing supper,—which is amongst them always *the* meal of the day. Towards sundown the *Tavaka* sounds again, and the day closes amid the echoes of village prayers from under their several banyan trees.

Thus day after day and week after week passes over us on Aniwa; and much the same on all the Islands where the Missionary has found a home. In many respects it is a simple and happy and beautiful life; and the man, whose heart is full of things that are dear to Jesus, feels no desire to exchange it for the poor frivolities of what calls itself "Society," which seems to find its life in pleasures that Christ cannot be asked to share, and in which, therefore, Christians should have neither lot nor part.

The habits of morning and evening Family Prayer and of Grace at Meat took a very wonderful hold upon the people ; and became, as I have shown elsewhere, a distinctive badge of Christian *versus* Heathen. This was strikingly manifested during a time of bitter scarcity that befell us. I heard a father, for instance, at his hut door, with his family around him, reverently blessing God for the food provided for them, and for all His mercies in Christ Jesus. Drawing near and conversing with them, I found that their meal consisted of fig leaves which they had gathered and cooked—a poor enough dish, but hunger makes a healthy appetite, and contentment is a grateful relish.

During the same period of privation, my Orphans suffered badly also. Once they came to me, saying, " Missi, we are very hungry."

I replied, " So am I, dear children, and we have no more white food till the *Dayspring* comes."

They continued, " Missi, you have two beautiful fig trees. Will you let us take one feast of the young and tender leaves ? We will not injure branch or fruit."

I answered, " Gladly, my children, take your fill ! "

In a twinkling each child was perched upon a branch ; and they feasted there happy as squirrels. Every night we prayed for the vessel, and in the morning our Orphan boys rushed to the coral rocks and eagerly scanned the sea for an answer. Day after day they returned with sad faces, saying, " Missi, *Tavaka jimra !* " (= No vessel yet).

But at grey dawn of a certain day, we were awoke by the boys shouting from the shore and running for the Mission House with the cry,—" *Tavaka oa ! Tavaka oa !* " (= The vessel, hurrah !)

We arose at once, and the boys exclaimed, " Missi, she is not our own vessel, but we think she carries her flag. She has three masts, and our *Dayspring* only two ! "

I looked through my glass, and saw that they were discharging goods into the vessel's boats ; and the children, when I told them that boxes and bags and casks were being sent on shore, shouted and danced with delight. As the first boat-load was discharged, the Orphans surrounded me, saying,

" Missi, here is a cask that rattles like biscuits! Will you let us take it to the Mission House ? "

I told them to do so if they could ; and in a moment it was turned into the path, and the boys had it flying before them, some tumbling and hurting their knees, but up and at it again, and never pausing till it rolled up at the door of our Storehouse. On returning I found them all around it, and they said, " Missi, have you forgotten what you promised us ? "

I said, " What did I promise you ? "

They looked very disappointed and whispered to each other, " Missi has forgot! "

" Forgot what ? " inquired I.

" Missi," they answered, " you promised that when the vessel came you would give each of us a biscuit."

" Oh," I replied, " I did not forget ; I only wanted to see if you remembered it ! "

They laughed, saying, " No fear of that, Miss ! ! Will you soon open the cask ? We are dying for biscuits."

At once I got hammer and tools, knocked off the hoops, took out the end, and then gave girls and boys a biscuit each. To my surprise, they all stood round, biscuit in hand, but not one beginning to eat.

" What," I exclaimed, " you are dying for biscuits ! Why don't you eat ? Are you expecting another ? "

One of the eldest said, " We will first thank God for sending us food, and ask Him to bless it to us all."

And this was done in their own simple and beautiful childlike way ; and then they *did* eat, and enjoyed their food as a gift from the Heavenly Father's hand. (Is there any child reading this, or hearing it read, who never thanks God or asks Him to bless daily bread ? Then is that child not a *white* Heathen ?) We ourselves at the Mission House could very heartily rejoice with the dear Orphans. For some weeks past our European food had been all exhausted, except a little tea, and the cocoa-nut had been our chief support. It was beginning to tell against us. Our souls rose in gratitude to the Lord, who had sent us these fresh provisions that we might love Him better and serve Him more.

The children's sharp eyes had read correctly. It was not

the *Dayspring*. Our brave little ship had gone to wreck on
6th January, 1873; and this vessel was the *Paragon*, chartered
to bring down our supplies. Alas! the wreck had gone by
auction sale to a French slaving company, who cut a passage
through the coral reef, and had the vessel again floating in the
Bay,—elated at the prospect of employing our Mission Ship
in the blood-stained *Kanaka*-traffic (= a mere euphemism for
South Sea slavery)! * Our souls sank in horror and concern.
Many Natives would unwittingly trust themselves to the *Dayspring*; and revenge would be taken on us, as was done on
noble Bishop Patteson, when the deception was found out.
What could be done? Nothing but cry to God, which all the
friends of our Mission did day and night, not without tears, as
we thought of the possible degradation of our noble little Ship.
Listen! The French Slavers, anchoring their prize in the
Bay, and greatly rejoicing, went ashore to celebrate the event.
They drank and feasted and revelled. But that night a
mighty storm arose, the old *Dayspring* dragged her anchor,
and at daybreak she was seen again on the reef, but this time
with her back broken in two and for ever unfit for service,
either fair or foul. Oh, white-winged Virgin, daughter of the
waves, better for thee, as for thy human sisters, to die and
pass away than to suffer pollution and live on in disgrace!

Dr. Steel had chartered the *Paragon*, a new three-masted
schooner, built at Balmain, Sydney, to come down with our
provisions, letters, etc.; and the owners had given a written
agreement that if we could purchase her within a year we
would get her for £3,000. She proved in every way a suitable vessel, and it became abundantly manifest that in the
interests of our Mission her services ought to be permanently
secured.

I had often said that I would not again leave my beloved
work on the Islands, unless compelled to do so either by the
breakdown of health, or by the loss of our Mission Ship and
my services being required to assist in providing another.
Very strange, that in this one season both of these events
befell us! During the hurricanes, from January to April, 1873,

---

* See Appendix D, "Kanaka Labour Traffic."

when the *Dayspring* was wrecked, we lost a darling child by death, my dear wife had a protracted illness, and I was brought very low with severe rheumatic fever. I was reduced so far that I could not speak, and was reported as dying. The Captain of a vessel, having seen me, called at Tanna, and spoke of me as in all probability dead by that time. Our unfailing and ever-beloved friends and fellow-Missionaries, Mr. and Mrs. Watt, at once started from Kwamera, in their open boat, and rowed and sailed thirty miles to visit us. But a few days before they arrived I had fallen into a long and sound sleep, out of which, when I awoke, consciousness had again returned to me. I had got the turn ; there was no further relapse ; but when I did regain a little strength, my weakness was so great that I had to travel about on crutches for many a day.

Being ordered to seek health by change and by higher medical aid, and if possible in the cooler air of New Zealand, we took the first opportunity and arrived at Sydney, anxious to start the new movement to secure the *Paragon* there, and then to go on to the Sister Colony. Being scarcely able to walk without the crutches, we called privately a preliminary meeting of friends for consultation and advice. The conditions were laid before them and discussed. The Insurance Company had paid £2,000 on the first *Dayspring*. Of that sum £1,000 had been spent on chartering and maintaining the *Paragon ;* so that we required an additional £2,000 to purchase her, besides a large sum for alterations and equipment for the Mission. The late Mr. Learmouth looked across to Mr. Goodlet, and said, " If you'll join me, we will at once secure this vessel for the Missionaries, that God's work may not suffer from the wreck of the *Dayspring*."

Those two servants of God, excellent Elders of the Presbyterian Church, consulted together, and the vessel was purchased next day. How I did praise God, and pray Him to bless them and theirs ! The late Dr. Fullarton, our dear friend, said to them, " But what guarantee do you ask from the Missionaries for your money ? "

Mr. Learmouth's noble reply was, and the other heartily re-echoed it—" God's work is our guarantee ! From them we will ask none. What guarantee have they to give us, except their faith in God? That guarantee is ours already."

I answered, " You take God and His work for your guarantee. Rest assured that He will soon repay you, and you will lose nothing by this noble service."

Having secured St. Andrew's Church for a public meeting, I advertised it in all the papers. Ministers, Sabbath School Teachers, and other friends came in great numbers. The scheme was fairly launched, and Collecting Cards largely distributed. Some of our fellow-Missionaries thought that the Colonial Churches should now do all these things voluntarily, without our personal efforts. But in every great emergency some one must take action and show the way, else golden opportunities are apt to slip. Committees carried everything out into detail, and all worked for the fund with great goodwill.

I then sailed from Sydney to Victoria, and addressed the General Assembly of the Presbyterian Church in session at Melbourne. The work was easily set a-going there, and willing workers fully and rapidly organized it through Congregations and Sabbath Schools.

Under medical advice, I next sailed for New Zealand in the S.S. *Hero*, Captain Logan. A large number of fast men and gamblers were on board, returning from the Melbourne Races, and their language was extremely profane. Having prayed over it, I said on the second day at the dinner-table, " Gentlemen, will you bear with me a moment? I am sure no man at this table wishes to wound the feelings of another or to give needless pain."

Every eye stared at me, and there was a general cry as to what I meant. I continued, " Gentlemen, we are to be fellow-passengers for a week or more. Now I am cut and wounded to my very heart to hear you cursing the Name of my Heavenly Father, and taking in vain the name of my blessed Saviour. It is God in whom we live and move, it is Jesus who died to save us, and I would rather ten times over you would wound and abuse me, which no gentleman here would think of doing, than profanely use those Holy Names so dear to me."

There was a painful silence, and most faces grew crimson,

25

some with rage, some perhaps with shame. At last a banker who was there, a man dying of consumption, replied with a profane oath and with wrathful words. Keeping perfectly calm, in sorrow and pity, I replied, looking him kindly in the face, " Dear Sir, you and I are strangers. But I have pitied you very tenderly, ever since I came on board, for your heavy trouble and hacking cough. You ought to be the last to curse that blessed Name, as you may soon have to appear in His presence. I return, however, no railing word. If the Saviour was as dear to your heart as He is to mine, you would better understand me."

Little else was said during the remainder of that meal. But an hour later Captain Logan sent for me to his room, and said, " Sir, I too am a Christian. I would not give my quiet hour in the Cabin with this Bible for all the pleasures that the world can afford. You did your duty to-day amongst these profane men. But leave them and their consciences now in the hands of God, and take no further notice during the voyage."

I never heard another oath on board that ship. The banker met me in New Zealand and warmly invited me to his house!

My health greatly improved during the voyage; but I was sorely perplexed about this new undertaking. A sum of £2,800 must be raised, else the vessel could not sail free for the New Hebrides. I trembled, in my reduced state, at the task that seemed laid upon me again. One night, after long praying, I fell into a deep sleep in my Cabin, and God granted me a Heavenly Dream or Vision which greatly comforted me, explain it how you will. Sweetest music, praising God, arrested me and came nearer and nearer. I gazed towards it approaching, and seemed to behold hosts of shining beings bursting into view. The brilliancy came pouring all from one centre, and that was ablaze with insufferable brightness. Blinded with excess of light, my eyes seemed yet to behold in fair outline the form of the glorified Jesus; but as I lifted them to gaze on His face, the joy deepened into pain, my hand rose instinctively to shade my eyes, I cried with ecstasy, the music passed farther and farther away, and I started up hearing a Voice saying, in marvellous power and sweetness, ' Who art thou, O great mountain ? Before Zerubbabel thou shalt become a plain." At this some will only smile. But to me it was a great and abiding consolation. And I kept repeating to myself, " He is Lord, and they all are ministering Spirits ; if He cheers me thus in His own work, I take courage, I know I shall succeed."

Reaching Auckland, I was in time to address the General Assembly of the Church there also. They gave me cordial welcome, and every Congregation and Sabbath School might be visited as far as I possibly could. The Ministers promoted the movement with hearty zeal. The Sabbath Scholars took Collecting Cards for " shares " in the New Mission Ship. A meeting was held every day, and three every Sabbath. Auckland, Nelson, Wellington, Dunedin, and all towns and Churches within reach of these were rapidly visited ; and I never had greater joy or heartiness in any of my tours than in this happy intercourse with the Ministers and People of the Presbyterian Church in New Zealand.

I arrived back in Sydney about the end of March. My health was wonderfully restored, and New Zealand had given me about £1,700 for the new ship. With the £1,000 of insurance money, and about £700 from New South Wales, and £400 from Victoria, besides the £500 for her support also from Victoria, we were able to pay back the £3,000 of purchase money, and about £800 for alterations and repairs, as well as equip and provision her to sail for her next year's work amongst the Islands free of debt. I said to our two good friends at Sydney :

"You took God and His work for your guarantee. He has soon relieved you from all responsibility. You have suffered no loss, and you have had the honour and privilege of serving your Lord. I envy you the joy you must feel in so using your wealth, and I pray God's double blessing on all your store."

Our agent, Dr. Steel, had applied to the Home authorities for power to change the vessel's name from *Paragon* to *Dayspring*, so that the old associations might not be broken. This was cordially granted. And so our second *Dayspring*, owing no man anything, sailed on her annual trip to the New Hebrides, and we returned with her, praising the Lord and reinvigorated alike in spirit and in body.

CHAPTER VIII.

PEN-PORTRAITS OF ANIWANS

A.D. 1874—1883.   ÆT. 50—59.

The Gospel in Living Capitals.—"A Shower of Spears."—The Tannese
Refugees.—Pilgrimage and Death of Namakei.—The Character of
Naswai.—Christianity and Cocoa-Nuts.—Nerwa the Agnostic.—
Nerwa's Beautiful Farewell.—The Story of Ruwawa.—Waiwai and
his Wives.—Nelwang and Kalangi.—Mungaw and Litsi Soré.—The
Maddening of Mungaw.—The Queen of Aniwa a Missionary.—The
Surrender of Nasi to Jesus.—Daylight Prayer-Meeting on Aniwa.—
Candidates for Baptism.—The Appeal and Testimony of Lamu.

I N Heathendom every true convert becomes at once a
Missionary. The changed life, shining out amid the
surrounding darkness, is a Gospel in largest Capitals which
all can read. Our Islanders, especially, having little to engage
or otherwise distract attention, become intense and devoted
workers for the Lord Jesus, if once the Divine Passion for
souls stirs within them. Many a reader, not making due
allowance for these special circumstances, would therefore
be tempted to think our estimate of their enthusiasm for the
Gospel was overdone ; but thoughtful men will easily perceive
that Natives, touched with the mighty impulses of Calvary,
and undistracted by social pleasures or politics, by literature
or business claims, would almost by a moral necessity pour all
the currents of their being into Religion, and probably show
an apostolic devotion and self-sacrifice too seldom seen, alas,
amid the thousand clamouring appeals of Civilization.

A Heathen has been all his days groping after peace of soul
in dark superstition and degrading rites. You pour into his
soul the light of Revelation. He learns that God is love, that
God sent His Son to die for him, and that he is the heir of

388

Life Eternal in and through Jesus Christ. By the blessed enlightenment of the Spirit of the Lord he believes all this. He passes into a third heaven of joy, and he burns to tell every one of this Glad Tidings. Others see the change in his disposition, in his character, in his whole life and actions ; and amid such surroundings, every Convert is a burning and a shining light. Even whole populations are thus brought into the Outer Court of the Temple ; and Islands, still Heathen and Cannibal, are positively eager for the Missionary to live amongst them, and would guard his life and property now in complete security, where a very few years ago everything would have been instantly sacrificed on touching their shores ! They are not Christianized, neither are they Civilized, but the light has been kindled all around them, and though still only shining afar, they cannot but rejoice in its beams.

But even where the path is not so smooth, nor any welcome awaiting them, Native Converts show amazing zeal. For instance, one of our Chiefs, full of the Christ-kindled desire to seek and to save, sent a message to an inland Chief, that he and four attendants would come on Sabbath and tell them the Gospel of Jehovah God. The reply came back sternly forbidding their visit, and threatening with death any Christian that approached their village. Our Chief sent in response a loving message, telling them that Jehovah had taught the Christians to return good for evil, and that they would come unarmed to tell them the story of how the Son of God came into the world and died in order to bless and save His enemies. The Heathen Chief sent back a stern and prompt reply once more, " If you come, you will be killed."

On Sabbath morning, the Christian Chief and his four companions were met outside the village by the Heathen Chief, who implored and threatened them once more. But the former said, " We come to you without weapons of war ! We come only to tell you about Jesus. We believe that He will protect us to-day."

As they steadily pressed forward towards the village, spears began to be thrown at them. Some they evaded, being all except one most dexterous warriors ; and others they literally received with their bare hands, striking them and turning them aside in an incredible manner. The Heathen, apparently thunderstruck at these men thus approaching them without weapons of war, and not even flinging back their own spears which they had turned aside, desisted from mere surprise, after having thrown what the old Chief called "a shower of spears." Our Christian Chief called out, as he and his companions drew up in the midst of them on the village Public Ground:

"Jehovah thus protects us. He has given us all your spears! Once we would have thrown them back at you and killed you. But now we come not to fight, but to tell you about Jesus. He has changed our dark hearts. He asks you now to lay down all these your other weapons of war, and to hear what we can tell you about the love of God, our great Father, the only living God."

The Heathen were perfectly overawed. They manifestly looked upon these Christians as protected by some Invisible One! They listened for the first time to the story of the Gospel and of the Cross. We lived to see that Chief and all his tribe sitting in the School of Christ. And there is perhaps not an Island in these Southern Seas, amongst all those won for Christ, where similar acts of heroism on the part of Converts cannot be recited by every Missionary to the honour of our poor Natives and to the glory of their Saviour.

Larger and harder tests were sometimes laid upon their new faith. Once the war on Tanna drove about one hundred of them to seek refuge on Aniwa. Not so many years before, their lives would never have been thus entrusted to the inhabitants of another Cannibal Island. But the Christ-Spirit was abroad upon Aniwa. The refugees were kindly cared for, and in process of time were restored to their own lands by our Missionary ship the *Dayspring*. The Chiefs, however, and the Elders of the Church laid the new laws before them very clearly and decidedly. They would be helped and sheltered, but Aniwa was now under law to Christ, and if any of the Tannese broke the public rules as to moral conduct, or in any way disturbed the Worship of Jehovah, they would at once be expelled from the Island and sent back to Tanna. In all this, the Chief of the Tanna party, my old friend Nowar, strongly supported our Christian Chiefs. The Tannese behaved well, and many of them wore clothing and began to attend Church ; and the heavy drain upon the poor resources of Aniwa was borne with a noble and Christian spirit, which greatly impressed the Tannese and commended the Gospel of Christ.

In claiming Aniwa for Christ, and winning it as a small jewel for His crown, we had the experience which has ever marked God's path through history,—He raised up around us and wonderfully endowed men to carry forward His own blessed work. Among these must be specially commemorated Namakei, the old Chief of Aniwa. Slowly, but very steadily, the light of the Gospel broke in upon his soul, and he was ever very eager to communicate to his people all that he learned. In Heathen days he was a Cannibal and a great warrior ; but from the first, as shown in the preceding Chapters, he took a warm interest in us and our work,—a little selfish, no doubt, at the beginning, but soon becoming purified, as his eyes and heart were opened to the Gospel of Jesus.

On the birth of a son to us on the Island, the old Chief was in ecstasies. He claimed the child as his heir, his own son being dead, and brought nearly the whole inhabitants in relays to see the *white* Chief of Aniwa ! He would have him called Namakei the Younger, an honour which I fear we did not too highly appreciate. As the child grew, he took his hand and walked about with him freely amongst the people, learning to speak their language like a Native, and not only greatly interesting them in himself, but even in us and in the work of the Lord. This, too, was one of the bonds, however purely human, that drew them all nearer and nearer to Jesus.

The death of Namakei had in it many streaks of Christian romance. He had heard about the Missionaries annually meeting on one or other of the Islands, and consulting about the work of Jehovah. What ideas he had formed of a Mission Synod one cannot easily imagine ; but in his old age, and when very frail, he formed an impassioned desire to attend our next meeting on Aneityum, and see and hear all the Missionaries of Jesus gathered together from the New Hebrides. Terrified that he would die away from home, and that that might bring great reverses to the good work on Aniwa, where he was truly beloved, I opposed his going with all my might.

But he and his relations and his people were all set upon it, and I had at length to give way. His few booklets were then gathered together, his meagre wardrobe was made up, and a small Native basket carried all his belongings. He assembled his people and took an affectionate farewell, pleading with them to be "strong for Jesus," whether they ever saw him again or not, and to be loyal and kind to Missi. The people wailed aloud, and many wept bitterly. Those on board the *Dayspring* were amazed to see how his people loved him. The old Chief stood the voyage well. He went in and out to our meeting of Synod, and was vastly pleased with the respect paid to him on Aneityum. When he heard of the prosperity of the Lord's work, and how Island after Island was learning to sing the praises of Jesus, his heart glowed, and he said, "Missi, I am lifting up my head like a tree. I am growing tall with joy!"

On the fourth or fifth day, however, he sent for me out of the Synod, and when I came to him, he said, eagerly, "Missi, I am near to die! I have asked you to come and say farewell. Tell my daughter, my brother, and my people to go on pleasing Jesus, and I will meet them again in the fair World."

I tried to encourage him, saying that God might raise him up again and restore him to his people; but he faintly whispered, "O Missi, death is already touching me! I feel my feet going away from under me. Help me to lie down under the shade of that banyan tree."

So saying, he seized my arm, we staggered near to the tree, and he lay down under its cool shade. He whispered again, "I am going! O Missi, let me hear your words rising up in prayer, and then my Soul will be strong to go."

Amidst many choking sobs, I tried to pray. At last he took my hand, pressed it to his heart, and said in a stronger and clearer tone, "O my Missi, my dear Missi, I go before you, but I will meet you again in the Home of Jesus. Farewell!"

That was the last effort of dissolving strength; he immediately became unconscious, and fell asleep. My heart felt like to break over him. He was my first Aniwan Convert—the first who ever on that Island of love and tears opened his heart to Jesus; and as he lay there on the leaves and grass, my soul soared upward after his, and all the harps of God seemed to thrill with song as Jesus presented to the Father this trophy of redeeming love. He had been our true and devoted friend and fellow-helper in the Gospel; and next morning all the members of our Synod followed his remains to the grave. There we stood, the white Missionaries of the Cross from far distant lands, mingling our tears with Christian Natives of Aneityum, and letting them fall over one who only a few years before was a blood-stained Cannibal, and whom now we mourned as a brother, a saint, an Apostle amongst his people. Ye ask an explanation? The Christ entered into his heart, and Namakei became a new Creature. " Behold, I make all things new."

We were in positive distress about returning to Aniwa without the Chief, and we greatly feared the consequences. To show our perfect sympathy with them, we prepared a special and considerable present for Litsi, his daughter, for his brother, and for other near friends—a sort of object lesson, that we had in every way been kind to old Namakei, as we now wished to be to them. When our boat approached the landing, nearly the whole population had assembled to meet us; and Litsi and the old Chief's brother were far out on the reef to salute us. Litsi's keen eye had missed old Namakei's form; and far as words could carry I heard her voice crying, " Missi, where is my father? "

I made as if I did not hear; the boat was drawing slowly near, and again she cried aloud, " Missi, where is my father? Is Namakei dead! "

I replied, " Yes. He died on Aneityum. He is now with Jesus in Glory."

Then arose a wild, wailing cry, led by Litsi and taken up by all around. It rose and fell like a chant or dirge, as one after another wailed out praise and sorrow over the name of Namakei. We moved slowly into the boat harbour; Litsi, the daughter, and Kalangi, his brother, shook hands, weeping sadly, and welcomed us back, assuring us that we had nothing to fear. Amidst many sobs and wailings, Litsi told us that they alldreaded he would never return, and explained to this effect:

" We knew that he was dying, but we durst not tell you. When you agreed to let him go, he went round and took farewell of all his friends, and told them he was going to sleep at last on Aneityum, and that at the Great Day he would rise to meet Jesus with the glorious company of the Aneityumese Christians. He urged us all to obey you and be true to Jesus. Truly, Missi, we will remember my dear father's parting word, and follow in his steps and help you in the work of the Lord ! "

The other Chief, Naswai, now accompanied us to the Mission House, and all the people followed, wailing loudly for Namakei. On the following Sabbath, I told the story of his conversion, life for Jesus, and death on Aneityum; and God overruled this event, contrary to our fears, for greatly increasing the interest of many in the Church and in the claims of Jesus upon themselves.

Naswai, the friend and companion of Namakei, was an inland Chief. He had, as his followers, by far the largest number of men in any village on Aniwa. He had certainly a dignified bearing, and his wife Katua was quite a lady in look and manner as compared with all around her. She was the first woman on the Island that adopted the clothes of civilization, and she showed considerable instinctive taste in the way she dressed herself in these. Her example was a kind of Gospel in its good influence on all the women; she was a real companion to her husband, and went with him almost everywhere.

Naswai, after he became a Christian, had a touch of scorn in his manner, and was particularly stern against every form of lying or deceit. I used sometimes to let jobs to Naswai, such as fencing or thatching, at a fixed price. He would come with a staff of men, say thirty or forty, see the work thoroughly done, and then divide the price generously in equal portions amongst the workers, seldom keeping anything either in food or wages for himself. On one occasion, the people of a distant village were working for me. Naswai assisted and directed them. On paying them, one of the company said, " Missi, you have not paid Naswai. He worked as hard as any of us."

Naswai turned upon him with the dignity of a prince, and

said, " I did not work for pay ! Would you make Missi pay more than he promised ? Your conduct is bad. I will be no party to your bad ways."

And with an indignant wave of his hand, he stalked away in great disdain.

Naswai was younger and more intelligent than Namakei, and in everything except in translating the Scriptures he was much more of a fellow-helper in the work of the Lord. For many years it was Naswai's special delight to carry my pulpit Bible from the Mission House to the Church every Sabbath morning, and to see that everything was in perfect order before the Service began. He was also the Teacher in his own village School, as well as an Elder in the Church. His addresses were wonderfully happy in graphic illustrations, and his prayers were fervent and uplifting. Yet his people were the worst to manage on all the Island, and the very last to embrace the Gospel.

He died when we were in the Colonies on furlough in 1875; and his wife Katua very shortly pre-deceased him. His last counsels to his people made a great impression on them. They told us how he pleaded with them to love and serve the Lord Jesus, and how he assured them with his dying breath that he had been "a new creature" since he gave his heart to Christ, and that he was perfectly happy in going to be with his Saviour.

I must here recall one memorable example of Naswai's power and skill as a preacher. On one occasion the *Day-spring* brought a large deputation from Fotuna to see for themselves the change which the Gospel had produced on Aniwa. On Sabbath, after the Missionaries had conducted the usual Public Worship, some of the leading Aniwans addressed the Fotunese; and amongst others, Naswai spoke to the following effect: "Men of Fotuna, you come to see what the Gospel has done for Aniwa. It is Jehovah the living God that has made all this change. As Heathens, we quarrelled, killed, and ate each other. We had no peace and no joy in heart or house, in villages or in lands; but we now live as brethren and have happiness in all these things. When you go back to Fotuna, they will ask you, 'What is Christianity?' And you will have to reply, 'It is that which has changed the people of Aniwa.' But they will still say, 'What is it?' And you will answer, 'It is that which has given them clothing and blankets, knives and axes, fish-hooks and many other useful things; it is that which has led them to give up fighting, and to live together as friends.' But they will ask you, 'What is it like?' And you will have to tell them, alas, that you cannot explain it, that you have only seen its workings, not itself, and that no one can tell what Christianity is but the man that loves Jesus, the Invisible Master, and walks with Him and tries to please Him. Now, you people of Fotuna, you think that if you don't dance and sing and pray to your gods, you will have no crops. We once did so too, sacrificing and doing much abomination to our gods for weeks before our planting season every year. But we saw our Missi only praying to the Invisible Jehovah, and planting his yams, and they grew fairer than ours. You are weak every year before your hard work begins in the fields, with your wild and bad conduct to please your gods. But we are strong for our work, for we pray to Jehovah, and He gives quiet rest instead of wild dancing, and makes us happy in our toils. Since we followed Missi's example, Jehovah has given us large and beautiful crops, and we now know that He gives us all our blessings."

Turning to me, he exclaimed, " Missi, have you the large yam we presented to you? Would you not think it well to send it back with these men of Fotuna, to let their people see the yams which Jehovah grows for us in answer to prayer? Jehovah is the only God who can grow yams like that ! "

Then, after a pause, he proceeded, " When you go back to Fotuna, and they ask you, 'What is Christianity?' you will be like an inland Chief of Erromanga, who once came down and saw a great feast on the shore. When he saw so much food and so many different kinds of it, he asked, 'What is this made of?' and was answered, 'Cocoa-nuts and yams.' 'And this?' 'Cocoa-nuts and bananas.' 'And this?' 'Cocoa-nuts and taro.' 'And this?' 'Cocoa-nuts and chestnuts,' etc., etc. The Chief was immensely astonished at the host of dishes that could be prepared from the cocoa-nuts. On returning, he carried home a great load of them to his people, that they might see and taste the excellent food of the shore-people. One day, all being assembled, he told them the wonders of that feast; and, having roasted the cocoa-nuts, he took out the kernels, all charred and spoiled, and distributed them amongst his people. They tasted the cocoa-nut, they began to chew it, and then spat it out, crying, ' Our own food is better than that!' The Chief was confused and only got laughed at for all his trouble. Was the fault in the cocoa-nuts? No; but they were spoiled in the cooking! So your attempts to explain Christianity will only spoil it. Tell them that a man must live as a Christian, before he can show others what Christianity is."

On their return to Fotuna they exhibited Jehovah's yam, given in answer to prayer and labour; they told what Christianity had done for Aniwa; but did not fail to qualify all their accounts with the story of the Erromangan Chief and the cocoa-nuts, with its very practical lesson.

The two Chiefs of next importance on Aniwa were Nerwa and Ruwawa. Nerwa was a keen debater; all his thoughts ran in the channels of logic. When I could speak a little of their language, I visited and preached at his village; but the moment he discovered that the teaching about Jehovah was opposed to their Heathen customs, he sternly forbade us. One day, during my address, he blossomed out into a full-fledged and pronounced Agnostic (with as much reason at his back as the European type!), and angrily interrupted me:

"It's all lies you come here to teach us, and you call it Worship! You say your Jehovah God dwells in Heaven. Who ever went up there to hear Him or see Him? You talk of Jehovah as if you had visited His Heaven. Why, you cannot climb even to the top of one of our cocoa-nut trees, though we can and that with ease! In going up to the roof of your own Mission House, you require the help of a ladder to carry you. And even if you could make your ladder higher than our highest cocoa-nut tree, on what would you lean its top? And when you get to its top, you can only climb down the other side and end where you began! The thing is impossible. You never saw that God; you never heard Him

speak ; don't come here with any of your white lies, or I'll
send my spear through you."

He drove us from his village, and furiously threatened
murder, if we ever dared to return.   But very shortly thereafter
the Lord sent us a little orphan girl from Nerwa's village.   She
was very clever, and could soon both read and write, and
told over all that we taught her.   Her visits home, or at least
amongst the villagers where her home had been, her changed
appearance and her childish talk, produced a very deep interest
in us and in our work.

An orphan boy next was sent from that village to be kept
and trained at the Mission House, and he too took back his
little stories of how kind and good to him were Missi the man
and Missi the woman.   By this time Chief and people alike
were taking a lively interest in all that was transpiring.   One
day the Chief's wife, a quiet and gentle woman, came to the
Worship and said, " Nerwa's opposition dies fast.   The story
of the Orphans did it !   He has allowed me to attend the
Church, and to get the Christian's book."

We gave her a book and a bit of clothing.   She went home
and told everything.   Woman after woman followed her from
that same village, and some of the men began to accompany
them.   The only thing in which they showed a real interest
was the children singing the little hymns which I had translated
into their own Aniwan tongue, and which my wife had taught
them to sing very sweetly and joyfully.   Nerwa at last got so
interested that he came himself, and sat within earshot, and
drank in the joyful sound.   In a short time he drew so near
that he could hear our preaching, and then began openly and
regularly to attend the Church.   His keen reasoning faculty
was constantly at work.   He weighed and compared everything
he heard, and soon out-distanced nearly all of them in his
grasp of the ideas of the Gospel.   He put on clothing, joined
our School, and professed himself a follower of the Lord Jesus.
He eagerly set himself, with all his power, to bring in a neighbouring Chief and his people, and constituted himself at once
an energetic and very pronounced helper to the Missionary.

On the death of Naswai, Nerwa at once took his place in
carrying my Bible to the Church, and seeing that all the people

were seated before the stopping of the bell. I have seen him clasping the Bible like a living thing to his breast, as if he would cry, " Oh to have this treasure in my own words of Aniwa ! "

When the Gospels of Matthew and Mark were at last printed in Aniwan, he studied them incessantly, and soon could read them freely. He became the Teacher in his own village School, and delighted in instructing others. He was assisted by Ruwawa, whom he himself had drawn into the circle of Gospel influence ; and at our next election these two friends were appointed Elders of the Church, and greatly sustained our hands in every good work on Aniwa.

After years of happy and useful service, the time came for Nerwa to die. He was then so greatly beloved that most of the inhabitants visited him during his long illness. He read a bit of the Gospels in his own Aniwan, and prayed with and for every visitor. He sang beautifully, and scarcely allowed any one to leave his bedside without having a verse of one or other of his favourite hymns, " Happy Land," and " Nearer, my God, to Thee."

On my last visit to Nerwa, his strength had gone very low, but he drew me near his face, and whispered, " Missi, my Missi, I am glad to see you. You see that group of young men ? They came to sympathize with me; but they have never once spoken the Name of Jesus, though they have spoken about everything else ! They could not have weakened me so, if they had spoken about Jesus ! Read me the story of Jesus ; pray for me to Jesus. No ! stop, let us call them, and let me speak with them before I go."

I called them all around him, and he strained his dying strength, and said, " After I am gone, let there be no bad talk, no Heathen ways. Sing Jehovah's songs, and pray to Jesus, and bury me as a Christian. Take good care of my Missi, and help him all you can. I am dying happy and going to be with Jesus, and it was Missi that showed me this way. And who among you will take my place in the village School and in the Church ? Who amongst you all will stand up for Jesus ? "

Many were shedding tears, but there was no reply ; after which the dying Chief proceeded, " Now let my last work on Earth be this—We will read a chapter of the Book, verse about, and then I will pray for you all, and the Missi will pray for me, and God will let me go while the song is still sounding in my heart!"

At the close of this most touching exercise, we gathered the Christians who were nearby close around, and sang very softly in Aniwan, "There is a Happy Land." As they sang, the old man grasped my hand, and tried hard to speak, but in vain. His head fell to one side—"the silver cord was loosed, and the golden bowl was broken."

Soon after his burial, the best and ablest man in the village, the husband now of the orphan girl already referred to, came and offered himself to take the Chief's place as Teacher in the village School; and in that post he was ably assisted by his wife, our "little maid," the first who carried the news of the Gospel life to her tribe, and inclined their ears to listen to the message of Jesus.

His great friend, Ruwawa the Chief, had waited by Nerwa like a brother till within a few days of the latter's death, when he also was smitten down apparently by the same disease. He was thought to be dying, and he resigned himself calmly into the hands of Christ. One Sabbath afternoon, sorely distressed for lack of air, he instructed his people to carry him from the village to a rising ground on one of his plantations. It was fallow; the fresh air would reach him; and all his friends could sit around him. They extemporized a rest—two posts stuck into the ground, slanting, sticks tied across them, then dried banana leaves spread on these and also as a cushion on the ground—and there sat Ruwawa, leaning back and breathing heavily. After the Church Services, I visited him, and found half the people of that side of the Island sitting round him, in silence, in the open air. Ruwawa beckoned me, and I sat down before him. Though suffering sorely, his eye and face had the look of ecstasy.

"Missi," he said, "I could not breathe in my village; so I got them to carry me here, where there is room for all. They are silent and they weep, because they think I am dying. If it were God's will, I would like to live and to help you in His work. I am in the hands of our dear Lord. If He takes me, it is good; if He spares me, it is good! Pray, and tell our Saviour all about it."

I explained to the people, that we would tell our Heavenly Father how anxious we all were to see Ruwawa given back to us strong and well to work for Jesus, and then leave all to His wise and holy disposal. I prayed, and the place became a very Bochim. When I left him, Ruwawa exclaimed, " Farewell, Missi; if I go first, I will welcome you to Glory; if I am spared, I will work with you for Jesus; so all is well!"

One of the young Christians followed me and said, " Missi, our hearts are very sore! If Ruwawa dies, we have no Chief to take his place in the Church, and it will be a heavy blow against Jehovah's Worship on Aniwa."

I answered, "Let us each tell our God and Father all that we feel and all that we fear; and leave Ruwawa and our work in His holy hands."

We did so, with earnest and unceasing cry. And when all hope had died out of every heart, the Lord began to answer us; the disease began to relax its hold, and the beloved Chief was restored to health. As soon as he was able, though still needing help, he found his way back to the Church, and we all offered special thanksgiving to God. He indicated a desire to say a few words; and although still very weak, spoke with great pathos thus :

" Dear Friends, God has given me back to you all. I rejoice thus to come here and praise the great Father, who made us all, and who knows how to make and keep us well. I want you all to work hard for Jesus, and to lose no opportunity of trying to do good and so to please Him. In my deep journey away near to the grave, it was the memory of what I had done in love to Jesus that made my heart sing. I am not afraid of pain,—my dear Lord Jesus suffered far more for me and teaches me how to bear it. I am not afraid of war or famine or death, or of the present or of the future; my dear Lord Jesus died for me, and in dying I shall live with Him in Glory. I fear and love my dear Lord Jesus, because He loved me and gave Himself for me."

Then he raised his right hand, and cried in a soft, full-hearted voice—" My own, my dear Lord Jesus! " and stood for a moment looking joyfully upward, as if gazing into his Saviour's face. When he sat down, there was a long hush, broken here and there by a smothered sob; and Ruwawa's words produced an impression that is remembered to this day.

In 1888, when I visited the Islands, Ruwawa was still devoting himself heart and soul to the work of the Lord on Aniwa. Assisted by Koris, a Teacher from Aneityum, and visited annually by our ever-dear and faithful friends, Mr. and Mrs. Watt, from Tanna, the good Ruwawa carried forward all the work of God on Aniwa, along with others, in our absence as in our presence. The meetings, the Communicants' Class, the Schools, and the Church Services are all regularly conducted and faithfully attended. " Bless the Lord, O my soul ! "

I am now reminded of the story of Waiwai, both because it was interesting for his own personality, and also as illustrating our difficulties about the delicate question of many wives. He was a man of great wisdom, and had in his early days displayed unwonted energy. His assistance in finding exact and idiomatic equivalents for me, while translating the Scriptures, was of the highest value.

He had been once at the head of a numerous people, but was now literally a Chief without a tribe. His son and heir was smitten down with sunstroke, while helping us to get the coral limestone, and shortly thereafter died. His only daughter was married to a young Chief. And at last, of all his seven wives only two remained alive.

He became a regular attender at Church, and when our first Communicants' Class was formed, Waiwai and his two wives were enrolled. At Communion time, he was dreadfully disappointed when informed that he could neither be baptized nor admitted to the Lord's Table till he had given up one of his wives, as God allowed no Christian to have more than one wife at a time. They were advised to attend regularly, and learn more and more of Christianity, till God opened up their way in regard to this matter; that it might be done from conscience, under a sense of duty to Christ, and if at all possible by peaceable and mutual agreement.

Waiwai professed to be willing, but found it terribly hard to give up either of his wives. They had houses far apart from each other, for they quarrelled badly, as is usual in such cases. But both were excellent workers, both were very attentive to the wants of Waiwai, and he managed to keep on affectionate terms with both. After all the other men on the island had, under the influence of Christianity, given up all their wives save one, Waiwai began to feel rather ashamed of being the conspicuous exception, or thought it prudent to pretend to be ashamed; and so he publicly scolded them both, ordering one or other to go and leave him, that he might be enabled to join the Church and be a Christian like the rest. But I learned privately that he did not wish either to go, and that he would shoot the one that dared to leave him. I remonstrated with him on his hypocrisy, warning him that God knew his heart. At last he said, that since neither of them would depart, he would leave them both and go to Tanna for a year, ordering one or other of them to get married during his absence. He did go, but on his return found both still awaiting him at their respective stations. He pretended to scold them very vigorously *in public*; but his duplicity was too open, and I again very solemnly rebuked him for double dealing, showing him that not even men were deceived by him, much less the all-seeing God. He frankly admitted his hypocrisy. He loved both; he did not want to part with either; and both were excellent workers!

In process of time the younger of the two women bore him a beautiful baby boy, about which he was immensely uplifted; and a short while thereafter the elder woman died. At her grave the inveterate talking instinct of these Islanders asserted itself, and Waiwai made a speech to the assembled people in the following strain: "O ye people of Aniwa, I was not willing to give up either of my wives for Jesus; but God has taken one from me and laid her there in the grave; and now I am called to be baptized, and to follow Jesus."

The two now regularly attended Church, and learned

diligently at the Communicants' Class. Both seemed to be very sincere, and Waiwai particularly showed a very gentle Christian spirit, and seemed to brood much upon the loss of family and people and tribe that had befallen him. His had been indeed a crushing discipline, and it was not yet complete. For, shortly before the Communion at which they were to be received into fellowship, his remaining wife became suddenly ill and died also. At her grave the old man wept very bitterly, and made another speech, but this time in tones of more intense reality than before, as if the iron had entered his very soul :

" Listen, all ye men of Aniwa, and take warning by Waiwai. I am now old, and ready to drop into the grave alone. My wives kept me back from Jesus, but now they are all taken, and I am left without one to care for me or this little child. I tried to deceive the Missi, but I could not deceive God. When I was left with only one wife, I said that I would now be baptized and live as a Christian. But God has taken her also. I pretended to serve the Lord, when I was only serving and pleasing myself. God has now broken my heart all to pieces. I must learn no longer to please myself, but to please my Lord. Oh, take warning by me, all ye men of Aniwa! Lies cannot cheat the great Jehovah God."

Poor broken-hearted Waiwai had sorrow upon sorrow to the full. We had agreed to baptize him and admit him to the Lord's Table. But a terrible form of cramp, sometimes met with on the Islands, overtook him, shrinking up both his legs, and curving his feet up behind him. He suffered great agony, and could neither walk nor sit without pain. In spite of all efforts to relieve him, this condition became chronic ; and he died at last from the effects thereof during our absence on furlough.

His married daughter took charge of him and of the little boy ; and so long as I was on Aniwa during his illness, I visited and instructed and ministered to him in every possible way. He prayed much, and asked God's blessing on all his meals ; but all that I could say failed to lead him into the sunshine of the Divine Love. And the poor soul often revealed the shadow by which his heart was clouded by such cries as these :

"I lied to Jehovah! It is He that punishes me! I lied to Jesus!"

Readers may perhaps think that this case of the two wives and our treatment of it was too hard upon Waiwai; and those will be the most ready to condemn us, who have never been on the spot, and who cannot see all the facts as they lie under the eyes of the Missionary. How could we ever have led Natives to see the difference betwixt admitting a man to the Church who had two wives, and not permitting a member of the Church to take two wives after his admission? Their moral sense is blunted enough, without our knocking their heads against a conundrum in ethics! In our Church membership we have to draw the line as sharply as God's law will allow betwixt what is Heathen and what is Christian, instead of minimizing the difference.

Again, we found that the Heathen practices were apparently more destructive to women than to men; so that in one Island, with a total population of three hundred and fifty, I found that there were twelve adult men over and above the number of women. As a rule, for every man that has two or more wives, the same number of men have no wives and can get none; and polygamy is therefore the prolific cause of hatreds and murders innumerable.

Besides all this, to look at things in a purely practical light, as the so-called "practical men" are our scornful censors in these affairs, it is really no hardship for one woman, or any number of women, to be given up when the man becomes a Christian and elects to have one wife only; for every one so discarded is at once eagerly contended for by the men who had no hope of ever being married, and her chances of comfort and happiness are infinitely improved. We had one Chief who gave up eleven wives on his being baptized. They were without a single exception happily settled in other homes. And he became an earnest and devoted Christian.

While they remain Heathen, and have many wives to manage, the condition of most of the women is worse than slavery. On remonstrating with a Chief, who was savagely beating one of his wives, he indignantly assured me, "We must beat them, or they would never obey us. When they quarrel, and become bad to manage, we have to kill one, and feast on her ! Then all the other wives of the whole tribe are quiet and obedient for a long time to come."

I knew one Chief, who had many wives, always jealous of each other and violently quarrelling amongst themselves. When he was off at war, along with his men, the favourite wife, a tall and powerful woman, armed herself with an axe, and murdered all the others. On his return he made peace with her, and, either in terror or for other motives, promised to forego and protect her against all attempts at revenge. One has to live amongst the Papuans, or the Malays, in order to understand how much Woman is indebted to Christ !

The old Chief's only brother was called Kalangi. Twice in Heathen days he tried to shoot me. On the second occasion, he heard me rebuking his daughter for letting a child destroy a beautiful Island plant in front of our house. He levelled his musket at me, but his daughter, whom we were training at the Mission House, ran in front of it, and cried, " O father, don't shoot Missi ! He loves me. He gives us food and clothing. He teaches us about Jehovah and Jesus ! "

Then she pled with me to retire into the house, saying, " He will not shoot you for fear of shooting me. I will soothe him down. Leave him to me, and flee for safety."

Thus she probably saved my life. Time after time he heard from this little daughter all that we taught her, and all she could remember of our preaching. By-and-bye he showed a strong personal interest in the things he heard about Jesus, and questioned deeply, and learned diligently. When he became a Christian, he constituted himself, along with Nelwang, my body-guard, and often marched near me, or within safe distance of me, armed with tomahawk and musket, when I journeyed from village to village in the pre-Christian days. Once, on approaching one of our most distant villages, Kalangi sprang to my side, and warned me of a man in the bush watching an opportunity to shoot me. I shouted to the fellow, " What are you going to shoot there ? This is the Lord's own Day ! "

He answered, " Only a bird."

I replied, " Never mind it to-day. You can shoot it to-morrow. We are going to your Village. Come on before us, and show us the way ! "

Seeing how I was protected, he lowered his musket, and marched on before us. Kalangi addressed the people, after I had spoken and prayed. In course of time they became warm friends of the Worship ; and that very man and his wife, who once sought my life, sat with me at the Lord's Table on Aniwa. And the little girl, above referred to, is now the wife of one of the Elders there, and the mother of three Christian children,—both she and her husband being devoted workers in the Church of God.

Litsi, the only daughter of Namakei, had, both in her own career and in her connection with poor, dear Mungaw, an almost unparalleled experience. She was entrusted to us when very young, and became a bright, clever, and attractive Christian girl. Many sought her hand, but she disdainfully replied, " I am Queen of my own Island, and when I like I will ask a husband in marriage, as your great Queen Victoria did ! "

Her first husband, however won, was undoubtedly the tallest and most handsome man on Aniwa ; but he was a giddy fool, and, on his early death, she again returned to live with us at the Mission House. Her second marriage had everything to commend it, but it resulted in indescribable disaster. Mungaw, heir to a Chief, had been trained with us, and gave every evidence of decided Christianity. They were married in the Church, and lived in the greatest happiness. He was able and eloquent, and was first chosen as a deacon, then as an Elder of the Church, and finally as High Chief of one half of the Island. He showed the finest Christian Spirit under many trying circumstances. Once, when working at the lime for the building of our Church, two bad men, armed with muskets, sought his life for blowing the conch to assemble the workers. Hearing of the quarrel, I rushed to the scene, and heard him saying, " Don't call me coward, or think me afraid to die. If I died now, I would go to be with Jesus. But I am no longer a Heathen ; I am a Christian, and wish to treat you as a Christian should."

Two loaded muskets were levelled at him. I seized one in each of my hands, and held their muzzles aloft in air, so that, if discharged, the balls might pass over his head and mine ; and thus I stood for some minutes pleading with them.

Others soon coming to the rescue, the men were disarmed ; and, after much talk, they professed themselves ashamed, and promised better conduct for the future. Next day they sent a large present as a peace-offering to me, but I refused to receive it till they should first of all make peace with the young Chief. They sent a larger present to him, praying him to receive it, and to forgive them. Mungaw brought a still larger present in exchange, laid it down at their feet in the Public Ground, shook hands with them graciously, and forgave them in presence of all the people. His constant saying was, " I am a Christian, and I must do the conduct of a Christian."

In one of my furloughs to Australia I took the young Chief with me, in the hope of interesting the Sabbath Schools and Congregations by his eloquent addresses and noble personality. The late Dr. Cameron, of Melbourne, having heard him, as translated by me, publicly declared that Mungaw's appearance and speech in his Church did more to show him the grand results of the Gospel amongst the Heathen, than all the Missionary addresses he ever listened to or read.

Our lodging was in St. Kilda. My dear wife was suddenly seized with a dangerous illness on a visit to Taradale, and I was telegraphed for Finding that I must remain with her, I got Mungaw booked for Melbourne, on the road for St. Kilda, in charge of a railway guard. Some white wretches, in the guise of gentlemen, offered to see him to the St. Kilda Station, assuring the guard that they were friends of mine, and interested in our Mission. They took him, instead, to some den of infamy in Melbourne. On refusing to drink with them, he said, they threw him down on a sofa, and poured drink or drugs into him till he was nearly dead. Having taken all his money (he had only two or three pounds, made up of little presents from various friends), they thrust him out to the street, with only one penny in his pocket.

On becoming conscious, he applied to a policeman, who either did not understand or would not interfere. Hearing an

engine whistle, he followed the sound, and found his way to
Spencer Street Station, where he proffered his penny for a
ticket, all in vain. At last a sailor took pity on him, got him
some food, and led him to the St. Kilda Station. There he
stood for a whole day, offering his penny for a ticket by every
train, only to meet with refusal after refusal, till he broke
down, and cried aloud in such English as desperation gave
him :

" If me savvy road, me go. Me no savvy road, and stop
here me die. My Missi Paton live at Kilda. Me want go
Kilda. Me no more money. Bad fellow took all ! Send me
Kilda."

Some gentle Samaritan gave him a ticket, and he reached
our house at St. Kilda at last. There for above three weeks
the poor creature lay in a sort of stupid doze. Food he could
scarcely be induced to taste, and he only rose now and again
for a drink of water. When my wife was able to be removed
thither also, we found dear Mungaw dreadfully changed in
appearance and in conduct. Twice thereafter I took him
with me on Mission work ; but, on medical advice, preparations were made for his immediate return to the Islands. I
entrusted him to the kind care of Captain Logan, who undertook to see him safely on board the *Dayspring*, then lying at
Auckland. Mungaw was delighted, and we hoped everything
from his return to his own land and people. After some little
trouble, he was landed safely home on Aniwa. But his
malady developed dangerous and violent symptoms, characterized by long periods of quiet and sleep, and then sudden
paroxysms, in which he destroyed property, burned houses,
and was a terror to all.

On our return he was greatly delighted ; but he complained
bitterly that the white men "had spoiled his head," and that
when it " burned hot " he did all these bad things, for which
he was extremely sorry. He deliberately attempted my life,
and most cruelly abused his dear and gentle wife ; and then,
when the frenzy was over, he wept and lamented over it.
Many a time he marched round and round our House with
loaded musket and spear and tomahawk, while we had to keep
doors and windows locked and barricaded : then the paroxysm

passed off, and he slept, long and deep, like a child. When he came to himself, he wept and said, "The white men spoiled my head! I know not what I do. My head burns hot, and I am driven."

One day, in the Church, he leapt up during Worship with a loud yelling war-cry, rushed off through the Imrai to his own house, set fire to it, and danced around till everything he possessed was burned to ashes. Nasi, a bad Tannese Chief living on Aniwa, had a quarrel with Mungaw about a cask found at the shore, and threatened to shoot him. Others encouraged him to do so, as Mungaw was growing every day more and more destructive and violent. When any person became outrageous or insane on Aniwa, as they had neither asylum nor prison, they first of all held him fast and discharged a musket close to his ear; and then, if the shock did not bring him back to his senses, they tied him up for two days or so; and finally, if that did not restore him, they shot him dead. Thus the plan of Nasi was favoured by their own customs. One night, after Family Worship—for amidst all his madness, when clear moments came, he poured out his soul in faith and love to the Lord—he said, "Litsi, I am melting! My head burns. Let us go out and get cooled in the open air."

She warned him not to go, as she heard voices whispering under the verandah. He answered a little wildly, "I am not afraid to die. Life is a curse and burden. The white men spoiled my head. If there is a hope of dying, let me go quickly and die!"

As he crossed the door, a ball crashed through him, and he fell dead. We got the mother and her children away to the Mission House; and next morning they buried the remains of poor Mungaw under the floor of his own hut, and enclosed the whole place with a fence. It was a sorrowful close to so noble a career. I shed many a tear that I ever took him to Australia. What will God have to say to those white fiends who poisoned and maddened poor dear Mungaw?

After a while the good Queen Litsi was happily married again. She became possessed with a great desire to go as a Missionary to the people and tribe of Nasi, the very man who had murdered her husband. She used to say, " Is there no Missionary to go and teach Nasi's people ? I weep and pray for them, that they too may come to know and love Jesus."

I answered, " Litsi, if I had only wept and prayed for you, but stayed at home in Scotland, would that have brought you to know and love Jesus as you do ? "

" Certainly not," she replied.

" Now then," I proceeded, " would it not please Jesus, and be a grand and holy revenge, if you, the Christians of Aniwa, could carry the Gospel to the very people whose Chief murdered Mungaw ? "

The idea took possession of her soul. She was never wearied talking and praying over it. When at length a Missionary was got for Nasi's people, Litsi and her new husband offered themselves at the head of a band of six or eight Aniwan Christians, and were engaged there to open up the way and assist as Teachers and Helpers the Missionary and his wife. There she and they have laboured ever since. They are " strong " for the Worship. Her son is being trained up by his cousin, an Elder of the Church, to be " the good Chief of Aniwa " ; so she calls him in her prayers, as she cries on God to bless and watch over him, while she is serving the Lord in at once serving the Mission family and ministering to the Natives in that foreign field.

Many years have now passed ; and when lately I visited that part of Tanna, Litsi ran to me, clasped my hand, kissed it with many sobs, and cried, " O my father ! God has blessed me to see you again. Is my mother, your dear wife, well ? And your children, my brothers and sisters ? My love to them all ! Oh, my heart clings to you ! "

We had sweet conversation, and then she said more calmly, " My days here are hard. I might be happy and independent as Queen of my own Aniwa. But the Heathen here are beginning to listen. The Missi sees them coming nearer to Jesus. And oh, what a reward when we shall hear them sing and pray to our dear Saviour ! The hope of that makes me strong for anything."

My heart often says within itself—When, *when* will men's eyes at home be opened ? When will the rich and the learned and the noble and even the princes of the Earth renounce their shallow frivolities, and go to live amongst the poor, the ignorant, the outcast, and the lost, and write their eternal fame on the souls by them blessed and brought to the Saviour? Those who have tasted this highest joy, " the joy of the Lord," will never again ask—*Is Life worth living?* Life, any life, would be well spent, under any conceivable conditions, in bringing one human soul to know and love and serve God and His Son, and thereby securing for yourself at least one temple where your name and memory would be held for ever and for ever in affectionate praise,—a regenerated Heart in Heaven. That fame will prove *immortal*, when all the poems and monuments and pyramids of Earth have gone into dust.

Nasi, the Tanna-man, was a bad and dangerous character, though some readers may condone his putting an end to Mungaw in the terrible circumstances of our case. During a great illness that befell him, I ministered to him regularly, but no kindness seemed to move him. When about to leave Aniwa, I went specially to visit him. On parting I said, " Nasi, are you happy? Have you ever been happy?"

He answered gloomily, " No! Never."

I said, " Would you like this dear little boy of yours to grow up like yourself, and lead the life you have lived?"

"No!" he replied warmly; "I certainly would not."

"Then," I continued, "you must become a Christian, and give up all your Heathen conduct, or he will just grow up to quarrel and fight and murder as you have done; and, O Nasi, he will curse you through all Eternity for leading him to such a life and to such a doom!"

He was very much impressed, but made no response. After we had sailed, a band of our young Native Christians held a consultation over the case of Nasi. They said, " We know the burden and terror that Nasi has been to our dear Missi. We know that he has murdered several persons with his own hands, and has taken part in the murder of others. Let us unite in daily prayer that the Lord would open his heart and change his conduct, and teach him to love and follow what is good, and let us set ourselves to win Nasi for Christ, just as Missi tried to win us."

So they began to show him every possible kindness, and one after another helped him in his daily tasks, embracing every opportunity of pleading with him to yield to Jesus and take the new path of life. At first he repelled them, and sullenly held aloof. But their prayers never ceased, and their patient affections continued to grow. At last, after long waiting, Nasi broke down, and cried to one of the Teachers, " I can oppose your Jesus no longer. If He can make you treat me like that, I yield myself to Him and to you. I want Him to change me too. I want a heart like that of Jesus."

He rubbed off the ugly thickly-daubed paint from his face ; he cut off his long heathen hair ; he went to the sea and bathed, washing himself clean ; and then he came to the Christians and dressed himself in a shirt and a kilt. The next step was to get a book,—his was the translation of the Gospel according to St. John. He eagerly listened to every one that would read bits of it aloud to him, and his soul seemed to drink in the new ideas at every pore. He attended the Church and the School most regularly, and could in a very short time read the Gospel for himself. The Elders of the Church took special pains in instructing him, and after due preparation he was admitted to the Lord's Table—my brother Missionary from Tanna baptizing and receiving him. Imagine my joy on learning all this regarding one who had sullenly resisted my appeals for many years, and how my soul praised the Lord who is " Mighty to save ! "

On my recent visit to Aniwa, in 1886, God's almighty compassion was further revealed to me, when I found that Nasi the murderer was now a Scripture Reader, ánd able to comment in a wonderful and interesting manner on what he read to the people When I arrived on a visit to the Island, after my last tour in Great Britain in the interests of our Mission, all the inhabitants of Aniwa seemed to be assembled at the boat-landing to welcome me, except Nasi. He was away fishing at a distance, and had been sent for, but had not yet arrived. On the way to the Mission House, he came rushing to meet me. He grasped my hand, and kissed it, and burst into tears. I said, " Nasi, do I now at last meet you as a Christian ? "

He warmly answered, "Yes, Missi ; I now worship and serve the only Lord and Saviour Jesus Christ.   Bless God, I am a Christian at last ! "

My soul went out with the silent cry, " Oh, that the men at home who discuss and doubt about conversion, and the new heart, and the power of Jesus to change and save, could but look on Nasi, and spell out the simple lesson,—He that created us at first by His power can create us anew by His love ! "

My first Sabbath on Aniwa, after the late tour in Great Britain and the Colonies, gave me a blessed surprise.   Before daybreak I lay awake thinking of all my experiences on that Island, and wondering whether the Church had fallen off in my four years' absence, when suddenly the voice of song broke on my ears !   It was scarcely full dawn, yet I jumped up and called to a man that was passing, " Have I slept in ? Is it already Church-time ?   Or why are the people met so early ? "

He was one of their leaders, and gravely replied, " Missi, since you left, we have found it very hard to live near to God ! So the Chief and the Teachers and a few others meet when daylight comes on every Sabbath morning, and spend the first hour of every Lord's Day in prayer and praise.   They are met to pray for you now, that God may help you in your preaching, and that all hearts may bear fruit to the glory of Jesus this day."

I returned to my room, and felt wonderfully " prepared " myself.   It would be an easy and a blessed thing to lead such a Congregation into the presence of the Lord !   They were there already.

On that day every person on Aniwa seemed to be at Church, except the bedridden and the sick.   At the close of the Services, the Elders informed me that they had kept up all the Meetings during my absence, and had also conducted the Communicants' Class, and they presented to me a considerable number of Candidates for membership.   After careful examination, I set apart nine boys and girls, about twelve or thirteen years of age, and advised them to wait for at least another year or so, that their knowledge and habits might be matured.

They had answered every question, indeed, and were eager to be baptized and admitted ; but I feared for their youth, lest they should fall away and bring disgrace on the Church. One of them, with very earnest eyes, looked at me and said, " We have been taught that whosoever believeth is to be baptized. We do most heartily believe in Jesus, and try to please Jesus."

I answered, " Hold on for another year, and then our way will be clear."

But he persisted, "Some of us may not be living then ; and you may not be here. We long to be baptized by you, our own Missi, and to take our place among the servants of Jesus."

After much conversation I agreed to baptize them, and they agreed to refrain from going to the Lord's Table for a year ; that all the Church might by that time have knowledge and proof of their consistent Christian life, though so young in years. This discipline, I thought, would be good for them ; and the Lord might use it as a precedent for guidance in future days.

Of other ten adults at this time admitted, one was specially noteworthy. She was about twenty-five, and the Elders objected because her marriage had not been according to the Christian usage on Aniwa. She left us weeping deeply. I was writing late at night in the cool evening air, as was my wont in that oppressive tropical clime, and a knock was heard at my door. I called out, *"Akai era ?"* (= Who is there ?)

A voice softly answered, " Missi, it is Lamu. Oh, do speak with me ! "

This was the rejected candidate, and I at once opened the door.

"Oh, Missi," she began, "I cannot sleep, I cannot eat ; my soul is in pain. Am I to be shut out from Jesus ? Some of those at the Lord's Table committed murder. They repented, and have been saved. My heart is very bad ; yet I never did any of those crimes of Heathenism ; and I know that it is my joy to try and please my Saviour Jesus. How is it that I only am to be shut out from Jesus ? "

I tried all I could to guide and console her, and she listened to all very eagerly. Then she looked up at me and said,

" Missi, you and the Elders may think it right to keep me back from showing my love to Jesus at the Lord's Table ; but I know here in my heart that Jesus has received me ; and if I were dying now, I know that Jesus would take me to Glory and present me to the Father."

Her look and manner thrilled me. I promised to see the Elders and submit her appeal. But Lamu appeared and pled her own cause before them with convincing effect. She was baptized and admitted along with other nine. And that Communion Day will be long remembered by many souls on Aniwa.

It has often struck me, when relating these events, to press this question on the many young people, the highly privileged white brothers and sisters of Lamu, Did you ever lose one hour of sleep or a single meal in thinking of your Soul, your God, the claims of Jesus, and your Eternal Destiny ?

And when I saw the diligence and fidelity of these poor Aniwan Elders, teaching and ministering during all those years, my soul has cried aloud to God, Oh, what could not the Church accomplish if the educated and gifted Elders and others in Christian lands would set themselves thus to work for Jesus, to teach the ignorant, to protect the tempted, and to rescue the fallen !

CHAPTER IX.

SECOND VISIT TO BRITAIN.

A.D. 1884—1885.   ÆT 60—61.

IN December 1883 I brought a pressing and vital matter before the General Assembly of the Presbyterian Church of Victoria. It pertained to the New Hebrides Mission, to the vastly increased requirements of the Missionaries and their families there, and to the fact that the *Dayspring* was no longer capable of meeting the necessities of the case,—thereby incurring loss of time, loss of property, and risk and even loss of precious lives. The Missionaries on the spot had long felt this, and had loudly and earnestly pled for a new and larger Vessel, or a Vessel with Steam Auxiliary power, or some arrangement whereby the work of God on these Islands might be overtaken, without unnecessary exposure of life, and without the dreaded perils that accrue to a small sailing Vessel such as the *Dayspring*, alike from deadly calms and from treacherous gales.

The Victorian General Assembly, heartily at one with the
Missionaries, commissioned me to go home to Britain in 1884,
making me at the same time their Missionary delegate to the
Pan-Presbyterian Council at Belfast, and also their representative to the General Assemblies of the several Presbyterian
Churches in Great Britain and Ireland. And they empowered
and authorized me to lay our proposals about a new Steam-
Auxiliary Mission Ship before all these Churches, and to ask
and receive from God's people whatever contributions they
felt disposed to give towards the sum of £6,000, without
which this great undertaking could not be faced.

At Suez, I forwarded a copy of my commissions from
Victoria, from South Australia, and from the Islands' Synod, to
the Clerks of the various Church Courts, accompanied by a
note specifying my home-address, and expressing the hope
that an opportunity would be given me of pleading this special
cause on behalf of our New Hebrides Mission.   On reaching
my brother's residence in Glasgow, I found to my deep amazement that replies awaited me from all the Churches, except
our own,—*i.e.*, the Free Church, which I call our own, as
having taken over our South Seas Mission when it entered
into Union with the Reformed Presbyterian Church, to which
I originally belonged, though now I was supported by the
Church of Victoria.   This fact pained me.   It is noted here.
An explanation will come in due course.

A few days after my arrival, I was called upon to appear
before the Supreme Court of the English Presbyterian Church,
then assembled at Liverpool.   While a hymn was being sung,
I took my seat in the pulpit under great depression.   But light
broke around, when my dear friend and fellow-student, Dr.
Oswald Dykes, came up from the body of the Church, shook
me warmly by the hand, whispered a few encouraging words
in my ear, and returned to his seat.   God helped me to tell
my story, and the audience were manifestly interested.   Again,
however, another indication of a rift somewhere, unknown
to me, was consciously or otherwise given, when both the
Moderator and Professor Graham, in addressing the Deputies
and referring to their Churches and speeches individually,
conspicuously omitted all reference to the New Hebrides and

the special proposal which I had brought before them.   Again
I made a note, and my wonder deepened.

Next, by kind invitation I visited and addressed the United
Presbyterian Synod of Scotland, assembled in Edinburgh.
My reception there was not only cordial,—it was enthusiastic.
Though as a Church they had no denominational interest
in our Mission, the Moderator, amidst the cheers of all the
Ministers and Elders, recommended that I should have free
access to every Congregation and Sabbath School which I
found it possible to visit, and hoped that their generous-hearted
people would contribute freely to so needful and noble a cause.
My soul rose in praise ; and I may here say, in passing, that
every Minister of that Church whom I wrote to or visited
treated me in the same spirit throughout all my tour.

Having been invited by Mr. Dickson, an Elder of the Free
Church, to address a mid-day meeting of children in the Free
Assembly Hall,—and the Saturday before the Meeting of
Assembly having now arrived without bringing any reply to my
note to be received and heard,—I determined to call at the
Free Church Offices, and make inquiries at least.   They
treated me with all possible kindness and sympathy, but
explained to me the strange perplexity that had been introduced into my case.   A letter had been forwarded to them
from the *Dayspring* Board at Sydney, intimating that the
Victorian Church had no right to commission me to raise a
new Steam-Auxiliary Ship without consulting them, and that
they placed their direct veto upon the Free Church authorities
in any way sanctioning that proposal or authorizing me to raise
the money.   Here, then, was the rift ; and many things that
had recently perplexed me were explained thereby.

Here is not the place to discuss our differences, nor shall
I take advantage of my book to criticise those who have no
similar opportunity of answering me.   But the facts I must
relate, and exactly as they occurred, to show how the Lord
overruled everything for the accomplishment of His own
blessed purposes.   Doubtless the friends at Sydney had their
own way of looking at and explaining everything ; and the
best of friends must sometimes differ, even in the Mission
field, and yet learn to respect each other, and work so far as

they can agree towards common ends in the service of the Divine Lord and Master.

My Commission was publicly intimated. Communication had also been made to the Church of New South Wales as to appointing me their second representative to the Pan-Presbyterian Council, in connection with my mission to Britain, but they replied that one would serve their purpose. And South Australia and Tasmania were both written to regarding the object of my visit to the home countries. But no note of dissent, no hint of disapproval from any quarter, was intimated to the Victorian Church, or in any sense, directly or indirectly, reached me till I heard of that so-called *veto* in the Free Church Offices at Edinburgh.

This intimation, just as I was entering the Assembly Hall to address a great congregation of children and their friends, staggered me beyond all description. The Free Church alone, in Scotland, now supported our New Hebrides Mission. From it I expected the principal contributions for the sorely-needed new Mission Ship. And now, by the action of the *Dayspring* Board at Sydney, the Free Church was debarred from acknowledging my three-fold Commission or in any direct way sanctioning my appeals. No sorer wound had ever been inflicted on me; and when I sat down on the platform beside Mr. Dickson, my head swam for several minutes, and faintishness almost overpowered me. But, by the time my name was called, the Lord my Helper enabled me to pull myself together; I committed this cause also with unfailing assurance to Him; and by all appearances I was able greatly to interest and impress the Children. At the close, my dear and noble friend, Professor Cairns, warmly welcomed and cheered me, and that counted for much amid the depressions of the day.

But when all were gone and we two were left, Mr. Dickson under deep emotion said, "Mr. Paton, that veto has spoiled your mission home. The Free Church cannot take you by the hand in face of the *veto* from Sydney!"

Having letters from Andrew Scott, Esquire, Carrugal, my very dear friend and helper in Australia, to Dr. J. Hood Wilson, Barclay Free Church, Edinburgh, I resolved to deliver them that evening; and I prayed the Lord to open up all my path, as I was thus thrown solely on Him for guidance and bereft of the aid of man. Dr. Wilson and his lady, neither of whom I had ever seen before, received me as kindly as if I had been an old friend. He read my letters of introduction, conversed with me as to plans and wishes (chiefly through Mrs. Wilson, for he was suffering from sore throat), and then he said with great warmth and kindliness :

"God has surely sent you here to-night! I feel myself unable to preach to-morrow. Occupy my pulpit in the forenoon and address my Sabbath School, and you shall have a collection for your Ship."

Thereafter, I was with equal kindness received by Mr. Balfour, having a letter of introduction from his brother, and he offered me his pulpit for the evening of the day. I lay down blessing and praising Him, the Angel of whose Presence was thus going before me and opening up my way. That Lord's Day I had great blessing and joy; there was an extraordinary response financially to my appeals; and my proposal was thus fairly launched in the Metropolis of our Scottish Church life. I remembered an old saying, Difficulties are made only to be vanquished. And I thought in my deeper soul,—Thus our God throws us back upon Himself; and if these £6,000 ever come to me, to the Lord God alone, and not to man, shall be all the glory!

On the Monday following, after a long conversation and every possible explanation, Colonel Young, of the Free Church Foreign Missions Committee, said, "We must have you to address the Assembly on the evening devoted to Missions."

But the rest insisted that, to keep straight with the Board at Sydney, no formal approval should be given of my proposals This I agreed to, on condition that the Committee did not publish the Sydney veto, but allowed it simply to lie on their table or in their minutes. Thus I had the pleasure and honour of addressing that great Assembly; and though no notice was taken of my proposals in any "finding" of the Court, yet many were thereby interested deeply in our work, and requests now poured in upon me from every quarter to occupy pulpits and receive collections for the new Ship.

Still I had occasional trouble and misunderstanding through

that veto during all my tour in Britain and Ireland. It pre-vented me particularly from getting access to the Free Church Foreign Missions Committee, or addressing them on one single occasion, though I pled hard to be allowed to do so and to explain my position. This I felt all the more keenly, as I laboured freely and for weeks, along with their noble Missionaries then at home on furlough, in addressing meetings in Glasgow, Aberdeen, Greenock, etc., chiefly for Sabbath Scholars, but from which I received no help directly in the matter of the Mission Ship. Doubtless they were trying to do their duty, and refusing to take either side; and that they thought they had succeeded appears from the following fact. When rumour reached Australia that my mission home had been under God a great success, a letter came to them from their Committee's agent in Sydney as to the "application" of the sum that had been raised by me, to which they replied :

" The Foreign Missions Committee of the Free Church of Scotland, in accordance with the action of the *Dayspring* Committee at Sydney, have from the first abstained from assisting Mr. Paton in this movement, believing that the question is one entirely for the Australian Churches."

At the meeting in the Assembly Hall of the Church of Scotland, which, along with others, I was cordially invited to address, the good and noble Lord Polwarth occupied the chair. That was the beginning of a friendship in Christ which will last and deepen as long as we live. From that night he took the warmest personal interest, not only by generously contribut-ing to my fund, but by organizing meetings at his own Mansion House, and introducing me to a wide circle of influential friends. Every member of his family took "shares" in the new Steam-Auxiliary Mission Ship, and by Collecting Cards and otherwise most liberally aided me ; and that not at the start only, but to the day of my departure—one of the last things put into my hand on leaving Britain being a most hand-some donation from Lord and Lady Polwarth to our Mission Fund—" a thank-offering to the Lord Jesus for precious health restored in answer to the prayer of faith."

Nor, whilst the pen leads on my mind to recall these Border memories, must I fail to record how John Scott Dudgeon, Esq.,

Longnewton, a greatly esteemed Elder of the Church, went from town to town in all that region, and from Minister to Minister, arranging for me a series of happy meetings. I shared also the hospitality of his beautiful Home, and added himself and his much-beloved wife to the precious roll of those who are dear for the Gospel's sake and for their own.

Her Majesty's Commissioner to the General Assembly for the year was that distinguished Christian as well as nobleman, the Earl of Aberdeen. He graciously invited me to meet the Countess and himself at ancient Holyrood. After dinner he withdrew himself for a lengthened time from the general company, and entered into a close and interested conversation about our Mission, and especially about the threatened annexation of the New Hebrides by the French.

There also I had the memorable pleasure of meeting, and for a long while conversing with, that truly noble and large-hearted lady, his mother, the much-beloved Dowager-Countess, well known for her life-long devotion to so many schemes of Christian philanthropy. At her own home, Alva House, she afterwards arranged meetings for me, as well as in Halls and Churches in the immediately surrounding district; and not only contributed most generously of her own means, but interested many besides and incited them to vie with each other in helping on our cause. I was her guest during those days, and never either in high or in humble station felt the ties of true fellowship in Christ more closely drawn. Despite frost and snow, she accompanied me to almost every meeting; and her letters of interest in the work, of sympathy, and of helpfulness, from time to time received, were amongst the sustaining forces of my spiritual life. When one sees noble rank thus consecrating itself in humble and faithful service to Jesus, there dawns upon the mind a glimpse of what the prophet means, and of what the world will be like, when it can be said regarding the Church of God on Earth,—" Kings *have become* thy nursing fathers, and their Queens thy nursing mothers."

My steps were next directed towards Ireland, immediately after the Church meetings at Edinburgh ; first to 'Derry, where the Presbyterian Assembly was met in annual conclave, and thereafter to Belfast, where the Pan-Presbyterian Council was shortly to sit. The eloquent fervour of the Brethren at 'Derry was like a refreshing breeze to my spirit ; I never met Ministers anywhere, in all my travels, who seemed more whole-hearted in their devotion to the work which the Lord had given them to do.

But the excitement over the Organ and Hymn question was too intense for me ; the debate threatened to degenerate into a wrangle ; and the marvellous way in which a stick or an umbrella was flourished occasionally by an impulsive speaker, to give action to his eloquence, was not a little suggestive of blows and broken heads. All ended quietly, however, and the decision, though not final, gave hope of an early settlement, which will secure alike the liberty and the peace of the Church. A trip to the South Seas, and a revelation of how God used the Harmonium and the Hymn, as wings on which the Gospel was borne into the homes and hearts of Cannibals, would have opened the eyes of many dear fathers and brethren, as it had opened mine ! No one was once more opposed, especially to instrumental music in the worship of God, than I had been ; but the Lord who made us, and who knows the nature He has given us, had long ago taught me otherwise.

I addressed the Assembly at 'Derry and also the Council at Belfast. The memory of seeing all those great and learned and famous men—for many of the leaders were eminently such —so deeply interested in the work of God, and particularly in the Evangelizing of the Heathen World and bringing thereto the knowledge of Jesus, was to me, so long exiled from all such influences, one of the great inspirations of my life. I listened with humble thankfulness, and blessed the Lord who had brought me to sit at their feet.

On the rising of the Council, I entered upon a tour of six weeks among the Presbyterian Congregations and Sabbath Schools of Ireland. It had often been said to me, after my addresses in the Assemblies and elsewhere, " How do you ever expect to raise £6,000 ? It can never be accomplished, unless you call upon the rich individually, and get their larger subscriptions. Our ordinary Church people have more than enough to do with themselves. Trade is dull," etc.

I explained to them, and also announced publicly, that in all similar efforts I had never called on or solicited any one privately, and that I would not do so now. I would make my appeal, but leave everything else to be settled betwixt the individual conscience and the Saviour—I gladly receiving whatsoever was given or sent, acknowledging it by letter, and duly forwarding it to my own Church in Victoria. Again and again did generous souls offer to go with me, introduce me, and give me opportunity of soliciting subscriptions; but I steadily refused—going, indeed, wherever an occasion was afforded me of telling my story and setting forth the claims of the Mission, but asking no one personally for anything, having fixed my soul in the conviction that one part of the work was laid upon me, but that the other lay betwixt the Master and His servants exclusively.

"On what then do you really rely, looking at it from a business point of view?" they would somewhat appealingly ask me.

I answered, "I will tell my story; I will set forth the claims of the Lord Jesus on the people; I will expect the surplus collection, or a retiring collection, on Sabbaths; I will ask the whole collection, less expenses, at week-night meetings; I will issue Collecting Cards for Sabbath Scholars; I will make known my Home-Address, to which everything may be forwarded, either from Congregations or from private donors; and I will go on, to my utmost strength, in the faith that the Lord will send me the £6,000 required. If He does not so send it, then I shall expect He will send me grace to be reconciled to the disappointment, and I shall go back to my work without the Ship."

This, in substance, I had to repeat hundreds of times; and as often had I to witness the half-pitying or incredulous smile with which it was received, or to hear the blunt and emphatic retort, "You'll never succeed! Money cannot be got in that unbusiness-like way."

I generally added nothing further to such conversations; but a Voice, deep, sweet, and clear, kept sounding through my soul —"The silver and the gold are Mine."

During the year 1884, as is well known, Ireland was the

scene of many commotions and of great distress. Yet at the
end of my little tour, amongst the Presbyterian people of the
North principally, though not exclusively, a sum of more than
£600 had been contributed to our Mission Fund. And there
was not, so far as my knowledge went, one single large subscription ; there were, of course, many bits of gold from those
well-to-do, but the ordinary collection was made up of the
shillings and pence of the masses of the people. Nor had I
ever in all my travels a warmer response, nor ever mingled
with any Ministers more earnestly devoted to their Congregations or more generally and deservedly beloved.

No man, however dissevered from the party politics of the
day, can see and live amongst the Irish of the North, without
having forced on his soul the conviction that the Protestant
faith and life, with its grit and backbone and self-dependence,
has made them what they are. Romanism, on the other hand,
with its blind faith and its peculiar type of life, has been at
least *one*, if not the main, degrading influence amongst the Irish
of the South and West, who are naturally a warm-hearted and
generous and gifted people. And let Christian Churches, and
our Statesmen who love Christ, remember—that no mere
outward changes of Government or Order, however good and
defensible in themselves, can ever heal the miseries of the
people, without a change of Religion. Ireland needs the pure
and true Gospel, proclaimed, taught, and received, in the South
as it now is in the North ; and no other gift, that Britain ever
can bestow, will make up for the lack of Christ's Evangel.
Jesus holds the Key to all problems, in this as in every land.

Returning to Scotland, I settled down at my headquarters,
the house of my brother James in Glasgow; and thence began
to open up the main line of my operations, as the Lord day by
day guided me. Having the aid of no Committee, I cast myself on Minister after Minister and Church after Church, calling
here, writing there, and arranging for three meetings every
Sabbath, and one, if possible, every week-day, and drawing-
room meetings wherever practicable in the afternoons. My
correspondence grew to oppressive proportions, and kept me
toiling at it every spare moment from early morn till bed-time.
Indeed, I never could have overtaken it, had not my brother

devoted many days and hours of precious time, answering letters regarding arrangements, issuing the " Share " receipts for all moneys the moment they arrived, managing all my transactions through the bank, and generally tackling and reducing the heap of communications and preventing me falling into hopeless arrears.

I represented a Church in which all Presbyterians are happily united ; and so, wherever possible, I occupied, on the same Sabbath day, an Established Church pulpit in the morning, a Free Church in the afternoon, and a United Presbyterian Church in the evening, or in any order in which the thing could be arranged to suit the exigencies of every town or village that was visited. In all my addresses, for I nowhere attempted ordinary sermonizing, I strove to combine the Evangelist with the Missionary, applying every incident in my story to the conscience of the hearer, and seeking to win the sinner to Christ, and the believer to a more consecrated life. For I knew that if I succeeded in these higher aims, their money too would be freely laid upon the altar of the Lord.

I printed, and circulated by post and otherwise, ten thousand copies of a booklet, " Statement and Appeal,"—containing, besides my Victorian Commission and my Glasgow address, a condensed epitome of the results of the New Hebrides Mission and of the reasons for asking a new Steam Auxiliary Ship. To this chiefly is due the fact, as well as to my refusing to call for subscriptions, that the far greater portion of all the money came to me by letter. On one day, though no doubt a little exceptional, as many as seventy communications reached me by post ; and every one of these contained something for our fund—ranging from " a few stamps " and " the widow's mite," through every variety of figure up to the wealthy man's fifty or hundred pounds. I was particularly struck with the number of times that I received £1, with such a note as, " From a servant-girl that loves the Lord Jesus " ; or " From a servant-girl that prays for the conversion of the Heathen." Again and again I received sums of five and ten shillings, with notes such as—" From a working-man who loves his Bible " ; or " From a working-man who prays for God's blessing on you and work like yours, every day in Family Worship." I sometimes regret that the graphic, varied, and intensely interesting notes and letters were not preserved; for by the close of my tour they would have formed a wonderful volume of leaves from the human heart.

I also addressed every Religious Convention to which I was invited, or to which I could secure access. The Perth Conference was made memorable to me by my receiving the first large subscription for our Ship, and by my making the acquaintance of a beautiful type of Christian merchant. At the close of the meeting, at which I had the privilege of speaking, an American gentleman introduced himself to me. We at once entered into each other's confidence, as brothers in the Lord's service. I afterwards learned that he had made a competency for himself and his family, though only in the prime of life; and he still carried on a large and flourishing business—but why? to devote *the whole profits*, year after year, to the direct service of God and His cause among men! He gave me a cheque for the largest single contribution with which the Lord had yet cheered me. God, who knows me, sees that I have never coveted money for myself or my family; but I did envy that Christian merchant the joy that he had in having money, and having the heart to use it as a steward of the Lord Jesus! Oh, when will men of wealth learn this blessed secret, and, instead of hoarding up gold till death forces it from their clutches, put it out to usury now in the service of their Master, and see the fruits and share the joy thereof, before they go hence to give in their account to God? One of the most appalling features in the modern Christian world, considering the needs of men and the claims of Jesus, is this same practice of either spending all for self, or hoarding all for self, alone or chiefly. Christians, who do so, seem to stand in need of a great deal of converting still!

Thereafter I was invited to the annual Christian Conference at Dundee. A most peculiar experience befell me there. Being asked to close the forenoon meeting with prayer and the benediction, I offered prayer, and then began, " May the love of God the Father——" but not another word would come in English; everything was blank except the words in Aniwan, for I had long begun to *think* in the Native tongue; and after a dead pause, and a painful silence, I had to wind up with a simple "Amen"! I sat down wet with perspiration. It might have been wiser, as the Chairman afterwards suggested, to have given them the blessing in Aniwan, but I feared to set them a-laughing by so strange a manifestation of the "tongues." Worst of all, it had been announced that I was to address them in the afternoon; but who would come to hear a Missionary that stuck in the benediction? The event had its semi-comical aspect, but it sent me to my knees during the interval in a very fever of prayerful anxiety. A vast audience assembled, and if the Lord ever manifestly used me in interesting His people in Missions, it was certainly then and there. As I sat down, a devoted Free Church Elder from Glasgow handed me his card, with "I.O.U. £100." This was my first donation of a hundred pounds, and my heart was greatly cheered. I praised the Lord, and warmly thanked His servant. A Something kept sounding these words in my ears, "My thoughts are not as your thoughts"; and also, "Cast thy burden upon the Lord, and He will sustain thee."

During my address at that meeting a coloured girl, not unlike our Island girls, sat near the platform, and eagerly listened to me. She was apparently about twelve years of age, and at the close she rose, salaamed to me in Indian fashion, took four silver bangles from her arm, and presented them to me, saying, "Padre, I want to take shares in your Mission Ship by these bangles, for I have no money, and may the Lord ever bless you!"

I replied, "Thank you, my dear child; I will not take your bangles, but Jesus will accept your offering, and bless and reward you all the same."

As she still held them up to me, saying, "Padre, do receive them from me, and may God ever bless you!" a lady, who had been seated beside her, came up to me, and said, "Please do take them, or the dear girl will break her heart. She has offered them up to Jesus for your Mission Ship."

I afterwards learned that the girl was an orphan, whose parents died of cholera; that the lady and her sister, daughters of a Missionary, had adopted her to be trained as a Zenana Missionary, and that she intended to return with them, and live and die to aid them in that blessed work amongst the daughters of India. Oh, what a reward and joy might many a lady who reads this page easily reap for herself in Time and Eternity by a similar simple yet far-reaching service! Take action when and where God points the way; wait for no one's guidance.

The most amazing variety characterized the gifts and the givers. In Glasgow a lady sent me an anonymous note to this effect: "I have been curtailing my expenses. The first £5 saved I enclose, that you may invest it for me in the Bank of Jesus. I am sure He gives the best interest, and the most certain returns."

From Edinburgh a lawyer wrote, saying, "I herewith send you £5. Take out for me two hundred shares in the Mission Ship. I never made any investment with more genuine satisfaction in all my life."

A gentleman, whose children had zealously collected a considerable sum for me by the Cards, at length sent me his own subscription, saying, "I enclose you £25, because you have so interested my children in Missions to the Heathen." The same friend, after hearing me plead the cause in Free St. George's, Edinburgh, sent me a most encouraging letter, and another contribution of £100.

In Glasgow a lady called at my brother's house, saying, "Is the Missionary at home? Can I see him alone? If not, I will call again." Being asked into my room, she declined to be seated, but said, "I heard you tell the story of your Mission in the City Hall, and I have been praying for you ever since. I have called to give you my mite, but not my name. God bless you. We shall meet in Heaven!" She handed me an envelope, and was off almost before I could thank her. It was £49 in bank-notes.

Another dear Christian lady came to see me, and at the close of a delightful conversation, said: "I have been thinking much about you since I heard you in the Clark Hall, Paisley.

I have come to give a little bit of dirty paper for your Ship. God sent it to me, and I return it to God through you with great pleasure." I thanked her warmly, thinking it a pound, or five at the most; on opening it, after she was gone, it turned out to be £100. I felt bowed down in humble thankfulness, and pressed forward in the service of the Lord.

Another lady, who sent for me to call, said : " I have heard of the sufferings and losses of the Missionaries on your Islands through the smallness of the Sailing Vessel. I am glad to have the opportunity of giving you £50 to assist in getting a Steam Auxiliary."

Many articles of jewellery—silver and gold ornaments, rings and chains—were also sent to me, or dropped into the Collecting plate. With the assistance of Christian gentlemen, and by the kindness of a merchant at once interested in our work and in the gold and silver trade, these were turned into cash on the most advantageous possible terms, and added to the Mission Fund.

Having an introduction to a London lady, then living in Edinburgh, I called, and was most kindly received because of our dear mutual friend Mrs. Cameron, of St. Kilda. After delightful Christian conversation, she retired for a minute, and returned, saying, " I have kept this for twelve months, asking the Lord to direct me as to its disposal. God claims it now for the Mission Ship, and I have great joy in handing it to you." It was another £100. I had been praying all that afternoon for some token of encouragement, especially as I went to that lady's house, and God's extraordinary answer, even while the prayer was still being uttered, struck me so forcibly that I could not speak. I received her gift in tears, and my soul looked up to the Giver of all.

The time now arrived for my attempting something amongst the Presbyterians of England. But my heart sank within me ; I was a stranger to all except Dr. Dykes, and the New Hebrides Mission had no special claims on them. Casting myself upon the Lord, I wrote to all the Presbyterian Ministers in and around London, enclosing my " Statement and Appeal," and asking a Service, with a retiring collection, or the surplus above the usual collection, on behalf of our Mission Ship.

All declined, except two. I learned that the London Presbytery had resolved that no claim beyond their own Church was to be admitted into any of its pulpits for a period of months, under some special financial emergency. My dear friend, Dr. J. Hood Wilson, kindly wrote also to a number of them, on my behalf, but with a similar result; though at last other two Services were arranged for with a collection, and one without. Being required at London, in any case, in connection with the threatened Annexation of the New Hebrides by the French,* I resolved to take these five Services by the way, and immediately return to Scotland, where engagements and opportunities were now pressed upon me, far more than I could overtake. But the Lord Himself opened before me a larger door, and more effectual, than any that I had tried in vain to open up for myself.

The Churches to which I had access did nobly indeed, and the Ministers treated me as a very brother. Dr. Dykes most affectionately supported my Appeal, and made himself recipient of donations that might be sent for our Mission Ship. Dr. Donald Fraser, and Messrs. Taylor and Mathieson, with their Congregations, generously contributed to the Fund. And so did the Mission Church in Drury Lane—the excellent and consecrated Rev. W. B. Alexander, the pastor thereof, and his wife, becoming my devoted personal friends, and continuing to remember in their work-parties ever since the needs of the Natives on the New Hebrides. Others also, whom I cannot wait to specify, showed a warm interest in us and in our department of the Lord's work. But my heart had been foolishly set upon adding a large sum to the fund for the Mission Ship, and when only about £150 came from all the Churches in London to which I could get access, no doubt I was sensible of cherishing a little guilty disappointment. That was very unworthy in me, considering all my previous experiences; and God deserved to be trusted by me far differently, as the sequel will immediately show.

That widely-known and deeply-beloved servant of God, J. E. Mathieson, Esq., of the Mildmay Conference Hall, had

---

* See Appendix E, "The Future of the New Hebrides."

invited me to address one of their annual meetings on behalf of Foreign Missions, and also to be his guest while the Conference lasted. Thereby I met and heard many godly and noble disciples of the Lord, whom I could not otherwise have reached though every Church I had asked in London had been freely opened to me. These devout and faithful and generous people, belonging to every branch of the Church of Christ, and drawn from every rank and class in Society, from the humblest to the highest, were certainly amongst the most open-hearted and the most responsive of all whom I ever had the privilege to address. One felt there, in a higher degree than almost anywhere else, that every soul was on fire with love to Jesus and with genuine devotion to His Cause in every corner of the Earth. There it was a privilege and a gladness to speak ; and though no collection was asked or could be expected, my heart was uplifted and strengthened by these happy meetings and by all that Heavenly intercourse.

But see how the Lord leads us by a way we know not ! Next morning after my address, a gentleman who had heard me, the Hon. Ion Keith-Falconer, handed me a cheque from his father-in-law for £300, by far the largest single donation at that time towards our Mission Ship ; and immediately thereafter I received from one of the Mildmay lady-Missionaries £50, from a venerable friend of the founder £20, from "Friends at Mildmay" £30 ; and through my dear friend and brother, J. E. Mathieson, many other donations were in due course forwarded to me.

My introduction, however, to the Conference at Mildmay did far more for me than even this ; it opened up a series of drawing-room meetings in and around London, where I told the story of our Mission and preached the Gospel to many in the higher walks of life, and received most liberal support for the Mission Ship. It also brought me invitations from many quarters of England, to Churches, to Halls, and to County Houses and Mansions.

Lord Radstock got up a special meeting, inviting by private card a large number of his most influential friends ; and there I met for the first time one whom I have since learned to regard as a very precious personal friend, Rev. Sholto D. C.

Douglas, clergyman of the Church of England, who then, and afterwards at his seat in Scotland, not only most liberally supported our fund, but took me by the hand as a brother and promoted my work by every means in his power.

The Earl and Countess of Tankerville also invited me to Chillingham Castle, and gave me an opportunity of addressing a great assembly there, then gathered together from all parts of the County. The British and Foreign Bible Society received me in a special meeting of the Directors ; and I was able to tell them how all we the Missionaries of these Islands, whose language had never before been reduced to writing, looked to them and leant upon them and prayed for them and their work—without whom our Native Bibles never could have been published. After the meeting, the Chairman gave me £5, and one of the Directors a cheque for £25 for our Mission Ship.

I was also invited to Leicester, and made the acquaintance-ship of a godly and gifted servant of the Lord Jesus, the Rev. F. B. Meyer, B.A. (now of London), whose books and booklets on the higher aspects of the Christian Life are read by tens of thousands, and have been fruitful of blessing. There I addressed great meetings of devoted workers in the vineyard ; and the dear friend who was my host on that occasion, a Christian merchant, has since contributed £10 per annum for the support of a Native Teacher on the New Hebrides.

It was my privilege also to visit and address the Müller Orphanages at Bristol, and to see that saintly man of faith and prayer moving about as a wise and loving father amongst the hundreds, even thousands, that look to him for their daily bread and for the bread of Life Eternal. At the close of my address, the venerable founder thanked me warmly and said, "Here are £50, which God has sent to me for your Mission."

I replied, saying, "Dear friend, how can I take it? I would rather give you £500 for your Orphans if I could, for I am sure you need it all!"

He replied, with sweetness and great dignity, "God provides for His own Orphans. This money cannot be used for them. I must send it after you by letter. It is the Lord's gift."

Often, as I have looked at the doings of men and Churches,

and tried to bring all to the test as if in Christ's very presence, it has appeared to me that such work as Müller's, and Barnardo's, and that of my own fellow-countryman, William Quarrier, must be peculiarly dear to the heart of our blessed Lord. And were He to visit this world again, and seek a place where His very Spirit had most fully wrought itself out into deeds, I fear that many of our so-called Churches would deserve to be passed by, and that His holy, tender, helpful, divinely-human love would find its most perfect reflex in these Orphan Homes. Still and for ever, amidst all changes of creed and of climate, this, *this* is "pure and undefiled Religion" before God and the Father!

Upper Norwood, London, is ever fresh in my memory, in connection with my first and subsequent visits, chiefly because of the faithful guidance and help amidst all the perplexities of that Great Babylon, so ungrudgingly bestowed upon me by my old Australian friends, then resident there, William Storrie, Esq., and his most excellent wife, both devoted workers in the cause of Missions abroad and at home. Great kindness was shown to me also by their Minister there; and by T. W. Stoughton, Esq., at whose Mission Hall there was a memorable and joyful meeting; and, amongst many others whom I cannot here name, by Messrs. Morgan & Scott, of the *Christian*,—all of whom I rejoiced to find actively engaged in personal service to the Lord Jesus.

But in this connection I must not omit to mention that the noble and world-famous servant of God, the Minister of the Tabernacle, invited me to a garden-party at his home, and asked me to address his students and other Christian workers. When I arrived I found a goodly company assembled under the shade of lovely trees, and felt the touch of that genial humour, so mighty a gift when sanctified, which has so often given wings to C. H. Spurgeon's words, when he saluted me as "the King of the Cannibals!" On my leaving, Mrs. Spurgeon presented me with her husband's "Treasury of David," and also "£5 from the Lord's cows"—which I afterwards learned was part of the profits from certain cows kept by the good lady, and that everything produced thereby was dedicated to the work of the Lord. I praised God that He had privileged me to meet this extraordinarily endowed man, to whom the whole Christian World is so specially indebted, and who has consecrated all his gifts and opportunities to the proclamation of the pure and precious Gospel.

But of all my London associations, the deepest and the most imperishable is that which weaves itself around the Honourable Ion Keith-falconer, who has already passed to what may truly be called a Martyr's crown. At that time I met him at his father-in-law's house at Trent; and on another occasion spent a whole day with him at the house of his noble mother, the Countess-Dowager of Kintore. His soul was then full of his projected Mission to the Arabs, being himself one of the most distinguished Orientalists of the day; and as we talked together, and exchanged experiences, I felt that never before had I visibly marked the fire of God, the holy passion to seek and to save the lost, burning more steadily or brightly on the altar of any human heart. The heroic founding of the Mission at Aden is already one of the precious annals of the Church of Christ. His young and devoted wife survives, to mourn indeed, but also to cherish his noble memory; and, with the aid of others, and under the banner of the Free Church of Scotland, to see the " Keith-Falconer Mission " rising up amidst the darkness of blood-stained Africa, as at once a harbour of refuge for the slave, and a beacon-light to those who are without God and without hope. The servant does his day's work, and passes on through the gates of sleep to the Happy Dawn; but the Divine Master lives and works and reigns, and by our death, as surely as by our life, His holy purposes shall be fulfilled.

On returning to Scotland, every day was crowded with engagements for the weeks that remained, and almost every mail brought me contributions from all conceivable corners of the land. My heart was set upon taking out two or three Missionaries with me to claim more and still more of the Islands for Christ; and with that view I had addressed Divinity Students at Edinburgh, Glasgow, and Aberdeen. Again and again, by conversation and correspondence, consecrated young men were just on the point of volunteering; but again and again the larger and better known fields of labour turned the scale, and they finally decided for China or Africa or India. Deeply disappointed at this, and thinking that God directed us to look to our own Australia alone for Missionaries for the New Hebrides, I resolved to return, and took steps towards securing a passage by the Orient Line to Melbourne. But just then two able and devoted students, Messrs. Morton and Leggatt, offered themselves as Missionaries for our Islands; and shortly thereafter a third, Mr. Landells, also an excellent man; and all, being on the eve of their Licence as preachers, were approved of, accepted, and set to special preparations for the Mission field, particularly in acquiring practical medical knowledge.

On this turn of affairs, I managed to have my passage delayed for six weeks, and resolved to cast myself on the Lord that He might enable me in that time to raise at least £500, in order to furnish the necessary outfit and equipment for three new Mission Stations, and to pay the passage money of the Missionaries and their wives, that there might be no difficulty on this score amongst the Foreign Mission Committees on the other side. And then the idea came forcibly, and for a little unmanned me, that it was wrong in me to speak of these limits as to time and money in my prayers to God. But I reflected, again, how it was for the Lord's own glory alone in the salvation of the Heathen, and for no personal aims of mine; and so I fell back on His promise, "Whatsoever ye shall ask in my Name," and believingly asked it in His Name, and for His praise and service alone. I think it due to my Lord, and for the encouragement of all His servants, that I should briefly outline what occurred in answer to these prayers.

Having gone to the centre of one of the great ship-building districts of Scotland, and held a series of meetings, and raised a sum of about £55 only after nine services and many Sabbath School collecting cards, my heart was beginning to sink, as I did not think my health would stand another six weeks of incessant strain; when at the close of my last meeting in a Free Church, an Elder and his wife entered the vestry and said, "We are deeply interested in you and in all your work and plans. You say that you have asked £500 more. We gave you the first £100 at the Dundee Conference ; and it is a joy to us to give you this £100 too, towards the making up of your final sum. We pray that you may speedily realize your wish, and that God's richest blessing may ever rest upon your head."

Glasgow readers will at once recognise the generous giver, J. Campbell White, Esq. (now Lord Overtoun), who rejoices, along with his dear wife, to regard himself as a steward of the Lord Jesus. My prayer is that they, and all such, may feel more and more "blessed in their deeds."

Another week passed by, and at the close of it a lady called upon me, and, after delightful conversation about the Mission, said, "How near are you to the sum required ? " I explained to her what is recorded above, and she continued, "I gave you one little piece of paper, at the beginning of your efforts. I have prayed for you every day since. God has prospered me, and this is one of the happiest moments of my life, when I am now able to give you another little bit of paper."

So saying, she put into my hand £100. I protested, "You are surely too generous. Can you afford a second £100 ? "

She replied to this effect, and very joyfully, as one who had genuine gladness in the deed, "My Lord has been very kind to me, in my health and in my business. My wants are simple, and are safe in His hands. I wait not till death forces me, but give back whatever I am able to the Lord now, and hope to live to see much blessing thereby through you in the conversion of the Heathen."

The name of that dear friend from Paisley rises often in my prayers and meditations before God. "Verily I say unto you, the Father that seeth in secret shall reward openly."

My last week had come, and I was in the midst of preparations for departure, when amongst the letters delivered to me was one to this effect :

"Restitution money which never now can be returned to its owner. Since my Conversion I have laboured hard to save it. I now make my only possible amends by returning it to God through you. Pray for me and mine, and may God bless you in your work ! " I rather startled my brother and his wife at our breakfast table by shouting out in unwontedly excited tones,—" Hallelujah ! The Lord has done it ! Hallelujah ! " But my tones softened down into intense reverence, and my words broke at last into tears, when I found that this, the second largest subscription ever received by me,* came from a converted tradesman who had now consecrated his all to the Lord Jesus, and whose whole leisure was now centred upon seeking to bless and save those of his own rank and class, amongst whom he had spent his early and unconverted days. Jesus said unto him, " Go home to thy friends, and tell them how great things the Lord hath done for thee, and hath had compassion on thee."

Bidding farewell to dear old Glasgow, so closely intertwined with all my earlier and later experiences, I started for London, accompanied by my brother James. We were sitting at breakfast at Mrs. Mathieson's table, Mildmay, when a telegram was put into my hands announcing the " thank-offering " from Lord and Lady Polwarth, received since our departure from Glasgow, and referred to on an earlier page. The Lord had now literally exceeded my prayers. With other gifts, repeated again by friends at Mildmay, the special fund for outfit and travelling expenses for new Missionaries had risen above the £500, and now approached £650.

In a Farewell Meeting at Mildmay the Lord's servants, being assembled in great numbers from all quarters of London, dedicated me and my work very solemnly to God, amid songs of praise and many prayers and touching " last " words. And when at length Mr. Mathieson, intimating that I must go, as another company of Christian workers were elsewhere waiting also to say Good-bye, suggested that the whole audience should stand up, and, instead of hand-shaking, quietly breathe their benedictory Farewell as I passed from the platform down through their great Hall, a perfect flood of emotion overwhelmed me. I never felt a humbler man, nor more anxious to hide my head in the dust, than when all these noble, gifted,

---

* A Christian lady in Sunderland has since contributed a donation of £1,000 through " The John G. Paton Mission Fund "—EDITOR.

and beloved followers of Jesus Christ, and consecrated workers in His service, stood up and with one heart said, "God speed" and "God bless you," as I passed on through the Hall. To one who had striven and suffered less, or who less appreciated how little we can do for others compared with what Jesus had done for us, this scene might have ministered to spiritual pride ; but long ere I reached the door of that Hall, my soul was already prostrated at the feet of my Lord in sorrow and in shame that I had done so little for Him, and I bowed my head and could have gladly bowed my knees to cry, "Not unto us, Lord, not unto us !"

On the 28th October, 1885, I sailed for Melbourne, and in due course safely arrived there by the goodness of God. The Church and people of my own beloved Victoria gave me a right joyful welcome, and in public assembly presented me with a testimonial, which I shrank from receiving, but which all the same was the highly-prized expression of their confidence and esteem.

During my absence at the Islands, to which I immediately proceeded, they unanimously elected me Moderator of their Supreme Court, and called me back to fill that highest Chair of honour in the Presbyterian Church. God is my witness how very little any or all of these things in themselves ever have been coveted by me; but how, when they have come in my way, I have embraced them with a single desire thereby to promote the Church's interest in that Cause to which my whole life and all my opportunities are consecrated—the Conversion of the Heathen World.

My Mission to Britain was to raise £6,000, in order to enable the Australian Churches to provide a Steam-Auxiliary Mission Ship, for the enlarged and constantly enlarging requirements of the New Hebrides. I spent exactly eighteen months at home; and when I returned, I was enabled to hand over to the Church that had commissioned and authorized me no less a sum than £9,000. And all this had been forwarded to me, as the free-will offerings of the Lord's stewards, in the manner illustrated by the preceding pages. "Behold, what God hath wrought !"

Of this sum £6,000 are set apart to build or acquire the

new Mission Ship. The remainder is added to wnat we call our Number II. Fund, for the maintenance and equipment of additional Missionaries. It has been the dream of my life to see one Missionary at least, with trained Native Teachers, planted on every Island of the New Hebrides, and then I could lie down and whisper gladly, " Lord, now lettest Thou Thy servant depart in peace ! "

As to the new Mission Ship, unexpected delay has arisen. First, there were differences of opinion about the best way of carrying out the original proposal. Then there had to be negotiations betwixt New South Wales and Victoria and the other Colonies, as to the additional annual expenditure for the maintenance of a Steam-Auxiliary, and how the same was to be allocated. Finally, perplexity as to the wisest course of procedure has deepened since the Colonial Government began to run Mail Ships regularly from Australia to Fiji, willing on certain terms to call at one or other harbour in the New Hebrides, which has raised the fresh problem of subsidizing their services so far, and, for the rest, securing merely an *inter-island* Steamer, under the management of the Synod there and the Colonial Churches, to be used exclusively in the interests of the Mission and for the welfare of the Missionaries and their families. Meantime, let all friends who are interested in us and our work understand—that the money so generously entrusted to me has been safely handed over to my own Victorian Church, and has been deposited by them at good interest in the bank, to be spent at their discretion in due time, when all details are settled, and, as nearly as possible in the altered circumstances, exclusively for the purposes for which it was asked and bestowed.

To me personally, this delay is confessedly a keen and deep disappointment. But here is not the place to discuss that matter further. The special work laid upon me has been accomplished. The Colonial Churches have now all the responsibility of the further steps. In this, as in many a harder trouble of my chequered life, I calmly roll all my burden upon the Lord. I await with quietness and confidence His wise disposal of events.   His hand is on the helm ; and whither He steers us, all shall be well.

But let me not close this chapter, till I have struck another and a Diviner note.   I have been to the Islands again, since my return from Britain.   The whole inhabitants of Aniwa were there to welcome me, and my procession to the old Mission House was more like the triumphal march of a Conqueror than that of a humble Missionary.   Everything was kept in beautiful and perfect order.   Every Service of the Church, as previously described in this book, was fully sustained by the Native Teachers, the Elders, and the occasional visit, once or twice a year, of the ordained Missionary from one of the other Islands.   Aniwa, like Aneityum, is a *Christian* land.   Jesus has taken possession, never again to quit those shores.   Glory, *glory* to His blessed Name !

CLOSING TESTIMONY.

WHEN pleading the cause of the Heathen and the claims of Jesus on His followers, I have often been taunted with being "a man of one idea." Sometimes I have thought that this came from the lips of those who had not even one idea!—unless it were how to kill time or to save their own skin. But seriously speaking, is it not better to have one good idea and to live for that and succeed in it, than to scatter one's life away on many things and leave a mark on none?

And, besides, you cannot live for one good idea supremely without thereby helping forward many other collateral causes. My life has been dominated by one sacred purpose; but in pursuing it the Lord has enabled me to be Evangelist as well as Missionary; He has enabled me, whilst seeking for needed money, to seek for and save and bless many souls,—has enabled me to defend the Holy Sabbath in many lands, as the God-given and precious birthright of the toiling millions, to be bartered away for no price or bribe that man can offer,—has enabled me to maintain the right of every child in Christian lands, or in Heathen, to be taught to read the blessed Bible and to understand it, as the Divine foundation of all Social Order, and the sole guarantee of individual freedom as well as of national greatness,—and has enabled me also to do battle against the infernal *Kanaka* or Labour Traffic, one of the most cruel and blood-stained forms of slavery on the face of the Earth, and to rouse the holy passion of Human Brotherhood in the Colonies and at Home against those who trafficked in the bodies and souls of men.

In these, as well as in my own direct labours as a Missionary, I probably have had my full share of "abuse" from the enemies of the Cross, and a not inconsiderable burden of trials

443

and afflictions in the service of my Lord ; yet here, as I lay
down my pen, let me record my immovable conviction that
this is the noblest service in which any human being can spend
or be spent; and that, if God gave me back my life to be lived
over again, I would without one quiver of hesitation lay it on
the altar to Christ, that He might use it as before in similar
ministries of love, especially amongst those who have never yet
heard the Name of Jesus.   Nothing that has been endured,
and nothing that can now befall me, makes me tremble—on
the contrary, I deeply rejoice—when I breathe the prayer that
it may please the blessed Lord to turn the hearts of all my
children to the Mission Field ; and that He may open up their
way and make it their pride and joy to live and die in carrying Jesus and His Gospel into the heart of the Heathen World !
God gave His best, His Son, to me ; and I give back my best,
my All, to Him.

PART THIRD.

CHAPTERS I.—II.

A.D. 1886—1897.

ÆT. 62—73.

PRELIMINARY NOTE.

THE "Story of my Life," so unexpectedly owned and blessed of God to multitudes in every Land, closed, when first published in 1889, with what I then regarded and described as my "Last" Visit to Britain, 1884–1885. It did not for one moment enter my mind, at that time, that world-wide travels were still before me, in the interests of our beloved Mission; or that I should ever again be called upon to lift my pen, in the further telling of my own Biography. So much so, that I then wrote something in the "farewell" to the reader, hinting not dimly that the *last* Chapter of all, yet to be added, would fall to be described by another hand than mine!

More than ten years have, however, since elapsed, and, "by the good hand of my God upon me for good," I am still hale and vigorous, rejoicing to serve my Redeemer by serving those whom He died to save and lives to bring to Glory. Wherefore, at the earnest and repeated entreaty of my dear brother, James, but for whom this book never could or would have been given to the world at all, I resume my pen to add a brief sketch of the Autumn of my life, that he may set it in order, and bring this *Autobiography* up to date. In many respects, I can unfeignedly say that I would rather bury all in oblivion, or keep it under the eye of my Saviour alone. But I dare not shrink from the door of Great Opportunity thus opened before me; and this, also, I humbly lay on the Altar to the glory of Jesus my Lord.

CHAPTER I

ROUND THE WORLD FOR JESUS.

A.D. 1886—1893. ÆT. 62—69.

From 1886 to 1892.—Tour Round the World.—Fire-Arms and Intoxi-
cants.—International Prohibition Proposed.—Deputies to America.
— Samoan Converts. — America and Hawaii. — San Francisco.—
Salt Lake City.— Chicago. — Niagara. — Pan-Presbyterian Council at
Toronto.—The Ruthven Imposture.—Sabbath Observance.—Rochester.
—New York.— Public Petitions.— Washington.— The Presbyterian
Assembly.—President Cleveland.—France's Withdrawal.—Dr. Joseph
Cook. — Dr. Blank. — Second Probation. — Chicago Exhibition. —
Canadian Presbyterian Church.—Two Months' Rush of Meetings.—
Incidents of Travel.—Impressions of Canada and the States.

FROM 1886 till 1892 my days were occupied, in the various
Colonies of Australasia, and in occasional visits to the
New Hebrides, practically in the same way as set forth again
and again in the preceding Chapters. Colony after Colony, and
Congregation after Congregation listened with ever-deepening
interest to the narrative of God's dealings with the Islanders,
and to the record of the effects produced by my relating these
incidents wherever my steps had been led in the interests of
Missionary Enterprise. If I have accomplished nothing else
by all these travels and toils, this at least has been accomplished, and I write it down to the praise of my blessed
Redeemer—there are Missionaries at this day labouring in
every Heathen Land, who have assured me that they first
gave themselves away to the glorious work, while drinking in
from my poor lips the living testimony from the New Hebrides
that the Gospel is still the power of God and the wisdom of
God unto Salvation ; and there are individual Christians, and
sometimes also Congregations of the Lord, now zealously sup-

447

porting Missionaries to the Heathen in all the great Mission fields of the world, who, till they heard the story of Cannibals won for Christ by our noble Missionaries on the New Hebrides, had foolishly branded the modern Christian Mission to the Heathen as the greatest imposture and failure of the Century. God has filled the ear and the eye of Christendom with the story of one of the smallest, yet most fruitful, Missions in one of the hardest and darkest fields on this Earth ; and the whisper of " imposture " has died for shame, while the arm of the scoffer falls paralyzed, and can no longer sling its stones of abuse. " Failure " has been blotted from the vocabulary of Missions and their Critics by the Story of the New Hebrides.

But in 1892, events which had been maturing through many years came to a crisis, the issue of which was that I was sent a TOUR ROUND THE WORLD in the Cause of Jesus, and for the sake of our beloved Islanders. A broadly-drawn picture of these things, without any attempt at details, seems all that is called for here. This I now set myself to give to the patient and indulgent reader of these pages, which after all contain only brief and fragmentary scenes out of a crowded and hurried life.

The occasion was this. The sale of Intoxicants, Opium, Fire-Arms and Ammunition, by the Traders amongst the New Hebrideans, had become a terrible and intolerable evil. The lives of many Natives, and of not a few Europeans, were every year sacrificed in connection therewith, while the general demoralization produced on all around was painfully notorious. Alike in the Colonial and in the Home Newspapers, we exposed and condemned the fearful consequences of allowing such degrading and destructive agencies to be used as barter in dealing with these Islanders. It is infinitely sad to see the European and American Trader following fast in the wake of the Missionary with opium and rum ! But, blessed be God, our Christian Natives have thus far, with very few exceptions, been able to keep away from the White Man's Fire-Water, that maddens and destroys. And not less cruel is it to scatter fire-arms and ammunition amongst Savages, who are at the same time to be primed with poisonous rum ! This were surely Demons' work.

To her honour, be it said, that Great Britain prohibited all her own Traders, under heavy penalties, from bartering those dangerous and destructive articles in trade with the Natives. She also appealed to the other trading Nations, in Europe and America, to combine and make the prohibition "International," with regard to all the still unannexed Islands in the Pacific Seas. At first America hesitated, owing to some notion that it was inconsistent with certain regulations for trading embraced in the Constitution of the United States. Then France, temporising, professed willingness to accept the prohibition when America agreed. Thus the British Trader, with the Man-of-War and the High Commissioner ready to enforce the laws against him, found himself placed at an overwhelming disadvantage, as against the neighbouring Traders of every other Nationality, free to barter as they pleased. More especially so, when the things prohibited were the very articles which the masses of the Heathen chiefly coveted in exchange for their produce ; and where keen rivals in business were ever watchful to inform and to report against him. If illicit Trading prevailed, under such conditions, no one that knows average Human Nature can feel any surprise.

By-and-bye, the *Australian New Hebrides Company*, with two Steamers plying betwixt Sydney and the New Hebrides, took up the problem. Having planted Traders and Agents on the Islands, they found themselves handicapped in developing business, and began a brisk agitation in the Australasian and English Press, either to have the Prohibition applied all round, or completely rescinded. We have never accepted that alternative, but resolutely plead for an International Prohibitive law, as the only means under God to prevent the speedy sweeping off into Eternity of these most interesting Races by the tide of what is strangely styled Civilization.

At length Sir John Thurston, Her Majesty's High Commissioner for the Western Pacific, whose sympathies all through have been on our side, advised that the controversy in the Newspapers cease, and that our Missions and Churches send a deputation to America to win the assent of the United States. Consequently, the next Federal Assembly of the Australasian Presbyterian Churches instructed two of its Professors in the Divinity Hall of Victoria, who were then visiting Britain, to return by America, and do everything in their power to secure the adhesion of the United States Government to the International proposal. Lest, however, these Deputies found themselves unable to carry out their instructions, the same Assembly appointed me as Deputy, with identical instructions, to undertake the task during the succeeding year.

Meanwhile, the General Assembly of Victoria appointed the Rev. Professor Rentoul, D.D., Ormond College, the Rev. Jas. M'Gaw and myself, to represent them at the Pan-Presbyterian Council to be held at Toronto in September, 1892, and thus was I altogether unexpectedly launched on what proved to be the biggest of all my Missionary journeys. I received three several Commissions. But that from my own Church of Victoria, signed by the Moderator of the General Assembly and the Convener of our Foreign Mission Committee, bears most closely on the succeeding narrative. It set forth that, besides being appointed by the Federal Assembly to the Council at Toronto, I was empowered to use all legitimate influence with the Government of the United States "for the suppression of the trade in Fire-Arms, Intoxicating Liquors, and Opium, in the New Hebrides Islands and other unannexed Groups in the Western Pacific." I was also "authorised to procure two Missionaries to serve in the New Hebrides Islands under this Church," and to receive, on behalf of the Committee, "any contributions offered for its Foreign Missions." So that I acted, and had good right to act, in the name and by the authority of my own Church, and of the Federated Churches of Australasia.

With my Fellow-Deputies, and accompanied so far on the journey by my wife and our beloved daughter, we sailed from Sydney for San Francisco per s.s. *Monowai*, on 8th August, 1892. We had a very agreeable voyage, Captain Carey and all on board striving to make others happy. At Auckland, on the 13th, we had the great delight of spending a few hours with our very dear friends, Mr. and Mrs. Mackie, while the ship was discharging and receiving cargo and mails; and, as she was leaving, several Ministers and other kind friends bade us Godspeed. Again, at Samoa, on the 18th, we had a few hours to spend, and were immensely gratified with the appearance of the Natives. They had a bright and healthy look as they came amongst the passengers with shells, operculums, and fans, their manner being characterised by a gentle grace, that comes only with the coming of Christ into a Savage man or woman. These, and the Rarotongans, and the people of Savage Islands, were amongst the first whom the London Missionary Society saw "flocking as the doves to their windows," from the hordes of Cannibalism. They are tall, vigorous and alert; and many of them are now teachers for Jesus, and preachers of the Gospel in New Guinea and other Heathen Islands. My heart overflows with love and praise whenever I gaze on such trophies of Redeeming Grace.

We reached Honolulu, the Hawaiian Capital, on the 25th, and spent nearly a whole day on shore. By a circuitous drive, and on remarkably good roads, we ascended a considerable hill and beheld the City spread before us with its Palace, Government Buildings, Mansions and Villas. Large and beautiful trees surrounded them all. Two Men-of-War and many other ships swung at anchor in the harbour, and the shimmering Sea completed a charming panorama. Smart and diligent Chinese were at work on every hand, side by side with the busy representatives of almost every Nationality, eager to profit by the passing visitors. The larger portion of the wharf seemed to be covered with Bananas for San Francisco, the bunches carefully bound up in dry leaves for shipping. I had never seen so many in all my life thus gathered together.

The Queen had been deposed or deprived of power. National interests were sacrificed in self-seeking and partisanship. One could not but sigh for some strong and righteous Government. They are a people capable of great things. Everything seems to invite America to annex the group; and it would be for the permanent welfare of all concerned.

On 2nd September, we arrived at San Francisco, after a delightful voyage. The society on board was most congenial. We had happy daily Religious Services, and I managed to secure about eight hours to myself out of every twenty-four for copying out translations, finishing my Dictionary of the Aniwan language, and other Mission work on which I was constantly engaged.

San Francisco is beautifully situated. Many of its streets run up and down what seemed very steep hills, and the principal highways are well supplied with Electric Cars. Your own language is spoken, indeed, but you feel at every turn, for all that, you are in a Foreign City. On Sabbath morning, the first thing I marked on leaving our Hotel was the joiners busy with saw and plane, as on any other day! The next was a multitude of people flocking to a place of Public Amusement, while others were going to Church. The mass of the inhabitants were either in pursuit of pleasure, or following their usual avocations. Even the City scavengers turned out with their carts, and were cleaning the streets on the Lord's Day!

Yet we soon learned that even there the Lord Jesus has many faithful servants living and working for His glory. Several Ministers, hearing of our arrival, found out our Hotel, and had us to assist them in their Services. I delivered three Addresses, walking considerable distances between, and refusing to use public conveyances, or deprive man or beast of rest for my convenience,—to the great astonishment of my guides and friends.

On Monday morning we visited the famous Seal Rocks, a short distance from the city. There you see them, under protection, safely wobbling up on the rocks and basking contentedly in the sunshine, or tumbling delightedly into the Sea. From a considerable distance you hear the strange, half-barking sound of their voices, like muzzled dogs. From the plateau and promenade of a lovely private Garden near by and open to the public, we had a magnificent view of the Sea and all the surrounding scenery.

The same day, our whole party were invited to address a meeting of Lady Workers, who carry on a Mission in the Chinese quarter of the City. A report was given, and some Converts from the Flowery Land sang hymns to Jesus. It was joyful to see this spiritual life;—for tokens were not awanting of a darker and sadder picture all around us, in the dens of vice and misery.

Guided, but not very wisely, by Cook's representative, we left San Francisco on 5th September. Though now travelling night and day, we halted a few hours at the famous Mormon

Settlement on 7th September. While looking at the grave of Brigham Young, a well-dressed old lady approached us and volunteered much information about her departed husband. He was one of the first settlers in the Salt Lake District, and had taken an active part in the building of the city and the Temple. She herself was a Mormon, and mourned that their glory was departing under the influence of the American laws. She was fervent in her defence of polygamy, but I noted that, with the Mormons as with the South Sea Savages, a separate house had to be provided for each wife! We saw their vast Temple, said to accommodate 15,000 persons, with tradesmen toiling busily to finish it, for the reception of Brigham Young on his speedy return to this Earth.

Replenishing our provision basket, as it was too expensive to take all our meals on board the train, our next run was to Chicago, which we reached on 10th September, and where we rested at a Hotel on the Sabbath Day. It was a day of tremendous storm and rain and no one of us ventured out even to Divine Service, especially as no Place of Worship was nigh at hand. Amongst our fellow-passengers from San Francisco had been a very kindly Christian man belonging to Chicago. He gave us every information, and on Monday showed us round the whole City by boat and car. We saw the Exhibition Buildings, lavishly expensive. The Horticultural Gardens were extensive and most interesting. In the Zoological Enclosure we saw a few remaining specimens of the Buffaloes, which once in myriads roamed the Prairies, but which Civilization has swept away.

Leaving Chicago, we arrived at Buffalo on the evening of the 13th September, and returned next day to Niagara, whence by train and steamboat we were bound for Toronto. We had already had a glimpse of the Falls, where the train halted for a few minutes at a convenient spot, and the view was grand! When next I gazed on the spectacle, nigh at hand, I am afraid almost to admit that I was rather disappointed. Too transcendent expectations beforehand, I suppose!

I left Mrs. Paton and our daughter at the Falls for a day, whilst I went on to Toronto to arrange for accommodation. What a blessing that I was guided to do so! A great Agricultural Show was being held there; and, on arriving in the evening, I found every Hotel and Lodging so crowded that I walked till midnight from one end of the City to the other, seeking in vain for a bed. At last one manager of a Hotel proposed to give me a "shake-down" in a Common Room, where twenty-two were to sleep that same night. But the Hotel-Keeper taking pity, and protesting that he could not allow me to "tumble into that crowded place," gave me the address of a private family who took in lodgers, to whom he commended me. With much difficulty, at that late hour, I found the street and the number. The owner, on hearing my appeal, said he had already "turned away thirteen," and that he had not a corner to receive me. I offered to pay him the highest charges, "merely to rest in the Hall all night," rather than to tramp the streets. Calling his wife, he said: "I have not the heart to turn this old man away! May he not sleep on the floor of our new empty Room?" Her answer was: "I have neither bed, nor bed-clothes, nor even a pillow to give him." But I was glad of the shelter over my head. A chair was brought in and placed in the middle of the floor. Kneeling, I thanked the Lord, and my hosts. Then, utterly worn out, I placed my travelling handbag for a pillow, rolled my clothes tightly round me, lay down, and enjoyed a most refreshing sleep.

Next morning I found my way to the Presbyterian Church Offices, where a cordial welcome awaited me, and news of ample accommodation for our comfort, all generously provided. Several invitations were pressed on me, but I accepted that of Mrs. Park, who had in the old days been a member of my Bible-class in the Green Street Mission, Glasgow, and it was a great joy to meet once more her sister and herself. The attention of many other friends was also very great, and far too devoted, making us feel ashamed at the love lavished on us.

At the Pan-Presbyterian Council I met and became acquainted with representative Ministers and Laymen from all parts of the world, but in specially large numbers from Canada and the United States. Along with Fellow-Deputies, I addressed the Assembly on Foreign Missions, and on the urgent reasons for my present visit to America. A Minister from the States at once rose and protested that there must be some mistake, that it was "an insult to their honour" to insinuate that they declined to join with Britain in such an International Prohibition! I repeated my statements, showed my Commission, and affirmed that it was certainly as I had represented. He telegraphed to the Authorities at Washington, and next day he courageously stood up in his place and admitted that he was wrong, and that I had correctly stated the facts. The action of that good and brave man, once for all, made the issue plain and cleared my future course.

I was proud of our Professor Rentoul, of Ormond College. He at once took a leading place in the Council. In wisdom, in vast learning, and in eloquent debate, he was the equal of the best men from all Presbyterian Christendom. I envied the Students who sit at the feet of such a noble Master in the School of Christ.

In response to my appeals, Ministers from Canada and the States began informing me how many collections they had given "for the New Hebrides Mission," and subscriptions "for building the new Mission Ship." I had never heard of these, and inquired to whom they had been given. They replied that it was to my "alternate," commissioned from the Presbyterian Church of Victoria! I assured them that my Church appointed no alternate, and that this person must be an impostor. A Committee was appointed to look into the matter. The eloquent pleader turned out to be a Roman Catholic student who had joined the Victorian Church, had been licensed and ordained as a Minister, had broken down in character, and disappeared from the Colony. Now, under a false name and forged credentials, representing himself as a Minister in full and honourable standing, and a Missionary who had been thirteen years in the New Hebrides, he was raising large sums of money ostensibly for our Mission, but applying it all to his own uses. His lectures were cleverly compounded out of my *Autobiography*, with wild adornments and fancies of his own. He had Collecting Cards for children and for adults; the minimum subscription on the latter being half-a-crown! His New Ship was to be sheathed in brass, and every subscriber of not less than £1 was to have his name engraved thereon!

One man informed us of giving £5 to have his Family Register completed on the sheath of brass!

Dr. Rentoul, by appointment, officially exposed and denounced this impostor on the floor of the Council. But, in these vast countries, a lie is hard to overtake and to extinguish. Letters continued to reach me from many quarters, and urgent appeals that I should sanction his arrest. At one place he drank for a week, after a series of Mission Meetings. The Ministers of Buffalo at length caused him to be arrested; and the Public Attorney, founding on his so-called credentials as my assistant, summoned me to appear before the Grand Jury at his trial. In a "blizzard," I travelled two nights and a day—one night the severest and coldest I ever endured—and reached my destination in time.

Having answered all questions by the Attorney and the Grand Jury, they asked me to see the prisoner, and testify whether he was the ex-Priest Riordan, now giving his name as Ruthven. I thereon handed the Attorney a pamphlet exposing the evils and errors of Popery, being three Lectures by V. H. Riordan, with his portrait on the front page. They all at once recognised him by this likeness. Nevertheless, I was enjoined to go and see him, and report what took place. He was behind an iron-grated door, and two ladies were conversing with him from without. Addressing him at once by his name, I said: "It grieves me to see you here in these circumstances, Mr. Riordan." Completely off his guard, he at once answered to his own name, and addressed me by mine: "And I am very sorry, Dr. Paton, to be here in such circumstances." This was enough! I reported what transpired, and the Jury took a hearty laugh at the simplicity of the interview. I was dismissed for the time.

In answer to the Prosecutor, he explained that when he renounced the errors of Popery, he assumed his mother's name for life—Ruthven; yet there they had his own pamphlet, with his real name, printed in Philadelphia less than two years before! Being committed for trial before the Supreme Court, he spent his time of waiting in abusing me from his cell through the pages of a Sunday newspaper, as "a drunkard" debauching my Sacred Office, and "a hireling" living by commission on the moneys raised for the Mission. So madly did he rage, that some suspected he was put up to do so, in order that his agent might work up a plea of insanity, if the case at last went against him.

At his trial, which occupied the greater part of three days, I was again cited to appear. The Jury found him "guilty," but strangely enough recommended him to mercy, and his lawyer pled for a money fine as the penalty. The Judge sternly refused. He had been found guilty in every count. His sentence would be "twelve months in prison with hard labour." That was "extreme leniency." It should have been "three years."

One would have thought that this should have extinguished him. But no! His imprisonment has expired. He is again at his lecturing and lying. Quite lately I saw a report of his appearing at a place called Dunmore. The Romanists mobbed him. In reply to their eggs and snowballs he fired a pistol into the crowd. The cry then rose, "Lynch the Renegade!" Ruthven, bounding through an open door, scaling fences, and crossing lots, managed to escape. But a warrant was at once issued for his apprehension, and doubtless he is proving the truth of one text, which he has listened to in vain: "The way of transgressors is hard."

During the Pan-Presbyterian Council, I addressed many meetings in the churches of Toronto and its suburbs, receiving, on one occasion, by the kindness of Dr. Parsons, a collection of two hundred dollars for our Mission. And, by the urgent request of many Ministers, I spent a considerable time after the Council in visiting the chief towns of Ontario, where I was cordially received everywhere, and had very great pleasure throughout the whole circuit.

Never, since I left the Christian Islands on the New Hebrides, such as Aniwa and Aneityum, have I seen the Sabbath Day kept so well, and the Churches so largely attended, as at Toronto and in the chief towns of Ontario. In that Capital, the Public-Houses are closed from seven o'clock on Saturday night till eight o'clock on Monday morning. No confectioners, tobacconists, fruiterers, or the like, are open on the Lord's Day.

The street Electric Car, and the Omnibus are at rest. All work-men are enjoying their Sabbath privilege, like other Citizens. And all this is carried through by the will of the People them-selves, and by the vigilance and influence of the servants of God. Surely, men of Christian principle, of grit, and of public spirit, could, by keeping their hand on the helm, secure in the same way the blessed Day of Rest for all, in every City through-out the Christian World.

By cordial invitations from many men of the highest rank in the Church of God throughout the States, I was pressed to occupy their Pulpits, and tell the story of our Mission to the Cannibals of the New Hebrides. They also formed a Committee of their own number to advise and help me in promoting the prohibition against trading with the Natives in Intoxicants and Fire-Arms. And the great-hearted Dr. John Hall, in order to give me a good start in New York, offered me his Pulpit for my first Sabbath there.

On the way, I had promised to spend an afternoon and evening at Rochester, with the Rev. Principal Osgood of the Baptist College. An extraordinary spirit of consecration seemed to rest on Professors and Students alike. My heart was overflowing with joy, to think of the type of Ministers and Missionaries certain to go forth from such a Home of Piety and of Learning.

Never can I express how much I owe to the genuine and brotherly friendship of Dr. Sommerville of New York, and his devoted lady. Not simply did they make their House my very Home, whensoever I chose to return to it, but they heaped on me every token of consideration and of helpful sympathy. Amidst his many cares, as a Minister of the Covenanting Church, and his literary labours, as Editor of the *Herald of Mission News*, he became Honorary Treasurer for me in the States, and according to his utmost ability opened up all my way, and helped me at every turn. They are for ever my dearly beloved friends in the bonds of Jesus Christ.

After my first two Sabbaths in New York, one in Dr. John Hall's Church, and one in Dr. Sommerville's, I had no difficulty in arranging for as much work, Sunday and Saturday alike, as my strength could overtake. One lady, who heard me in Dr. Hall's, sent me one thousand dollars, as from "Elizabeth Jane." In addressing the Chamber of Commerce, the Doctor himself announced clearly the special object of my visit to America, and described the features of our Mission. This, being fully reported in the Public Press, woke a wide-spread interest, and invitations poured in upon me from all branches of the Church, excepting only the Romish and the Unitarian.

The way to Washington, and to influence with the Governing Authorities, was prepared for me thus. Being a stranger and only a poor Missionary, I asked every Public Meeting, held on any day except Sabbath, to forward a Petition to the President and the Congress, signed by the Chairman, in favour of the Prohibition of Intoxicants and Fire-Arms, as barter by American Traders on the New Hebrides, or other unannexed Islands in the Pacific. The Daily Press reported all these Petitions. The Public became thoroughly interested. And even the Authorities were expecting my appeal in person. Nay, I cannot but regard it as of the Lord that my first Sabbath in Washington happened to be in the pulpit of Dr. Bartlet, where I, altogether unknown to myself, was pleading the cause before the Chief Secretary of the Government. He sent me fifty dollars for the Mission, invited me to lunch with his family, and gave me ample opportunity, by answers to many questions, to state all the case, and to deepen all round the growing interest in our Mission.

On the forenoon of the following Sabbath, I occupied the pulpit of Dr. Hamlin, and the President of the United States heard my story and appeal. Many Senators and Members of Congress, having matters thus rehearsed, were able to weigh the question carefully, before I made my official statement at all. The President declared himself quite frankly to be deeply interested, and willing to expedite in every possible way the negotiations with Britain. It emerged that in the British reply there was a new clause, empowering one of the contracting parties to license Traders, under certain circumstances, to sell Intoxicating Drinks. The President struck his pen through that clause, and at once returned it, insisting on its excision. Had Britain agreed to this, President Harrison would then have signed the Treaty. But, alas, week after week elapsed, and no reply came. A new Election took effect, and President Cleveland was installed at the White House.

My Advisory Committee in America now insisted that I must wait till the new Government's arrangements were all completed, and once more press my appeal. I resumed my work of addressing Public Meetings every week day, and Congregations every Sabbath Day, always sending, from the former, Petitions to the President and Congress regarding the proposed Prohibition on the Islands. I had also private interviews with many leading Politicians. To all I pointed out that, as America was now united with Britain in the Dual Protectorate of Fiji, we only sought the extension of prohibition on that Group to the Group of the New Hebrides.

Constantly engaged in these Mission interests, I planned my second visit to Washington to take place at the same time as the General Assembly of the Presbyterian Church of the United States. I had the honour to address it on Foreign Missions, and to preach before a number of Congregations during its sittings, for a very deep interest was manifested in the wondrous workings of God on the New Hebrides.

I was introduced to the new President, when the General Assembly went in procession to do him honour. Both he and Mrs. Cleveland welcomed me to America, and, a few days after, they invited me to lunch at the White House, privately, that they might question me freely regarding the Islanders and our work. They both seemed to me to be genuine followers of the Saviour, and sincerely interested in the salvation of the Heathen World.

The Presbyterian Assembly thereafter appointed a large Deputation of its leading men to accompany me in laying officially before the Government our grievance regarding Fire-Arms and Intoxicants, and pleading that the United States should unite with Britain in the prohibition of all trading with Natives in the same. In order to save time, and secure lucidity, Professor Hodge carefully prepared and read our statement. The President expressed himself as deeply interested, and requested the document to be left with him for reference. We anxiously awaited the result; but the final reply from Britain was still delayed. Our hearts grew sore with hope deferred!

In course of time I was informed at the British Colonial Office in London, that as France and Russia had withdrawn from the proposal, the negotiations were for the present suspended. France, for years, postured before the world as ready to enforce this prohibition, if America would; and now, when America was ready, France withdrew! Still, on the highest of all moral grounds, let us plead with America, Germany, and Britain, already united in their triple Protectorate of Samoa, to extend the same prohibition to the New Hebrides, and the other unannexed Islands in the Western Pacific. If they would do so, the other Powers interested could scarcely fail to agree, and France would be ashamed to stand before the world as the only Civilized Nation, exploiting the bodies and souls of poor Savages by trading with them in Fire-Arms and Drink for mere godless greed of gold!

In Boston, the Ministers of all the Reformed Churches, having formed a representative Committee, organized a series of meetings, and cordially invited me to address them. Dr. Joseph Cook and his gifted wife gave me a public reception, to which many of the leading Citizens, as well as Professional men, were invited, and where I answered all sorts of questions regarding Missions in general, and the New Hebrides in particular. I was also twice introduced to the audiences at his famous Monday Lectures; and my replies to testing problems, there submitted, were printed in *Our Day*, and woke not a little interest in the work of God amongst the Cannibals of the Southern Seas. To all these generous friends at Boston, I am for ever indebted, but very specially to John Gilchrist, Esq., an office-bearer in the Presbyterian Church, who toiled in the cause incessantly, and whom may the Lord Jesus richly recompense!

One curious experience befell me there, outside the range of my ordinary work. A "Temperance Union" of Women engaged me to address a Working Folks' Meeting on a Sabbath afternoon, in what they called the Peoples' Church. When I arrived, nearly half of the large Platform was occupied with ladies scraping away and tuning their violins, large and small!

A lady occupied the chair, and introduced Dr. Blank, a Unitarian or rather an Infidel, who was to speak for ten minutes, and then leave the meeting in my hands. He knew that I had to leave within an hour, and drive to another meeting, but he went on and on, tracing a Carpenter all through his life to exhausted old age, manifestly stirring up class against class, and sowing the seeds of infidelity. At last, he wound up by picturing the Carpenter, outworn and ready to die, sitting with his wife and children around the table at their evening meal, taking the bread and breaking it and saying: "Eat ye all of it, for this is my body broken for you; this do in remembrance of me, for I have worn out my life for your sakes." Whereon, his wife poured out the tea, and said: "If the bread is your body broken for us, this tea is my blood shed for you; drink ye all of it in remembrance of me, as I have spent my life in toiling for you."

Being able to stand it no longer, I turned to the ladies behind us and said aloud: "Who is this blasphemer that you have set up to speak to the people? He is simply belching out Infidelity, and setting man against man. This is a black disgrace to you all!" He paused a moment, and then said: "I wish this Congregation to understand that, in what I have just said about the Carpenter and his bread, I throw no slight on the name or memory of one who thus parted from his followers long ago"—and thereon he resumed his seat, having spoken for nearly the whole hour. Reply was impossible for lack of time, and my expected Address was crushed aside. But, ere I left the Platform, I uttered a few burning words, and the whole audience seemed to go with me. I denounced all setting of the poor against the rich, as alien to the spirit of Jesus. I branded as an insult to the Divine Saviour of the world the blasphemer's parody of the Lord's Supper, to which we had been treated. I warned these Temperance workers that, in bringing such a teacher of Abstinence before the people, they were degrading the cause which they desired to promote. And finally, I summoned them to remember that we must all appear before the Judgment Seat of Christ, and implored them, and Dr. Blank amongst the rest, to seek pardon and acceptance at the feet of

Jesus now, that they might find their Judge was also their Saviour in the last awful day! A hasty Benediction was pronounced, at the Chairwoman's request. I hurried from the Church, greatly shocked, but encouraged by the handshake and the "God bless you!" of many whom I passed. There was one small consolation which I unfeignedly enjoyed—the fiddling ladies had no opportunity of displaying their skill on that Lord's Day!

While I was in America many minds were being troubled with ideas regarding what is styled the "Second Probation." At one of his famous Monday Lectures, Dr. Joseph Cook put to me, on the Platform, the following amongst other questions : "How would Missionaries, teaching the Second Probation, succeed with the Cannibals on your Island?" My reply was : "How can they succeed on such terms anywhere? Our Cannibals would say,—If we have a second chance hereafter, let us enjoy our present pleasures and risk the future!" Again he asked : "How would Missionaries holding that doctrine, but promising not to teach it, succeed amongst them?" I replied : "Hypocrites are a poor set everywhere, but especially in the Mission Field. How could a man succeed in teaching what he did not believe? Cannibals, like Children, are quick to discern insincerity ; and such a man could do no good, but only evil amongst them." Joseph Cook and his like-minded wife appeared to be noble instruments in the hand of God, for the defence of truth and righteousness.

During this supplementary series of Meetings I happened to reach Chicago during the Great Exhibition. Dr. Macpherson greatly helped me, and arranged all my work. The City was crowded with visitors from all the World. There were many things in the Big Show that one would have liked to see ; but when I learned how its Directors, in violation of their agreement with the Government, opened it on Sabbath and turned the Lord's Day into a Saturnalia of sports and amusements, I positively declined to enter within its gates. They made a huge noise about accommodating the working men, but they really sought mere selfish gains. They filled the streets with advertising cars, with flags flying from each, announcing their theatres and shows, desecrating the Holy Day. Thank God such Heaven-defying conduct was condemned from many a Protestant Pulpit, and the Congregations warned against countenancing such a sinful and shameful Vanity Fair!

The Directors, having secured President Cleveland to open the Exhibition, desired him to go from Washington by special train on the Sabbath Day. Their plan was to utilize the occasion by enormous Excursions from all quarters on the Day of Rest. But the God-fearing Presbyterian President went with a usual train on Saturday, took up his residence at a Private Hotel, and showed his disapproval of their tactics by declining their projected ovation. On Sabbath morning he attended worship at Dr. Macpherson's Church. A Baptismal Service was intimated for the afternoon. The President again attended. He opened the Exhibition officially, but left the City as privately as he had come to it, and this rebuke was not misunderstood by the Community, and was greatly appreciated by decided Christians, to whom the rest of the Day of God is a Heavenly heritage for all the creatures of Earth, which no man may lawfully alienate or impair.

To a man like myself, the results brought a certain retribu-tive joy. The rush of Foreigners, after the first two or three Sabbaths, was soon over. Then it was discovered that the masses of the Working People of Chicago absented themselves on the Lord's Day, knowing well that it was not for their benefit that this thing was done, but merely to coin money out of them. Finding that, instead of a gain, the opening on the Sabbath was a deadly loss, the Managers proposed to close it, but found themselves tied hand and foot by their own past action at law. Conspicuously, the City suffered through the vices and crimes thereby fostered ; and will continue to suffer ; for such evil cannot be swept away with the temporary build-ings of the Exhibition. Doom seemed to overtake the authors speedily. One of the leaders was cruelly shot ; and the gates were at last closed in silence, and apparently in shame!

Very varied were the means adopted, by interested friends, to arrest attention on the New Hebrides, and create enthusiasm in their cause. One very memorable occasion was at Pittsburg, where J. I. Buchanan, Esq., gave a great dinner, to which he invited the Owners and Editors of all the local Newspapers, to meet the New Hebrides Missionary. After I had addressed them, they tackled me with questions regarding the Islanders, and on all conceivable aspects of work for Christ amongst Cannibals. Most of them got deeply interested; and, next day, the whole Press of the City was full of the Mission, and of the reasons for our seeking the Prohibition of Fire-Arms and Intoxicants as articles of trade amongst the Natives.

I had now visited the leading Towns in all the Northern States, and not a few on the borders of some of the Southern States, being everywhere received by Ministers and People with exceeding kindness and exceptional liberality. My next anxiety was to be present at the Assembly of the Canadian Presbyterian Church, and I therefore decided to leave the work undone, which was daily being pressed upon me throughout the States, and to hasten thither. This was surely of God's guidance; at least I reverently think so; for I reached the Assembly Hall, all unknown to myself, on the night of their Foreign Mission Report; and the first thing I heard was an "Overture" from Nova Scotia, urging the Assembly to hand over their three Missionaries on the New Hebrides to the Australian Churches, which were now "both able and willing to support them"!

The Assembly received me very cordially. The Moderator invited me to speak immediately after the Overture had been presented. I conveyed to them the greetings of our Church, and of our Synod on the Islands, and reported in general terms on the Home and Foreign Missions in Australasia. Then I turned to the Moderator, and asked on whose authority it was declared that the Australian Churches were both able and willing to take over the Nova Scotian Mission on the New Hebrides, with its annual cost of about £1300. The question was put to the Assembly. There was a significant silence for several moments, and then some one feebly replied: "On Dr. Geddie's." I retorted, that surely the author of the Overture was ashamed of it, when he sought to palm it on the honoured father of our Mission, now many years resting in his grave! I demonstrated, by irrefragable facts and figures, that the Australian Churches were in no position to undertake this additional expense; and, further, I insisted that to give up this specially-honoured Mission would be one of the greatest losses to the spiritual life of their own Congregations and Sabbath Schools. It was the Mother of all their Missions! It was the Mission which had wakened in them all the Missionary spirit they now possessed!

The Moderator emphatically protested, from the Chair, that he hoped the General Assembly "would hear no more of such a proposal." Yet the agitation is carried on, from what creditable motive it is very hard to see. The Editor of their *Mission Record*, with a few men of similar spirit at his back, seems to have determined to cut the connection betwixt Nova Scotia and the New Hebrides, and to close by violence one of the noblest chapters in that Church's history. They have written to the Australian Churches on the matter, and I venture to predict that their answers will be more emphatic than even my instantaneous protest. The nobler spirits in Nova Scotia ought to squelch out this miserable agitation, which is killing the Missionary enthusiasm and curtailing the liberality of their Church.

Surrounded by a multitude of devoted Ministers and Elders, I agreed to remain two months in Canada, and address as many Meetings every day of the week as could possibly be crowded into time and space. To relieve the pressure on Mission Funds in Nova Scotia, I offered to give up twenty days entirely to them, with all the proceeds from every Meeting. They received, I understand, above £500; and I trust that by my Addresses, one at least every day and four or five every Sabbath, all the Funds of all these Congregations prospered and continue to prosper; for I humbly and gratefully recognise the fact that God has used me not for one Mission but for all Missions, and not through one Church but through all His Churches.

The series of Meetings, up to Quebec, was mapped out at the Assembly, and the whole of the arrangements were entrusted to the Rev. J. W. Mitchell of Thorold, a man of deep devotion and of untiring zeal. Our Treasurer was A. K. Macdonald, Esq., Toronto, to whose kindness also we were profoundly indebted. Countless applications poured in upon us. It was no uncommon thing to address two or even three Meetings daily, and to travel long distances between them by conveyance and rail. On Sunday we delivered never less than three Addresses, but more frequently five, and sometimes even seven, including the Bible Classes and Sabbath Schools. It was dreadfully exhausting work. Sometimes I hesitated, fearing every day would be my last. But again my vigour returned, and my heart hungered to overtake all that I possibly could, knowing that the time was short. Besides, in this tour as always, the getting of Collections, however anxiously desired for our Mission, was never my primary aim; but always the saving of souls, by the story of the New Hebrides. For that cause I would gladly die. But I did not die; and there was given a new illustration of the meaning of that inspired saying —"The joy of the Lord is your strength"—the work, which is our *joy*, uplifts rather than oppresses us!

The incidents of these journeys would fill a goodly volume. But I had neither the leisure nor the inclination to record them day by day. One or two specially impressed themselves on my memory, however, and may here be glanced at.

On one occasion, after a long Railway ride, I found myself set down on the wrong side of a flooded River, the bridge having been swept away. The Station-Master pointed us to a boat, kept by a farmer, which, if we reached, might ferry us over. But two huge fields betwixt us and the spot were flooded with the overflow, and these had to be crossed. A young lady, a gentleman, and I, all equally eager to get to the other side, resolved to try. We waded to the Boat-Landing, and reached it in a very bedraggled state. There the boat had been left, awaiting some one's return, but the farmer was across the River. None of us felt very brave about the experiment of rowing across the racing current! Our fellow-traveller, nevertheless, resolved to try. Minimizing my warning about rowing a long way up in the quieter water, and then slanting across with the sweep of the current, he went up only a little, and quickly plunged in. His boat was whirled away like a cork. We held our breath, while the young farmer on the opposite bank kept shouting and gesticulating, running down the River, and guiding the rower as best he could. It was with a sigh of thankful relief that we saw the traveller stand up at last on the farther side, safe but badly shaken.

The farmer now took the oars in hand, and with his great strength and greater skill ferried first one and then the other across in safety, but not without peril. In a high light cart he mounted us and bore us securely across another field, through three feet of water if not more, and planted us gladly at his fireside. There the lady waited, that her dripping clothes might be dried, and the other traveller found his way to his desired haven. But, the hour of my Meeting having already arrived, I hastened to address them, with clothes soaked through and through, and was immediately thereafter driven to another town at a distance of several miles. Without any opportunity of proper refreshment, or of getting clothes dried or changed, I spoke for an hour and a-half to a large Public Meeting there, and then retired for the night. My clothes were hung up to dry. I had to start by train very early next morning. When I dressed, the damp of yesterday's drenching still hung about them, and made me shiver. For two days my bones and muscles felt very sore, and the dread of severe rheumatic fever hung over me. But I sustained myself with the assurance that the Great Physician would take care of me, since none of this had been brought on by selfish pleasure, or self-willed obstinacy, but in devotion to His Will and in doing His work. I suffered no further harm, and carried through all the Meetings, praising Jesus my Saviour.

On another occasion I was for a time seriously perplexed. A kind Minister drove me, after conducting several Meetings under his charge, to join the Night Train at a lonely crossing. Arrangements had been made at Headquarters to set me down, pick me up, and set me down again at such places, in order to reach certain Meetings, and thence go on my way to others, with the least possible loss of time. Being duly despatched by my friend, I was set down, in the darkness, at such a crossing, where was neither sight of any house, nor sound of any human being. The Guard, in manifest pity, exclaimed, "I don't know, sir, what you can do here! I am extremely sorry to leave you. But, for God's sake, keep off the line. The Express follows. The rails are wet, and you might never hear her! Someone will surely meet you. Good-bye!"

His Train soon disappeared into the darkness. I tried to

rest, sitting on my travelling bag, but it was too cold, and rain began to fall. Marching about to keep up the circulation, I kept hallooing as loudly as I could every few moments, but no sound came in reply. Worn out and greatly disheartened, I at last put both hands to my mouth and began the Australian *Koo-ee! Koo-ee!* and sustained it with all the breath and strength I possessed. By-and-bye, in the pauses, I heard a faint and far reply, like the echo of my own voice. It drew nearer and nearer in response to my cry, and at last grew into the salutation of a glad human voice. It was the Minister, appointed to meet me, who now emerged out of the darkness. There were two crossings in the district, and they had left me at the wrong one! He had tied his horse to the fence, and followed my cries through the night. We stumbled our way back, and were ere long welcomed to his cosey Manse; and I tucked myself into a warm bed as soon as possible. Not without praising our Heavenly Guide, I soon fell into a deep and sweet sleep, and felt able next Sabbath morning for any amount of Meetings. The Holy Day proved to be exceptionally busy, and exceptionally happy; for I was with a good and true Minister of Jesus Christ, and that transforms all work into joyful fellowship.

Once the shaft of our engine broke, and the train stood still. The Guard advised all the passengers to leave and take to the fields across the fence. I decided to stick by the train. A messenger started on the rails behind and another in front, and each ran with all his might, waving the red flag and shouting. But the Engineers never lost their heads for a moment. They screwed and hammered and chiselled; they unloosed one part and pitched it up among the coals; they fixed and adjusted another, in the most mysterious ways, as it seemed to me. And in a very short time, to the delight and amazement of all, that train began to move slowly ahead, and crept on steadily to the nearest Station, one side of the engine only being in working order. The alarm of all was very great, as an Express was due behind us and might any moment have crashed upon the scene. "Our Father knoweth."

At another time I was travelling, by rail, a great distance *to* address a Mid-Day Meeting. Only one hour was free, and then I must join another train. Two or three Stations before reaching the former destination, a gentleman surprised me, exclaiming, "Dr. Paton, here is your Lunch! You will not have a minute for food either before or after the Meeting. Leave the jug and plates at any Station, and they will be returned. Good-bye and God bless you!" I looked on this excellent meal with very curious sensations, as if it had dropped to me out of the Hand that feeds the ravens; and I prayed my Saviour to bless the good-hearted giver.

I may here record that this period of my life was fuller of constant stir and excitement, rushing from Meeting to Meeting, and from Town to Town, than any other through which, heretofore, I had ever passed, without one single day of rest, or almost an hour of breathing space. I do not think it is exaggeration to say that, on an average, during these months, I must have addressed ten Meetings on the ordinary days of the week and five every Sunday. I certainly know that, during many special weeks, the numbers far exceeded these. Blessed be God, who so marvellously sustained me through it all. When my throat got a little husky, my only medicine was a sip of pure Glycerine, a little bottle of which I always carried with me. My daily diet was always, by choice, the simplest and homeliest food which I could obtain—a plate of porridge with milk, a cup of tea with bread and butter, and a very moderate amount of flesh meat of any kind, often for days together none at all. And my only stimulant was—the ever-springing fountain of pure joy in the work of my Lord and Saviour Jesus Christ!

One thing was at first a great worry to me, but at length solved itself very happily. I cannot, with any conscience, use cars, cabs, trains, or steamboats on the Lord's Day, except under such an emergency of "necessity or mercy," that my Lord, if He met me on the way, would declare me "blameless." On beginning in America, it was enforced on me from every quarter that I must use these conveyances on the Sabbath, owing to enormous distances, or find my mission an utter failure. My one answer was: "No working man or woman shall ever accuse me at the Bar of God for needlessly depriving them of their Day of Rest, and imperilling or destroying their highest welfare." Shoulders were shrugged knowingly, heads shaken rather pityingly, and gentle appeals made to yield for the sake of the higher interests of the Mission. But I held my ground unfalteringly. It became known that I would not use such conveyances, and that I sturdily trudged from Meeting to Meeting on foot, all through the Lord's Day. Immediately the private carriages of friends of Jesus and His Mission were placed largely at our disposal; and, in all cases, I pled for such arrangements as gave the horse its rest, and the man his opportunity of worship. Whensoever I was necessitated to hire for the Lord's Day, it was invariably so planned that not only was proper food duly provided for man and beast, but the driver was invited and encouraged to join in the Service of the House of God. I pray my Lord to accept my life-long testimony and practice on this supremely important matter, and to use it for the preservation of the blessed Day of Rest as the inalienable heritage of all His toiling creatures,—next to the gift of His own Son, one of the most priceless of all His boons to the Human Race!

The time had come that I must say farewell to Canada and the States. It was the first time I had ever seen these new and marvellous Lands. My soul was not unaware of their beauties, nor unresponsive to their grandeur of scenery. But my whole time and strength were otherwise required; and I turned not aside from the call of my Lord. He knows that my heart rejoices in all the wonders of His Power, not the less that I spend myself in proclaiming the greater wonders of His Grace. All my recollections of intercourse with the Ministers and the People of the New World are abidingly sweet, and move me to bless the Lord for the God-fearing, Bible-loving, and Sabbath-keeping Nations that have sprung from our British Race. From the highest to the humblest they received me with royal welcome, and heard me with loyal sympathy. Their help was generous, and was gladly given. Their interest in the work of God was genuine, and was frankly displayed. And their delight in listening to the story of the salvation of the South Sea Cannibals, made me firm in the assurance that they themselves already know within their own souls the unspeakable worth of Jesus!

CHAPTER II.

THE HOME-LANDS AND THE ISLANDS.

A.D. 1894—1897.   ÆT. 70—73.

Arrival in Great Britain.—Requisitions.—Professors and Students.—*Day-spring* Scheme.—Ten Years' Delay.—Gideon's Fleece Experiment. —Two Memorable Cheques.—The "John G. Paton Mission Fund." —The *Dayspring* Disaster.—Mission Work on all the Islands.

I EMBARKED from New York for Liverpool, per the new and magnificent s.s. *Campania.* The vibrations of that vessel were more fearful than anything I had ever experienced in all my travels. There was some defect, which I hear has since been remedied. I was scarcely conscious of ever sleeping at all, and the ship seemed to be constantly on the eve of shaking herself into fragments! On the voyage I made the acquaintance of very dear friends, bearing my own name; whose Home at Liverpool by-and-bye received me lovingly; and where also I met the learned and honoured Principal Paton of Nottingham.

My arrival in Britain revealed to me, immediately and amazingly, how times had changed since my previous visit, only ten years before. *Then* I had many difficulties to face in arranging for public meetings, especially in England, as set forth in a previous Chapter. Many a weary day's tramping I had, even in Scotland where something was known about the Mission to the New Hebrides, passing from Minister to Minister, and pleading, frequently all in vain, for the use of their Pulpits and for access to their Congregations. But since then, by my brother's insistence, the story of my life had gone through the Land in my *Autobiography*. I was no longer treated as a stranger, but as the dearly beloved friend of everyone who had read my book. Blessed be God, who used it for His glory, and gave our Mission appeal everywhere an open door, such as never in my most hopeful hours had my faith even dreamed !

Now, hundreds of invitations poured in on my British Committee, all Honorary Helpers who grudged no amount of labour and pains. I found a Series of Meetings already arranged for me, covering the principal towns and cities of the United Kingdom,—Mr. Watson of Belfast taking charge in Ireland, Mr. Langridge in England, and my brother James, with his Honorary Secretary, arranging for Scotland, and acting as General Director of the Mission. When those had been fairly overtaken, the additional applications had risen to several hundreds more than could possibly be faced, unless I prolonged my stay for years. My Committee at one time found themselves dealing with a mass of 500 invitations ! A selection had to be made of the more important and populous centres for the Services on the Lord's Day, and one or two Meetings each day during the week in the smaller surrounding towns ; but even then the disappointments were many and grievous ; and not more so to them than to me ; for I did passionately desire to tell every human being the story of the Gospel on the New Hebrides, that other and still other souls might be won thereby for Jesus my Lord.

One very precious feature of my tour was this :—the manner in which Ministers and Christian workers of all the Churches united to welcome me, and gave very practical support to this Presbyterian Mission. Frequently, the invitation was signed by all the Ministers of the district, excepting only the Roman Catholic ; and my prayers rose daily to my Lord that my humble presence might be one of the means in His loving hand of paving the way for a closer union amongst the Members of His Redeemed Flock. I was much touched by the requisition that came to me from my well-beloved Dumfries, with the names of all the Ministers, and full of tender references to my early associations with the Queen of the South, as in our boyhood we loved to call her !

The Congregations, on week days not less than on Sabbaths, filled the largest Public Halls and Churches in each locality ; with frequent overflow Meetings, at which I had to speak for fifteen minutes or so, and then leave them in the hands of others, whilst I drove or ran to the principal Meeting, now opened and awaiting my Address. During the two years of my Tour, I addressed very nearly 1400 audiences, ranging from a few hundreds to five and six thousand each, and in doing so I travelled over many thousands of miles, on foot and in every kind of conveyance that is used in the English-speaking world.

The Chairmen at my various Meetings represented every type of Christian worker, and all social grades, from the godly Tradesman, evangelizing in his quiet Mission Hall, up through Ministers and Mayors, Provosts and Members of Parliament, Bishops and Archbishops, to Lords and Dukes and other Peers of the Realm. Under this rush of the Missionary Spirit, many conventional barriers were broken down, so that I was, even on Sunday, invited to give my Address from the very Pulpit in Episcopal Churches, as for example in the Pro-Cathedral at Manchester. On week days, this was a not infrequent experience.

These things, and all my opportunities of usefulness, thus unexpectedly thrust upon me, at the close of a long life of toil and self-denial and sacrifice for Jesus, I devoutly laid at His feet, and implored Him to use me only for His glory. And I can truly say that I never felt more deeply humbled, all my days, than at the close of some of those almost unparalleled Missionary Meetings, when I was alone with my Saviour after all was over, and thinking of my lowly Home and all the way by which the God of my father had led me, from these hours of hardship to this day of triumph. Fame and influence laid me lower and lower yet, at the feet of Jesus, to whose grace alone everything was due.

Never were these feelings more present with me than when I was called upon to tell the story of our Mission before the learned Professors and eager Students, at so many Universities, Colleges, Theological Halls, and similar Institutes. I have a note of at least sixty-three Seats of Learning, including Princeton and the most famous Colleges in America, as well as Oxford and Edinburgh, Cambridge and Glasgow at Home, where some of the greatest living Masters in every department, such as my own world-famous Professor, the now venerable Lord Kelvin,

listened to my testimony as to the power of the Gospel to make
new Creatures of the South Sea Cannibals and build them up
into the likeness of Jesus Christ.   I trespassed not into *their*
spheres, where I would have been a child and an ignoramus
compared with them ; and they, on the other hand, treated *me*
with profound respect, and even occasionally with demonstrative
appreciation, in that sphere of the moral and spiritual, the work
of the Christ-Spirit and its influence on the lowest and most
degraded of human beings, wherein I had some right to speak
with authority.   This was my " one " talent, in the presence of
such men ; and I " traded " with it, that the Name of my Saviour
might be honoured more and more, in the Halls of Letters, and
in the Temples of Art and Science.

By the general desire of my fellow-Missionaries on the New
Hebrides, I had visited Britain ten years before, for the express
purpose of raising if possible £5000 for a new *Dayspring*,
larger than the old, and with Steam Auxiliary Power.   By the
blessing of God on my humble pleading, and very largely in
direct answer to prayer, for I called on no one privately for
donations, there came to us in twelve months the large sum of
£10,000, of which more than one half reached us by post.
My Church in Victoria, to whom I rendered an account of all,
set apart £6000 for the new Mission Vessel, the interest to be
added to capital till such time as she might be built ; while the
remaining £4000 were devoted to the obtaining and supporting
of additional Missionaries for the New Hebrides.

But a new difficulty had emerged, and created not only delay
all these years, but no small measure of regrettable dissension ;
and that was how to maintain the Ship, and keep her floating
in the service of the Mission ; for the *Dayspring*, not being
allowed to trade, had been wholly maintained by the Sabbath
Schools of the Churches having Missionaries on the New
Hebrides.   The sum which they had raised annually, each
Church in its allotted proportion, amounted to £1500, or
rather more ; and it was manifest that the Steam Auxiliary
would cost at least £1000 extra per annum.   Unfriendly
critics doubled that charge, and some prophesied even treble ;
but level-minded experts limited it to £1000, and the actual
facts of experience, as to cost of maintaining the *Morning Star*

and the *Southern Cross*, in these same Pacific Seas, tallied with their estimates.

The burning question, therefore, had been how to raise this *extra* sum for *Dayspring* Maintenance. Our Victorian Church proposed to increase her quota from £500 to £750, and issued appeals to the other co-operating Churches to make a similar advance. It did not seem too much to expect, in the interests of the Mission, all whose operations had trebled since the original responsibility was allocated; but they pled inability to comply, and so the project hung fire for ten years and more, experiments being meanwhile made in other arrangements for the Maritime Service of the Mission, and new interests of various kinds being thereby created, which have not tended to unity and peace in the management of the New Hebrides. There is peril also incurred to the highest spiritual interests of the Mission, which I daily pray God, in His loving-kindness and mercy, to be pleased to avert!

Without ascribing anything but the most ordinary motives in the world to those who opposed the getting of a new *Dayspring*, the situation that thus grew up is perfectly transparent. The Australian New Hebrides Company was employed to do the work of our Mission by their Trading Ships. In 1895—*e.g.*, we paid to them the large sum of £2451, 8s. 1d.; all found money, for, without us, these Ships in their outgoing trip to the Islands would have sailed comparatively empty. To secure a Ship of our own would be, therefore, to deprive the Company of this handsome subsidy; and it is but Human Nature, and implies no necessary dishonour, that the shareholders and their Ministerial and Missionary friends should have become the keenest and even bitterest opponents of the new *Dayspring*. Further, the headquarters of the Company being at Sydney, and the subsidy for our Mission, as well as the money for the upkeep of our Missionaries and their families, being consequently expended almost exclusively there, it is, from the world's point of view, equally natural to anticipate that the very heart and centre of the opposition has been in New South Wales, and has concentrated itself in the Advisory Committee which sits at Sydney and is known as *The Dayspring Board.* All this, I say, was only to be expected, if the whole transaction is to be weighed and measured by the standards of men of the World, instead of being put into the balances of Jesus Christ, and estimated in the light of the spiritual and eternal interests of the Islanders whom He has committed to our care.

With great plausibility, this selfish opposition sought to commend itself to a wider circle by a Patriotic plea. If we did not support the Trading Company, it would fail, and the French might come on the scene and annex the New Hebrides! The facts of history were forgotten or ignored, with their ominous lesson, that other influences than trade must be brought into action to save these Islands from France. Did the tide of British trade, on the Loyalty Islands, on Madagascar, and the like, prevent their annexation by France? Certainly not! True, it will be a terrible calamity, not only to our Mission but to Australasia, if France is permitted to annex the New Hebrides; but, while she is openly preparing the way for that fatal step, Britain and her Colonies mock at all our warnings, and treat the whole matter with indifference, if not contempt. New South Wales and Victoria have even withdrawn those modest subsidies from Colonial Trading Ships, whereby their Governments might have continued to manifest some little desire to save the New Hebrides from the maw of Popish France!

Even if the horror of French Annexation were to overtake us, it might be rationally contended that our Mission, instead of being implicated with the existence of a rival Trading Company, would receive more favourable consideration, if we had a Steam Auxiliary Ship devoted entirely to spiritual services, ministering to, say, twenty-four Mission Families, with their Lay Assistants and all belongings and dependents.

But, after all, such reasonings do not even touch the very heart of the matter; and men who never go deeper than these cannot understand our aims, and are in no position to criticise them, however loudly they may abuse or oppose us. It is the spiritual and eternal welfare of our poor Islanders that is at stake, in the question of *Dayspring* or no *Dayspring;* at least that is my immovable conviction, and, apart from that, no argument on the other side has or can have much consideration at my hands. With a Mission Ship of our own, for the

New Hebrides, as for every other Mission in these Pacific seas, we can visit our Stations, as the interests of God's work may require; we can visit and cheer the Native Teachers at their lonely outposts amongst Heathen Villages; we can deliberately visit and open up Pioneer Stations, where Heathenism still reigns, and plant there our young Missionaries and their Helpers; we can dissociate our Ship and her crew from the drunkenness, profligacy, and profanity of the ordinary crews of Trading Vessels; we can prevent the sale of Fire-Arms and Intoxicants, in barter with the Natives; and, in a single word, we can make the Mission Ship, in all her ways and surroundings, an adjunct to the work of the Missionary, and a herald of the Kingdom of God among the Islanders, alike on God's Day of Rest, and on every day of the week—and all this in a manner and to a degree, that is not within human possibility if we be deprived of our own *Dayspring*, and thrown back upon ordinary Trading Ships. This, and this alone, goes to the bottom of the whole controversy.

Consequently, the men who opposed us never seriously denied what we here affirm, or attempted to answer our arguments. On the contrary, they practically gave away the whole case by perilling everything on the question of expense. All we urged might be unassailably true, but the cost was prohibitory! The money could not be raised, or, if it could, it would be positively sinful to spend so much on such a Mission! My blood often tingled to my finger tips, to hear this urged by self-indulgent and purse-proud men, who spent every year, on the pleasures of this perishing life, more than all that was required for the *Dayspring* and the four and twenty Mission Families, and the hundred thousand New Hebrideans, to whom she was to minister as the white-winged Servant of the Gospel of Jesus. Nor was my mood much calmer when this same thing was urged by Ministers and Office-Bearers of the Church, at Home and in the Colonies, who carry on their labours amidst the inspiring surroundings and associations of their happier lot; who criticise Missions and their management from the safe and cosey retreat of their libraries and armchairs; who by post and telegraph are in touch with those most dear to them every day, yea, every hour; and many of whom never denied

themselves one of the necessities of life, nor one of their own
perhaps foolish luxuries, for the sake of the Lord Jesus and
His cause,—never allowed themselves to suffer, even to the
extent of one poor pennyworth, even for the length of one
passing day, for the love they bore to God or to their
fellows. I fear that I am an impatient reasoner, when
creatures of this type cross my path. Alas, they too much
abound, to the shame of the Church, and for the scorn of the
World !

Coming back, therefore, to Britain, with these ten years of
delay to be accounted for, I did in all my Addresses frankly
avow, that, in my judgment the main obstacle, if not the only one,
was the lack of this extra £1000 per annum for Maintenance.
Friends on every side started up, and thrust upon me the
proposal, that those who had subscribed the money to build
the Ship were quite willing to subscribe yearly to assist
in maintaining her. I took the whole matter to my Lord in
special prayer. It was borne in upon me to let the proposal be
fully known, and I felt myself bound to conclude that if, in a
spontaneous way, the sum of £1000 were provided, with any
hope of permanent interest, to renew it from year to year, *that*
would be to me at least the demonstration of the Gideon's
Fleece, that God, who had through His people presented the
Ship to our Mission, was opening up a way for her yearly
Maintenance.

A Circular Letter on the *Dayspring* Maintenance Fund was
accordingly drawn up, and issued to all correspondents and
supporters by my British Committee. Certificates for Three-
Penny Shares in the *Dayspring*, to be renewed annually, were
widely circulated in Sabbath Schools. And, without further
organization or appeal, the answer to our prayers was almost
instantaneously forthcoming. My Honorary Treasurer had the
needed £1000 already paid, and sufficient promises for the
immediate future. We were empowered to promise this for
Maintenance, if the *Dayspring* were duly placed on the scene.
If not, the money was to be returned to the donors, or by them
allocated to other departments of the Mission enterprise. If,
in all this, we had not the guidance of God, I know not how to
trace His hand !

Other Providential signs were not awanting. I called one day, at Liverpool, on a generous Christian gentleman, to thank him personally for a sum of £50 sent to the Mission. The thought or purpose of seeking more money from him had never once entered my brain! He questioned me carefully about the needs of the Mission, the accommodation of the proposed Ship, and all our plans. Then he closed our interview thus: "I am convinced that you cannot buy or build a sufficient Mission Vessel for £6000, and I wish you to add this in order to secure a larger and a better Ship." He handed me his cheque for £1000! In tears of joy, I thanked God and His dear servant, but hinted something about preferring it rather for the first year's Maintenance Fund, but he repeated that this was to secure a larger and a better Ship, adding: "Receive this as from God, and the other will come also."

Again, my dear friend Lord Overtoun, who had presided over two Meetings that were addressed by me, entered one morning into a Railway Car by which I was travelling, and sat down beside me. At the close of a happy and very friendly conversation, he added: "Lady Overtoun and I gave you £200 towards the building of the Mission Ship; and now, after talking the matter over, we have resolved to give you £100 per annum for five years to help to pay for her Maintenance."

My soul overflowed with praise to God, and with thanks to those whose hearts were thus in His keeping. To me, and to all my fellow-Helpers, it seemed to be plainly the will of the Lord. We reverently believed that this was God's doing, and no mere plan of ours. He had given the *Dayspring* in a present to the New Hebrides; and now He had provided for her Maintenance. We were convinced at that time, and, despite all that has happened since, we are still convinced, that the Divine voice was infallibly saying, Go forward!

I returned to Victoria in the autumn of 1894. To the Assembly of the Presbyterian Church at Melbourne I gave my first public account of my Tour Round the World as their Missionary and Representative. At the close of my address, I handed to the Moderator a cheque for £12,527, 4s. 2d., as the fruit of the Collections and Donations at my Public Meetings

—the offerings of the people of God from all these lands, to be used for completing the evangelization of the New Hebrides. To this I added a deposit of £1000,—part of the profits of my book, but for the time locked up in our Australian Banks. As this money all came to me through those Congregations and Assemblies which I addressed as Missionary Representative of the Church in Victoria, I regarded it as belonging to my Church and as placed entirely under their control. I had no right to exercise any further authority over it, save only thus far, that it could not honourably be spent in any other way than on the New Hebrides Mission. The donors had again and again protested that they wanted to hear me on that Mission and on nothing else—that they had many other opportunities of giving to the other great Missions in India, China, and Africa, and that what they gave through me was for the New Hebrides. I handed over the money; I delivered their message; and there, so far, my responsibility ceased.

But that sum, vast as it may seem, represented only half the generosity of the Churches of Britain and America during these three fruitful years. Side by side with Public Collections and the like, another stream of liberality had been constantly flowing. The readers of my *Autobiography*—now published not only in a single volume Popular Edition, and in an Edition for Young Folks, but even in a Penny Edition, which circulated in tens of thousands, especially in connection with my Lectures and Addresses—responded liberally to the appeal of my British Committee, and poured donations into their hands or mine, almost entirely by post, till, from readers of my book alone, *The John G. Paton Mission Fund (see Appendix* F.), gave me on leaving a cheque for £12,000. These donations were placed entirely at my personal disposal, under one condition only—that I must use them for the extension of Mission work on the New Hebrides. For the management of this sum, I obtained the sanction of the General Assembly to the preparation of a legal Deed. It is held by the Finance Committee of the Victorian Church, under those conditions,—that I only can operate on it for the extension of the work of God on the New Hebrides, while I live; and that after my decease they can use it, but only for these same purposes; thus fulfilling, as faithfully as may be, the wishes of those Christian souls who sent this money to me from all corners of the world.

In addition to these two large branches of our *General Fund*, there had come to myself or to my British Committee very considerable sums for Special Funds. Notably these two:— the *Native Teachers' Fund*, designed to pay a small yearly salary, formerly of £6, but now beginning at that figure and after two years' faithful service rising to £8, to each of those Converts to whom God had given the capacity and the call to become Helpers to the Missionary in School and Church, and in many cases Pioneers of the Cross where no white Missionary had ever gone: and also, the *Dayspring Maintenance Fund*, already referred to and described. The latter of these two was, of course, retained in the hands of the British Committee at my call, till such time as the Churches and the Mission Synod decided for or against a Mission Vessel. The former they continue to administer, at my direction and under my sanction, through one of the Missionaries on the Islands, who acts as their treasurer and agent. So far as the annual donations will allow, we freely grant to every Missionary all the assistance in our power for the training and maintaining of these Native Evangelists, many of whom are destined to become the future Pastors of the people. Up till now our difficulty has been to find enough of suitable and reliable Native Teachers to be allocated to the Churches, Bible Classes, Sunday Schools, and individual Christians, willing to support them. But we hope for great things from the TRAINING COLLEGE recently opened on Tangoa under Dr. Annand, one of our ablest and most devoted Missionaries ; and my British Committee have undertaken to pay the salary of his Assistant, £150 per annum, with my cordial approval. Many prayers are uplifted daily for this Missionary Institute on the New Hebrides, at the very heart and centre of these Cannibal Isles, that the Lord God would own it and send forth thence trained and consecrated Evangelists to build up and to rule the New Hebridean Church of Christ in the days that are to be,—no longer under European tutelage, but under Native Pastors. We would glory to lead on to that consummation, and then to pass to other fields of labour !

It is but right for me to mention, though most readers

are already aware of it, that all my Helpers and Fellow-Workers at Home and in America give their time and strength freely and gladly, without thought of any reward except the joy of the service. All actual outlays incurred in the on-carrying of the various schemes are, of course, met out of what we call the *General Fund;* but every other penny, that comes to them or to me, goes directly to the extension of the Gospel on the New Hebrides. Each donation or subscription is acknowledged in our little quarterly magazine known as *Jottings,* a copy of which is posted to all our correspondents and supporters, and which is now the bond whereby God keeps us together and sustains our interest in this work—another development, not so much of our seeking, as rather thrust upon us by the necessities of the work of the Lord, which so increased that my Helpers could in no other way overtake the correspondence, or circulate the Mission news so eagerly desired. It is thus that those who unfeignedly seek to serve are led on by the Master Himself. The Pillar of Cloud and Fire still marches before us; but, alas, how many have lost the power to behold it!

I praise God every day of my life for all these dear supporters and correspondents, far scattered in every Land, but one in heart for the salvation of the New Hebrides. Through their generosity, my British Committee with my joyful approval have undertaken, in addition to the support of Native Teachers and the subsidy for Maintenance of *Dayspring,* to defray the entire cost of two Missionaries and their wives, and also two Lay European Assistants. Nay, if the generosity of friends should continue, they are at the moment of my writing hopefully contemplating the support of a third Missionary, with, if possible, a Lay Assistant also. These are surely God-honouring fruits from the planting of my humble book in hearts that love the Lord, and from the zeal and devotion and extraordinary gifts of our Honorary Organizing Secretary—with whom, and with all our Helpers everywhere, we reverently say, Glory to God and not unto us!

Our loving God orders everything well. But for that Fund handed over by me to the Victorian Church, I know not what would have become of the New Hebrides Mission during the intervening years, since the crash of our Australian Banks and the consequent terrible financial depression. Thousands and tens of thousands of our people were literally ruined. Money could not be obtained, even for the ordinary and inevitable expenses of our Congregations. Ministers' stipends were, on almost every hand, temporarily reduced. The Foreign Mission Committee's income fell so terribly, that nearly everything was consumed in meeting the claims of the Mission to the Aborigines and to the Chinese. In 1895 the contributions to the *Dayspring Fund* fell in Victoria from £500 to £200, and even that was raised with difficulty. In fact, but for our Fund, the salaries of several of the Missionaries and Native Teachers would of necessity have been cancelled, and our forces withdrawn from the field. God be praised, that calamity was averted! All our Army for Jesus have been maintained at their posts; nay, additional Pioneers have actually, despite these depressions, gone forth and pierced the Kingdom of Darkness here and there with shafts of Gospel light.

On my return to Victoria all these schemes, and particularly the new proposals as to the *Dayspring*, were fully laid before the General Assembly of the Presbyterian Church at Melbourne. Though the Ship was offered as a free gift to the Mission, and the additional £1000 *per annum* was now provided, without laying one farthing of financial burden on them or on any of the Churches concerned, yet our Victorian Church resolved to proceed with great deliberation, and to carry, if possible, the approval of all parties concerned. They entered into correspondence with each of the seven other Churches co-operating in the New Hebrides, and with each of the Missionaries on the Islands, and agreed to instruct the building of the Ship only if all, or a clear majority, cordially approved. More than ten years ago, all had sanctioned the raising of the money for a new and larger Steam Auxiliary Ship, and that sanction had never been withdrawn. But many things had happened since then; and it was at least brotherly and considerate, if not absolutely obligatory, to confer with them all ere proceeding further.

The vast majority of the Missionaries at once re-affirmed their approval of the scheme. All the Churches concerned, except one, either cordially approved or left the matter to the free decision of the Australasian Churches and the Missionaries on the field, in which decision they intimated that they would heartily concur. The one exception was the Church of New South Wales, influenced, as already indicated, by its close association with the Trading Company, though doubtless from motives entirely honourable, so far as individuals were concerned. What is known as *The Dayspring Board*, with its headquarters at Sydney, was also strongly opposed, and for similar reasons, too manifest to need specification here. But I cannot regard the opposition of that Board as either defensible or requiring to be taken into account at all. It is simply an Advisory Committee. It neither raises any money for the Ship nor for the Mission. It is the Executive, at most, of the Mission Synod and the Churches concerned; and its proper and only function is to carry out, in a helpful and business-like way, the instructions received from the Missionaries. It is absurd, therefore, that such a Board should have any vote on the question of a *Dayspring* or no *Dayspring*, any more than would a paid Agent executing the orders of the Missionaries for articles of merchandise. A delicate sense of honour should have made them feel this, and act accordingly, instead of becoming, as they did, not only avowed opponents of the scheme, but, in some cases, even bitter partisans and unscrupulous antagonists. For myself, I frankly say that the opposition of a Board so constituted should not only be discounted, but should be wholly ignored.

The Victorian Church, therefore, through its Foreign Mission Committee, ordered the *Dayspring*. She was built by Messrs. Mackie & Thomson on the Clyde, under the instructions and the personal supervision of John Stephen, Esquire, of Linthouse. Better, more skilled, more reliable advice could not be obtained in Britain. It was all gratuitously and ungrudgingly given for the sake of the Mission, and we felt deeply indebted for the same. The new Steam Auxiliary *Dayspring*, on her completion, was exhibited to friends, subscribers, and Sabbath Scholars, at Glasgow, at Ayr, at Belfast, at Douglas, and at Liverpool. Thousands upon thousands of people flocked to see the little Missionary Ship, and to wish her God-speed. She was universally admired. The Public Press commented on her trim appearance, substantial workmanship, and perfect adaptation to the service for which she was destined. She had been built and equipped within the £7000 set apart for her construction. She had every necessary accommodation for Officers and Crew, for Missionaries and their Families, and for Native Teachers; and when she sailed away from Liverpool, the representatives of my British Committee, upon whom had lain the heavy burden of all the details, praised God that the plans and toils of so many years had at last been brought to so auspicious an issue. It marked the beginning of a new era, it was hoped, in the Conversion of the New Hebrides, and the little Ship was borne away on the wings of prayer and praise!

She performed the Ocean voyage to the highest satisfaction of all her Officers. At Melbourne she was welcomed with much enthusiasm. On her first trip to the Islands, the hearts of our Natives thrilled with great joy at the sight of their own Gospel Ship. On her second visit, her powers and capacities were most severely tested, and her adaptability to the needs of the Mission. She had to call at all our Stations, and carry up to Aneityum all the members of the Mission for the Annual Synod in the month of May. She had on board fifty passengers, forty adults, and ten children, exclusive of the Native Teachers and their families, and, after the Synod, she had to carry all these back again to their several scattered Stations. It was the unanimous and decided opinion of all concerned, that, during no previous Synod Trip under any service, had we ever enjoyed the same comfort and the same happiness. There was thanksgiving, on every hand. The dissensions of the past were buried. The Mission Synod had now their own Ship; and they unitedly resolved to turn her to the best possible account in the Cause of Jesus and for the speedy Evangelizing of the New Hebrides. Our hearts were at rest. We turned aside to other labours, thanking God that in all this many prayers had been answered, many tears had borne precious fruit. The *Dayspring* was the crown and complement of our Missionary Enterprise for the salvation of these Islands—God bless her!

Our dear little Mission Ship performed her third trip also with perfect safety, and with much satisfaction to all the Missionaries. Her new Captain, who had formerly been her first

Officer, and who in his earlier days had sailed these same Seas in the *Southern Cross*, was a great favourite alike amongst the Missionaries and the Natives; thoroughly capable, firm yet gentle, deserving and commanding universal respect. The Ship had, as the result of experience, been in some matters overhauled and re-adjusted, to meet special requirements; and her fourth Voyage was entered upon with hope and joy. She was loaded with provisions for the Missionaries and their Families, with wood for the building of their Houses and Schools, and with whatsoever was most urgently required by them for three months to come. So that at every Station, on every Island, the eyes of our beloved Missionaries and their Converts were eagerly looking out across the Seas for the flag of the dear little *Dayspring*.

Alas, they looked in vain! She struck on an uncharted reef, not far from New Caledonia,—a disaster against which no skill and no experience could guard, in those not yet thoroughly explored and ever-changeful Seas. Her Officers and Crew did everything that men could do to save her, and struggled on till all hope had perished. With sore hearts, they at last provisioned and manned the two boats, and committed themselves to the deep—agreeing on certain general lines of action, that, please God, they might again come together and be rescued. In a very short time, after they had withdrawn, a high wind and a heavy sea working together completed her destruction, and they beheld the dear little *Dayspring* plunging head-foremost from the reef into the Sea, and disappearing, masts and all, within the hungry Ocean.

The Captain's boat ran to an island for safety, and was, ere long, picked up, and he and all his men safely returned to Australia. The other boat had a dreadful voyage. More than once she was overturned, and left them all struggling in the Sea. For fourteen days and nights, without almost any food, without any possibility of rest, bareheaded in a broiling sun, the poor fellows endured suffering and untold distress; till, at length, by a well-nigh miraculous Providence, they ran ashore on the coast of Queensland, and were saved. Blessed be God, though our dear little *Dayspring*, with all her belongings, her Library, her Mission Harmonium, Lord Kelvin's magnificent

Compass, and the books, the furnishings, and the food of our beloved Missionaries, lay sleeping in the Ocean's bed—no father's or mother's heart was wrung with the memory of some precious Son buried with her there.   We were all spared that agony, and we continue to praise God that the wreck of the *Dayspring* cost not a single human life.

It does not need that I should inform the Reader of the preceding pages that this wreck was, in all the circumstances, one of the bitterest sorrows of my life.   I am not ashamed, considering my views of its spiritual value as the Handmaid of the Gospel in completing Christ's Mission on the New Hebrides, to confess that I showed as much emotion, though in a different way, when I heard the sorrowful news, as did the Christian Natives at Lenukel, when they rolled themselves in anguish on the sands, and set up a death-wail as if they had lost their dearest friend.   It requires very little imagination to realize the scene, as the news was borne from Isle to Isle, and to hear one long, deep, and heart-breaking cry resounding throughout the New Hebrides—"Alas for the Gospel Ship! Alas for our dear little *Dayspring!*   Alas for the white-winged Herald of the Cross!"

For one, though firmly believing that her loss was a great blow to all the higher interests of our Mission, I was able to say: "The Lord gave and the Lord hath taken away:"—but yet, God forgive me, it was very hard to add: "Blessed be the Name of the Lord."   But never, in my deepest soul, did I for a moment doubt that in His hands all must be well. Whatever trials have befallen me in my Earthly Pilgrimage, I have never had the trial of doubting that perhaps, after all, Jesus had made some mistake.   No! my blessed Lord Jesus makes no mistakes!   When we see all His meaning, we shall then understand, what now we can only trustfully believe, that all is well—best for us, best for the cause most dear to us, best for the good of others and the glory of God.   Still, my tears would flow when I thought of the dear little *Dayspring*, the fruit of ten years of prayers and toils, the gift of God's people throughout the world to our beloved Mission, tumbled from that reef and lying at the bottom of the Sea.   And I felt comforted to think that He, who wept with the mourning

Sisters at the grave of Lazarus, did not rebuke their tears, but soothed them by weeping with them—"Jesus wept."

Wisely or otherwise, all parties seemed to embrace at once the conclusion that this Shipwreck should furnish the occasion for re-considering the whole question of a Mission Vessel or no Mission Vessel for the New Hebrides. For the time, arrangements had again to be resumed for the services of the Trading Company; and the interval was to be utilized in consulting the Mission Synod on the Islands, and the Churches concerned, in the light of the experience gained, whether another *Dayspring* should be built or not. I must openly affirm that this policy never commended itself to my judgment, nor even yet can I see its wisdom. With the Insurance, though limited to the inadequate sum of £2000 much against my will by the Committee at Melbourne, and with the other Funds for the *Dayspring* still on hand, besides the Free-Will Offerings that poured in on us from friends everywhere, we could have ordered and paid for a New Ship without one hour's delay. We had the assent of the Churches and the approval of the Missionaries, and should have gone forward, as if the wreck had never happened. God seemed Himself to be clearly pointing the way. Within a few hours, after the disaster was cabled to Britain, a lady in London sent a cheque for £1000 to my Home Committee, "to build or buy a new and larger ship!" Other generous offers were also pressed upon us; and the money is at this moment lying in the Bank awaiting a decision. We could then, and can now, present to the Mission another *Dayspring*, as a free gift from those throughout the world to whom God has endeared the Mission on the New Hebrides.

But I was powerless to resist the policy of delay, the consequences of which I cannot but fear, whatever the ultimate decision may be, as highly disastrous to our Mission. Should the vote be in favour of another Ship, the delay will have so damped the interest of supporters, that my British Committee may find it extremely difficult to revive subscriptions and secure the promised £1000 *per annum* towards the Maintenance Fund. Should the vote be unfavourable, the dissension amongst the Missionaries and the Churches, and the see-saw policy in the Management of the Mission, will so shake the confidence of the Christian Public, that all our funds are bound to suffer, and the welfare of the Mission be seriously crippled. I do, therefore, most earnestly pray and hope that there may be unity, at whatever cost to my personal predilections; for the spectacle of a disloyal Minority, undermining and destroying the work of the Majority, is enough to bring on our cause the contempt of men, if not also the curse of God. And at the same time, I cannot but fervently desire that the mind of the Synod on the Islands and of the Churches in the Colonies, at Home, and in Nova Scotia, may be clear and decided in favour of a Mission Ship, for the highest welfare of the Church of God on the New Hebrides.*

Experience has demonstrated that a perfectly suitable Vessel can be constructed for, say, £8000, that is, fifty tons larger than the Ship we have lost. Experience has further demonstrated that she can be maintained for £2500 per annum, or even less. Our opponents must therefore lay aside their speculative figures, and cease to say that her building may cost £10,000, and her yearly maintenance not less than £5000. The *Dayspring* lived long enough to slay these two wild fabrications. Now then, let them be buried with her in the Sea! It is purely and simply a question of whether, in the interests of the Kingdom of God on the New Hebrides, and in order to cut off our work there from all degrading association with Sabbath-breaking and grog-selling Trading Ships, we should or should not accept the free-will offerings of the People at Home to build for us, and to help us to maintain, a Mission Ship of our own. I never can believe it possible to imagine any other answer but one—if that issue were clearly contemplated, and judgment pronounced, *apart* from all other considerations, whether personal, self-interested, or merely worldly.

Thus far, as part of my Life-Story, and that every reader may comprehend my aims, it seemed necessary to explain, to argue, and even to criticise. But all further reference here is needless. Ere this page is published, the final decision will

---

* The Synod on the Islands (May, 1897) have voted *for* a New Mission Ship by a majority of 13 against 2.—ED.

probably have been announced. I can truly say that my Lord knows how sincerely I desire a clear and final decision, whether for or against another**Dayspring;* and that, such having been given, I pledge myself beforehand to accept it as His will, and, under it, to do all that in me lies to promote during my remaining days, the true welfare of the Mission of Christ to the New Hebrides. *Dayspring,* or no *Dayspring,* these souls must be won for Jesus!

And now, since this in all human probability is the closing Chapter of my humble Life, so far as it shall ever be written by me, therefore ere I lay down my pen, let me dwell with unalloyed delight on a few pictures of facts that rise before me, illustrative of the work of God at large throughout the New Hebrides. In all my journeyings, and in all my talks and writings, though of necessity personal experiences bulked somewhat largely, yet every candid hearer or reader will bear witness that I was eager and careful to pay unstinted honour to all my fellow-labourers on these Islands; many of whom, men and women too, I truly regard before God as amongst the noblest Servants of the Lord Jesus that I have ever known, or expect to know, on this Earth. God be with them, one and all; and though, on questions of policy and management, some of them may differ from me, I would gladly spend my last ounce of strength in promoting the spiritual interests of their work at every Station, and contributing to their personal happiness and prosperity, if it be in my power in any way to do so. All this, on both sides, we thoroughly know and understand, as becometh the Ambassadors of Christ to the Heathen World. I am never happier than when, as now, I try to picture the work of God on all the Isles of the New Hebrides, and show our friends and supporters in every Land some of the fruits of their money and their prayers.

At North Santo, we see Mr. Noble Mackenzie and his wife with hope and faith unfurling the Banner of the Cross; and Dr. and Mrs. Sandilands at Port Philip, Big Bay, on the same great Island, by healing and by teaching, pioneering for Jesus. Mr. Bowie and his wife, from the Free Church of Scotland, are taking possession of South Santo in the name of Christ; and if the Mission Synod agrees to plant his brother, Dr. Bowie,

---

* See page 496.

along with his wife, sent out this year by my British Committee, on East Santo, as seems desired—this, the largest and most northerly island of the Group, with its many languages and its unknown thousands of inhabitants, will at last be ringed round with fire,—the fire of love to Jesus and to the souls of the Heathen.

Another great Island, with several languages, has in recent years been surrounded by the soldiers of the Cross, and claimed for Christ—Mr. Watt Leggatt and his devoted wife at Aulua, Mr. Frederick J. Paton at Pangkumu, and Mr. Boyd at South West Bay—uniting their threefold forces to bring vast and populous Malekula to the feet of Jesus. Already most hopeful beginnings have been made. Christian Churches, with a few Converts, have been planted at these three Stations—the nucleus, we trust, of living branches on Earth of the Living Body of our Living Lord in the Heavenly World.

Tanna, also, has been afresh assaulted, in the name of God. Mr. Gillies and his wife are on their way to assist and to succeed Mr. Watt at Kwamera and Port Resolution; Mr. Thomson Macmillan has entered upon the field at Wiasisi, from which Mr. Gray had to retire; and Mr. Frank H. L. Paton and his devoted wife, along with their Lay Assistant, Mr. Hume, have opened a Pioneering Mission at Lenukel, on the Western coast, entirely supported by the funds of my British Committee. And our hopes beat high that Tanna, often described as the hardest Mission field in the Heathen World, is on the eve of surrendering to the Gospel of Jesus, which the fierce Tannese have so long and so savagely resisted.

To join the noble band of younger Missionaries, Dr. Agnew has also gone to the New Hebrides, an experienced and gifted and most attractive Missionary at Home, and destined, we believe, to be a fruitful worker for Jesus in the Foreign field. The preliminary expenses connected with several of these, such as Medical and other outfit, passage money to Australia, and the like, have been gladly borne by my British Committee, thereby relieving the Churches of all initial outlays, and encouraging them to undertake their permanent support. We press forward still, never thinking we can lawfully rest till every Tribe on the New Hebrides shall have heard, each in their own language, in their Mother Tongue, the old and ever new and deathless story of Redeeming Love.

These, however, are but beginnings. Our older Stations showed, in 1895, a record of work done and sufferings borne for Jesus that might well make all Christians thrill with praise. Take a few examples only.

During the year, Mr. Michelsen of Tongoa, one of the most successful Missionaries in the field, baptized and admitted to the Lord's Table 200 Converts; while 200 more under his tuition and that of Mrs. Michelsen were being prepared for the same holy privileges. God has given them in all nearly 2000 Converts from amongst these Cannibals, who are being built up into the faith and service of Jesus Christ. Alas, since the Queensland Government, in defiance of the solemn Protest of the Chiefs, opened this Island to the Labour-recruiting Ships, hundreds of their best and most hopeful Native Helpers have been seduced as *Kanakas* to the Sugar Plantations—and the Missionary and the Islanders alike regard them as virtually dead; so very few will ever return! Mr. Michelsen has thirty Native Teachers or Evangelists, with 1850 pupils attending the Mission Schools. During the same year, the Converts collected from amongst themselves £25, and handed it over for the promotion of the Gospel of Christ; so that the labours of this devoted servant of God, for sixteen years, are being crowned with many tokens of blessing.

It is believed amongst us that few Missions in the World show more interesting fruits of Evangelistic enterprise than Nguna and its Islets, under the fostering pastorate of Mr. Milne and his most devoted and gifted wife. There are 750 Communicants on the Church's Roll, 1700 regularly attending the Worship of God, and at least 2000 in all who have turned from Heathenism and adopted the habits of Christian Civilization. There are thirty Native Teachers, for whose support the Native Church raised £155, 8s. 11d. in 1895, besides giving Arrowroot for Mission purposes valued at £120. They had thirty-seven Christian Marriages during the year, and 100 Candidates for Membership in the

Communicants' Class. Nay, most marvellous of all, the Church of Nguna has thirty-eight of its married couples who have gone forth as Native Teachers and Mission Helpers to other Islands—a Missionary Church called out of Heathenism, thus joyfully and instinctively sending forth from its own bosom Missionaries into the Heathenism beyond. Surely I am warranted in saying, to the praise of Jesus and of His servants, that this is a glorious record for five and twenty years!

On Epi, Mr. Fraser, having laboured fourteen years, had 137 Members on his Communion Roll, and 128 Candidates in his Communicants' Class; 27 Native Teachers, with 1000 at the Day Schools, and 1250 at the Sabbath Schools; and his people collected amongst themselves £34 for Mission purposes. Since then, and every day, the tide of prosperity is rising on the side of Christianity, and all these figures are steadily increasing. Mr. Smail is on the other side of the same Island, and has, as the result of six years' devotion to his work, 36 Communicants in his Church, 13 Candidates for Membership, 14 Native Teachers, and 500 daily attending their Schools. They gave £7 for the work of the Mission.

Erromanga, where five Missionaries were murdered, and two of them devoured by the Cannibals, is now a Christian Island. There are 300 Communicants, 12 Elders, 40 Native Teachers, and 1750 attending the Schools — practically the whole population. Mr. Robertson and his devoted wife have been honoured of God, in completing this grand work, during the last four and twenty years.

And so on all round the Group, Island after Island being brought by patient, devoted, and rational expenditure of time, and affection, and all Gospel influences, to the knowledge of the Christian life, and thereby to Civilization. There are still four or five great Centres of Heathenism untouched. When God sends us Missionaries for these, it will then only be a question of time coupled with pains and prayer, till all the New Hebrides in all their Babel tongues, shall be heard singing the praises of Redeeming Love. May my blessed Saviour spare me to see the full Dawn, if not the perfect Noon, of that happy Day!

It is easy to raise the shallow cry that the New Hebrides

Mission is overmanned, as compared with India, China and Africa, as some, and very specially the same men who most keenly oppose the *Dayspring*, are persistently doing. We might answer by retort,—Your own Towns and Villages are overmanned; why not resign your charges, and go to the millions of Heathendom? But we leave that retort to others, and reply: There are differences in all these fields of enterprise, which demand specific adaptation of means to ends, and we fearlessly declare, in the face of all Christendom, that God Himself has approved of our system by the almost unparalleled results. We plant down our European Missionary with his staff at a given Station. We surround him with Native Teachers, who pioneer amongst all the Villages within reach. His life-work is to win that Island, or that People, for God and Civilization. He masters their Language, and reduces it to writing. He translates and prints portions of the Bible. He opens Schools, and begins teaching the whole population. He opens a Communicants' Class, and trains his most hopeful Converts for full membership in the Church. And there he holds the fort, and toils, and prays, till the Gospel of Jesus has not only been preached to every creature whom he can reach, but also reduced to practice in the new habits and the new religious and social life of the Community. In this way has Aneityum been won for Christ, and thoroughly Christianized; and Aniwa, and Erromanga, and Efatè, and Nguna, and Tongoa, and several adjoining Isles. And, humanly speaking, there is no other way in which these Tribes and Peoples can be evangelized. The next stage will be that of the Native Pastorate, with a very few superintending European Missionaries—a stage on which, for instance, my own Aniwa has long since practically entered, the Elders carrying on all the work of the Church, with an occasional visit from a neighbouring Missionary. But the foundations of Civilization and of Christianity must either be laid and solidly built up by a Missionary for each of these Peoples, or they will never be laid at all.

Let our Churches then go forward on the lines which God the Lord hath blessed. Complete the pioneering work on the New Hebrides, bring the Gospel within reach of every creature there, and then set free your money and your men to do the

₅ame elsewhere. But even in India and in China and in Africa, with their countless millions, learn a lesson from the work on the New Hebrides. Plant down your forces in the heart of one Tribe or Race, where the same Language is spoken. Work solidly from that centre, building up with patient teaching and life-long care a Church that will endure. Rest not till every People and Language and Nation has such a Christ-centre throbbing in its midst, with the pulses of the New Life at full play. Rush not from Land to Land, from People to People, in a breathless and fruitless Mission. Kindle not your lights so far apart, amid the millions and the wastes of Heathendom, that every lamp may be extinguished without any of the others knowing, and so leave the blackness of their Night blacker than ever. The consecrated Common-sense that builds for Eternity will receive the fullest approval of God in Time.

Oh that I had my life to begin again ! I would consecrate it anew to Jesus in seeking the conversion of the remaining Cannibals on the New Hebrides. But since that may not be, may He help me to use every moment and every power still left to me to carry forward to the uttermost that beloved work. Doubtless these poor degraded Savages are a part of the Redeemer's inheritance, given to Him in the Father's Eternal Covenant, and thousands of them are destined through us to sing His praise in the glory and the joy of the Heavenly World ! And should the record of my poor and broken life lead any one to consecrate himself to Mission work at Home or Abroad that he may win souls for Jesus, or should it even deepen the Missionary spirit in those who already know and serve the Redeemer of us all—for this also, and for all through which He has led me by His loving and gracious guidance, I shall, unto the endless ages of Eternity, bless and adore my beloved Master and Saviour and Lord, to whom be glory for ever and ever.

NOTE TO PAGE 491.—The General Assembly at Melbourne (November 1897) resolved by a majority of one to delay for twelve months before deciding either for or against a new *Dayspring*. —EDITOR.

FAREWELL TO THE READER.

READER, Fare-thee-well! Thou hast companied with me —not without some little profit, I trust; and not without noting many things that led thee to bless the Lord God, in whose honour these pages have been written. In your life and in mine, there is at least one *last* Chapter, one final Scene awaiting us,—God our Father knows where and how! By His grace, I will live out that Chapter, I will pass through that Scene, in the faith and in the hope of Jesus, who has sustained me from Childhood till now. As you close this book, go alone before your Saviour, and pledge yourself upon your knees by His help and sympathy to do the same. And let me meet you, and let us commune with each other again, in the presence and glory of the Redeemer. Fare-thee-well!

APPENDICES.

APPENDIX A.

(*See page* 18.)

(*See page* 18.)

The following Poem appeared in *Life and Work* for September 1890. The Editor is emboldened to hope, through the uncommon interest shown by all readers in this First Chapter of the *Autobiography*, that he will be pardoned for giving these verses, founded thereon, a more permanent connection with the Book, by reproducing them here.

A WHITE-SOULED PEASANT.

By the Rev. JAMES PATON, B.A., Glasgow.

Founded upon the first chapter of the *Autobiography* of John G. Paton, Missionary; particularly the pen-portrait there drawn of his saintly father.

"Never, in temple or cathedral, on mountain or in glen, can I hope to feel that the Lord God is more near, more visibly walking and talking with men, than under that humble Cottage roof of thatch and oaken wattles." (Part First, Ch. I.)

A WHITE-SOULED Peasant of the olden time,
    God-freighted, Angel-guarded,
Here lived and made a poor man's life sublime—
Luminous with Christ-light from the spirit-clime,
    By flesh-veils scarce retarded.

His fresh young heart, inspired by Mother's prayers
    Godward and Christward gladly,
Saw and began to mount those Bethel Stairs
That lift our feet above the sins and cares
    Which most men follow madly.

From early Teens far past Three-score-and-ten
    For God he hungered, thirsting;
The God-glow on his face attracted men,
And children gazed and smiled, as if again
    Christ's eyes were on them bursting!

For forty years dear old Torthorwald saw
　　Christ's life his life uplifting;
And neighbours marked that Cottage Home with awe,
Where life for God flowed on with scarce a flaw,—
　　Storm-tossed but never drifting.

The "But" and "Ben" and "Inner Chamber" shone,
　　Through Poortith hard and trying;
Yet not with light of human love alone,
But also love that bound them to the Throne
　　Of Jesus,—Love undying!

There sons and daughters flourished, thence went forth,
　　And far and near were scattered;
But morn and even by that Altar Hearth
He met them—gathered in from all the Earth—
　　There distance nothing mattered.

The Mother and the Children, one and all,
　　However torn and sundered,
He bore right in where seraph footsteps fall,
And with the Everlasting Arms did them enthrall—
　　While Angels peered and wondered.

Toiling for daily bread, not this world's gear,
　　His days and years sore cumbered;
But Psalms and Holy Songs sustained his cheer,
And kindly deeds with Christ-light shining clear
　　His hours and moments numbered.

From farm and cot, four * Parishes around,
　　The sick and dying sought him;
Death's terrors vanished, when the silver sound
Of his high praises rang through depths profound
　　To Jesus who had bought him.

His eyes spoke Gospels; and his countenance
　　With soul-light beamed benignly;
His happy face did God's dear love enhance,
And trembling souls—rapt into holy trance—
　　Rose on Faith's wings divinely.

---

* Torthorwald, Tinwald, Mouswald, and Lochmaben.

The lapse of years, full seventy and seven,
    At length brought death to claim him ;
Kind Nature squared accounts and found them even—
A life well spent, a passage clear for Heaven,
    No record left to shame him.

A ᴜeath-bed ? Nay, this scene where Angels wait,—
    Gateway to Glory rather !
The body gently slips from off its mate,
And falls asleep ; the soul, upborne elate,
    Returns to God the Father.

Lift up your heads, O ye Eternal Gates,
    Jesus His trophy bringeth !
High song of saint and seraph there awaits
The King of Glory's triumph o'er the fates,
    And loud the Anthem ringeth.

Hush, O my soul ! Back from such ravishment !
    Swoon not till God's time cometh ;
Fulfil thy day's darg ; and, when strength is spent,
Lie down in Arms of Christ, and rest content
    Till trump of Judgment boometh.

O white-souled Peasant of the olden time,
    I thank God for thy story ;
Memories of thee like bells of Christmas chime
And cheer our souls unfalteringly to climb
    The stairs that lead to Glory.

APPENDIX B.

(See page 69.)

NOTES ON THE NEW HEBRIDES.

By the Editor.

The South Seas—so named by Vasco Nugnez de Balboa, who in 1513 first saw the Ocean on the other side of Darien, and marched into it as far as he durst, waving his sword, and taking possession of it in the name of his master, the King of Spain.

The Pacific Ocean—so named by Ferdinand Magellan, who

in 1521 sailed westwards in his *Victory* seven thousand miles, and found the sea exceptionally *peaceful*—for that trip at least.

The NEW HEBRIDES—so named by Captain Cook, who in 1773 first fully explored and described the whole of the group. As far back, however, as 1606, Captain Pedro Fernandez de Quiros had landed on the largest and most northerly island of the group. He at once fancied it to be the great *Southern* Continent, deemed to be essential to balance the great Continents of the North, and eagerly looked for both by sailors and men of science. He named the bay *Vera Cruz*,—the river that flowed into it, *Jordan*,—and the city which he founded there, *New Jerusalem*. The land itself he called by the preposterous designation of *Tierra Australis del Espiritu Santo*. In 1768 a French Explorer, Bougainville, sailed round *Santo*, discovering that it was but an island, and through the *Straits* that still bear his name; whereon, finding many islands all around, he re-baptized them *L'Archipel des Grandes Cyclades*. But Cook, being the first who sailed in and out amongst all the group, and put on record the most faithful descriptions and details, which to this hour remain generally authoritative, considered himself entitled to name them the *New Hebrides;* and history since has been well pleased to adopt his views, seeing, doubtless, the geographical analogy betwixt the multitudinous scattered isles and islets of the *old* Hebrides and those of the *new*.

From Santo in the north to Aneityum in the south, a distance of about 400 miles, there are scattered over the Ocean thirty islands, twenty being well inhabited, and eleven of them being of considerable size, from Aneityum, which is forty miles in circumference, to Santo, which measures seventy miles by forty. The Islands lie 1,000 miles to the North of New Zealand, 1,400 miles North-East from Sydney, 400 miles West of Fiji, and 200 East of New Caledonia. The population is now estimated at 70,000; but, in the early days of Missions, before Traders and Kanaka-collectors, and the new Epidemics of Civilization (!) had decimated them, their numbers were certainly three times greater.

The general appearance of the Islands is that of a range of mountains bursting up out of the sea, clothed with forests, and severed from each other by deep valleys, through which the tides now flow. They are all volcanic in origin; in some cases, the lava has poured itself out over a bed of coral, and the mountains have reared themselves up on a coral base; but in others, the volcano, bursting through, has borne the coral rocks to the tops of the hills, and even piled them on mountain summits. The fires are still active on Tanna, Ambrym, and I opivi—the volcano

on Tanna being now, as in the days of Cook, a pillar of cloud by
day and of fire by night, a far-shining lighthouse for the sailor,
kindled by the finger of God Himself. The climate is moist and
humid, with a thermometer seldom below 60° and seldom above
90° in the shade; what they call the Rainy Season is their worst
and hottest weather; and the vegetation is tropical in its
luxuriance.

On one Island may be found a hundred varieties of ferns alone.
The damara or kauri-pine, so prized in New Zealand, grows
there, as also the bread-fruit tree, the banana, the papua-apple,
the chestnut, and above all the cocoa-nut, which for refreshing
drink competes with the vine of other lands, and for varied uses
and services to man almost rivals the very palm-tree of Palestine.
The sandal-wood, for its sacred odours and idol incense, has been
almost swept entirely away,—as much as £70,000 worth being
carried off from Erromanga alone!

Among native foods, the yam and the taro hold the foremost
place, not inferior to our finest potatoes; besides the banana, the
sugar-cane, the bread-fruit, and the cocoa-nut, which flourish to
perfection. Their arrowroot is in some respects the finest in
the world, and is kept only for special uses as yet, but may
develop into a great and valuable industry, as Commerce opens
up her markets and stretches out her hands. The English
cabbage has been introduced and grows well; also the planting
of cotton and of coffee.

The scarcity of animals is marvellous. The pig, the dog, and
the rat are their only four-footed creatures; and some affirm that
the rat is the alone indigenous quadruped in all the New Hebrides.
Lizards and snakes abound, but are declared not to be poisonous.
There are many small and beautiful pigeons, also wild ducks and
turkeys, besides multitudes of ordinary fowls. Goats have now
been largely introduced, as well as sheep, and various European
animals. Fish, of course, swarm in millions around the shores,
and a whaling station on Aneityum sent into the market £2,000
worth of oil in a year.

The Natives are practically quite naked, till induced by the
Missionary to "wear a shirt"—the first sign of renouncing
Heathenism and inclining towards Christianity. They are
Cannibals of a very pronounced type, and Savages without any
traces of civilization, except those connected with war (!),—
without a literature, and almost without a religion, except only
the dread of evil spirits, the worship of ancestors, and the lowest
forms of fetishism, as to trees, stones, etc. They are partly
Malay and partly Papuan,—a mixture of Ham and of Shem,—

some with hair crisp and woolly, stuck full of feathers and shells, others with hair long and wavy, twisted into as many as 700 separate whipcords on a single head, and taking five years to finish the job! Their bows and arrows, tomahawks, clubs, and spears are sometimes elaborately carved and adorned; and they can twist and weave grasses and fibres into wondrously beautiful mats, bags, and girdles. They make bracelets out of shells, sliced and carved in marvellous ways, as also ear-rings and nose-rings; and in many similar methods they show some savage sense of beauty.

Polygamy, with all its accompanying cruelties and degradations, universally prevails. Infanticide is systematically practised; and even the dispatch of parents, when they grow old and helpless. Widows are put to death on almost every island, to bear their husbands company into the spirit world. There is not an unmentionable vice hinted at in Romans i. which is not unblushingly practised on those Islands, wheresoever the Gospel has not dawned.

For the best published information on all these subjects, consult (1) the work by Dr. John Inglis, "IN THE NEW HEBRIDES" (Nelson & Sons, 1887),—Reminiscences of noble Missionary Service for three-and-thirty years; and (2) the work by Dr. Steel of Sydney, founded on a Cruise amongst the Islands in the Mission Ship, and entitled "THE NEW HEBRIDES AND CHRISTIAN MISSIONS" (Nisbet & Co., 1880).

APPENDIX C.

(*See page* 219.)

THE PRAYER OF THE TANNESE,
WHO LOVE THE WORD OF JEHOVAH
TO THE GREAT CHIEF OF SYDNEY.

[*Written at the urgent request and dictation of the Missionary's friends on Tanna to be presented to the Governor of New South Wales. Literally translated by me, John G. Paton.*]

To the Chief of Sydney, the servant of Queen Victoria of Britannia, saying—We great men of Tanna dwell in a dark land. Our people are very dark hearted. They know nothing good.

Missi Paton the man, Missi Mathieson the man, and Missi Mathieson the woman, have dwelt here four yams (= years) to teach us the worship of Jehovah. Their conduct has been straight and very good; therefore we love these three Missionaries, and the worship of Jehovah which they three have taught us, the Tannese.

Alas! a part, as it were; only three of our Chiefs, whose names are Nauka, Miaki, and Karewick, besides Ringian, Enukarupi, Attica, and Namaka, they and their people hate the worship and all good conduct like that which the Word of Jehovah teaches us and the people of all lands. These men all belong to four Villages only. They have stolen all Missi's property; they have broken into his house. They have cut down his bananas. They have scolded and persecuted him; and they desire to kill Missi and to eat him, so that they may destroy the Worship of God from the land of Tanna.

We hate exceedingly their bad conduct, and pray you, the Great Chief of Sydney, to punish these dark Tannese, who have persecuted Missi, who have deceived Missi, who have altogether deceived the Great Chief (= Commodore Seymour) and the Chief (= Captain Hume) of the Men-of-war, and who deceived the Chief and the Missionaries in the *John Williams*, who murdered one of Missi Paton's Aneityum Teachers, who fought Missi Turner and Missi Nisbet, who killed Vasa and his Samoan people, who killed the foreigners, who have now fought and driven away our three Missionaries. Their conduct has been exceedingly bad. They destroy the Kingdom of Tanna, kill the people and eat them, and are guilty of bad conduct every day. Our hearts hate their bad conduct; we are pained by it.

Therefore we earnestly pray you, the Chief of Sydney, to send quickly a Man-of-war to punish them, and to revenge all their bad conduct towards Missi. Then truly we will rejoice; then it will be good and safe for the three Missionaries to dwell here, and to teach us, men of the devil. Our hearts are very dark; we know nothing; we are just like pigs. Therefore it is good for Missi to teach us the Word and the Worship of Jehovah the Great King. Long ago He was unknown here. Missi brought His knowledge to us.

Our love to you, the Great Chief of Sydney, the servant of Queen Victoria, and we earnestly pray you to protect us, and to protect our Missionaries and the Worship of God in our land, the land of Tanna. We weep for our Missionaries. They three gave us medicine in our sickness, and clothing for our bodies; taught us what is good conduct, and taught us the way to

Heaven. Of all these things long ago we had no knowledge whatever ; therefore we weep, and our hearts cling to these three, our Missionaries. If they three are not here, who will teach us the way to Heaven? Who will prevent our bad conduct? Who will protect us from the bad conduct of foreigners? And who will love us, and teach us all good things?

Oh, compassionate us, Chief of Sydney! Hold fast these three, our Missionaries, and give them back to us, and we will love you and your people. You and your people know the Word of Jehovah ; you are going on the path to Heaven ; you all love the Word of Jehovah. Oh, look in mercy on us, dark-hearted men, going to the bad iand, to the great eternal fire, just like our fathers who are dead !

May Jehovah make your heart and the hearts of your people sweet towards us, to compassionate us and to look in mercy on our dark land ; and we will pray Jehovah to make you good, and give you a rich reward.

The names of us, the Chiefs of Tanna, who worship towards Jehovah :

Yarisi,	× his mark.	Manuman,	× his mark.
Ruawa,	× his mark.	Nuara,	× his mark.
Kapuka,	× his mark.	Nebusak,	× his mark.
Taura,	× his mark.	Kaua,	× his mark.
Faimungo,	× his mark.	Nowar,	× his mark.

Publishers' Note

Three of the appendices which appeared in the twelfth Popular edition are dated and therefore have been omitted from this edition. The subjects were "The Kanaka Traffic", "The Future of the New Hebrides" and "The John G. Paton Mission Fund". References to these appendices have not been deleted from the index.

INDEX.

INDEX.

SOME OTHER
BANNER OF TRUTH
TITLES

FIVE PIONEER MISSIONARIES

There are few more thrilling periods of church history than the great missionary movement which stretched from the eighteenth into the nineteenth century. Recognising that Jesus Christ was the missionary sent by the Father, and that the Bible is the *Magna Carta* of missions, men like Henry Martyn, John G. Paton, John Eliot, David Brainerd and William Chalmers Burns left home, family and love for the sake of Christ and to spread his good news. The narratives of their monumental labours and sufferings and their strong longings to see Christ glorified in the salvation of the nations make awe-inspiring and God-honouring reading.

Five Pioneer Missionaries tells the story of each of these servants of God, in doing so it not only outlines some of the great biblical principles of missions, but also challenges Christians today to live lives completely dedicated to serving Jesus Christ wherever he calls us to go.

ISBN 0 85151 117 1
352pp. Paperback

THE LIFE AND LETTERS OF
HENRY MARTYN

John Sargent

John Sargent's *Memoir of Henry Martyn* (1781-1812), after its first publication in 1819, went through repeated reprints and new editions (on both sides of the Atlantic) and was arguably the most influential missionary biography of the last century.

As the first Anglican graduate to put the work of evangelism and Bible translation in India before all the prizes which his brilliant Cambridge career had opened to him, Martyn was bound to receive attention. But it was the story of what happened after he left England in 1806 which became, through Sargent's biography, the most unforgettable part of his short life.

In spiritual sympathy with his subject Sargent (1780-1833) is far ahead of the later biographers of Martyn. His is one of the great books, to be not only read but felt. Many have risen from its pages in a state of 'deep and sober ecstasy of true religious feeling' and determined to follow Christ more faithfully.

ISBN 0 85151 468 5
480pp. Paperback

AUSTRALIAN CHRISTIAN LIFE
FROM 1788

Iain H. Murray

Australian Christian Life is an introduction to a remarkable period of history. While Australia's first white community—convicts and their military gaolers—arrived from England with the name of Christian, it contained few who gave thought to either their own spiritual need or to that of the indigenous Aborigine population. Nominally 'Christian', the early colony was largely licentious, brutal and pagan; the least likely of all places to be a successful mission field.

But Christian history is a history of surprises. From such unpromising beginnings an heroic form of resolute, self-sacrificing yet 'singing' Christianity began to make its way. From among soldiers, convicts, merchants, new settlers and, at long last, Aborigines also, churches came into existence which powerfully affected the greater part of the entire population. These pages show that when Christians are faithful to apostolic truth and to apostolic methods they will always, sooner or later, know apostolic success.

ISBN 0 85151 524 X

384pp. Cloth-bound. Illustrated

CHRISTIANITY AMONG THE NEW ZEALANDERS

William Williams

New Zealand has a priceless Christian heritage. For three or four decades following the establishment of a mission by Samuel Marsden in 1814 a work of grace occurred which ranks second to none in the annals of missionary endeavour. Even before systematic colonisation began in the 1840s a large number of Maori people had left off the 'unfruitful works of darkness' and had begun to display a form of Christianity seldom seen since apostolic times. Instrumental in bringing about this change was a handful of Protestant, evangelical missionaries. *Christianity Among the New Zealanders* is a moving account of the remarkable events of those times, written by one who was an eyewitness of much that is recorded.

As a testimony from history this rare work is important in its own right. More than that, however, it has inspiring lessons on Christian witness and demonstrates that the only hope for the world today is the same message which accomplished such a transformation in 'the land of the long white cloud'.

ISBN 0 85151 566 5
398pp. Cloth-bound. Illustrated

THE LIVES OF ROBERT AND JAMES HALDANE

Alexander Haldane

Written by one of the Anglican evangelical leaders of the last century, this volume tells the remarkable story of the author's father, James Haldane (1768-1851) and uncle, Robert Haldane (1764-1842). Members of the Scottish aristocracy, James was a captain with the East India Company and Robert the owner of Gleneagles and other estates in Perthshire when they were converted in the last decade of the 18th century. Thereafter the two brothers became identified for the next fifty years with many of the foremost evangelical enterprises.

Robert Haldane gave himself to the spread of the gospel in Scotland and in Europe. His remarkable visit to Geneva in 1816 led to a widespread awakening and, ultimately, to the publication of his *Exposition of the Epistle to the Romans.*

James Haldane, pre-eminently a preacher, was an itinerant evangelist and, through 52 years, an influential pastor in Edinburgh. Both men believed that the blessing of God on their labours 'was designed as an encouragement to those who should cast away worldly policy, and setting before them nothing but the glory of God, rest boldly on the blessing promised, both to the written and spoken word.'

ISBN 0 85151 567 3
728pp. Cloth-bound

A VISION FOR MISSIONS

Tom Wells

Foreign Missionary endeavour sometimes appears hesitant, even half-hearted before the problems of this age. Poverty and famine, national religious and cultural issues, and above all the weakness of the 'Christian' West have thrown doubt on the work of missions as it was once understood.

Tom Wells writes with the conviction that Christians must come back to first principles. Human need and world conditions are not the starting point. The gospel is a call to know and worship God, and the primary conviction of the messenger must be that God is worthy to be known. The missionary vision must begin with the vision of God. Only then can the Church truly respond to the command to 'declare his glory among the nations'.

This is a challenging book, and equally relevant to Christians at home or abroad. It treats missionary endeavour not as a separate interest but as basic to Christianity itself. By reference to Brainerd, Carey and Martyn the author also shows the true inspiration which lay behind the missionary movement of the 18th and 19th centuries.

ISBN 0 85151 433 2
160pp. Paperback

THE ST. ANDREWS SEVEN

Stuart Piggin & John Roxborogh

Occasionally, in the annals of Christian history, the heroic stories of long-forgotten movements of God's Spirit are rediscovered. This little book contains the narrative of such a movement in the nineteenth century. Its chief characters are the great Thomas Chalmers, and six of his students. The influence in later life of these six young men, especially in India, was to be far beyond their wildest expectation, even in their teenage enthusiasm to serve Christ to the ends of the earth.

In this extraordinary account, Stuart Piggin and John Roxborogh, both experts in the field of missions, trace vividly and popularly the story—the aspirations, fears, doubts, struggles, opposition, sorrows, triumphs—of these six most gifted and dedicated young Christians. In moving simplicity they recount the astonishing influence of one of their number who died before he could fulfil his heart's ambitions, but whose life led the others to the profound conviction that 'only one thing seemed to matter: to discover God's will and do it'. *The St. Andrews Seven* not only restores their name from obscurity, but also challenges the church of today to put aside its mediocrity and respond obediently to Christ's great commission.

ISBN 0 85151 428 6
144pp. Large Paperback

THE PURITAN HOPE
Revival and the Interpretation of Prophecy

Iain H. Murray

Today the Church's hope in respect of her mission of discipling all nations is in eclipse. The world gives Christianity no future and evangelicals themselves doubt whether the cause of Christ can ever attain to a greater triumph before his Second Advent. Must the prospects for succeeding generations be darker than those of today? Can we ever expect any period of history to intervene before the Advent of Christ? How can readiness for Christ's coming be consistent with the belief that revivals are yet to be given to the Church? Such questions are brought to the fore in this book and the author, employing both exposition of Scripture and much historical and biographical material, sets out the case for believing that it is not 'orthodox' to indulge in gloom over the prospect for Christianity in the world.

ISBN 0 85151 247 X
328pp. Paperback. Illustrated

For further details and a free illustrated catalogue please write to:
THE BANNER OF TRUTH TRUST
3 Murrayfield Road, Edinburgh EH12 6EL
P.O. Box 621, Carlisle, Pennsylvania, 17013, U.S.A.